Another Steven Soderbergh Experience

Another Steven Soderbergh Experience

Authorship and Contemporary Hollywood

by MARK GALLAGHER

University of Texas Press Austin

Requests for permission to reproduce material from this work should be sent to:
    Permissions
    University of Texas Press
    P.O. Box 7819
    Austin, TX 78713-7819
    http://utpress.utexas.edu/about/book-permissions

♾ The paper used in this book meets the minimum requirements of ANSI/NISO
Z39.48-1992 (R1997) (Permanence of Paper).

LIBRARY OF CONGRESS CATALOGING-IN-PUBLICATION DATA

Gallagher, Mark, 1968–
  Another Steven Soderbergh experience : authorship and contemporary
Hollywood / by Mark Gallagher. — 1st ed.
      p.   cm.
  Includes bibliographical references and index.
  ISBN 978-0-292-74421-9 (cloth : alk. paper)
    1. Soderbergh, Steven, 1963—Criticism and interpretation.   I. Title.
  PN1998.3.S593G36   2013
  791.4302'33092—dc23

                                                                2012026740

doi:10.7560/744219

Contents

Contents

Acknowledgments

Like Soderbergh's work, this book represents a collaboration with many talented and generous people. Thanks to my irreplaceable colleagues in the Department of Culture, Film and Media at the University of Nottingham, in particular Paul Grainge, Roberta Pearson, Julian Stringer, Luke Robinson, Gianluca Sergi, and Paul McDonald. Many former colleagues at other institutions encouraged the project during its long gestation, including Dan Wojcik and Kathleen Karlyn at the University of Oregon; Edward Jones, Leonard Leff, and Jeff Walker at Oklahoma State University; Jack Boozer and Niklas Vollmer at Georgia State University; Brad Prager at the University of Missouri; and Grace An at Oberlin College. Jim Burr at the University of Texas Press showed unimaginable patience for the finished product. Special thanks also to those who read draft chapters or gave other essential support, especially Rikke Schubart, Stephanie Lewthwaite, Paul Jenner, Sharon Monteith, Jake Smith, Chi-Yun Shin, Pam Golden, Kevin Gallagher, and Karen Eng. Further thanks to close friends who endured my ceaseless ear-bending about Soderbergh's work and other film-culture esoterica, including Michael Pebworth and Lindsay Schubert, Aron Golden and Lisa Schultz, Nate Nichols and Fran Salafia, Peter and Cindy Witkow, Luci Hackbert and Seth Friedman, Andy Deck, Jon Burgerman, Bernard Radfar, Kirstin Stiebel, Erich Reed, and Susannah Beck. Thanks as well to Carl Spence of the Seattle International Film Festival for a very informative interview about festival programming that has helped me anchor some of this book's claims.

Portions of two chapters were previously published in different forms. Part of Chapter 2 appeared as "Discerning Independents: Steven Soderbergh and Transhistorical Taste Cultures" in *American*

Independent Cinema: Indie, Indiewood, and Beyond (edited by Yannis Tzioumakis, Claire Molloy, and Geoff King, London: Routledge, 2012). A portion of Chapter 5 appeared as "Male Style and Race in the Neo-Retro Heist Film" in *Millennial Masculinity: Men in Contemporary American Cinema* (edited by Timothy Shary, Detroit: Wayne State University Press, 2012). Thanks to the editors for their permission to include this material.

Most essentially, thanks to Steven Soderbergh for his detailed fact-checking of the draft manuscript, and for granting me much of his valuable time for a wide-ranging discussion on filmmaking and art. Finally, my eternal gratitude to Elaine Roth for sharing ten years of Soderbergh's oeuvre and other stimuli, and for graciously leaving the project in my capricious hands.

Another Steven Soderbergh Experience

Introduction

Across his nearly thirty-year career as a screen-industry professional, filmmaker Steven Soderbergh has proven himself one of the most dynamic figures in the U.S. film industry, a prolific director and producer of blockbuster entertainments, idiosyncratic art films, low-budget video experiments, and television series. We can see the characteristic diversity of his work by bracketing an interval of his career. For the sake of illustration, I begin by briefly surveying his work between late 2004 and early 2006, one of many densely productive periods in his creative life. In September 2004, the omnibus international art film *Eros* debuted at the Venice and Toronto film festivals, with Soderbergh as director, cinematographer, and editor of one of its three segments. The Toronto festival, and the Telluride festival earlier in the month, also screened the low-budget independent *Keane*, executive-produced by Soderbergh as a product of the Section Eight production company he co-managed with actor George Clooney. Early December saw the opening of star-ensemble studio film and sequel *Ocean's Twelve*, with Soderbergh as director and cinematographer. The film quickly became a commercial hit, ultimately grossing over $350 million worldwide. Next, in January 2005, the television series *Unscripted*, another Section Eight effort executive-produced by Soderbergh, began its run on HBO. The same month, the experimental film *Symbiopsychotaxiplasm: Take 2 1/2*—directed by William Greaves, a leading figure in black independent cinema since the 1960s—premiered at the Sundance Film Festival, with Soderbergh again credited as executive producer. Soderbergh earned additional executive-producer credits on five Section Eight films released in 2005, including Academy Award contenders *Syriana* and *Good Night, and Good Luck*. Meanwhile, in the realm of home video,

Soderbergh contributed co-commentary tracks to the DVD releases of *Point Blank* (1967) and *The Yards* (2000), interviewing directors John Boorman and James Gray, respectively. Also in 2005, he wrote the foreword to a book about the indie-rock band Guided by Voices, fellow travelers in hugely prolific output (and whose frontman, Robert Pollard, would contribute the score to Soderbergh's next film, *Bubble* [2005]).

At the end of our surveyed time frame, in January 2006, Soderbergh earned notice again for the national release of *Bubble*,[1] though not for his multi-hyphenate work as director, cinematographer, and editor. Instead, the digital-video effort attracted industry interest for its simultaneous release in theaters, on pay-per-view television, and on DVD. While not naming Soderbergh directly, National Association of Theatre Owners president John Fithian labeled this arrangement a "death threat" to exhibitors. Following *Bubble*'s release, Soderbergh would not receive another screen credit for a full six months, until the release of *A Scanner Darkly* (2006), another Section Eight project he executive-produced. And probably more to the comfort of Fithian and other exhibitors, Soderbergh's follow-up feature as director was *The Good German*, a part-homage to *Casablanca* (1942) that premiered at the end of 2006. Though that film earned only a limited release and consequently was not a box-office success, Soderbergh returned temporarily to the list of high-grossing directors with *Ocean's Thirteen* (2007), and he has continued to alternate between star-driven features and more esoteric projects.

Soderbergh's work illuminates many trends in industry practice, media authorship, technologies of film and television production and distribution, and motion-picture aesthetics. His features have been shot on 35mm film as well as digital video. His filmography includes popular blockbusters, prestige studio pictures, standard-setting independent films, and extensive experimental work. He has directed numerous adaptations, remakes, and sequels. He has worked in television as series creator, producer, and director. In some of the films he directed in the 1990s, and in all since 2000's *Traffic*, he has served pseudonymously as cinematographer, and usually as uncredited camera operator, too. On many he has served as editor as well, also under a pseudonym. Also, alongside other scripting efforts, he wrote the screenplays for *sex, lies, and videotape* (1989) and for *Schizopolis* (1996), in which he played the lead role as well. His many roles in film and television production evidence nearly all categories of screen authorship.

Another Steven Soderbergh Experience argues for the opportunities afforded to the creative individual within contemporary screen industries. Soderbergh is in many respects a unique figure—no other industry professionals work so prominently in so many genres, modes, media, and areas of technical expertise. At the same time, his myriad efforts typify contemporary media-industry practice, in which production entities, distribution platforms, and creative labor increasingly cross-pollinate. Dispensing with the romantic model of the film author as visionary artist struggling against the crass commercial system, this book considers anew the possibilities for collaboration, entrepreneurship, and artistry in entertainment industries. Equally significantly, it emphasizes continuity across historical periods and industrial modes, challenging long-accepted distinctions between independent and studio films, between film and television authorship, between theatrical and home-video releases, and more. While such categories retain some utility in marking critical and industrial boundaries, they fail to account for the diverse production and reception practices of contemporary Hollywood and the surrounding media environment.

Soderbergh's expansive industrial activity allows us to reframe long-standing approaches to screen authorship. Many authorship studies proceed from questions about the origins of textual meaning, asking what signs of authorship films reveal. Inferred auteur sensibilities cement particular critical-reading strategies, and authorship as a concept or practice gains utility only insofar as it helps unpack textual meanings. While Soderbergh's films and other output are rich in signification, this book asks instead what comprises the work of a screen author in contemporary Hollywood. Thus, my focus is less "what do texts mean?" than "what do authors do?" While I devote substantial attention to specific films and television programs made with Soderbergh's input, I concentrate on his position as industrial agent, collaborative creative practitioner, and energetic participant in contemporary film culture.

The highly collaborative nature of Soderbergh's filmmaking practice attunes us as well to circuits of boutique practitioners. The 1990s saw the rise of a corporate-subsidized boutique cinema, made up of production companies and small- to medium-budget films supported by major studios, which can provide production financing, studio facilities and equipment, and established distribution networks. Hollywood (and New York City) boutiques include such companies as Sony Pictures Classics, Fox Searchlight, Focus Features, HBO Films, and the now defunct Picturehouse, Fine Line Features, and USA Films. Soderbergh's films have long been associated with this category. His debut fiction feature, the independently produced *sex, lies, and videotape*, was distributed successfully by Miramax, spurring that company's 1993 acquisition by Disney. Two of Soderbergh's directorial efforts of the mid-1990s, *King of the Hill* (1993) and *The Underneath* (1995), were produced or distributed by Universal's Gramercy Pictures unit, prior to Universal's creation of the Focus Features division. Similarly, while Warner Bros. produced *Ocean's Eleven* (2001) and its sequels, that studio's now-defunct boutique division, Warner Independent Pictures, distributed four films from Soderbergh's Section Eight production company. Soderbergh's films exemplify the increasingly similar production and distribution strategies of films regarded as wholly "independent" and those produced with financing or supervision from entities linked to multinational media conglomerates. Aesthetic distinctions once taken for granted—between high-concept and character-driven cinema; between the image and sound designs of studio releases and those of indie or art cinema—similarly blur in Soderbergh's films. Soderbergh-directed efforts include stylized, modestly budgeted studio releases such as *The Underneath* and expensive independent productions such as *Che* (2008). These and other works demonstrate the fluidity of filmmaking styles and production personnel across familiar categories of "studio" and "independent." Soderbergh's recurrent team of collaborators—including assistant director Gregory Jacobs, production designer Philip Messina, sound editor Larry Blake, and others—might be understood as a close-knit group of boutique practitioners adaptive to disparate filmmaking challenges and not defined wholly by overarching production categories.

Reflecting what I characterize later as a boutique sensibility catering to boutique tastes, Soderbergh's ongoing career provides an illuminating model of so-called independent cinema's dissemination into the mainstream in the 1990s. In their modes of production and distribution, their aesthetics and narratives, and their reception among U.S. and global audiences, Soderbergh's films and television productions reveal entertainment industries' openness to innovation and experimentation. Rather than pursuing a chronological, project-by-project appraisal of his work, this book considers Soderbergh's work in three distinct but related ways: (1) as specific texts exemplifying creative authorship across disparate modes and media; (2) as works in dialogue with film history and with production modes and aesthetics long associated with low-budget, commercially marginal cinema; and (3) as boundary-pushing examples of screen-media convergence, new production technologies, and exhibition and distribution strategies. Through a focus on a dynamic creative individual, I seek to highlight the variegated

practices and output of contemporary U.S. screen industries, colloqui-
ally known as Hollywood. Soderbergh and his many projects construct
a particular boutique brand, that of a figure who performs multiple
creative roles in collaboration but who is viewed as exercising sufficient creative control to merit the attribution of primary authorship. I
interrogate as well the myriad discourses that contribute to the production of Soderbergh's screen-author profile. *Another Steven Soderbergh
Experience* attends to the overall process of author construction and to
its consequences for screen producers, consumers, and the industries
connecting them.

The book pursues historical, political, and economic analysis of
contemporary U.S. screen industries while retaining a precise focus on
Soderbergh's many projects and collaborations. Its overall focus is on
authorship, namely on Soderbergh's role as creative individual active
at all levels of production and distribution. Part One, "Soderbergh and
American Cinema," positions the contemporary filmmaker in relation
to the modes and output of mainstream and marginal cinema that
precede him. Chapter 1 takes up Soderbergh's symbolic reputation as
standard-bearer of independent cinema. This chapter examines the
distribution and reception of *sex, lies, and videotape*, and Soderbergh's
relationships with major studios following its critical and commercial success. It also narrates his initial 1990s efforts as independent
producer of projects both within and outside major studios. Chapter
2 investigates the explicit dialogues that Soderbergh and his works
conduct with film history, with canonical and offbeat texts, and with
the creative personnel of U.S. and international cinema. This chapter
links Soderbergh's work to the vibrant U.S. and European cinemas of
the 1960s and 1970s, repeated points of reference for him as for countless other filmmakers and the historians and critics who unite them in
film-cultural discourse.

Part Two, "Authoring and Authorization," investigates the work
that screen authorship entails, and the ways film reception recognizes
Soderbergh's creative contributions. It looks at the work *of* authorship
and the corollary efforts of cultural intermediaries such as reviewers to
label that work *as* authorial—or auteurist—practice. Chapter 3 examines the processes of creative authorship through production analysis of
numerous films directed by Soderbergh. This core chapter documents
the creative practices of Soderbergh and his recurring collaborators,
highlighting in the process the consistency of practice for both studio-
funded and independently produced films. The discernible presence of

similar creative practices in films made for different, and differently capitalized, production companies indicates the need for challenges to the established studio/independent binary. To probe further the discursive power and limits of the "independent" appellation, Chapter 3 also addresses Soderbergh's location-filming efforts and his global profile. It considers his production work outside the U.S., his collaborations with international creative workers and industries, and his status—or lack thereof—as a consecrated global auteur. Returning to domestic contexts, it analyzes critics' and location-shoot witnesses' recognition of Soderbergh and his collaborators' creative activity. Chapter 4 continues the investigation of critical reception, assessing the ways critical discourses have granted Soderbergh the status of individual most directly responsible for the textual features and meanings of the films on which he is credited as director. This chapter surveys efforts to define Soderbergh in auteurist terms, and the benefits that critics and other film-cultural intermediaries gain from constructing Soderbergh as an auteur director even in the face of strong evidence of industrial collaboration.

Most viewers encounter Soderbergh's work at the level of the text, and so Part Three, "Soderbergh and Textuality," identifies the textual characteristics of Soderbergh's films as director, and their generic and intertextual dialogues with previous films and other media texts. Critics and scholars have argued that Soderbergh has shown strong commitments to overtly progressive filmmaking—among other efforts, granting leading roles to African-American and Latino performers, casting nonprofessionals in *Bubble*, directing the pop-leftist *Erin Brockovich* (2000), and executive-producing *Far From Heaven* (2002), the high-profile film about race and sexuality from New Queer Cinema pioneer Todd Haynes. Partly in contrast, Soderbergh films such as *Traffic* have provoked debate for their contradictory or problematic representations of politics, race, gender, and class. Chapter 5 takes up issues of textuality and representation, considering how textual elements acquire significance based on discursive positionings, regimes of style, and a range of viewing protocols. Relatedly, this chapter reassesses the utility of textual criticism, asking how textual critiques of representation bear on viewing practices. Chapter 6—focused on film genres, adaptations, and remakes—considers particular Soderbergh films' intertextual, intermedial dialogues with their many preexisting sources. The chapter addresses the ways intertextual discourses position the films for critical and popular reception, as well as the ways

Soderbergh's consistent reconfiguration of existing texts contributes to his authorial persona.

Soderbergh's creative signature is not only intertextual but also transmedia. Part Four, "Soderbergh and Screen Industries," argues for Soderbergh's unique role in contemporary media industries, emphasizing his efforts across media platforms and distribution networks. Virtually no U.S. filmmakers have worked simultaneously in mainstream genre cinema, low-budget independent cinema, and television. His mainstream Hollywood features since the late 1990s have been marked by an original combination of filmmaking sensibilities, demonstrably indebted to numerous eras in American popular film as well as to filmmakers and movements in international art cinema. His casts include marquee names, indie-film stalwarts, and nonprofessionals. In addition, the Section Eight production company he ran with Clooney through 2006 produced other critically or financially successful films such as *Insomnia* (2002), *Far From Heaven, Good Night, and Good Luck*, and *Michael Clayton* (2007).

To account for this extensive activity, Part Four examines Soderbergh's creative work beyond feature-film directing. Chapter 7 looks to his small-screen projects, projects that foreground narrative and formal experimentation consistent with his film work, but that also exploit television's serial nature. Like many contemporary filmmakers—including Steven Spielberg, Robert Altman, Jerry Bruckheimer, James Cameron, and Michael Mann—Soderbergh moved to the small screen amid a period of critical acclaim and box-office success. In 2003, he served as co-creator, producer, and director of the HBO political series *K Street*; and in 2005, he was a co-producer of *Unscripted*, alongside Clooney and Grant Heslov. Chapter 8 concentrates on Soderbergh's own efforts as producer for Section Eight's projects and others. His films have been co-produced by his own production company, by boutique divisions of major studios, and by the major studios themselves. As his work demonstrates, contemporary U.S. film and television industries offer opportunities for creative industrial practice, boutique productions, and collaboration among corporate, major-studio interests and those of autonomous artist-filmmakers. Soderbergh's ability to work both within and outside the boundaries of major-studio filmmaking—at levels of production, distribution, and exhibition—attests to the fluidity of contemporary, transnational media systems. His collaborative efforts as filmmaker and producer unsettle existing paradigms of media authorship and indicate the need for new, flexible models that account for the complexity of contemporary screen industries. To develop such a model, this chapter considers Soderbergh's extensive activity on DVD commentaries alongside his producing work. Both forms of labor—material production work and discursive performance—constitute a practice of associative authorship that connects Soderbergh to a range of other films and filmmakers.

Chapter 8, like the book overall, seeks not only to establish Soderbergh's position in contemporary screen culture but also to distill and analyze the myriad aspects of media production that make possible his enormous breadth of undertakings. Soderbergh has established himself as a virtual media brand, with high-profile involvement in nearly all forms of contemporary production and spare time to provide DVD commentaries for films he did not direct (such as the 1970 war satire *Catch-22* and the low-budget 1993 drama *Clean, Shaven*), to create new edits of still others (*Keane*'s DVD release includes a separate cut of the film edited by Soderbergh), and to write the occasional book or book introduction. The book's conclusion uses the particular example of Soderbergh to consider how industries and ancillary institutions circulate authorial brands across film-cultural discourse. As a final case study, the conclusion surveys new-media discourses' constructions of Soderbergh surrounding *Che*'s international release in 2008 and 2009. With *Che*, as we will see, official and unofficial agents reference Soderbergh's creative signature to amass different kinds of cultural capital. For a first-person understanding of that signature, I turn also to Soderbergh himself, who generously consented in summer 2011 to a lengthy interview that appears in full as this book's Appendix, and which I hope sheds further light on the relations among artistic temperament, practice, and output. But first, to illustrate Soderbergh's artistic and industrial position in more depth, I turn to a different use of his creative signature, accompanying the modest yet highly experimental feature *Bubble*.

Bubble and Multiplatform Film Distribution

Over the course of Soderbergh's career, screen industries have expanded and contracted at sometimes dizzying rates. Writing in the *New York Times* in 2009, Michael Cieply claims that,

> The glory days of independent film, when hot young directors like Steven Soderbergh and [Quentin] Tarantino had studio executives tangled in fierce bidding wars at Sundance and other celebrity-studded festivals, are now

barely a speck in the rearview mirror. And something new, something much odder, has taken their place.[2]

This "something much odder" refers to emerging models of film circulation, including individual filmmakers' self-distribution of their works, their social-networking efforts, and other unconventional means of four-walled as well as online presentation. Cieply name-checks Soderbergh but does not mention him further in the ensuing discussion, and yet, Soderbergh has shown deep investments in many of these new circulation models. To tease out some of the key dynamics of Soderbergh's work, I begin with a case study of *Bubble*, focusing on its novel exhibition and distribution strategy and Soderbergh's role in promoting the simultaneous multiple-platform release. This case study also permits attention to two other aspects of filmmaking practice that characterize Soderbergh's work: use of high-definition digital-video cameras rather than film cameras, and work with nonprofessional actors. These features of *Bubble* exemplify the innovative, experimental dimension of Soderbergh's work but also bleed into the production method and aesthetics of his mainstream studio features. *Bubble* underlines, too, the role of the branded author in circulating discrete texts across multiple exhibition platforms.

As surveyed above, *Bubble* represents one of Soderbergh's many projects between work on *Ocean's Twelve* and *Ocean's Thirteen*. Working as director, camera operator, and editor, Soderbergh shot *Bubble* with a small cast of nonprofessional actors and a minimal crew. It played on thirty-two U.S. screens at its widest release, while the *Ocean's* films each played on between 3,500 and 4,000 screens in the U.S. alone. Beyond Soderbergh's A-list pedigree and creative method, *Bubble* deserves attention for its simultaneous theatrical, pay-television, and DVD release. In this it exemplifies the ongoing efforts of U.S. media industries to expand distribution pathways to reach diffuse audiences worldwide. The growth of multiplatforming as an exhibition practice promises to transform critical understandings of textuality and consumption. *Bubble*—DVD artifact, made-for-TV movie, arthouse theatrical release, and experimental film promoting the brand of its well-known director—further erodes organizing binaries such as film vs. television texts, theatrical vs. domestic consumption, and conceptions of discrete film, television, and DVD industries altogether.

Academic and industrial definitions of media texts have in recent years emphasized platform specificity, or the ways textual properties accommodate the requirements of distinct media such as theatrical

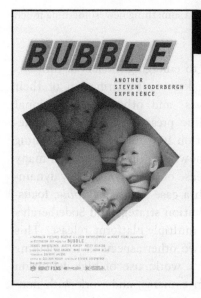

The promotional poster for *Bubble* (2005) relies on Soderbergh's name as a key marketable asset.

film, television, DVD, and portable devices. As feature films circulate among these media in narrower time frames—for example, as the interval between theatrical and home-video releases shrinks—textual features and promotional discourses increasingly address multiple reception groups simultaneously. As a low-budget digital-video feature with a prominent Hollywood director but no stars, and without major-studio support but with a well-financed and well-publicized distributor, *Bubble* earns a curious industrial position mixing innovation and convention. *Bubble* merges existing techniques of realist filmmaking (including location shooting and improvisation) with newer modes of production and distribution (including digital-video shooting and its cross-platform release), suggesting one model for the circulation of entertainment texts in post-theatrical and post-studio eras. Released with the slogan "Another Steven Soderbergh Experience," *Bubble* also suggests ways the author function can facilitate cross-platform circulation in a crowded marketplace. *Bubble* relies on its brand author as a promotional device, rather than foregrounding such elements as stars, genres, visual spectacle, or sequels and series (all of which studios or smaller producers have used to market other Soderbergh-directed efforts).

Bubble was shot quickly in small-town West Virginia and Ohio, and exhibits a low-tech HD-video aesthetic.[3] For the sake of convenience, we may persist in labeling *Bubble* a "film," even as this designation is arguably inaccurate given its limited circulation as a 35mm print. *Bubble*'s narrative concerns the friendships and rivalries of three workers at a small plastic-doll factory: a middle-aged woman and a young couple, all lower-middle class. The film is altogether minimal, with a storyline that features just one notable incident, an unobtrusive solo-guitar soundtrack, and a 73-minute running time, barely feature length. Its aesthetic could be characterized as stylized realism: many scenes play out in long takes with no camera movement, while others employ amplified, ambient location sound or anti-realist color. The film includes two particularly subjective interludes in which the older protagonist, Martha (Debbie Doebereiner), appears surrounded by darkness, with only her face and torso illuminated by blue-tinted lighting, and with a series of direct-address shots and extreme close-ups showing her fixed stare. In its production context and textual features, *Bubble* exemplifies regional filmmaking. The production is highly local, shot entirely in one semi-rural area and using existing actors, locations, and costumes. The film could also be categorized as vérité or personal cinema, with cast members playing versions of themselves (as screen tests included on the DVD indicate), albeit with narrative additions such as criminal behavior. The film fits too under the all-purpose "independent film" banner, given its no-frills aesthetic and its theatrical release from Magnolia Pictures, distributor of small independent releases, documentaries with crossover appeal, and foreign genre films.

Bubble inaugurated a planned six-film series contracted by Soderbergh with HDNet Films, the production arm of the mini-conglomerate 2929 Entertainment, owned by entertainment moguls Todd Wagner and Mark Cuban. Soderbergh's name thus contributes to HDNet's emerging brand of "day-and-date" multiplatform releases. Trade commentary on *Bubble* accentuates not director Soderbergh or any aspect of the film's content, but instead its novel U.S. release pattern.[4] Production and distribution occur across 2929 Entertainment's multiple divisions: producer HDNet Films, the Landmark Theatres chain, pay-per-view channel HDNet Movies, and DVD distributor Magnolia Home Entertainment. The Wagner/Cuban company's diverse profile (which includes another specialty cable channel, HDNet) exemplifies Patricia Zimmermann's claim that "independent narrative film needs to . . . be rethought as a form of cinema that moves across different platforms and through different audiences and economies."[5] Zimmermann's carefully argued work retains terms such as "film" and "cinema" even as the parameters of her study go well beyond celluloid production and theatrical exhibition. The case of 2929 Entertainment further complicates the term "independent" as well. While as a production entity it hardly challenges any of the established media conglomerates, it benefits from its principals' substantial capital and existing media and entertainment holdings, which also include part-stakes in Canadian-based producer/ distributor Lions Gate Entertainment, the post-Miramax Weinstein Company, and a U.S. professional sports franchise. Wagner and Cuban became billionaires through technology-sector entrepreneurship, and Cuban has earned further media celebrity through reality-television appearances and his visible courtside presence as majority owner of the NBA's Dallas Mavericks. With eBay founder Jeff Skoll and Moviefone founder Andrew Jarecki also working in independent film,[6] this sector of the global entertainment industry is thoroughly embedded in existing networks of multinational capitalism.

Entertainment conglomerates and smaller media producers share, too, a strategic interest in promotional branding of creative workers. Soderbergh, whose work ranges from mass-release theatrical blockbusters to experimental shorts on limited-distribution compilation DVDs, perfectly embodies this industrial strategy. Soderbergh's most successful efforts, the *Ocean's* trilogy and *Erin Brockovich*, have been star-driven genre films that mass audiences may not associate with a particular director. (Instead, stars such as George Clooney and Julia Roberts dominate those films' promotional campaigns.) And in a 2008 interview, Universal's former worldwide chief of marketing, David Weitzner, offers a commonsensical critique of the notion of film directors as marketable assets: "It's pomposity on the part of studios to think that the public is going to respond to an advertising message that says to see the film because it's from the director of another film."[7] Yet in smaller productions targeted at niche and cinephile viewerships, particular creative workers do carry brand-name appeal. In Soderbergh's case, this appeal is fashioned not only from discrete texts bearing his name but also from a range of discursive practices, many demonstrating what John Caldwell terms "industrial reflexivity," or reflexive industrial practice.[8] Soderbergh's reflexive practices occur in DVD commentaries, production diaries and book introductions, interviews in niche periodicals such as *Film Threat*, and shepherding of multiple reissues of American underground films through executive-producer roles.

Journalists and other industry analysts invoked *Bubble*'s multiplatform release to speculate about the future of film distribution and exhibition.[9] While the Hollywood trade press was both curious and sanguine about the experiment,[10] the community of exhibitors reacted negatively. Many U.S. theaters and chains refused to exhibit *Bubble* because of its home-video availability, and many press outlets circulated Fithian's description of multiplatform releases as a "death threat" to cinemas, a declaration he had made nearly six months before *Bubble*'s release, in regards to a remark from Disney chairman Robert Iger.[11] Recalling a still-earlier event of perceived industry crisis, the hand-wringing over circulation of DVD screeners during the 2003 Academy Awards season, Barbara Klinger observes that "cinema's ability to be so easily reproduced for nontheatrical exhibition still manages to introduce the specter of chaos, a looming circumvention of tradition and regulation that can arouse Hollywood's protective reaction."[12] In the case of *Bubble*, executive producer Cuban served as the vocal advocate of multiplatform distribution, leaving Soderbergh to give more low-key interviews about the film's distribution and content.

Trade-press coverage of *Bubble*'s release is notable for its assumption that *Bubble* is primarily a feature film that enjoys a simultaneous release on pay television and DVD (the latter of course principally viewed on television screens). No commentator suggests that *Bubble* might be a television text that enjoys separate theatrical screenings. Even in the evolving convergence landscape, theatrically released cinema provides the locus for recognition of industrial, economic, and aesthetic transformations. As Zimmermann argues further, "films are the nodal points of circulating commodities,"[13] and theatrical releases facilitate the proliferation of commodities across a range of media and time frames (i.e., industry-dictated release windows). Myriad taste cultures and institutional preferences continue to bolster film's status as the pinnacle of screen artistry and creative labor. In trade- and especially popular-press coverage, creative professionals' film-industry work overshadows their efforts in television and other media. Despite Soderbergh's involvement in two HBO series, he is rarely identified as a television practitioner, or as anything but a "filmmaker" or "director," in trade- or popular-press coverage.

Even as convergence threatens to upset the hierarchy in which film stands above television, DVD, and web-based and portable media, discursive formations continue to privilege old media. Industry and academics do increasingly regard authorship as a cross-platform phenomenon, with many creative workers hailed as "auteurs" in both film and television, or television and new media.[14] However, involvement in theatrically released feature films continues to carry greater cachet than achievement in other media. All these points echo Caldwell's argument that "Hollywood's production communities perpetuate the largely symbolic, hierarchical model of film as artistry versus electronic media as commerce. Practitioners achieve very real benefits when this discourse of distinction circulates."[15] A different approach to the text *Bubble* and the phenomena of its production and distribution, then, would be to view it as a television or digital production that is also distributed outside conventional broadcast or narrowcast windows.[16] In fact, the architecture of *Bubble*'s online promotional forums partly achieves this inversion or leveling. The websites of the various companies under the 2929 Entertainment umbrella make no particular distinctions regarding their primary industry or the exhibition site for their produced content. *Bubble*'s own official website simply includes links to the various pathways through which audiences might experience the text, with information about DVD purchase, subscriber-television schedules, theatrical screenings, and ancillary streaming-video content ranked in effect equally on the webpage. Nonetheless, it is telling that its production company, whose output consists exclusively of productions shot on digital video, and that are consumed primarily in DVD form, should be named HDNet *Films*.

In whatever medium we choose to categorize it, *Bubble*'s production and distribution link it to opposing terms in multiple binaries that surround screen media: analog/digital, realism/stylization, amateur/professional, location/dispersion, experience/artifact, and more. While evidencing what Soderbergh calls "site-specific" filmmaking,[17] it also circulates more freely than conventional studio releases or independently distributed features. In this respect, it can be positioned within either of two distinct phases in Hollywood's development. Aida Hozic proposes a chronology of Hollywood history that begins "in the studio," largely moves "on location," and now exists "in cyberspace."[18] At the level of production, *Bubble* remains emphatically on location (small-town West Virginia and Ohio). Its distribution and exhibition cross media platforms and thus geographic space as consumers experience it in different locations. However, *Bubble* does not circulate freely in the global arena. Its DVD release was limited to the North American Region 1/NTSC format,[19] and outside the U.S., it received theatrical screenings only at select film festivals. Clearly, multiplatform releases and the convergent-media environment hardly guarantee access to global audiences. *Bubble* faced tangible obstacles in the form of a lack of ready buyers for worldwide theatrical distribution rights and rights issues as well as hardware and software restrictions for the DVD release.[20]

While its theatrical returns and DVD sales were modest,[21] in many respects *Bubble* carries a near-ideal pedigree for a multiplatform release to arthouse cinemas, niche cable channels, and cinephilic DVD consumers. Soderbergh, still identified with the U.S. independent-cinema boom thanks to the canonization of *sex, lies, and videotape*, is arguably *Bubble*'s principal exploitable element. The film show-cases no other A-list talent such as screenwriters or producers, and its superficial description—"site-specific" digital-video production with a partly improvising amateur cast—makes it comparable to innumerable backyard family videos and student films. On the other hand, in the realm of DVD content, Soderbergh is a prolific figure. His multiple creative efforts as filmmaker, producer, and commentator make him a veritable cottage industry of ancillary material, supplying interviews or commentaries for DVD releases of films as diverse as *The Third Man* (1949), *Catch-22*, mid-budget Miramax release *The Yards*, the Chinese war drama *Devils on the Doorstep* (2000), and many others. Active, too, in such areas as niche-market DVD shorts, intra-industry promotion of digital filmmaking, and anti-piracy advocacy, Soderbergh is the reflexive industrial practitioner par excellence. Caldwell argues that vocal, visible industry self-scrutiny circulates an impression of transparent practice, and *Bubble* further exemplifies this phenomenon. The *Bubble* website features Soderbergh in a streaming-video inter-view about the film and its multiplatform release, and the DVD extras include a co-commentary with fellow director Mark Romanek (not involved in *Bubble*'s production), the lead performers' screen tests, and a segment in which they spend time in their homes and hometown accompanied by *Bubble*'s screenwriter, Coleman Hough. Together these features promise to open up the production process to diverse audiences. Consequently, the feature *Bubble* becomes in effect an add-on to the recreated immersion in the production process. Ancillary content creates sufficient added value that the centrality of the feature itself diminishes. In lieu of any generic or narrative descriptors, the name-checking of Soderbergh and the "Another Steven Soderbergh Experience" tagline on the promotional poster and DVD sleeve fore-ground the branded author exclusively.

While multiplatform releases have subsequently increased through such efforts as the Independent Film Channel's "IFC on Demand" and "Festival Direct" services (carried by the major cable provider Comcast since 2008), the example of *Bubble* indicates the substantial institu-tional and attitudinal hurdles to their success. Soderbergh's second work in the multiple-film contract with HDNet Films, *The Girlfriend*

Experience (2009), earned some notoriety through the casting of video-porn star Sasha Grey but otherwise remains in the category of small independent releases. It was unveiled in rough-cut form at Sundance in 2009 (tied to the twentieth anniversary of *sex, lies, and video-tape*'s premiere at Sundance's precursor, the U.S. Film Festival), then received limited U.S. theatrical and DVD distribution from Magnolia. Meanwhile, other HDNet Films output remains in categories long associated with U.S. independent cinema: offbeat documentaries and erotically charged dramas that play in festival screenings at Sundance and elsewhere and earn limited releases in boutique cinemas. (In fact, this profile more or less describes a number of Soderbergh's 1990s efforts as director as well.) Nonetheless, the evolving HDNet/Magnolia/2929 enterprise and other companies' "day-and-date" or digital-distribution initiatives underscore the significance of industrial negotiations as films and filmmakers seek to establish relationships with North American and international audiences.

Investigation of these new exhibition initiatives may further our awareness of the possibilities and limits of screen-media circulation, and our recognition of authoring figures' positions within global circulation networks. This brief case study demonstrates, I hope, some of the ways the transmedia author Soderbergh has pursued innovative screen practice. We may now circle back to the start of his career, probing his associations with commercial independent cinema since the 1980s, his evolving authorial persona, his thoroughgoing collaborative practice, and his carefully cultivated position as intermediary in global screen cultures.

Part One

Soderbergh and American Cinema

Chapter 1

Sex, Lies, and Independent Film

The success of *sex, lies, and videotape* at the Cannes and U.S. (a.k.a. Sundance) film festivals and in commercial release earned Soderbergh indelible associations with the discourses and institutions of U.S. independent cinema on a global stage. Measured in terms of commercial visibility, Soderbergh's career floundered for much of the 1990s. The limited impact of his post–*sex, lies* features stood as an apparent object lesson in the pitfalls of Hollywood authorship. For example, one 1998 profile, subtitled "The Return of Steven Soderbergh," describes him as "the indie hero whose films nobody goes to see."[1] While the view of Soderbergh as icon of independents obscures U.S. independent cinema's long history, Soderbergh's debut feature may rightly be credited with ushering in the 1990s boom in independent-cinema production and distribution. *sex, lies, and videotape* featured prominently in entertainment-press commentary upon its release and in subsequent popular histories of independent cinema. This chapter identifies the conditions that facilitated the 1990s indie-film boom, as well as Soderbergh's specific contributions through film direction, collaborative production, and promotion. The chapter also considers Soderbergh's relationships with major studios and independent producers in the early 1990s. While his early films as director bore the hallmarks of independent cinema in subject, style, and distribution, some were in fact produced or distributed by "mini-major" boutique divisions created or acquired by major studios. Soderbergh's second feature, *Kafka* (1991), appeared as a co-production from small U.S. independent Baltimore Pictures and two French production companies. He then began a relationship with Universal, whose Gramercy Pictures imprint distributed his next two directing efforts, *King of the Hill* and

The Underneath. Even his low-budget experiment *Schizopolis*, which received almost no theatrical release and which was shot on film stock donated by a fellow filmmaker,[2] owed its financing to Universal's advance purchase of home-video rights and its payment to Soderbergh of a fee for another project in development.[3] Also during this period, Soderbergh directed the 1996 adaptation of a Spalding Gray stage monologue, *Gray's Anatomy*, a transnational collaboration of two television producers, the UK's BBC and the U.S.'s Independent Film Channel (and with U.S. theatrical distribution from the independent Northern Arts).

I argue in this chapter that Soderbergh's 1990s work exemplifies U.S. and European film industries' sustenance of a range of idiosyncratic filmmaking modes and styles. As many commentators have noted, during this period conglomerate studios moved increasingly toward blockbuster or tentpole releases with large production and marketing budgets (e.g., the *Batman* franchise of 1989 and beyond, and the *Jurassic Park* series beginning in 1993). Consequently, smaller producers filled gaps for ostensibly adult fare with low- to medium-budget ($1 million to $10 million) films, films then often acquired for distribution by companies in which major studios had controlling investments or owned outright. As in Hollywood's post–Paramount Decree era, a substantial number of films in wide circulation came from independent producers, with studios operating chiefly as distributors rather than directly managing the creative process of production.[4] Such decentralization of production meant that even films released under studio logos could manifest the creative impulses of small production teams.

I do not mean here to endorse the crude binary that posits studio production as artless and profit-driven against the auteurist paradise of independent filmmaking, but merely to indicate industrial structures outside the studio sector that encourage definitively artisanal production modes. These production determinants include small production partnerships often responsible for only single films; production financing earned through such strategies as pre-sales to European television markets, further reducing executive oversight; creative personnel assembling for single productions and then dispersing; and location filmmaking often distant from the production centers of Los Angeles and New York. Often film-school trained, the acclaimed 1980s independent filmmakers worked largely within the parameters of narrative fiction, hewing closely to realist convention and linear storytelling norms, and their films still draw on exploitable elements such as genres and stars. This loose template offered substantial latitude for experimentation in narrative, performance style, image and sound aesthetics, and subject matter. Marginal and radical filmmaking traditions abounded: documentary, artists' video, black underground filmmaking, gay and lesbian cinema, and numerous other movements and modes. Commercial independent cinema occupied a border space between real or imagined mainstreams and margins.[5] As industry and assemblage of creative workers, commercial independent cinema showed affiliations with studio personnel and practices as well as with the milieus of underground and experimental film and video. Though Soderbergh was not involved with key sub-strands of U.S. independent cinema in the 1990s, he took on new patron roles in the 2000s, as other chapters in this book discuss.

Soderbergh's films have been central to the fabrication of the discursive formation "indie film" and to the development of major studios' boutique divisions. One such company, Warner Independent Pictures, during its existence from 2003 through 2008 produced or distributed many of the films from Soderbergh's Section Eight production company.[6] Earlier, Soderbergh's initial success in the independent sector enabled him to find backing for a series of commercially disappointing medium-budget films through the late 1990s. Even discounting the cachet that *sex, lies, and videotape* garnered Soderbergh in the years after its release, it becomes clear that executives at various levels of U.S. and European film industries in the 1990s continued to support creative filmmaking and attached few preconditions to their support. Throughout his 1990s interviews, Soderbergh recounts few stories of executive interference, though aesthetic compromises distinguish his work from the start of his career. A 1989 *Rolling Stone* profile, for example, describes in passing the pragmatic relationship between Soderbergh and *sex, lies, and videotape*'s key production financier: "He wanted to shoot the movie in black and white, but RCA/Columbia insisted on color."[7] Soderbergh retrospectively affirms this compromise, suggesting that to proceed according to his initial preference would have been a "huge mistake. A fatal mistake."[8] Soderbergh did spar with executives who envisioned explicit sex scenes and female nudity,[9] but they ultimately accepted his choice to withhold graphic imagery. Overall, Soderbergh's work through the late 1990s shows studios' and independent production companies' intermittent patronage of highly author-driven filmmaking partly irrespective of audience and profit considerations. To gain a close view of Soderbergh's relationship with industry personnel and mediating critical institutions, this chapter devotes particular attention to the intra-industry response to

Soderbergh's work through the mid-1990s, a formative period for mainstream recognition of independent film.

Identifying the semantic battles and practical complications of the term "independent" as applied to commercial U.S. film productions, Yannis Tzioumakis argues that "American independent cinema" is best understood not as an empirical category but as a discourse, "a discourse that expands and contracts when socially authored institutions . . . contribute toward its definition at different periods in the history of American cinema."[10] His book *American Independent Cinema* traces the development of independent cinema both as discourse and as identifiable if consistently disputed industrial formation. Rather than reproducing Tzioumakis's cogent historical narrative, in this chapter I wish to demonstrate how Soderbergh's creative efforts contribute to, and are framed by, 1980s and 1990s commercial-cinema discourses. Framings of Soderbergh's films demonstrate the taste allegiances and industrial narratives spread by industry personnel and by intermediaries such as entertainment reporters and film-review journalists.

Niche Filmmaking and Codependence in 1980s Hollywood

Thanks to the growth of numerous companies and institutions, the relationship between independent filmmakers and corporate-controlled film studios changed significantly in the 1980s. Key independent-cinema institutions emerged to lend visibility to disparate strands of U.S. filmmaking. The now-venerable Sundance Film Festival began in 1978 as the Utah/U.S. Film Festival and in 1985 came under the administration of the Sundance Institute, which had been formed in 1981. (The festival's name remained the U.S. Film Festival through 1990.[11]) In 1986, the U.S. nonprofit Film Independent began giving its Independent Spirit Awards.[12] Beyond these institutional efforts to raise the profiles of films and filmmakers, distribution of independent films exploded in the mid-1980s, with the number of independently distributed films nearly doubling from 1984 to 1986.[13] Major studios' distribution of independent productions did not jump so measurably; instead, independents invested more heavily in production and distribution. New or growing companies such as Carolco, Orion, New World, Vestron, and others began bold production-financing efforts on the strength of individual successes (such as 1982's *First Blood* for Carolco and 1986's *Platoon* for Orion) and on the potential for profit in the emerging home-video market.[14] Lacking adequate capitalization or otherwise unable to weather periodic slumps, most of these companies were soon absorbed by larger conglomerates or folded outright. The 1990s witnessed similar growth and contraction among independent producers and distributors, with the surviving companies those with long-term arrangements with established studios or conglomerates—Miramax with Disney, New Line with Warner Bros., Gramercy Pictures and October Films with Universal (these, though, both later casualties of mergers and restructurings at the parent company), and others.

Soderbergh's entry into Hollywood industries occurred not through independent film but through network television. A young and uncredentialed writer and would-be director, he began industry work as an editor on the NBC series *Games People Play* (1980–1981), then earned his first feature credit for directing and editing Yes's concert documentary *9012LIVE* (1985), a hybrid music- and film-industry production that earned Soderbergh a Grammy nomination. Though he amassed no further production credits in the 1980s, one of his scripts drew interest from independent Outlaw Productions, who negotiated a production deal with him for a different script that would eventually become *sex, lies, and videotape*. Outlaw gained production financing by pre-selling U.S. home-video rights to RCA/Columbia Home Video and overseas exhibition and video rights to Virgin. As many have narrated, the film screened at 1989's U.S. Film Festival, where it attracted distributors' interest. At the following month's American Film Market, Miramax acquired the film's remaining rights, including U.S. theatrical distribution.[15]

From the outset, Soderbergh's filmmaking practice was less independent than codependent. Partly lost in the narrative of a scrappy young talent casting about for financial support and eventually striking gold is the fact that Soderbergh's key backers were divisions of major entertainment conglomerates. *9012LIVE* was produced by Atlantic Records, controlled by the Warner Entertainment conglomerate (preceding the 1990 merger that created Time Warner). Meanwhile, RCA/Columbia Home Video, the principal financier of *sex, lies, and videotape*, represented a partnership of Columbia Pictures and electronics giant RCA.[16] Soderbergh claims as well to have made the short film *Winston* (1987)—a narrative of sexual unease used as a demo reel to attract investors—with money received from a TriStar scriptwriting commission.[17] Thus, as with countless other "independent" successes, entertainment-conglomerate capital explicitly supported Soderbergh's work. While these entities played almost no creative role during *sex, lies, and videotape*'s production, their backing was essential to the execution of the $1.2 million film. Soderbergh's other well-below-the-line work during his initial residence in Los Angeles similarly relied on subsidiaries of major studios. Such industrial interconnectedness renders the concept of economic independence altogether suspect. Meanwhile, relying on the examples of Soderbergh and others, we may preserve notions of creative independence, but only by compartmentalizing filmmakers' experiences, regarding conglomerate-derived paychecks as irrelevant to specific artistic sensibilities. If we abandon this fragile conceit, we gain instead a fair picture of Soderbergh as a creative worker supported from the beginning of his career by entertainment conglomerates in screen, music, and technology industries.

Film history abounds with cases of filmmakers alternating between studio and independent projects. The familiar principle of "one for the studio, one for yourself" suggests that creative workers operate with dual, opposing consciousnesses: a work-for-hire mindset that involves no personal artistic stake, and a work-for-love or work-for-art perspective that entails passionate commitment and creative satisfaction. As later chapters discuss, Soderbergh and his collaborators repeatedly move among large- and small-scale productions. Tiny, shoestring productions inarguably differ from well-financed, large-scale efforts. Production scales dictate substantially different working conditions in terms of pace of production and overall production timeframes, quality and abundance of technical resources, comfort levels and compensation for cast and crew, producer oversight based on economic considerations, and more. A large production scale dictates a need to speak to a wide viewership, limiting the creative innovation that may be evident on smaller projects. Compelling cases can be made for small-scale projects facilitating distinct artistic sensibilities in ways larger productions cannot, but creative professionals routinely work across production scales in a range of artistic roles. For example, as a writer-director John Cassavetes crafted highly contained films such as *Shadows* (1959) and *Faces* (1968) infused with a realist sensibility, while highlights of his acting career include stylized crime films such as *The Killers* (1964), the cartoonish war epic *The Dirty Dozen* (1967), and supernatural horror such as *Rosemary's Baby* (1968). However Cassavetes asserted his artistic integrity and justified his professional choices, his performances in studio productions were essential to the steady progression of his directorial career. His romantic enshrinement as uncompromising independent filmmaker should not overshadow his broader profile as film-industry professional. Efforts to demarcate spheres of artistic engagement and disengagement—on the part of film critics, historians, distributors, and cinephile communities overall—perpetuate untenable binaries about the nature of creative labor in U.S. and global film industries.

Soderbergh's professional profile includes areas of creative autonomy as well as economic dependence and codependence. Industrial analyses of contemporary Hollywood show the increasingly interconnected networks of ownership and investment in screen-media production, distribution, and exhibition. (Audio and print media of course participate in and extend these networks.) Writing on studio-affiliated specialty divisions (and borrowing a concept from Mike Wayne), Geoff King argues for the so-called "Indiewood" sector as emblematic of "subsidiary capitalism."[18] In this post-Fordist practice, independent producers act as proxies for conglomerate interests, resulting in expanded reach of independent productions as well as those productions' own incorporation of explicitly commercial logics. Recognition beyond the narrowest niche community depends on engagement with some facet of comprehensive commercial networks. Understanding Soderbergh as a figure embedded in creative-industry networks can take us beyond the somewhat limiting paradigms of studio and independent filmmaking, as well as beyond the unsophisticated if romantic construct of the rebel-auteur filmmaker.

The concept of the creative individual embedded in commercial networks foregrounds numerous economic and artistic relationships. Filmmakers' and critics' scorn for contemporary conglomerate-studio production often sits aside celebrations of those same studios' output in other eras, with late-1960s and early-1970s New Hollywood a locus of collective esteem. (Invariably, the celebrated industry is the countercultural one behind *Bonnie and Clyde* [1967] and *Easy Rider* [1969] rather than the dinosaur responsible for *The Love Bug* [1969] and *Airport* [1970].) Material differences do indeed distinguish contemporary Hollywood from its romanticized forebear. Repeatedly invoked drags on creative autonomy include, for example, the rise of test marketing and of talent-agency packaging. Many corporate structures of the New Hollywood era—or "Hollywood Renaissance," for those who regard the term "New Hollywood" as synonymous with 1980s conglomeration[19]—nonetheless remain relatively intact, though now embedded more visibly in dispersed networks of transnational capital.

The 1980s encompasses the emergence of filmmakers such as John Sayles and Spike Lee, and the rise and decline of independent producers and distributors such as Island and Cinecom (as well as the larger independent companies noted above). These artistic and industrial arcs coincide with increasingly codependent relationships between independent filmmakers and conglomerating studios as well as the growing recognition and significance of niche viewerships. One impetus behind (or byproduct of) the fabrication of the "independent cinema" discourse was to lend distinction to small films that would otherwise have low marketplace visibility, lacking well-known stars, lavish production values, or readily exploitable genre elements. The label "independent film" offers cultural currency similar to that associated with another long-present niche commodity, "foreign film," and helps distinguish small U.S. films from glossier mainstream-Hollywood competition. Geoff King identifies the perceived logic of marketing films as niche products: "By choosing to view speciality rather than mainstream films . . . consumers are associating themselves . . . with a particular social-cultural domain based on varying degrees of differentiation from mainstream cinema, culture, and society."[20] The construction of this niche as a site of cultural esteem depends in turn on a negative construction of the mainstream, for which Hollywood supplies a convenient avatar.

What Are You Rebelling Against?

Accounts of U.S. cinema often emphasize interpersonal conflict (e.g., artist vs. executive) and artistic integrity, contributing to false binaries and distorting the work of commercial filmmakers overall. In journalistic and academic commentary on contemporary Hollywood, numerous key terms tend to be reproduced without interrogation. Buzzwords such as "outsiders," "rebels," and "mavericks" are particularly prevalent. Most of the beloved "mavericks" of popular film history, whether New Hollywood figures such as Francis Ford Coppola or younger filmmakers such as Spike Lee, gain recognition when their films achieve critical and commercial visibility. Hence the ever-narrower taxonomies of rebels or outsiders in cinephilic taste cultures that privilege exclusivity or obscurity, Coppola's or Lee's outsiderness differing qualitatively from that of Jonas Mekas or Charles Burnett, for example.[21] If the mindset of mavericks or rebels involves opposition to studio goals of commercial success, then such figures should logically produce resolutely un- or anti-commercial films. Film journalism as well as some academic criticism paradoxically celebrates groups of avowed rebels whose names— Fincher, Tarantino, Rodriguez, and many others—are familiar because of, not in spite of, their commercial success. In critical practice, the term "rebel" designates men (and never women) whose names accompany successful films in which critics discern any creative sensibility distinguishable from an understood mainstream. When characterized by persona rather than textual output, the rebel distinction emerges from narratives of limited compromise within corporate structures. In either case, rebels still meet a range of professional standards during production activity and in the provision of commercial works (or completion of the main body of that work, subject to refinement in postproduction).

Hollywood has historically thrived on the combination of institutionalized risk aversion and cyclical creative innovation. Thus, the term "Hollywood maverick" can be viewed as either redundant (in that Hollywood practice necessarily involves novelty and differentiation) or oxymoronic (in that actual mavericks do not willingly join themselves to commercial, hierarchical institutions). Still, numerous accounts of independent filmmakers who have successfully integrated studio-production or commercial-exhibition spaces explicitly celebrate the construct of the rebel or maverick. Greg Merritt titles his independent-cinema history *Celluloid Mavericks* (1999) and defines independence in the narrowest sense, via films wholly removed from studio and conglomerate networks (though this distinction cannot exclude films whose creative personnel might work separately on major-studio projects). In *The Sundance Kids*, subtitled "How the Mavericks Took Back Hollywood," James Mottram initially interrogates the term maverick, noting its potential incompatibility with commercial entertainment labor. He ultimately justifies its use with the simple claim that the filmmakers he studies meet part of the *OED*'s definition of the word: they are "unorthodox and open-minded."[22] Sharon Waxman's *Rebels on the Backlot* builds its simpler argument into a longer subtitle: "Six Maverick Directors and How They Conquered the Hollywood Studio System." Waxman's hyperbolic work offers no particular justification for its claims, asserting instead that the Indiewood directors she profiles "shared a collective disdain for a studio system designed to strip them of their voices and dull their jagged edges."[23] Her formulation betrays the continued impulse to demonize the "studio system" long after its erosion in the 1950s and the industrial shift to dispersed, independent production across Hollywood. Meanwhile, the most well-known popular-historical account of the late-1980s and 1990s indie-film boom, Peter Biskind's *Down and Dirty Pictures*, does not specifically name its subjects as rebels. Setting its overall tone, though, the book's first sentence links the era in question to the 1970s New Hollywood, and to Biskind's own 1998 book on that era, *Easy Riders, Raging Bulls* (which does use the rebel-hero trope for its own assertive subtitle, "How the Sex-Drugs-and-Rock 'n' Roll Generation Saved Hollywood").

Discursive connections among particular filmmakers, the broad category of independent film, and ideologies of rebellion and integrity hold sway even when contradictions loom large. The very concept of "Sundance," for example, merges underground or outsider discourses with those absolutely central to institutional Hollywood. The increasing visibility of the Sundance Film Festival and its related Sundance Institute led to assertions that by 1990, the festival already had become dominated by Hollywood-studio interests.[24] Few such critiques observed that the institute's co-founders included long-established studio directors Sydney Pollack and Robert Redford, or that the institute and festival both take their name from the 20th Century Fox release (though ostensible independent production) *Butch Cassidy and the Sundance Kid* (1969), which grossed over $100 million in theatrical release and positioned Redford as one of the industry's top stars. The film's success, and Redford's subsequent compensation on studio-backed films, enabled his continued investment in the tony Sundance ski resort as well as in the nonprofit filmmaking institute and the festival. Far from being an anti- or off-Hollywood maverick, Redford embodies middle-brow Hollywood prestige and has long served as an industry gatekeeper. Across his career, his Sundance associations have aligned him with independent-sector output without impeding his profitable position in the Hollywood mainstream.

Creative, professional, and economic networks linking art-minded filmmakers to post-Fordist conglomerates are active in the present and also were during the mid-1980s emergence of independent film as a visible market category. Many of the films that form the canon of 1980s independent cinema—i.e., those repeatedly invoked by cinephile communities and in academic and popular histories—show close links with major-studio interests. Numerous celebrated careers demonstrate such links. Before and after gaining acclaim as an independent writer-director, John Sayles earned screenwriting credits on productions from large independents, well-capitalized mini-majors, and conglomerate units including CBS (both television and film) and Warner Bros. These contract efforts gave him the financial security to pursue ostensibly personal projects that afforded him creative autonomy. And even as many of his 1980s features received independent distribution, the boutique imprint United Artists Classics distributed his second film,

Lianna (1983), and Paramount distributed his third, *Baby It's You* (1983).²⁵ To cite another case, Spike Lee's debut feature *She's Gotta Have It* (1986) was independently produced and distributed, though he worked next with Columbia for *School Daze* (1988). Lee also pursued a parallel career in television commercials, working with corporations such as Nike and advertising agencies such as the conglomerate unit DDB Needham. Some well-known independent filmmakers did operate in the 1980s and early 1990s principally in networks not linked to media-conglomerate holdings. Jim Jarmusch released *Stranger Than Paradise* (1984) through the mid-sized independent Samuel Goldwyn Company, and worked with the similarly scaled Island Pictures on his next film, *Down by Law* (1986, the same year as Island's release of *She's Gotta Have It*). Mini-major Orion Pictures distributed Jarmusch's 1989 feature, *Mystery Train*, through its Orion Classics imprint, and mini-major New Line, before its part-acquisition by Time Warner, distributed *Night on Earth* (1991) through its Fine Line subsidiary. Jarmusch has since joined conglomerate networks by association, working with major performers such as Johnny Depp and Bill Murray.

Beyond the economic and professional networks linking conglomerates and artisans, filmmakers and critics repeatedly invoke creative affiliations between the New Hollywood and contemporary independent cinema. This discourse rarely assesses the similarities or differences in industrial structure, distribution practices, and exhibition contexts across the two demarcated eras. Biskind's *Down and Dirty Pictures* declares itself a "sequel" to *Easy Riders, Raging Bulls* and asserts 1990s independent filmmakers as "spiritual and aesthetic heirs" to the New Hollywood.²⁶ Waxman's *Rebels on the Backlot* similarly opens by connecting New Hollywood and 1990s filmmakers, declaring the latter "self-conscious heirs to the mantle of directors such as Coppola, Bogdanovich, and Friedkin," the "older visionaries" linked to "a new generation of visionary talents."²⁷ Mottram's *The Sundance Kids* asserts the same connection, observing that the directors he surveys "share a debt to the 1970s and have at least one filmmaker from that era essential to their work."²⁸ Filmmakers themselves do cite such influences repeatedly. In 1989 interviews, Soderbergh accepts comparisons to *Five Easy Pieces* (1970) and *Carnal Knowledge* (1971), extending them to include his own attachment to *The Conversation* (1974) and other films demonstrating to him "maturity and control."²⁹ (Journalists give less space to Soderbergh's kinship with Richard Lester, the iconoclastic American expatriate director not easily locatable within the New Hollywood narrative.) David O. Russell, in a 1995 interview, similarly proclaims a desire to make films in the spirit of *Five Easy Pieces*, *Carnal Knowledge*, *Harold and Maude* (1971), and their aesthetic kin.[30] And in promoting *Rushmore* (1998), Wes Anderson established a further link with New Hollywood discourse by visiting the retired Pauline Kael, a key critical voice of the late 1960s and 1970s.[31] These discursive strategies permit young filmmakers to locate their work in a continuum of U.S. (and sometimes European) film history and to issue calls to older viewers enamored of 1960s and 1970s studio productions but possibly disenchanted by contemporary releases.

The discursive celebration of New Hollywood does not abide deep interrogation of the conditions that marginalized its filmmakers, particularly their penchant for expensive, career-damaging failures such as Friedkin's *Sorcerer* (1977) and Coppola's *One From the Heart* (1982). New Hollywood accounts also tend to overlook studios' inability to market such films to receptive demographics. The "spiritual heirs" designation depends on the construction of New Hollywood filmmakers as hungry and experimentation-minded, not as indulgent squanderers of vast studio resources. Notably, virtually all the filmmakers cited as inspirations, mentors, or guides by "Sundance kids" such as Soderbergh and Russell worked almost exclusively under the oversight of major studios, both before and after those studios were acquired by diversified conglomerates. All worked on numerous projects with substantial economic, logistical, and material resources at their disposal. These included production budgets at the far north end of studio expenditure in the 1970s and early 1980s, expansive studio facilities staffed by hundreds of technicians and support workers, and opportunities for location shooting in remote or under-resourced areas requiring massive logistical planning and construction (e.g., Mike Nichols's production of *Catch-22* in Mexico; Friedkin's of *Sorcerer* in locations including Jerusalem and Central America; and Coppola's in the Philippines for *Apocalypse Now* [1979]). Many celebrated New Hollywood filmmakers were studio-funded from early in their careers, while the heralded 1980s independents initially were not. It is hardly surprising, then, that 1990s filmmakers' discourses of New Hollywood creativity often fail to mention the already-conglomerating studios themselves. Putatively visionary or maverick movements do not gain from acknowledging their ties to shareholder-beholden megacorporations. The discursive construct of the "independent spirit" further obscures this historical relationship. Institutional promotional efforts such as the Independent

Spirit Awards enshrine and effectively commoditize this spirit, facilitating its subsequent usage by studio imprints.

Just as New Hollywood's ostensible rebels and visionaries intermittently oversaw massive transnational productions backed by conglomerate capital, so studios periodically granted license to uncommercial filmmakers throughout the 1970s and 1980s. Stephen Prince notes of 1980s Hollywood that many of its celebrated filmmakers "moved in and out of production and distribution deals with major studios while making resolutely nontraditional films. This phenomenon demonstrates the flexibility of the industry as well as its ability to absorb unconventional talents and niche market products."[32] Neither enthusing over Hollywood's openness to innovation nor decrying studios' cannibalizing tendencies, Prince's formulation suggests ways industries find uses for creative talent. While the numerous histories of 1980s U.S. film document a range of conflicts, what emerges in total is a picture of globalizing media industries seeking to produce viably commercial screen art. Rather than operating as enemies of artistry, Hollywood in the 1980s as in other periods routinized practices to ensure the steady supply of creative talent. Indeed, many artistically minded filmmakers gained stature through their efforts within existing and emerging distribution structures.

While some film workers aggressively defend their supposed distance from Hollywood's industrial practices, many professionals navigate small- and large-scale productions to ensure their continued employment in an industry defined by itinerant labor. Warren Buckland notes the prevalence in contemporary Hollywood of "temporary network[s] of freelance workers, or independent contractors."[33] The continued livelihood of these contractors depends on their professional engagement in the larger, more permanent networks in which they and others participate. Assessing Hollywood's cultural-industrial geography, Allen Scott concludes as well that post–studio era reorganization of Hollywood labor has resulted in a freelance-contractor system, "with shifting, temporary teams of creative workers and associated technical workers engaging with one another in personalized, open-ended systems of interaction."[34] Narratives of cooperation and compromise also distinguish Soderbergh's work in the 1990s, with production histories revealing conflicts with executives as well as relationships of patronage and support. Throughout the volatile early- and mid-1990s, a period characterized by continuous industry reshuffling and the emergence and demise of many large and small producers and distributors,

Soderbergh continued to work steadily as a feature-film director, producer, and sometimes writer-for-hire.

Negotiation as Artistry in 1990s Independent Cinema

Approaching Soderbergh's late-1980s and 1990s work through the prism of collaboration and negotiation, we see some of the ways industrial practices and discourse construct his authoring roles and his comprehensive creative activity. Overall, Soderbergh's early- and mid-career efforts demonstrate fairly consistent creative practice, indicating the degree to which a range of production determinants still allow marked flexibility in commercial filmmaking. As with many other filmmakers referred to interchangeably as part of "independent," "Indiewood," or "studio-independent" circles, Soderbergh exemplifies the transit and relationships of the creative individual embedded in commercial networks. Production histories detail his negotiations with a range of industry intermediaries, including production and distribution executives, mini-major moguls such as Harvey Weinstein, and others. Balancing desires for artistic autonomy with those for circulation of completed films, filmmakers such as Soderbergh devote considerable professional effort to negotiations over the financing, distribution, and exhibition of their works. Abundant discourse on film production apprehends dealmaking as somehow extrinsic to production activity, the sole province of managers and talent agents. However, Soderbergh's agency in negotiations reminds us that industry dealmaking forms a fundamental component of creative production practice.

In his work on media professionals' activity in the new century, John Caldwell investigates the creative role of studio executives, arguing that "the 'suits' in film/television continue to find ways to emulate the 'creatives' in Los Angeles's entertainment work worlds."[35] He subsequently extends the comparison: "Like creative workers, management types must publicly exploit and master flexibility and creative deal making to move from one company to others."[36] Beyond highlighting management's own creative self-fashioning, Caldwell's analogy enables us to recognize anew the managerial and negotiating roles that filmmakers play. Filmmakers act as manager-negotiators not just during production but also in project development, during efforts to secure distribution, and in the separate professional activities that promote and extend their personal brands. (Soderbergh's 1990s script doctoring, which maintains his intra-industry creative presence even if not earning him screen credits, exemplifies this last tendency.) Viewing Soderbergh's professional maneuvers in the 1990s, what is remarkable is not the public footprint of his completed features but his ability to remain visible inside the industry, in contention for feature projects alongside directors much more commercially successful at the time.[37] Though his economic value dwindled with the poor commercial outcome of each feature after *sex, lies, and videotape*, he retained substantial cultural capital, attractive to studio and mini-major executives seeking distinction by association with critically esteemed filmmakers. Geoff King identifies executives' "own personal investments and the articulations through which they distinguish themselves from their colleagues in the commercial mainstream"[38] as key to understanding the activity of industrial agents working at the intersection of commercial and art cinema. Such a phenomenon is not restricted to 1990s cinema. In a 2009 glossing of industry trends, *Variety* editor Peter Bart argues that "the ranks of the studios contain many executives who have sophisticated tastes and who, left to their own devices, would make art-house films."[39] Years before the contraction of this sector and of studios' boutique divisions, Soderbergh's cultural capital enabled him to join industry players in ongoing creative negotiations.

In interviews during *sex, lies, and videotape*'s successful theatrical run, Soderbergh foregrounds the actions of multiple executives and negotiators alongside his own artistic sensibility. While many interviewers probe his biography, others seek information on production collaborators, prompting Soderbergh to explain, "I had several producers who played crucial roles at different times,"[40] a narrative he repeats in other interviews. He extols three of the film's five named producers for specific on-site production supervision and for essential efforts in securing distribution deals.[41] He repeatedly credits Outlaw Productions' Bobby Newmyer with the RCA/Columbia Home Video contract, Nancy Tenenbaum with the overseas-rights contract with Virgin that generated further capital, and John Hardy of his native Baton Rouge with on-set production (Hardy subsequently served as a co-producer on most of Soderbergh's features through 2004). While Soderbergh isolates these individuals in discussions of production logistics rather than creative decisions, their negotiating roles entail the same kinds of creative performances that industrial and critical discourses associate with the artistry of filmmaking. For example, Soderbergh attributes one deal specifically to a producer's performance: "Nancy Tenenbaum negotiated single-handedly the universal rights with Virgin by simply showing them the script and her enthusiasm."[42] Dynamic personal energies thus acquire a status equal to the Oscar-nominated screenplay of the film discursively designated as an individual auteur's work. Meanwhile, Soderbergh praises executives' awareness of commercial considerations. He compliments Hardy, for example, with the claim that "[h]is tastes are very commercial and mainstream in a good way."[43] Soderbergh's own narrative, circulated in a range of niche, national, and international forums, constructs a continuum of filmmaking practices that ignores binary oppositions between creative and economic choices.

Soderbergh's career continued in the 1990s thanks to the support of various industrial agents. Consistent with his penchant for naming production executives and other collaborators in interviews, many of Soderbergh's interviews reference his agent throughout the 1990s, Pat Dollard (who took up the position following the accidental death in summer 1989 of Soderbergh's original agent, Pat's older sister Ann Dollard, in the midst of *sex, lies, and videotape*'s pre-production and negotiations over its financing).[44] Narratives of Soderbergh's career credit Pat Dollard with strong influence over Soderbergh's subsequent creative efforts, in particular identifying Dollard as the intermediary responsible for transmitting to Soderbergh the long-dormant screenplay for *Kafka*, "a script by Lem Dobbs that Dollard had given him as an example of good screenwriting technique."[45] While most accounts of agents and managers frame them as invasive figures detrimental to the creative process, they can also be viewed as key intermediaries, industrial actors who bridge creative and managerial roles.[46] A lengthy *Vanity Fair* profile of Pat Dollard asserts of Soderbergh's earlier work with Ann that "[t]heir meeting wasn't so much a typical agent-client encounter but the start of an intense creative collaboration."[47] Though it is tempting to dismiss such assertions as breathless journalistic excess, they nevertheless discursively position managerial workers as co-constituents of creative projects. Periodically this positioning matches that of avowed maverick filmmakers, who accomplish artistic goals through force of will. The Dollard profile further alleges that "*Traffic* was [Pat] Dollard's biggest coup. Dollard is credited by Soderbergh and others with getting the film made after it fell apart during pre-production."[48] Such a narrative declares a managerial figure an essential member of a collaborative creative team on a large-scale independent production. (Notably, too, Dollard's industrial negotiations proceed irrespective of studio/independent distinctions.) As is common industry practice, the film does not grant Dollard a screen credit, the official index of creative or technical contribution.

Managers and agents make suitable candidates for elevation to artist status owing to their similarities to filmmakers: all are to an extent freelance workers, acting on behalf of fellow individuals rather than exclusively within a single corporate entity. (The Dollards did work within agencies—Ann with Leading Artists, and Pat replacing her there, then moving to William Morris and later to the management division of Propaganda Films—but these companies were not beholden to global shareholders.) Soderbergh's 1990s work shows studio executives fostering his creative pursuits as well. Numerous accounts of his 1990s projects note the consistent support of Universal's Casey Silver, culminating in Silver seeking out Soderbergh as director for *Out of Sight* despite the commercial failure of two previous films produced for the Gramercy Pictures division part-owned by Universal.[49] Soderbergh's interactions with Silver began in the mid-1980s, during Silver's tenure as a TriStar production executive. Moving to Universal, Silver approved Soderbergh as director for *King of the Hill*, which Soderbergh had begun developing alongside producer Barbara Maltby, who worked with the support of Robert Redford's Wildwood Enterprises.[50] Silver and Universal subsequently approached Soderbergh to involve him in its remake of *Criss Cross* (1949)—which became the Gramercy release *The Underneath*—despite telling Soderbergh before production that "maybe there wasn't an audience for this kind of film" in the U.S.[51] Working later with executives at Jersey Films (housed on the Universal lot, and with whom the studio had a development deal), Silver successfully lobbied for Soderbergh as director of *Out of Sight*, overcoming Jersey's objections.[52] These tangled enterprises illuminate production networks in which creative and managerial activities overlap substantially. Also like the vaunted maverick filmmakers, Silver maintained interest in Soderbergh's creative capacities in spite of their historically selective commercial appeal. Moreover, Silver's own career arc—from screenwriter to production assistant to executive at multiple companies (Simpson/Bruckheimer Films, TriStar, and Universal) to independent producer—highlights the fluidity of Hollywood practice and interactions between individual and conglomerate interests.

Like other intermediaries, Silver deserves credit for channeling filmmakers' creative energies into specific projects, both as independent dealmaker and as producer responsive to parent-company dictates. As Silver's industrial labor encompassed creative as well as negotiating roles, so Soderbergh's own creative profile broadened in the 1990s to include managerial responsibilities. In addition to his work as director and writer or script doctor, he earned producing credits on a range of mid-budget independent films. Working both alongside filmmaker friends and as guarantor of corporate interests, Soderbergh acted as producer for the comedy *The Daytrippers* (1996; produced and distributed by the Canadian independent Cinépix), as one of multiple producers for New Line's $40 million comedy-fantasy *Pleasantville* (1998), and as executive producer for the Goldwyn Company's spare art-noir *Suture* (1993). Each project involved lengthy advance negotiations as well as production and postproduction supervision.[53] He also broadened his collaborative networks with other filmmakers, joining like-minded directors Alexander Payne, Spike Jonze, David Fincher, and Sam Mendes in 2001 to form the f64 film collective, aimed at collaborative production in the manner of the short-lived Directors Company of the 1970s.[54] The f64 project did not go forward, but Soderbergh's networking labor continued through the Section Eight production company he co-founded the previous year.

Soderbergh remained enshrined in the 1990s discourse of independent cinema even as his ongoing work was not among the period's celebrated independent productions either critically or commercially. Nonetheless, he and his work circulated among key figures at production and distribution companies, and he remained in consideration for numerous projects of different scales. Alongside Paramount producer Scott Kramer, he worked extensively in script development on a never-filmed adaptation of *A Confederacy of Dunces*.[55] He worked in development also on *Human Nature* (2001), eventually realized as a Fine Line release with Michel Gondry as director.[56] Baltimore Pictures, co-producer of *Kafka*, offered Soderbergh the director's role for *Quiz Show* (1994) despite *Kafka*'s poor performance; after maneuvering not involving Soderbergh, Robert Redford eventually directed,[57] with Disney's Hollywood Pictures division as co-producer. Miramax famously acquired and distributed *sex, lies, and videotape*, but despite this early support, Soderbergh worked only sporadically with the company in later years. Miramax handled distribution for *Kafka*, and Soderbergh did script doctoring for the 1997 Miramax releases *Nightwatch* and *Mimic* (receiving screen credit for the former but not the latter). Soderbergh also negotiated with Miramax in the 1990s regarding distribution of *Schizopolis* and development of other projects such as a Charlie Chan film, but no deals occurred.[58] Miramax's reputation subsequently grew with its financing from Disney beginning in 1993 and its concurrent relationship with writer-director Quentin Tarantino, whose 1994 hit *Pulp Fiction* exemplified yet another strain of independent cinema, the formally unconventional (if not explicitly radical or original) genre film. Meanwhile, Soderbergh's relatively small studio-supported productions such as *King of the Hill* earned modest critical acclaim if no particular commercial spark. Soderbergh's own narrative of his 1990s work is as a series of failed experiments, periods of creative stagnation, and the renewal offered by the monologue adaptation *Gray's Anatomy* and in particular the low-budget, limited-release *Schizopolis*.

Locating "Early Soderbergh"

Years after the industrial negotiation required to complete a series of feature films with different companies, Soderbergh has engaged in continued discursive maneuvering, using his early output to maintain an evolving creative profile. Interviews and promotion reference these early features to historicize Soderbergh's work, to fortify the construct of Soderbergh as a mature auteur filmmaker, and to testify to both the vibrancy and rootedness of contemporary film culture. Soderbergh's appraisal of his own career arc changes over time, with different artistic tendencies foregrounded depending on the discursive forum (DVD commentary, press conference, cinephile publication, mainstream newspaper interview, and so forth) and on his own creative and promotional agendas. In 2002, for example he played on the reputation of *sex, lies, and videotape* during promotion of the digital-video effort *Full Frontal*. He not only repeatedly evoked the comparison between the two works, but also told one interviewer that "it's how I would make *sex, lies, and videotape* today,"[59] immunizing himself and his debut feature from judgment. (That is, anyone unimpressed with the 1989 film might remain curious about Soderbergh's evolving poetics.) Similarly, in 2009, with periodic invocations in the entertainment press of *sex, lies, and videotape*'s twentieth anniversary, the film contributed to promotion of the low-budget production *The Girlfriend Experience*, which premiered as an anonymous "sneak preview" at Sundance in January 2009, the day after an anniversary screening of *sex, lies*.

Soderbergh has periodically critiqued or disavowed his early features, attesting to his own shifting artistic sensibility. His retrospective comments also provide a narrative of authorial progression. In a 1995 interview, for example, he asserted that "[i]n fifteen years, people will look back at my first four films and they will realize that they were just a preface to the book that I am only now starting to write."[60] Whether evidencing remarkable self-awareness or shocking hubris, Soderbergh's statement demonstrates one way filmmakers themselves draw on their completed works' cultural capital for later engagements with industries. In another case, Soderbergh returned his second feature, *Kafka*, to entertainment-press discourse in early 2005, during a period of multifaceted creative activity including direction, production of multiple features, and shorts of varying production scales. Appealing to cinephile constituencies, he told a UK interviewer about ongoing work re-editing *Kafka* for future DVD release, noting, "I'm doing it for my own interest—to see if I can make something out of it that I'm happier with."[61] Soderbergh's remark preempts continued negative appraisals of the older film. His reference to it also implicitly acknowledges a regional constituency, reminding the British publication's readers that he has made films in and about Europe. The assertion of private, unheralded reworking of a previous effort also emphasizes Soderbergh's own status as a creatively invested artist, crucial during the overseas release cycle of *Ocean's Twelve*, which had performed well in the U.S. in its somewhat earlier release there but did not receive particularly favorable reviews.

Soderbergh's 1996 feature, *Schizopolis*, also contributed to the maintenance of his creative profile some years after its debut. With a tiny theatrical run in 1997 (including a screening at the off-Sundance festival Slamdance), then a low-profile VHS release in 1999, the film earned a Criterion DVD release in October 2003, with abundant new material including Soderbergh's commentary track. The Criterion release, while directed principally to cinephile markets, rejuvenated Soderbergh's 1990s work and brought Soderbergh product to market at nearly the midpoint of the more-than-two-year period between theatrical releases of Soderbergh's features *Solaris* (opening in November 2002) and *Ocean's Twelve* (opening in December 2004). *Schizopolis* was repurposed yet again in autumn 2008, when Slamdance organizers sponsored a screening of the film at New York's IFC Film Center, with Soderbergh as a featured speaker.[62] The event served partly as a cross-promotion for the upcoming *Che*, distributed in the U.S. by IFC Films at the end of the year.

Lacking a critical mass of press commentary, Soderbergh's early- to mid-1990s features were on initial release not shaped discursively into a coherent auteurist oeuvre. When pressed, Soderbergh repeated in interviews the connective thematic thread of "main characters that are out of sync with their environments,"[63] but their range of genres and aesthetics, along with their sometimes ill fit with perceived cultural and pop-cinematic trends, discouraged efforts to reconstitute the films as part of an agreed zeitgeist or authorial persona. Periodic reappraisals located each film, and sometimes Soderbergh himself, alongside particular developments in Hollywood or independent cinema or larger spheres of cultural production. A brief consideration of these early features' textual elements and release climates will help locate them in the late-1980s to mid-1990s commercial landscape.

sex, lies, and videotape's singular achievement was perhaps simply to appear in the late-1980s film marketplace, its fairly slow pacing and mixture of dramatic, erotic, and comic elements suitably removed from the main of concurrent film production to distinguish it in critical and commercial milieus. It follows a married couple in which a lawyer, John (Peter Gallagher), conducts a not-particularly-discreet affair with his wife's sister (Andie MacDowell plays the melancholic wife, Ann, with Laura San Giacomo as the oversexed sister, Cynthia). The arrival of Graham (James Spader), a friend from John's past, reveals and upsets this troubled triangle. Graham's sexual problem—he can be aroused only by mediated female disclosure and not by actual sexual activity, so he videotapes women talking about sex—involves him emotionally with both women. After a series of dramatic crises and revelations, Ann leaves her adulterous husband for an apparent future with the jobless but pleasingly unrepressed Graham, whose sexual problem she has managed to cure. The film seeks to engage viewers through dramatic dialogue and character interiority rather than incident. Its abundance of conversations about sex and the human condition elicited critical comparisons to the films of French filmmaker Eric Rohmer such as *My Night at Maud's* (1969) and *Chloe in the Afternoon* (1972). As a cultural commodity, its constituent elements included location production far from Hollywood; a narrative of the work and romantic lives of white, middle-class, heterosexual characters in their twenties and thirties; and a cast of local Baton Rouge performers, newcomers, and actors with some visibility in prior studio and independent productions. These elements not only mark its similarity to numerous small films across the history of American cinema but also anticipate an array of similarly composed 1990s (and newer) works. Some commentators retrospectively linked Soderbergh's contemplative character study to Indiewood's plethora of navel-gazing comedy-dramas. Biskind, for example, asserts the symbolic importance of *sex, lies, and videotape* winning the Palme d'Or at Cannes over the otherwise heralded *Do the Right Thing* (1989), arguing that "the triumph of *sex, lies* over *Do the*

Right Thing ratified the turn away from the angry, topical strain of the indie movement that had its roots in the 1960s and 1970s toward the milder aesthetic of the slacker era."[64]

Embodying neither the "angry, topical" nor the "slacker" sensibility, Soderbergh's sophomore feature, *Kafka*, was logistically and formally ambitious, though finally substantially less commercial than *sex, lies*. Soderbergh has explained it as the product of a filmmaker overinvested in formalism. The film also manifests Soderbergh's dialogue with cinema history. Indeed, its setting and aesthetic—old-world Prague framed in Expressionist style—show its explicit debt to celebrated film-historical modes and to films such as *Nosferatu* (1922) and in particular *The Third Man* (1949). In constructing a narrative around writer and office-worker Kafka (Jeremy Irons), who occupies a milieu similar to that of Franz Kafka's own works, particularly *The Trial* (1925) and *The Castle* (1926), the film parades high-art credentials. At the same time, it offers a pulpy conspiracy plotline, abundant black humor as well as occasional slapstick, and arch performances from Irons, Theresa Russell, Ian Holm, and others. *Kafka* bears comparisons to analogous works appearing in the months following its release. The similarly executed *Shadows and Fog* (1991), Woody Allen's own *Third Man* homage, represents a particular point of intersection. Meanwhile, *Kafka*'s conceit of a writer inhabiting the imaginative milieu of his own work recurs in David Lynch's *Naked Lunch* (1991), which adapts William Burroughs's 1959 novel. Like *Kafka*, *Naked Lunch* adapts the work of a writer whose appeal bridges literary and cult communities. With *Kafka* grossing only one-tenth of its production budget (an $11 million budget and a $1.1 million gross), distributor Miramax did not capitalize on its serendipitous connections to the two proximal releases from established North American auteur directors. Soderbergh's own limited career to that point further discouraged auteurist framings, though numerous reviewers did remark with perplexity or regret on the film's substantial departure from the style and mode of *sex, lies, and videotape*.

Soderbergh changed course again with *King of the Hill*, adapting A. E. Hotchner's 1972 memoir of a Depression-era midwestern childhood. The production returned Soderbergh to U.S. location filming, this time in and around St. Louis, the setting of Hotchner's book. Having relied on Lem Dobbs's complex and homage-laden script for *Kafka*, Soderbergh returned to a writing role for *King of the Hill*, earning sole credit for his adapted screenplay. The finished film's address might be termed magical realist, with a mostly restrained performance style and a stylized color palette favoring reds, yellows, and browns, which Soderbergh likens to painter Edward Hopper's.[65] Soderbergh's only film to date featuring a child protagonist, *King of the Hill* immerses viewers in the materially impoverished but imaginatively rich life of the preteen Aaron (Jesse Bradford), who faces hunger, social ostracism, and romantic misadventure after his parents abandon him and his younger brother. It earned comparisons to a pair of historical films released around the same time: "a cross between *Barton Fink* and *This Boy's Life*."[66] Though the two other films are set respectively in the early 1940s and mid-1950s, again Soderbergh was identified as belonging in the company of acclaimed filmmakers or prestige films. *Barton Fink* (1991), from Soderbergh's near-contemporaries Joel and Ethan Coen, also won the Palme d'Or at Cannes. Meanwhile, *This Boy's Life* (1993), based on Tobias Wolff's memoir of a turbulent childhood, achieved a profile not much higher than *King of the Hill* despite a leading role from Robert De Niro and a wide Warner Bros. release in 773 theaters.[67]

Soderbergh's historical dialogue continued with his next directorial effort, *The Underneath*, set in the present but remaking the 1949 film noir *Criss Cross* (or adapting again Don Tracy's 1934 novel of the same title, as will be discussed in Chapter 6).[68] Soderbergh did not develop the project but did earn a screenplay credit (alongside Daniel Fuchs, screenwriter of the original film). The remake showcases a luckless gambler, Michael (*sex, lies, and videotape*'s Peter Gallagher, in a rare leading role), returning to the ex-wife, Rachel (Alison Elliott), and relatives he had abandoned years earlier when fleeing gambling debts. Michael attempts to rebuild his life and former romance but finds himself involved in an armored-car heist that goes badly awry, reprising the fatalism of the original film and of classical noir generally. Rather than reviving noir's characteristic chiaroscuro lighting (which might have extended *Kafka*'s neo-Expressionism and marked Soderbergh as a particular kind of visual stylist), *The Underneath* applies a palette of artificial greens and blues for many sequences. This stylized visual field serves the film's narrative structure, which relies on extensive cross-cutting among three different time periods: a generalized present, the period just preceding the dissolution of Michael and Rachel's earlier relationship, and the pivotal time frame of the heist sequence. (The emphatic color-coding also anticipates the cinematography of later Soderbergh-directed films such as *The Limey* [1999] and *Traffic*.)

The Underneath opened one week after a higher-profile noir remake, 20th Century Fox's *Kiss of Death* (1995), directed by the intermittently acclaimed Barbet Schroeder. With neither film a commercial or critical success, no critical consensus emerged to link them as products of notable filmmakers. Jonathan Rosenbaum's lengthy omnibus review of the two works in the *Chicago Reader* draws numerous parallels among Soderbergh's films but refers to Schroeder only once in passing. Like some other critics, Rosenbaum isolates a trend of neo-noirs based on these two films and on other efforts such as *Pulp Fiction* and October Films's minor indie hit *The Last Seduction* (1994). While locatable within a neo-noir production cycle, Soderbergh's film lacks the ironic address or straightforward people-behaving-badly appeals of Tarantino's and John Dahl's films, perhaps limiting connections with youth or college-age markets whose patronage contributed to 1990s independent films' commercial prospects. Todd McCarthy's *Variety* review underscores the film's inattention to market considerations: "At many important steps along the way . . . helmer has tilted this tale of trust and betrayal away from its more conventionally commercial suspense and sex angles and toward a more complexly cerebral and analytical reading. . . . Soderbergh has curiously crimped the story's most exploitable genre ingredients."[69] Proving that independent films too may live or die on such terms, *The Underneath* opened in only twenty-one theaters, where its returns of barely more than $500,000 (on an estimated $6.5 million budget) halted any expansion into wider release.[70]

Years later, Soderbergh acknowledged a narrowness of vision that may have contributed to his films' inability to connect with viewers. Recalling his earlier work in a 2002 interview, he claimed, "I'd become a formalist. . . . *The Underneath* was the sort of nadir of that kind of filmmaking to me, that sort of constructed, hermetically sealed way of working."[71] Hypothetically, to continue as a formalist might have endowed Soderbergh with a stable, recognizable authorial imprint. Instead, his work then and beyond thwarts reception strategies that involve easy recognition of authorship. In tandem with or distinct from genre preferences, cinephilic and fan interest often take shape around auteurist paradigms. Those with particular cultural or subcultural interest in cinema often make viewing choices based on the work of favored directors. The cult or mass appeal of *Reservoir Dogs* (1992) or *The Usual Suspects* (1995), for example, stokes long-term interest in subsequent films with Tarantino or Bryan Singer as director. Arguably, no such watershed film exists in Soderbergh's oeuvre. Moreover, his stylistic shifts and the varying roles he plays on film productions (i.e., different variants of multi-hyphenate roles) mean that viewers must perform additional cultural labor if they wish to track Soderbergh's career. Even the "preface" of Soderbergh's first four features includes an abundance of story types and structures, visual styles, tones, genres, and more. Critical work may discern an organizing authorial sensibility in these works, as professional reviewers periodically do. However, the effort required to catalog such a sensibility indicates the qualitative differences between Soderbergh's combined feature-film output and the strongly branded work of filmmakers such as Tarantino, Spike Lee, the Coens, or other contemporaries.

Soderbergh's 1990s work dovetails with some prevailing trends of popular independent and studio filmmaking, but splinters in other ways. As hip crime films proliferated, he retroactively disowned his own noir feature *The Underneath* and moved into experimental filmmaking, and as Miramax's star rose, he worked more with Universal/PolyGram subunit Gramercy. While Universal's *Out of Sight* was Soderbergh's first feature produced for the major branch of a studio rather an independent company or boutique division, his next feature, 1999's *The Limey*, was a production of the independent Artisan Entertainment, newly renamed and reconfigured the previous year and moving from home-video to theatrical distribution and also into production. Though *The Limey* was a small indie hit, Artisan's distribution of the phenomenally successful *The Blair Witch Project* also in 1999 made Soderbergh's film a relative footnote in the history of the company (which later came close to bankruptcy and was acquired in 2003 by Lionsgate).

The Emerging Post-Indiewood Discourse

The discourses of cinephile culture have already begun reshaping. The 1960s and 1970s New Hollywood was regarded, particularly in retrospect, as a reaction against the bloated studio productions of the late 1950s and early- to mid-1960s. Independent cinema of the 1980s was then constructed, or reconstructed, as a response to the bloated studio productions of the 1970s. Next, 1990s independent-cinema successes were cast as responses to studios' formulaic genre pictures of the 1980s, and in the new century, hybridized Indiewood productions have been framed as fresher variants of genre-film production, determinedly quirky efforts such as *Juno* (2007) seen as more vibrant than presold properties such as *Scooby-Doo* (2002). More recently, emergent niche trends such as mumblecore and microcinema can be positioned as responses to an Indiewood sector perceived as insufficiently oppositional or authentic. In autumn 2008, as part of the London Film Festival, the by turns stodgy and trend-conscious British Film Institute programmed a film series entitled "Indiewood Is Dead . . . Long Live the New, True Indies," with promotional copy highlighting poor fortunes for "faux-indies" (though without attributing the term to any specific companies or films).[72] Many of the films screened—including *Frozen River* (2008) and *Wendy & Lucy* (2008)—were contained, low-budget dramas focused on the interpersonal relationships of the alienated or socially marginal, recalling independent films of the early and mid-1980s.

While a veritable poster child for Indiewood filmmaking, Soderbergh has also pursued microscale production through efforts such as *Bubble* and *The Girlfriend Experience*, his larger efforts facilitating the smaller films' creative risk-taking and his name recognition contributing to their innovative distribution strategies. Soderbergh's filmmaking practice challenges the artificial distinctions created by such new labels as "new, true indies." Filmmakers seeking both creative satisfaction and commercial viability will continue to operate in the border territory that he and some of his peers occupy. Individual filmmakers may not find wholly autonomous zones within commercial industries, but they can position themselves strategically at intersections of creative enterprise and industrial power. Building on arguments concerning New Hollywood/Indiewood kinships, the next chapter considers ways Soderbergh and other filmmakers claim strategic positions by harnessing film history's symbolic capital.

Chapter 2

Hollywood Authorship and Transhistorical Taste Cultures

Through investigation of Soderbergh's 1990s activity, the preceding chapter has argued that he was and remains one of many contemporary filmmakers who gesture toward historical eras and modes to articulate their creative sensibilities and mobilize interest in their work. Some filmmakers gravitate repeatedly to particular movements and modes, as evident, for example, in Peter Bogdanovich's multiple homages to the classical studio era of the 1930s and 1940s or Guy Maddin's reworkings of 1910s and 1920s silent-cinema aesthetics. Others, including Soderbergh, cast a wider net through their film output and discourse outside filmmaking, expressing multiple affinities across screen media past and present. This chapter investigates Soderbergh and his works' dialogues with film history, with canonical and offbeat texts, and with a range of creative personnel in U.S. and international cinema. Soderbergh and the entertainment press have drawn connections between his work and numerous films and filmmakers of the 1960s and 1970s New Hollywood and European art cinema, in particular directors such as Jean-Luc Godard, Richard Lester, John Boorman, Mike Nichols, William Friedkin, and Sidney Lumet. Soderbergh has also positioned himself in relation to the Hollywood studio system and its 1940s output. The textual features, production practices, and discursive positionings of Soderbergh's work attest to historical continuities as well as industrial transformation.

Chapter 3's case study of *The Good German* considers Soderbergh's dialogue with classical Hollywood and 1940s cinema. Meanwhile, this chapter investigates Soderbergh's reference points in 1960s and 1970s U.S. and European cinema. These repeatedly invoked affinities both consolidate the earlier period's canon and underscore the era's significance for subsequent filmmakers. In her exploration of film canons, Janet Staiger reminds us:

> Even filmmakers are involved in canon formation. Those films chosen to be reworked, alluded to, satirized, become privileged points of reference, pulled out from the rest of cinema's predecessors.[1]

Soderbergh's most recurrent discursive and aesthetic engagements have been with a constellation of American films and filmmakers, works of the transatlantic migrant filmmakers Lester and Boorman, a group of Western European art-cinema directors, and related political thrillers such as *The Battle of Algiers* (1966) and *Z* (1969). Motivated by the robustness of "the New Hollywood" as a construct in U.S. popular and trade-press discourse, this chapter pursues in most detail Soderbergh's links to American films and filmmakers. *Schizopolis*, for example, contains homages to Lester, the Britain-based American who was also the subject of a book-length interview conducted by Soderbergh. Also, as consistently acknowledged by Soderbergh, *The Limey* owes an explicit debt to *Point Blank*, the first Hollywood feature directed by the British/Irish Boorman (who shares a commentary track with Soderbergh on the *Point Blank* DVD). The following year, during production of *Traffic*, Soderbergh invoked Friedkin and Lumet among others, and the film adopts the multiple-storyline style of many films directed by Robert Altman. The 2002 *Full Frontal* experiments with narrative and performance in ways evocative of the low-budget 1968 work *Symbiopsychotaxiplasm: Take One*, the sequel to which Soderbergh later executive-produced. Even the popular *Ocean's Twelve* borrows the setting and form of 1960s European thrillers. Analyzing film texts and historical and discursive contexts, I consider how Soderbergh-directed films manifest his demonstrated interest in 1960s and 1970s cinema. These films both benefit from and feed back into the film press's circulation of the view of the New Hollywood and contemporaneous movements as particular high-water marks of commercial cinema.

As Chapter 1 has argued, late-1960s and early-1970s American cinema has served as a frame of reference for generations of filmmakers, critics, and scholars. Whatever the accuracy of claims about the supposed golden age of American cinema, invocation of the practices, output, and abstracted spirit of this age repeatedly serves to legitimate contemporary films and filmmakers working firmly in the Hollywood mainstream as well as at the furthest margins of independent American cinema. In interviews, DVD commentaries, and other forums, Soderbergh himself has repeatedly compared his works and interests to those of earlier filmmakers distinguished by both artistic adventurousness and popular success. Entertainment and trade publications have similarly venerated the late-'60s/early-'70s era of American cinema and used it to distinguish contemporary filmmakers' sensibilities and to evaluate particular films, including Soderbergh's. The intertextual deployment of New Hollywood signposts in films such as *Schizopolis*, *The Limey*, and *Traffic* participates in the broader formation of cinephilic taste cultures. The case of Soderbergh helps indicate film journalists' and cinephiles' critical investments. We can see through his films and their critical framings that canonized texts and periods continue to organize understandings of filmmaking and film culture. Soderbergh's films, and the discourses they engender, indicate how taste cultures take shape across history, and around shared investments in particular modes of production, creative sensibilities, and film texts.

Transhistorical Poetics and Creative Capital

Connections between contemporary and historical cinemas take numerous forms, including industrial, aesthetic, and discursive relationships. Industrial relationships link filmmakers and producing companies over time based on company organization as well as production technologies and personnel. For example, Soderbergh's *The Underneath* relates to *Criss Cross* not only as a remake, or an adaptation of the same novel, but thanks to the ownership of both properties by Universal, still in existence though in a different form in 1995 than in 1949. Aesthetic relationships involve explicit textual correlations among screen works across history, expressed through narrative and thematic similarity as well as aspects of visual style, editing, and sound. Discursive relationships include filmmakers' linkages of their own works to preceding output across cinema history, as well as assertions to the same effect from producers and marketing personnel, and from film critics and other receivers. (This last category includes the bulk of auteurist film criticism, concerned not only with identifying a filmmaker's personal style but also with legitimating filmmakers through connections to other designated auteurs.) Aesthetic and discursive relationships exist partly in tandem, to the extent that aesthetic choices are articulated and contextualized through discourse.

Prompted by discursive claims, this chapter identifies specific points of aesthetic intersection and the rationale for and consequences of those intersections. Rationale can include personal, nostalgic affiliations with perceived golden ages; creative decisions made with the intent of producing contemporary but lasting cinematic art; desires among the various communities of studio executives, the entertainment press, and cinephile consumers to secure and enhance cultural capital; and production determinants such as budgetary constraints that might impel a filmmaker toward creative strategies associated with past rather than current filmmaking practice. Aesthetic intersections can realign views of contemporary and historical film texts, producing artists and industries, and reception communities. Transformations of discourse also occur through these reconfigured understandings. Before turning to questions of film discourse, I address matters of aesthetics and poetics.

Recognition of intertextual aesthetic affiliations follows from creators' stated intents as well as from individual viewers' judgments. Film reception involves a range of subjective, sense-making activities, including not only value judgments but also contextualization practices such as situating individual films in relation to the past texts that form part of a viewer's total media experience and library of taste preferences. Hypotheses about aesthetic kinship can highlight continuities and discontinuities in cinema's address to viewers. The establishment of such points of intersection contributes to a historical poetics and helps reveal how film texts distinguish themselves in the marketplace of artistic production, irrespective of other shaping factors such as promotion and reception.[2] Moreover, films' stylistic allegiances indicate what creative activities entertainment industries support and thus what resources they make available to filmmakers. As Henry Jenkins argues, "historical poetics' consideration of authorship requires attention to the range of formal choices available to directors and the conditions under which authorial expression occurs. . . . Attention to formal norms can locate the competing voices which constitute the film's production."[3] Production entities varyingly support filmmaking that combines present and past working methods and aesthetics. Studying transhistorical arcs, we see film texts and industries negotiating between contemporaneity and historicity. Popular cinema's industry discourse has long trumpeted technological innovation and promised viewers state-of-the-art experiences with each new release. At the same time, explicit or inferred links to past modes may engage viewerships nostalgic for such modes or regarding them as novel (as do, for example, the many viewers of films such as *Star Wars* [1977] or *Raiders of the*

Lost Ark [1981] unfamiliar with the 1940s film serials the newer films' styles and sensibilities invoke).

Film texts mobilize viewers' personal archives in diverse ways and for many reasons. Commenting on distributors' uses of a range of texts from cinema history, Barbara Klinger observes that "[t]he resurrection of artifacts is, of course, an integral activity of all institutions associated with the arts."[4] Evocations of past films and film culture can concentrate interest around particular zones of consumption, drawing attention to "the entertainment past"[5] rather than the totality of a historical period. In addition to activating past film culture as a possible commodity to be consumed (or reconsumed), films can invoke previous eras of artistic production to burnish their own credentials and appeals. For example, in reprising the narrative template and screwball sensibility of *Bringing Up Baby* (1938), Peter Bogdanovich's *What's Up, Doc?* (1972) distinguishes itself as an heir to an esteemed comic tradition and sets itself apart from its marketplace competitors. Textual and discursive signs of aesthetic continuity, or viewer inferences of such continuity, implicitly attest to the quality of newer works. These links also constitute part of a newer film's appeals and meanings, inseparable from its other textual characteristics. *The Limey*, for example, in casting Terence Stamp, using a sixties-rock soundtrack, and borrowing structural elements of films such as *Point Blank* along with its central figure of a stubborn male avenger, marks itself as a hybrid text merging contemporary and historical sensibilities. (Though my goal is not to catalog the totality of possible intertextual connections, I would note that *The Limey*'s aggrieved-parent narrative also aligns it with such films as *Get Carter* [1971], which features an avenging surrogate father, if not with the more sadistic *Death Wish* [1974].) While one approach to this form of intertextuality is to regard it as postmodernist pastiche, my interest is less in the implications of referential play than in the particular ways filmmakers and industries gather and deploy cultural capital for artistic and economic ends.

Films and film commentators perform substantial tastemaking work through their assertions of intertextual affinity. Klinger's discussion of media industries' uses of the past, including analysis of the cable channel American Movie Classics (AMC), underscores ways industrial framings can romanticize not only film history but also larger historical narratives. The institutional and industrial enshrinement of New Hollywood cinema achieves a related if not identical effect. Rather than rewriting the dominant narratives of U.S. culture in the 1960s or

1970s—i.e., narratives of the turbulent, vibrant 1960s and the malaise-ridden 1970s—the invocation of selective films and filmmakers of the period affirms Hollywood studio output as artistically adventurous and lasting. Paradoxically, the enshrined era coincides almost exactly with the advent of conglomerate Hollywood (if that era commences with Gulf + Western's 1966 acquisition of Paramount), overlooked in discourse about artistic renaissance. Discursive celebration of the pre-1975 New Hollywood also rewrites the film-historical narrative to foreground individual artists and textual artifacts, obscuring the film industry's continued, near-disastrous declines in audiences and revenues through this period. As film historians have recognized, by the late 1960s cinema had effectively ceased to exist as a truly popular medium, with cinemagoing no longer a dominant leisure activity and film culture consequently far less central to American life than during the peak years immediately after World War II.

The canon formation occurring through popular and critical discourse from the 1990s onward rewrites New Hollywood history in other ways, neglecting a range of films persistently regarded as socially unacceptable as well as numerous curiosities that attracted large audiences but were soon relegated to historical-footnote status. The net effect of discursive canon-formation has been to marginalize the remarkable U.S. box-office performance of many documentaries, foreign films, and low-budget independent features. In their place stands a now-familiar grouping of films, many independently produced but largely studio-distributed. Formation of critical and popular canons necessarily involves selection and exclusion, but the process reveals existing power relationships even as it endows new players with cultural capital. The dominant narrative of the New Hollywood years circulated by filmmakers and film journalists does not include successful documentaries of semi-exotica such as *Chariots of the Gods* (1970), seventeenth overall in theatrical rentals in its 1974 U.S. release, and the even more successful *In Search of Noah's Ark* (1976), ninth overall at the U.S. box office in 1976.[6] Independent distributors also took advantage of loosening censorship rules and availability of theatrical venues to profit from circulation of sexually explicit films. The Swedish sex drama *I Am Curious (Yellow)* (1967), the soft-porn *The Stewardesses* (1969), and the semi-documentary *Sexual Freedom in Denmark* (1970; despite its title, a U.S. production) all ranked in the top twenty theatrical rentals during their U.S. release years. The vogue for pornography continued into the 1970s, famously with the wide mainstream visibility of two hardcore films, 1972's *Deep Throat* ranking seventh at the box office and 1973's *The Devil in Miss Jones* ranking tenth or eleventh.[7] Awareness of pornography's mainstream success has not been explicitly suppressed, merely pushed to the side in favor of signposting of separate trends such as blaxploitation. Retrospective accolades for blaxploitation demonstrate one way a range of studio-produced or distributed features may be recuperated into progressive narratives of changing Hollywood representation.

Overall, revisionist histories of 1960s and 1970s Hollywood tend to elevate critically sanctioned films such as *Five Easy Pieces* and *Carnal Knowledge*, both ranking similarly in box-office performance to the films noted above (the former ranked fourteenth in 1970 rentals, the latter eighth in 1971). Both feature canonized directors (Bob Rafelson and Mike Nichols, respectively) and stars (Jack Nicholson in both, and musician Art Garfunkel in the latter) involved in even more successful films in other years. Both also come from respected distributors: Columbia Pictures for the former, the major independent Avco Embassy for the latter. Films of such pedigrees contribute to coherent narratives of Hollywood's output and its prominent industrial figures. The slow accretion of the New Hollywood canon successfully disavows a range of films and industrial agents that had temporarily competed with studio and major-independent releases. Not unexpectedly, the critical canon withholds celebration of a range of successful but formulaic disaster thrillers such as *Earthquake*, along with many popular family films such as *The Life and Times of Grizzly Adams* (both 1974; fourth and seventh, respectively, in annual revenues). Still, the canon remains fundamentally conservative. It marginalizes other popular output subject to long-term disrepute, including softcore and overseas erotica. Critical recognition of these successful, low-budget independent and foreign films might transitively weaken the artistic reputation and perceived originality of the avowedly gritty, adventurous 1960s and 1970s films now canonized. A subgenre such as blaxploitation can easily be critically separated from New Hollywood touchstones such as *Five Easy Pieces*, and the occasional hits from the American International Pictures exploitation stable long ago gained legitimacy with many AIP veterans' entry into the Hollywood mainstream. In contrast, the softcore and foreign films share with canonized New Hollywood studio releases the traits of topicality, sexual frankness, and a range of formal devices contributing (if inadvertently) to realist aesthetics, including 16mm and handheld cinematography, location shooting, anti-illusionistic performance, and more.

In many ways and for many reasons, then, 1990s and subsequent commentary rehabilitates earlier studio output as artistically rich and rewarding. Such discourse counters the competing evidence that much of the now-enshrined New Hollywood was simply unpopular, unappealing to audiences and unprofitable for studios. Latter-day promotion of the New Hollywood era differs strategically and in its consequences from the "rampant utopian historicism" that Klinger identifies in AMC and other institutions' promotional efforts.[8] The latter-day New Hollywood celebration produces an equally selective historical account, however. It relies on one criterion (a new critical consensus of artistic value) to eclipse another (the empirical evidence of the industry's diminished popular resonance). This narrative shifts understandings of film culture away from audiences and cultural appeal, and toward discrete production workers and texts. Ironically or fittingly, Soderbergh's films have faced criticism for replicating this narrative—that is, for showcasing their makers' interest in past films and filmmakers rather than delivering contained, satisfying viewing experiences to audiences. For example, J. Hoberman observes that Soderbergh's two-part 2008 feature *Che* "has struck some critics as essentially self-reflexive—that is, as a movie essentially concerned with its own making."[9] Similarly, numerous reviewers of *The Good German* found it to foreground its reworking of 1940s production technology at the expense of viewer engagement.[10]

The Good German engages its 1940s milieu by reviving the aesthetics and filmmaking technology of wartime studio productions. At the same time, unburdened by the Production Code or the weight of 1940s ideology, the film makes claims for greater authenticity through profanity, explicit sexuality, and a downbeat narrative. In contrast, the many films that revive the supposed New Hollywood aesthetic tend not to interrogate the 1960s and 1970s as such. Instead, discourses about late-1960s and 1970s cultural permissiveness often evolve into assertions of similar freedoms in popular filmmaking. Likewise, accounts of the era's turbulence and disorder cohere conveniently with tendencies located in filmmaking practice and film texts. Peter Biskind's 1998 popular history *Easy Riders, Raging Bulls* represents just one of many accounts of chaotic industrial practice. Its abundant anecdotes recount corporate mismanagement and accompanying disregard for studio oversight, wasteful spending, drug use, sexual promiscuity and adultery, and other exploitation of human and natural resources. Rather than attesting to a lamentable breakdown of professional standards, such accounts contribute to a narrative of cultural relevance and authenticity. Films thus become doubly reflective of culture, reproducing historically ennobled cultural imperatives—free love, turning on, sticking it to The Man, and many more—at the level of production as well as in texts themselves. Many successful films, from *The Jungle Book* (1967) and *Paint Your Wagon* (1969) to *Benji* (1974) and *Earthquake*, do not belong to this ostensibly countercultural narrative and are thus easily excised from the canon of maverick artistry. While invoking the aesthetics of the period and the work of particular filmmakers, contemporary Hollywood professionals tend to create implicit boundaries between celebrated New Hollywood films and surrounding cultural and industrial practices. Commercial and professional imperatives may inhibit the celebration of anarchic production methods and countercultural values. Both proved problematic for the industry. Cost overruns on many 1970s productions sabotaged profitability even of films with reasonably high box-office receipts, from *Tora! Tora! Tora!* (1970) to *The Black Hole* (1979). Also, as already noted, the industry's economic fortunes and its embeddedness in mass culture reached almost their absolute low point amid the late-1960s and early-1970s cultural climate, even as studios found new or growing adult and student markets following the 1966 dissolution of the Production Code.

In spite of the risks of certain countercultural associations, filmmakers and film institutions stand to gain by aligning themselves with some variant of popular-historical views of the 1960s or 1970s. Numerous commercial industries have successfully constructed the 1960s and 1970s as freewheeling, idealistic, impassioned, or simply remarkable times in U.S. history and culture. Categorized as the counterculture era, the Vietnam era, the Watergate era, or in other ways depending on the chosen chronological boundaries and events signposted, the 1960s and 1970s have been repeatedly repurposed to manufacture and profit from baby-boomer nostalgia and younger generations' curiosity. Partly owing to films' narrative and representational qualities, though, cinema institutions' invocations of the past must contend with different kinds of cultural baggage than do other commodities. The narrower association with romanticized artist-filmmakers helps to circumvent negative ideological associations of the overarching cultural epoch. This restricted association serves, too, to legitimize contemporary practitioners and texts as parts of valued artistic and industrial traditions.

At the same time, filmmakers' and critics' assertions of links between New Hollywood or European New Wave films and those of the 1990s independent-cinema vogue separate the newer works from the full continuum of screen history. As noted in Chapter 1, much discourse surrounding U.S. independent cinema fails to connect 1980s and 1990s filmmakers and movements. In the 1990s independent cinema's turn away from the earnest, social-issue driven films seen to distinguish 1980s independent cinema, and toward the violent genre narratives abundant in low-budget production before the 1980s, partly explains this discontinuity in film historiography. Moreover, in critical and practitioner discourse, those issue-driven films tend not to cluster into coherent movements, largely owing to the lack of promotion of designated auteur directors. Soderbergh's own collaborator Lem Dobbs reproduces this selective view in an early profile of Soderbergh. Dobbs, the article asserts, "suspects one reason [for Soderbergh's early acclaim] may have been the dearth of serious new film makers in the 80's."[11] Dobbs continues:

> You used to have waves of talent, whether it was the Nouvelle Vague from France in the 60's or when you had the young Bogdanovich, Scorsese and Coppola all at once in the 70's. Now, there hasn't been a wave in so long that Steven Soderbergh became a one-man wave.[12]

Speaking in 1991, just before the heralded explosion of "indie" film, Dobbs lashes together unspecified French New Wave filmmakers, New Hollywood auteurs, and Soderbergh himself without challenge or comment from his interviewer. This à la carte view of film history would persist throughout subsequent accounts of popular independent cinema.

A range of ideological and commercial imperatives underpins the ongoing linkage of contemporary cinema with New Hollywood and European New Wave output. In venerating New Hollywood figures, numerous groups may secure cultural capital. Contemporary filmmakers, the companies and industries that fund and may profit from their work, and the ancillary institutions that produce film criticism and entertainment journalism can all achieve real or symbolic benefits. Klinger observes that "[m]edia industries have long struggled to achieve the kind of symbolic capital or accumulated prestige that characterizes high art. Hollywood's history is marked by repeated efforts to align itself with respectability."[13] In this respect, the critical construct "Hollywood Renaissance" serves even better to create associations of artistic flowering. Like the other Renaissance, the Hollywood version may be seen as likely to persist in cultural memory for hundreds of years. Discursive invocations of the New Hollywood and its output maintain the era's presence in the public sphere. Meanwhile, contemporary films that revisit stylistic hallmarks of select 1960s and 1970s films recraft and perpetuate a New Hollywood aesthetic. Of course, the majority of late 1960s and early 1970s films do not closely match the aesthetics of such frequently invoked touchstones as *Bonnie and Clyde* or *The Conversation*. Hence a corpus of films that arguably did not coalesce into a broad-based tradition or a set of stylistic norms unites through a contemporary project of taxonomy and quotation.

Soderbergh has repeatedly cited a cluster of films already endowed with the commercial and artistic capital of value to a filmmaker whose work ranges across production scales and modes. For example, references to the French/Algerian political thriller *Z* during promotion of *Traffic* link Soderbergh and his work to political, art-cinema, and auteurist frameworks but also to resolutely commercial ones. *Z* ranks fifteenth among U.S. theatrical releases in 1969; showcases two of the period's leading international stars, Yves Montand and Jean-Louis Trintignant; and features a director, Constantin Costa-Gavras, who later worked on numerous Hollywood studio productions, including *Missing* (1982), a commercial success that also won Costa-Gavras an Oscar for his adapted screenplay. Invoking *Z*, Soderbergh gains the kudos of political, art, and international cinemas. He also crucially links his own practice to earlier films earning profit and measurable prestige (i.e., industry awards and not just critical praise) in wide domestic release. Soderbergh's promotion of *Traffic* included references as well to *The Battle of Algiers*, not a commercial hit on its initial U.S. release in 1967 but acquiring a strong critical reputation over time. And while in 2000, *The Battle of Algiers* did not exist strongly in public discourse, its much-reported 2003 screening at the Pentagon and its subsequent 2004 theatrical re-release returned it to both hard-news and entertainment-press discourse. Having participated also in a featurette on the 2005 Criterion DVD of *The Battle of Algiers*, Soderbergh had done the groundwork for reception forums to continue the analogy. Predictably then, numerous reviews of his leftist epic *Che* drew comparisons to the 1966 film. Soderbergh's repeated references to *The Battle of Algiers* over the years thus contribute to prefigurative understandings of *Che*, particularly useful given *Che*'s very limited advertising and other official promotion. And perhaps most cannily, across his career Soderbergh has repeated the narrative of his youthful obsession with *Jaws* (1975), including scores of theatrical viewings and excited devouring of production commentary.[14] Anecdotes of this formative moment appear in numerous interviews early in his career, helping position him not as a rarefied art filmmaker but as a devotee of resolutely commercial studio productions. Like many other filmmakers of his generation, Soderbergh safely articulates kinships with a range of already-canonized New Hollywood films and European works successful in U.S. release. These affiliations may in turn resonate with cinema connoisseurs, mainstream fans, fellow industry workers, studio executives, and independent financiers.

Comparative Aesthetics and Discourses of Authorship

By citing 1960s and 1970s cinema in interviews and other forums, Soderbergh and other filmmakers perform taste preferences and aesthetically frame their own completed films. These discursive framings constitute one of many strategies for organizing diverse production teams, film aesthetics, and viewer responses into narrow constellations of textual significance and authorial presence. Soderbergh calls on 1960s and 1970s films and filmmakers as aesthetic references and as cues for successful creative practice in commercial industries. While often taking on historical subjects and settings, Soderbergh's films consistently exploit contemporary production resources and modes of distribution and exhibition. These films borrow production methods, performance styles, formal devices, thematic hallmarks, and more from preceding films, not as backward-looking homage but in service of contemporary film art. Thanks to developments in film restoration technology, continued industrial and popular interest in historical film culture, the growth of high-quality (if not archivally stable) collection media such as DVD, and the proliferation of small-screen exhibition platforms, contemporary filmmakers may engage in actual and intertextual dialogues with sectors of cinema history in ways not possible in previous eras. Through these dialogues, hybrid authorial personas that incorporate transhistorical, interpersonal affiliations take shape.

Screen authorship always constitutes a series of dialogues for filmmakers—dialogues with financiers and other production executives, with fellow creative workers, with agents of the entertainment press and critical institutions (including museums and the academy), and directly or indirectly with media audiences. The phenomenon of authorship also includes dialogues with past films and filmmakers, whether occurring in a semi-public forum such as the DVD commentary, in a private relationship such as mentoring, or in a multitude of production practices concerned with creative decision-making.

However, discourses surrounding authorship tend to isolate individual creative workers both from their immediate production teams (requisite for assigning individual authorship) and from larger industrial and commercial systems (thus circumventing the problem of commerce, or locating artistic oases in commercial deserts). Auteurist film criticism in particular has sought to locate individual artists outside, or permanently at odds with, the commercial industries that support them. A narrow focus on discrete film texts, with an accompanying selective blindness to the evidence of collaboration supplied by opening and closing credits, facilitates the subjective elevation of individual filmmakers to auteur status. While acts of critical intervention depend on a corpus of completed films, auteurist discourse only sporadically contextualizes filmmakers in wider historical continuums of screen creativity. Acknowledging such associations risks dilution of the alleged originality, integrity, and above all singularity of a designated artistic vision. Filmmakers who acknowledge artistic forebears gain cultural capital and produce maps for recognition of their own work but also open themselves to accusations of derivativeness. Auteur status thus depends on strategic affiliation in measured combination with discourse affirming artistic integrity and originality.

The collaborative and comparative phenomena of authorship link creative workers through a range of contexts. The creative work of screen authorship brings together single films' production teams, usually within larger industrial units such as production companies or studios that employ creative workers temporarily, serially, or on long-term contracts. Creative labor also depends on geographic associations based on districts, cities, regions, nations, and transnational clusters. Temporal contexts also define authorship and collaboration, with Soderbergh, for example, as a "Sundance kid" or a "1990s filmmaker" in various critical discussions. Finally, as this chapter has argued already, authorship depends on aesthetic collaboration, whether direct or indirect, expressly articulated or subject to linkage through reception activity and discourse. Most commentators of course seek evidence of authorship, collaborative or otherwise, through close attention to screen texts. Recognizing the numerous caveats and problematics that accompany hypotheses of aesthetic correspondence, we can nonetheless use textual analysis to identify transhistorical affinities in Soderbergh's films, buoyed by knowledge of their director's multivalent interests in 1960s and 1970s films and taking further cues from surrounding promotional and critical discourse.

A focused comparison of New Hollywood and contemporary film texts requires evidence of shared features. Across a wide range of discursive forums, Soderbergh has signposted numerous films and filmmakers as models for his artistic goals, production and post-production decisions, and overall creative practice. Like many cinephiles and filmmakers, Soderbergh's publicly expressed tastes appear omnivorous. However, a constellation of popular and art-cinema films and filmmakers dominates his spoken public discourse if not his actual production practice. Merging cinephile and gearhead sensibilities, Soderbergh's discourse about cinema runs heavily to formal concerns such as film stock, lenses and cameras, lighting, production design, and art direction, along with logistical choices. At the same time, he articulates considerable investments in his own and others' storytelling choices, including narrative structure, character construction, exposition and dialogue, spatial continuity, and more. In his formal preferences and their execution in his screen work, Soderbergh routinely gravitates toward the range of aesthetic features Henry Jenkins categorizes as emblematic of a "Hollywood 'New Wave'" emergent from 1965 onward. Jenkins includes "location shooting, improvisational acting, and self-conscious experimentation with swish pans, repeated actions, zooms, jumpcuts, over-amplified sounds, colour filters, extreme deep focus, intimate close-ups, freeze frames, hand-held camera, split screen, jazz scoring and sound-image mismatches, a grab-bag of devices borrowed from the European New Wave movements."[15] Jenkins's list encompasses a range of disparate filmmaking modes and production scales, and might fairly categorize a multitude of feature films, from no-budget amateur projects to massive epics, produced worldwide across nearly the last fifty years. Though Jenkins and many filmmakers point to 1960s European cinema as a point of departure, the formal strategies Jenkins identifies appear also in films of the postwar American avant-garde, in 1950s and 1960s low-budget exploitation productions such as AIP's, and in countless other film and television works that adopt the stylistic practices David Bordwell categorizes as "intensified continuity."[16]

The aesthetic and discursive associations of Soderbergh's films depend in large part on the efforts of particular performers and technicians across multiple productions. Cinematographer Ed Lachman, for example, oversaw the stylized color world of *The Limey* as well as the more realist *Erin Brockovich*. *The Limey*'s editor, Sarah Flack, worked, too, with Soderbergh on *Schizopolis* and *Full Frontal*, contributing to each film's nonlinear structure. Even as they overlap with the stylistic norms of numerous movements and eras, the Hollywood and European New Wave aesthetic hallmarks that Jenkins lists figure prominently in Soderbergh's films. Thanks to the contexts promoted by Soderbergh and screenwriter Lem Dobbs, as well as the iconic significance of its lead players and much of its supporting cast, *The Limey* deserves particular consideration as a text situated in transhistorical aesthetic networks. Already granted some attention in academic film criticism,[17] the film remains an ideal sample for this chapter's arguments thanks to its explicit articulation of the transhistorical relationship between 1960s and 1970s New Waves and contemporary U.S. boutique productions.

Other Soderbergh-directed features engage strongly with 1960s and 1970s filmmaking contexts as well. Among his mid-career work, *Schizopolis* and *Traffic* figure significantly in this regard, though their different promotional and reception contexts result in less emphasis on transhistorical situation in the discourse surrounding them. *Schizopolis* received virtually no promotion upon its initial release, removing it from major circuits of film-cultural discourse. Later, with a 2003 DVD release from the Criterion Collection, known more for prestige reissues of art-cinema classics than for contemporary releases, *Schizopolis* became a kind of historical artifact itself, complicating potential efforts to locate it alongside earlier filmmaking traditions. Moreover, its particular points of reference speak to specialized niches within cinephilic circles, niches narrower yet than the overall Criterion reception community. These reference points include Lester's mid- to late-1960s directorial work (such as the Beatles vehicles *A Hard Day's Night* [1964] and *Help* [1965] and the New Hollywood feature *Petulia* [1968]) and metanarrative psychodramas such as the *Symbiopsychotaxiplasm* pairing (1968 and 2005), these latter circulating principally via Criterion's own 2006 DVD.[18] Meanwhile, critical discourse firmly situated *Traffic* in terms of war-on-drugs topicality, partly a result of the casting of numerous standing politicians and political commentators. Soderbergh and intermediaries periodically noted the film's aesthetic roots in late-1960s U.S. and European political cinema and 1970s thrillers such as *The French Connection* (1971) and *All the President's Men* (1976). *Traffic*'s high public profile, including a year-end release positioning it for Academy Awards contention, encouraged a framing of the film in broad discourses of topicality and precluded a narrower situation alongside historical antecedents. (Among other omissions, the film received only passing comparisons to its own source text, the

1989 UK television miniseries *Traffik*, until that series' rebroadcast on U.S. television in 2001.)

As a mid-budget independent release, *The Limey* did rely on historical associations as a major strand of its promotional discourse, creating resonances for traditional art-cinema audiences of adult cinephiles. In interviews surrounding its release, Soderbergh described the film as "*Point Blank* and *Get Carter* remade in the style of Alain Resnais."[19] This analogy creates associations with two iconic crime films—one a New Hollywood production and a Paramount release, though with a British director; the other a production of MGM's British division and an MGM release in the U.S.—and the French New Wave filmmaker whose work included arthouse standouts of the 1950s and early 1960s. Film-critical discourse has constructed the reputation of Resnais's films, in particular *Hiroshima Mon Amour* (1959) and *Last Year at Marienbad* (1961), in terms of stylized imagery and elliptical narration derived from the so-called *nouveau roman*. Resnais's name evokes further viewing challenges because of his films' allusive or explicit references to historical crises, including the post–nuclear attack Japan footage in *Hiroshima Mon Amour* and the documentary images of Holocaust victims in *Night and Fog* (1955). Consequently, the Resnais reference in promotion of *The Limey* frames Soderbergh's film in terms of formal experimentation within high-cultural artistic modes. The simultaneous analogies to the more accessible if still iconic or cult crime films broaden *The Limey*'s aesthetic affiliations and thus mobilize additional viewerships and viewing cues. Notably, *Point Blank* itself has a nonlinear narrative structure, returning like *The Limey* to a handful of key events at various points in its running time. Hence, the Resnais analogy is somewhat superfluous, but facilitates situation of *The Limey* in cinephile contexts, useful given its U.S. release principally in arthouse venues (with distribution from the small but then-flush company Artisan). *The Limey* debuted at the 1999 Cannes Film Festival, played also at Toronto's, and received a tiered global release from a number of distributors, so the high-cultural and British and continental film references shrewdly promote the film in ways resonant with region-specific cultural interests.

While linked to numerous films and filmmakers from the U.S., Britain, and France, *The Limey*'s references cluster around the late-1960s and early-1970s period of proliferating New Waves in global cinema. The film's casting and its approach to character further this temporal specificity. Lead actors Terence Stamp and Peter Fonda carry strong "'60s baggage," as Dobbs asserts on a DVD commentary,[20] and supporting players include subcultural film icons Barry Newman (star of 1971 countercultural road movie *Vanishing Point*) and Joe Dallesandro (the lead actor in many of the Paul Morrissey/Andy Warhol films of the late 1960s through the mid-1970s). *The Limey*'s reuse of many scenes of the 1967 British film *Poor Cow*, directed by Ken Loach and co-starring a young Stamp, extends its intertextual, transhistorical aesthetic pedigree. Casting choices also help the film interrogate the era informing it, particularly through the construction of Fonda's character, Terry Valentine, a music mogul who occupies a cloistered, upper-class milieu. Valentine's cultural allegiances remain tied to the 1960s, contributing to his inability to live ethically in the present. (The film pivots on his cover-up of the accidental death of a young girlfriend, leading to his pursuit by her father, Wilson [Stamp's character].) DVD commentary by Soderbergh and Dobbs suggests that the original screenplay pursues a further thematic interest in the 1960s, with numerous scenes and dialogue sacrificed in the editing room. In a discussion of filmmaking intentionality, Deborah and Mark Parker argue based on *The Limey*'s commentary that Dobbs "laments the excision of material that would have made the film a meditation on the spirit of the 1960s—long sequences that . . . would have articulated something about the legacy of this era."[21] They attribute the existing film to "Soderbergh's ultimate decision in the editing process, that a film incorporating the 1960s material would be less successful than one cast more in the mold of a stylish thriller."[22] On the actual commentary, Soderbergh refers not to a desire to limit the film's 1960s context but instead a choice to streamline exposition and curb backstory. Dobbs's scripting of further character development through dialogue and incident remains somewhat at odds with the various intertextual framings he and Soderbergh offer in the commentary track. They cite numerous films that foreground character through setting, tone, gestural language, and performance rather than through narrative events and heavy dialogue: the elegiac westerns *Ride the High Country* (1962) and *The Hired Hand* (1971), the downbeat neo-noirs *The Long Goodbye* (1973) and *Night Moves* (1975), and the existential road film *Vanishing Point*.

The Limey's Wilson combines the existential outlook of many of these films' heroes with the singular motivation of the protagonists of revenge films such as *Death Wish* and *Rolling Thunder* (1977), constructing multiple links to New Hollywood characterization. (Similarly dual-purpose protagonists appear in the films of Soderbergh's near-contemporaries Gus Van Sant and Jim Jarmusch, who have also articulated interest in New Hollywood cinema or the late-1960s/early-1970s era.) The completed film characterizes Wilson through minimal bio-graphical information—he is a criminal, a father, and British—and a surplus of personal style: a loping walk sometimes filmed in slow motion, a penchant for blunt violence, and a disarming unwillingness to modulate his behavior in any context. This last trait serves the film's editing style, which repeatedly cross-cuts scenes in different times and locations with Wilson as the figure of intersection. In numerous sequences, the sound of Wilson's rambling monologues and his conver-sations with other characters bridges cuts. His voice and thus his aural authority supply a key element of formal organization. The cross-cut scenes use dialogue as punctuation, cutting at the end of characters' spoken sentences, or use Cliff Martinez's ambient score to link shots. Shots of the same characters tend to be paired as well, as for example with two subsequent shots of de facto native informant Eduardo (Luis Guzman) at different times as he converses with Wilson. Wilson's over-arching narrative presence chiefly motivates the editing design.

Soderbergh's and Dobbs's claims for the film contribute to wider rec-ognition of its hybrid, transhistorical aesthetic. In using sound bridges and a mobile central character to stitch together scenes across narrative time, *The Limey* recalls the Boorman-directed *Point Blank*. As already noted, Soderbergh references *Point Blank* explicitly in his trade-press promotion of *The Limey*; and later, on the shared *Point Blank* DVD commentary track of 2005, he remarks to Boorman that "while I was preparing *The Limey*, I was watching *Point Blank* a lot."[23] Curiously, less than five minutes into *The Limey*'s own commentary track, Dobbs discounts the idea of *Point Blank* as a key template, claiming instead the farther-ranging but more rarefied influence of filmmakers Godard and Resnais alongside 1960s experimental films generally (without naming any specific titles in this category). Soderbergh nonetheless offers generic and thematic signposts, such as the violent revenge films *Get Carter* and *Rolling Thunder* and the complicated caper film *The Organization* (1971). At the same time, he defines these 1970s films as cold in sensibility, cueing viewers to regard *The Limey* as a comparatively more emotionally immersive experience. Invocations of the French filmmakers contribute indirectly to a similar goal. Even for cinephiles, the names Godard and Resnais conjure associations of rigorous films that may create substantial viewer distance. Rather than embracing the French New Wave's connoisseurial pedigree, Soderbergh claims of his directing and editing method that "I'm interested in ways to reveal character that are unorthodox, so nonlinear storytelling is a useful tool."[24] Thus a hybrid aesthetic takes shape both textually and in the filmmakers' shaping discourse. Soderbergh forges links in genre, thematics, and narrative situations to 1970s crime films, but proposes that *The Limey* does not reproduce the cold sensibility of those earlier works. Similarly, an affinity for the high-art nonlinearity of Resnais and Godard is leavened with promises of character-driven narrative. Textually, *The Limey* generally fulfills the promises made on its behalf in Soderbergh's and Dobbs's multiple discussions. It distills a range of film-historical aesthetic strategies into form and content exploitable in the late-1990s cinema marketplace. Overall, as a text and in discourse, *The Limey* merges its contemporary creators' production efforts with a range of artistic precedents, interrogating historical attitudes from the perspective of the present.

Many of *The Limey*'s formal strategies situate it clearly within the contexts of 1990s and turn-of-the-millennium independent or Indiewood releases. While at some level discernible as commercially risky or experimental, the film's nonlinearity links it structurally to the hugely successful *Pulp Fiction*. Given that film's theatrical success and its continued circulation in popular culture throughout the 1990s, its overtly out-of-sequence narrative aids viewer recognition and industry acceptance of nonlinearity in later genre films. Despite Tarantino's own rehearsed affection for Godardian aesthetics, *Pulp Fiction* brings nonlinear storytelling well into the commercial mainstream. The year after *The Limey*'s release, the reverse-linear *Memento* became the first successful release of independent distributor Newmarket Films. *Memento*'s principal structural device is its temporal complexity. The film gives an explicit motivation for this structure, locating viewers within its memory-deficient protagonist's damaged subjectivity. Thus its complex narrative differs from art-cinema nonlinearity, which tends not to be explicitly motivated by character psychology. In the realm of character, charismatic British criminals surfaced in other UK productions picked up by U.S. distributors, including *Lock, Stock and Two Smoking Barrels* (1998), with a successful U.S. release in 1999 from distributor Gramercy; another mid-budget independent, *Sexy Beast* (2000), successfully distributed by Fox Searchlight; and the higher-profile U.S./UK Columbia co-production *Snatch* (2000), also from *Lock, Stock* writer-director Guy Ritchie. While this cycle recalled for some critics the circa-1970 heyday of British crime films such as *Performance* (1970) and *Villain* (1971), the newer films eschew specific film-historical cues such as iconic casting (*The Limey* aside) or period settings. Situated within this grouping of late-1990s and early-2000s films, *The Limey* can appear less an heir to New Wave cinema than part of contemporary genre cycles of crime, revenge, or neo-noir films.

The Limey's aesthetic contemporaneity derives, too, from its complex sound design and its cinematography. Sound experiments occur with some regularity in New Hollywood productions, with films directed by Robert Altman using extensive overlapping dialogue in pursuit of dynamic realism, and films such as *Point Blank*, *Performance*, and *The Conversation* pursuing art-cinema expressiveness through subjective or otherwise stylized sound. While *The Limey*'s sound mix connects conversations in multiple locations and at different times, it also contributes to clarity of character and themes. Arguably in contrast to the stylized sound of 1960s and 1970s productions, sound in *The Limey* facilitates narrative clarity and viewer engagement. In its visual field, stylized lighting and color link it to a range of expressive New Hollywood films but also to numerous anti-realist productions in intervening years. Particularly in scenes featuring Stamp, daytime exteriors appear in bright sunlight, verging on washed-out. This expressive treatment of Los Angeles's apparently unrelenting sunshine emphasizes the out-of-placeness of the single-minded "limey" Wilson. Warmer but still stylized nighttime blues reproduce the neo-noir look of Soderbergh's previous *The Underneath* and *Out of Sight* (those films, notably, with Elliot Davis rather than Lachman as cinematographer). Interior scenes feature expressive lighting and color as well. An early, violent confrontation in a seedy company office uses unfiltered fluorescent light that bathes its subjects in sickly, artificial greens and blues. To contrast this environment, scenes of Wilson meeting with his late daughter's friend and voice coach, Elaine (Lesley Ann Warren), include warm reds and oranges, demonstrating his awkward passage into a more everyday, feminine-coded milieu. Warm lighting also sets the mood for intimate conversation scenes in which Wilson narrates to Elaine episodes of his young parenthood, cueing the interspersed fragments from *Poor Cow*. The realist color and flat lighting of the earlier film contrast sufficiently with the present-tense scenes to establish temporal distance, but the color palette and visual rhythms mesh sufficiently to connote both spaces as parts of Wilson's subjectivity. The 1967 and 1999 images are visually distinct enough to enable recognition, yet not so dissimilar as to disrupt viewer engagement. Complicating these associations, extensive handheld camera work underscores narrative tensions as the film moves toward the confrontation between its iconic male leads. *The Limey*'s frequent use of handheld camera aligns it with a range of

New Hollywood and European New Wave precedents—per Jenkins's identification of that recurrent device in his listing of New Hollywood techniques—but also with evolving norms in contemporary screen media. Handheld camera work distinguishes the low-budget *The Blair Witch Project* (1999) and energizes much of Soderbergh's *Traffic*, while matriculating swiftly to television thrillers such as *24* (2001–2010) and simultaneously across contemporary genre-film production.

Critical responses to *The Limey* strongly emphasize the film's intertextual historical associations rather than its cohesion with late-1990s aesthetic norms. Reviewing the film in *Variety*, Emanuel Levy asserts that "[a] key scene alludes to Stamp's landmark late-'60s movies: Wyler's *The Collector* and Pasolini's *Teorema*. Indeed, the two lead performances mirror key roles Stamp and Fonda have played in the past 30 years."[25] Charles Taylor's review in *Salon* similarly underlines historical connections, naming numerous 1960s Stamp roles and a range of other 1960s and 1970s art-Hollywood films, with particular comparisons to *Point Blank*. Such emphases follow not only from the film's casting and thematics, but also from the demographics of U.S. film critics, with many reviewers at major publications in the late 1990s having come of age in the 1960s, amid the flowering of world cinema on U.S. screens. This trade demographic partly explains the impulse to view contemporary cinema through the lens of 1960s and 1970s cinephilia. At the same time, in articulating networks of references to films and filmmakers, particularly anointed auteurs such as

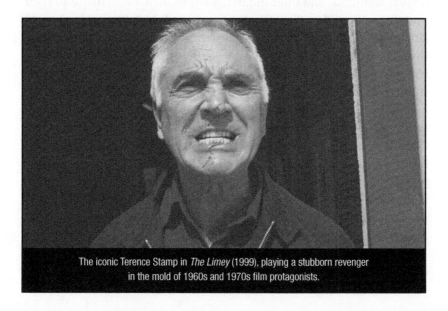

The iconic Terence Stamp in *The Limey* (1999), playing a stubborn revenger in the mold of 1960s and 1970s film protagonists.

Pasolini, critics secure cultural capital for themselves, their profession, and film culture generally. With its own proliferation of touchstones onscreen and in its filmmakers' discourse, *The Limey* offers a platform for critical dispensation of the kinds of film-cultural knowledge that build esteem for critics themselves. Intermediary industrial categories such as arts journalism create multiple incentives for their own agents to amass cultural capital and hail its dissemination. The work and discourse of historically aware filmmakers such as Soderbergh takes advantage of such taste considerations, even as it positions commercial texts in wider discursive fields to mobilize popular interest.

Film journalists are at once cultural producers, mobilizing professional skills to produce reportage and analysis, and consumers, amassing cultural capital through their own intake of commercial-artistic commodities, capital then reinvested in their professional labor. Filmmakers, too, operate in spheres both of cultural production and consumption. (Consider the French word *cinéaste*, which designates both film workers and film consumers.) Filmmakers' academic and professional training as well as leisure activity can include thorough engagement with textual artifacts across screen history. Their industrial position also affords them direct or indirect contact with other manifestations of industrial history—with filmmaking technology; with companies, institutions and other industrial constructs; and with past filmmakers through social or work interaction, study via studio archives, production biographies, and more. Filmmakers' intertextual and intra- and inter-industrial engagements contribute to their overall taste profiles. Filmmakers acquire and deploy taste markers to strengthen professional relationships with other creative workers and thus to manage their further prospects in arenas of production. These affiliative markers contribute as well to filmmakers' public authorial silhouettes. Ancillary workers such as film journalists can participate in parallel networks, building their own authorial credentials through the creative-intellectual labor of compiling screen-historical information into transhistorical grids. The cases surrounding Soderbergh and historical cinemas point to strategic efforts, undertaken by creative workers and other cultural agents with industrial investments, to profit from affinities with various sites of cultural esteem. (Chapter 4 investigates in more detail the role of film journalists as cultural and industrial intermediaries.)

Though temporally distant, the corpus of films and discourse that comprise 1960s and 1970s New Waves, art cinemas, renaissances, and other lauded categories can be accessed by producer-consumers in various forums and put to numerous uses. Pierre Bourdieu, writing of the profit gained from semi-public intellectual activity such as art-cinema patronage, notes the elite value of such practice: elites "expect the symbolic profit . . . from the work itself, from its rarity and from their discourse about it . . . , through which they will endeavour to appropriate part of its distinctive value."[26] Beyond the strategic use of taste commodities for class positioning, cultural workers can reinvest symbolic profit into subsequent creative pursuits, creating long-term feedback loops that ensure their continued employment and a secure position in artistic hierarchies. Contemporary films' and film culture's repurposings of film history can also accumulate cultural value through the implicit merit attached to demonstrations of historical awareness. From other vantages, these references represent aesthetic plunder and derivation.

The sheer volume of Soderbergh's textual and extratextual intersections with different eras of global film history can counter accusations of wholesale derivativeness. Semi-canonical films and filmmakers of the New Hollywood and 1960s European cinema—Godard and Antonioni in particular—repeatedly appear as signposts for Soderbergh's work and discourse. At the same time, in his extensive work as director, producer, patron, and more, Soderbergh has forged professional and discursive links with myriad film-historical eras. Historical backdrops for his own films as director have included circa-1920 Prague in *Kafka*, the Depression-era Midwest in *King of the Hill*, postwar Germany in *The Good German*, and revolution-era Latin America—late-1950s Cuba and mid-1960s Bolivia—in *Che's* two parts. These films and others show affinities with corresponding filmmaking movements, including German Expressionism, classical Hollywood cinema, 1960s Third Cinema agitprop, and more. As patron, Soderbergh's name has been used to "present" such works as Godfrey Reggio's *Naqoyqatsi* (2002) and the 2007 theatrical and DVD reissue of Charles Burnett's *Killer of Sheep* (1977). The connections to the experimental documentarian Reggio, best known for *Koyaanisqatsi* (1982), and to black underground filmmaker Burnett position Soderbergh as a connoisseur and patron of diverse strands of U.S. filmmaking far removed from Hollywood. Relatedly, the support for *Killer of Sheep's* restoration can defend Soderbergh's reputation against charges of anti-progressive race representation in films such as *Out of Sight* and *Traffic*.[27]

In addition to contributing production financing for *Naqoyqatsi*,[28] Soderbergh was credited as its executive producer, and his other, extensive producing work has linked him to further strands of esteemed film-historical practice. As executive producer of *Far From Heaven*, Todd Haynes's revision of Douglas Sirk's glossy yet contestatory 1950s melodramas, Soderbergh gains affiliation with a high-water mark of classical-Hollywood auteurism. Soderbergh earned the same credit on George Clooney's *Good Night, and Good Luck*, a film about television journalism printed in a rich black-and-white, modeled in part on Sidney Lumet-directed political melodramas such as *12 Angry Men* (1957) and *Fail-Safe* (1964). Through the affiliation with Clooney's film, Soderbergh furthered his intermediate position between film and television industries. In addition, *Good Night, and Good Luck*, like Soderbergh's own *The Good German*, merges existing archival footage into its fictionalized narrative. Through both productions, then, Soderbergh gains credence as a filmmaker conscious of the processes and implications of transhistorical engagement at multiple levels of production, textuality, and discourse.

Soderbergh's dialogues with film history, conducted with the support of other industry agents and ancillary figures, may be viewed as a substantial component of creative industrial activity. Screen authors can forge links to past artworks and movements to create profitable synergies at both ends: the older works enriching the status of the contemporary artist, and the contemporary artist's imprimatur augmenting the profile of the historical artifact or era. Such engagements can also complicate existing hierarchies and comparative judgments of historical periods. The film-historical past remains unstable, subject to appropriation, canon reformation, and other shifting criteria of industrial and popular value. Likewise, contemporary cultural agents— filmmakers, mediators such as professional reviewers, and broader viewing constituencies—respond to historic texts, discourses, and aesthetic clusters in unpredictable and finally unmanageable ways. Woven into contemporary film texts and discourses, reflexive and intertextual homages do not simply reconstruct past films and film culture. Such materials' producers, repackagers, intermediaries, and receivers pursue differing if not always competing agendas. Repurposing of cultural materials always carries opportunities for reception according to highly subjective, impressionistic criteria. Aesthetic repurposings remain contested and multivalent, and the polyvocality of film discourse precludes any official consensus concerning management of intertextual repositionings and re-presentations.

As a potent, visible industrial actor, Soderbergh's significance lies partly in his willingness to ignore or resist a range of venerable taste categories. While returning along with many other filmmakers and commentators to well-mapped golden ages of 1960s and 1970s cinema, he works in so many forms and modes as to disable coherent appraisal. In what reads as frustration at the inability to locate Soderbergh within convenient auteurist frameworks, J. Hoberman begins one review of a Soderbergh work with the claim that "Steven Soderbergh has no particular stylistic signature and one of the most uneven oeuvres imaginable."[29] Similarly, David Thomson weighs in on Soderbergh's critical practice with the critique that "[w]hat hangs over Soderbergh is the fatal notion that he can do some films for himself and some for the business."[30] Thomson claims that two Soderberghs exist, one a serious, auteur filmmaker, the other overseeing "entertaining genre films that have no directorial personality." Thomson's characteristically blunt view locates Soderbergh in familiar, uncomplicated evaluative categories. Soderbergh's creative practice and his discussions about filmmaking pose fundamental challenges to those categories. The "fatal notion" hangs not over Soderbergh but rather the critic Thomson, who in privileging the subjective construct of "personality" confirms his profession's continued reliance on auteurist methodologies.

Omnivorous Taste, Hybrid Authorship

Having worked repeatedly with the constructs of late-1960s and early-1970s cinema, Soderbergh has amassed sufficient cultural cachet to pursue idiosyncratic projects engaging with a range of film-historical formations. Notably, these projects include works in dialogue with film culture just preceding the so-called Hollywood Renaissance, that is, with one of the less (if not the absolute least) esteemed eras in Hollywood history. Having displayed affinities with political cinema in the mode of *The Battle of Algiers* and art cinema à la Godard and Resnais, Soderbergh's willingness to direct a remake of the maligned post-classical film *Ocean's Eleven* (1960) itself constitutes a form of experimentation. Soderbergh and Warner Bros. have engaged in adaptive reuse of the original film, though in carefully negotiated ways. Discourse surrounding the remade *Ocean's Eleven* invokes the original only sparingly. This management of promotional and reception climates protects the newer film from substantial associations with a text bearing a poor critical reputation as one in a series of uninspired Rat Pack showcases, and lacking name recognition overall except among select older viewerships. As an extension of a significant taste profile, such affiliations should carry only negative value, lacking either high-cultural or subcultural esteem and thus undermining a laboriously cultivated taste persona.[31] However, the very notion of a filmmaker known for character-driven and sometimes political independent cinema directing a remake of a notoriously indulgent star vehicle may create a strongly positive impression of ironic distance suitable to affirm Soderbergh's status as a wide-ranging, unpredictable talent.

Some years later, such an impression was bolstered through Soderbergh's publicized plans to direct *Cleo*, a 3-D musical Cleopatra biopic, the project recalling for many commentators the notorious 1963 film *Cleopatra*, the year's top box-office draw[32] but also one of the industry's most storied failures thanks to its exorbitant production costs. Further positioning the new venture at the margins of respectability but centrally within pop-culture history, during pre-production Soderbergh declared of the project, "It's sort of like *Viva Las Vegas* meets *Tommy*."[33] Soderbergh thus signposts two further touchstones, linking the project safely to two of popular music's most successful artists—Elvis Presley and The Who—as well as to high-performing films from two distinct eras.[34] Writing on corporate agents' framings of film-historical artifacts, Klinger reminds us that industries and institutions may influence but do not control popular memory: "the work of the cine-museum does not monopolize the social production of memory; memory is a contested terrain."[35] Present-day media consumers may straightforwardly embrace the Elvis/Las Vegas strand of mainstream popular culture or the varying iterations of the classic-rock opera. Others may find irony in these asserted points of intersection, deflecting questions of highbrow taste and laying the groundwork for favorable reception. As with the *Ocean's* films, any hostile responses to the *Cleo* project could be seen as evidence of biases of cultural elites. The perceived uninterest in elite taste criteria locates Soderbergh's authorial credentials in a realm of omnivorous connoisseurship, granting his production teams and his films access to myriad sources of commercial capital.

Soderbergh's diverse associations lend him abundant subcultural capital as well. His disparate output amounts to actualization of "what if?" fantasies for cinephile constituencies and positions him strongly within circuits of subcultural exchange. Paradoxically, his occasional immersion in disreputable, square subjects—Las Vegas casino culture, the entertainer Liberace (subject of another project, *Behind the Candelabra*, in development for HBO Films), or the combination of Cleopatra, 3-D, and the musical—disengages his work from the taste preferences of urban, cosmopolitan elites. This idiosyncratic refusal of understood taste categories places Soderbergh positively at a remove both from trends in independent cinema and from prestige-mainstream currents. Soderbergh's proliferating discursive and production activity construct an unorthodox but no less distinctive authorial persona. This persona makes substantial use of his status as intercultural agent, connecting the diverse agendas of past and present filmmakers, film cultures across history, and a range of taste strata. This hybrid creative formation productively destabilizes boundaries such as those demarcating discrete film-historical eras. Soderbergh's career highlights ways filmmakers and film cultures interact with dynamic constellations of elite, mass-cultural, and subcultural capital. The next chapter looks further at mediated professional relationships, addressing the experimentation, location work, and collaboration evident in Soderbergh-guided productions and the implications of those activities for understandings of screen authorship.

Part Two

Authoring and Authorization

Chapter 3

Authorial Practice, Collaboration, and Location Production

While forging artistic affiliations with a range of historical forebears in U.S. and global cinema, Soderbergh has since early in his career sought to maintain professional partnerships with many of his contemporaries as well. In Soderbergh's work world, as other chapters of this book demonstrate, discursive affiliations repeatedly evolve into collaborative production relationships. The strong emphasis on collaboration in Soderbergh's discussions of filmmaking highlights the interconnection of creative relationships in screen-media production. These relationships in turn reveal the inadequacies of the casual privileging of directors as the focal points of claims about film authorship. This chapter uses production analysis and different strands of reception commentary to illuminate Soderbergh's authorial practice, his collaborations with particular industry professionals, and the terms on which his films are understood as authored work. The cases here investigate authorship at three different levels of magnification: as framed in terms of creative experimentation on U.S. productions of contrasting scales, as a transportable feature of an international production, and as a category constructed or perceived locally amid production activity. In each case, not only filmmaking teams but also a multitude of cultural agents and intermediaries contribute to discourses about screen authorship. First, I focus on production of *The Good German*, along with its promotion as simultaneous film experiment and classical homage. In the film's production and circulation, numerous forms of authorial practice are manifest, promoted, or discounted. To recognize the variety of Soderbergh's activities, I also return briefly to *Bubble*, a more contained experiment involving a different span of industrial attributes and authorial work. The chapter's second and third sections address location filmmaking in disparate contexts: the production of *Che* in multiple Spanish-speaking countries, and the filming of much of *The Informant!* in the U.S. Midwest. These productions raise different questions about authorial practice and local communities' perception of and relationship to that practice. Through case studies of production work on films both large and small, I argue for a new, nuanced understanding of industrial categories and authorship. The chapter suggests the ways the auteur label, tied to the casually understood binary of studio versus independent film, serves as a convenient heuristic around which to organize cinephilic discussions but limits recognition of production labor and collaborative film artistry. Blanket designations such as "auteur film" fail to account fully for the diverse ways production teams perform, and viewing publics recognize, the art and work of filmmaking.

In addressing Soderbergh's specific practice as screen author, the chapter has two goals. First, it outlines a system of collaborative authorship in contemporary screen production. Second, through consideration of that system, it argues that contemporary Hollywood and a critical mass of international screen producers remain receptive to experimental practice and to filmmaking initiatives in diverse locations worldwide. As already discussed, Soderbergh remains a filmmaker well known within industry and cinephile circles, though he is hardly a household name on the order of, for example, Spielberg or Tarantino. A wide variety of production entities and financiers have continued to fund Soderbergh's semi-experimental work even when that work at the pre-production stage shows limited commercial prospects, and even when those entities have no economic stake in Soderbergh's other explicitly mainstream and commercial projects. While experimentation is key to Soderbergh's collaborations, the phenomenon of authorship deserves broader consideration first.

Authorship is a multiply defined and strongly contested term. At one level it refers to acts of *creation* and creativity—to author is to make something. But authorship is also a category of attribution. In collaborative artistic production in particular, authorship depends on recognition. In cinema, the auteur label, bestowed by others, elevates filmmakers from the category of industrial workers to artists. To author films is to make art, and artistry depends on external judgment to be recognized as such. Some claim artist or auteur status for themselves, but such claims remain subject to external debate. Soderbergh himself has been reluctant to describe his filmmaking practice as art. "I am a filmmaker," he declared in congressional testimony in 2009, "and so by some loose definition I'm an artist."[1] One can be a filmmaker, a maker of films, without being acknowledged as an author per se, or particularly as an auteur.[2] Recognition as an author calls upon a second quality of authorship: that of *authority*, of control over the process of creation. Authorial control requires that production teams establish a chain of creative command, grant decision-making power to particular individuals, or allow particular co-creators to stand to account for an artwork during or after its composition. For collaborative, principally industrial artworks such as motion pictures, authorship involves processes of creation, management, negotiation, and recognition. This chapter, accordingly, considers different ways authoring occurs in film production and achieves recognition. It first looks to Soderbergh and his collaborators' experimentation on a studio product, and the processes of author recognition encompassing that film and Soderbergh's preceding micro-budget independent work. It next explores ways Soderbergh's work method adapts to international conditions and ways particular films and filmmakers secure positions in global film cultures. Finally, it considers how witnesses to a localized film production apprehend the activities of a film shoot as collaborative or authored. In all, it interrogates authorship and film culture according to the terms established so far in this book: filmmaking as collaborative process, negotiation with industry agents, dialogue with historical artifacts and creators, and engagement with viewing publics through texts and discourse. Through theorization and case studies, I argue for a model of collaborative authorship that recognizes the conditions of contemporary screen practice.

Copyright law and other regimes of intellectual property measure authorship according to contracts and corporate ownership, while arts scholars tend to define authorship through interpretive acts. To ground this book in production categories, I propose four conditions under which single individuals merit the attribution of primary authorship of a screen text: (1) demonstrable evidence of supervision of production elements; (2) creative collaboration with the same individuals across a body of films; (3) multi-hyphenate activity, or demonstrated investment in multiple aspects of the production and postproduction process; and (4) work within the art-cinema sector, in small-scale production, or in another industrial formation allowing a high degree of creative autonomy. I address these conditions across this book, emphasizing the shapes production work, reception activity, and screen texts themselves take when viewed through the prism of authorship.

Soderbergh's ability to work both within and outside the boundaries of major-studio filmmaking—at levels of production, distribution, and exhibition—attests to the fluidity of contemporary, transnational media systems. These dynamic artistic practices constitute screen authorship, if not its recognition. Constructions of authorship depend on visibility: box-office success, critical commentary, or a substantive presence at international festivals, in art cinemas, or in other realms of cinephile culture. Recognition in any of these categories can generate the industrial and critical interest crucial to the circulation of an authorial reputation. Our first area of attention, the collaborative production of *The Good German* and the promotional rhetoric that accompanies it, exemplifies ways key discourses construct screen authorship. The language of authorship brings together producers, texts, and viewers. Thus, understanding of discursive practices illuminates the industrial systems that support filmmakers and filmmaking, and the cultural work that screen texts do.

Re-Theorizing Authorship: Promotion, Collaboration, and the Manufacture of Auteurs

With George Clooney and Cate Blanchett as its leads, *The Good German* was promoted by Warner Bros., perhaps predictably, as a star vehicle and a wartime romance in the classical Hollywood style. It was also framed, much less predictably given its not-meager $32 million production budget and its co-financing by investment consortium Virtual Studios, as an experiment for its producers and for audiences. Somewhat surprisingly too, Soderbergh and Warner Bros. did not promote *The Good German* in terms of topicality. Its wartime-reconstruction narrative might have easily been framed as an allegory for ongoing U.S. involvement in Iraq and Afghanistan. Another Clooney-affiliated black-and-white production, *Good Night, and Good Luck*, released the previous year by Warner Independent Pictures and also from Soderbergh and Clooney's Section Eight production company, did use topicality as a promotional tool, comparing its world of brave journalists to present political and news-media environments. Instead, *The Good German*'s promotion showcases the film's relationship to World War II–era films and filmmaking, and also, perhaps most unusually for a mainstream studio release, its stylistic and thematic experimentation. This framing facilitates a view of Soderbergh as someone involved in artistic practice, whether or not the resulting film is itself seen as an artwork.

In his many interviews publicizing *The Good German*, Soderbergh returns repeatedly to the notion of experimentation. He invokes not only the use of 1940s technology and the construction of a 1940s aesthetic for the film—appealing perhaps to cinephiles or to nostalgic filmgoers enamored of classical-Hollywood style—but also the desire to experiment with style and narrative.[3] In particular, Soderbergh signposts the film's use of profanity and its realist treatment of sexual behavior. Five minutes after it begins, the film features a scene of semi-consensual rear-entry sex between stars Blanchett and Tobey Maguire, and generous helpings of profanity appear across the film. The foregrounding of rough sex, coarse language, and above all the notion of film as experiment serve quite different purposes than the promotion of the film as classical-Hollywood homage. Textually, the film includes numerous allusions to films such as *Casablanca* and *The Third Man*. The promotional campaign makes such allusions as well; for example, the poster graphic of *The Good German* is an almost exact reproduction of *Casablanca*'s. However, Soderbergh's repeated claims of experimentation suggest a very different rationale for the film.

The term "experiment" deserves some clarification. Soderbergh's feature films do not enter the realm of experimental video that encompasses such artists as Bill Viola, Douglas Gordon, and Matthew Barney. Most of his work remains commercially released narrative features.

At left: The iconic promotional poster for *Casablanca* (1942).
Right: The promotional poster for *The Good German* (2006) closely mirrors *Casablanca*'s.

Nonetheless, his ongoing efforts with digital video as well as film, with black-and-white production, and with other production and post-production processes, locate his creative work within the climate of innovation that periodically defines Hollywood studio production—in the 1920s with sound, the 1930s with color and deep-focus cinematography, the 1950s with widescreen processes, and so forth. Present discursive conceptions of Hollywood highlight the industry's risk aversion via genre-film production, franchises, presold properties, and other efforts regarded as contrary to artistic experimentation. Yet even as Soderbergh has been associated with virtually all the *bêtes noires* linked to contemporary Hollywood—genre films, star vehicles, franchises, remakes, and sequels—he has also been granted considerable artistic autonomy. His manner of experimentation differs from that undertaken for museum and gallery contexts, yet the efforts of Soderbergh and many other popular commercial filmmakers undermine false binaries of Hollywood as site of artistic stagnation, under whose shadow vanguard experimental artists toil without fanfare.

For *The Good German*, Soderbergh's relationship with Warner Bros. allowed him and his crew to conduct virtual film-school exercises during production. These include shooting in black-and-white with obsolete lenses, lighting, sound equipment, and visual effects, and calling for a stylized, non-contemporary performance style.[4] Additionally, during its production, Soderbergh, who did not attend film school, screened for his cast and crew such films as *Mildred Pierce* (1945), *Out of the Past* (1947), and *The Third Man*, films that appear on many university film syllabi. Such efforts may appear contrary to popular notions of Hollywood studios' cost- and audience-consciousness. Yet film screenings during production—not just of production dailies but of past films—form part of the combined professional and film-cultural activity that accompanies many film productions. Directors (and less often, cinematographers) choose films that provide visual, cultural, or performance-based frames of reference for ongoing productions. Soderbergh's efforts transform studio production facilities into well-appointed film-school classrooms, but this tendency is not at all unique to Soderbergh's productions. Attention to the global economic logic of the U.S. film industry can obscure the fact that studios regularly support filmmakers' efforts to locate their work in a historical continuum of screen art.

One might expect the latitude afforded Soderbergh and his crew to be an idiosyncratic arrangement with a single studio or production company. However, Soderbergh has directed films for nearly every major Hollywood studio and high-profile independent producer. He has worked with Warners, Columbia, Universal (and its Focus Features imprint), 20th Century Fox, Miramax (both before and after its acquisition by Disney), Lionsgate, and the now-defunct Artisan and USA Films. His films have been produced as well by smaller companies such as Participant Media (for *The Informant!* and *Contagion* [2011]), Magnolia Pictures (for *Bubble* and *The Girlfriend Experience*), HBO, and even the BBC (co-producer, with the Independent Film Channel, of the stage adaptation *Gray's Anatomy*). His partnerships with studios continued even after films he directed were critical and commercial failures. Universal, for example, produced or distributed four of his films as director, with only the last, *Erin Brockovich*, achieving commercial success. Warners reputedly created its Warner Independent Pictures boutique imprint partly to accommodate Soderbergh specifically. In short, numerous financing sources and distribution channels remain available to filmmakers whose interests are not restricted to easily marketable, risk-averse genre productions.

Before turning to issues of creative collaboration, I raise one further point regarding *The Good German*'s distribution. With its A-list cast but U.S. gross of only $1.3 million, we might regard the film as a substantial failure. However, from its limited opening in December 2006 through its final theatrical bow in April 2007, the film played in a total of only 66 U.S. theaters, compared to nearly 3,600 theaters for the subsequent Soderbergh-directed, Clooney-starring effort, *Ocean's Thirteen*. In other words, Warners distributed *The Good German* no more widely than a small independent film; following disappointing reviews for its New York and Los Angeles openings, the film was not given a wide release. The clearest sign of studio economic imperatives is the decision not to distribute and promote the film across the U.S. *The Good German*'s performance indicates that studios may finance the production of unconventional films, but will not necessarily support their distribution.[5]

Its studio's mercurial distribution practices notwithstanding, *The Good German* offers a particularly rich case of artistic collaboration. The film adapts a 2001 novel, combines 1940s and contemporary technologies, and makes substantial use of footage of postwar Berlin gathered from Russian, German, and U.S. archives. Notably, the film's status as adaptation and its appropriative use of archival film contribute to its double framing as allusion to 1940s practices and as contemporary experiment. Interviews with Soderbergh surrounding the film's release encourage this view of the production and the film.

With the support of ancillary institutions such as entertainment journalism, global film industries foreground film directors principally to enable coherent choices for film patrons, and secondarily to organize understandings of textual meaning. Directors' prominent but not all-encompassing roles in film production liken them to sports teams' designated captains, who give post-game interviews. In both situations, single individuals are asked to account for a group performance, much of which they do not govern at all. And in both situations, news industries and receivers grant some credence to the spokesman's claims. At risk of overextending the sports analogy, I note that Soderbergh's team features Soderbergh himself playing nearly all front-court positions, with his recurring collaborators filling out most of the others (aside from screenwriting roles—Soderbergh has never worked with the same screenwriter more than twice). Soderbergh and Clooney dominate press coverage of the film.[6] Screenwriter Paul Attanasio, writer of the critically acclaimed *Quiz Show* (1994) and *Donnie Brasco* (1997) in addition to numerous popular thriller adaptations, receives some mentions but is never quoted in articles surrounding the film's release. Collaboration is a bald fact of commercial screen production, yet screen-cultural discourse tends to withhold discussion of collaboration in favor of inaccurate but easily apprehensible foregrounding of solitary authorial agents. In his theorization of collaborative film authorship, Robert Carringer argues that "[c]ollaboration analysis has two phases. The first entails the temporary suspension of single-author primacy . . . to appraise constituent claims to a text's authorship. In the second phase, the primary author is reinscribed within what is now established as an institutional context of authorship."[7] For numerous reasons, much popular and industrial discourse on cinema strongly maintains notions of single, and single-minded, authors. If we recognize Soderbergh's own activity as predominantly collaborative, we can better understand creative production practices and the narratives of those practices that various institutions circulate. Attention to institutional contexts demonstrates the richness both of the industrial system and of the creative workers operating within it.

Multiple collaborators can be said to constitute part-authors of film and television texts bearing Soderbergh's name. On *The Good German*, in addition to directing, Soderbergh served as cinematographer, lead camera operator, and film editor, but other major roles went to longtime collaborators.[8] At the time of its release, the film represented his second collaboration with composer Thomas Newman, his fourth with costume designer Louise Frogley, his eighth with set decorator Kristen Toscano Messina, his ninth with production designer Philip Messina, his fourteenth effort with assistant director and producer Gregory Jacobs, and his sixteenth film with sound editor Larry Blake. Soderbergh worked with each of these collaborators, aside from Newman, on later films as well. Screen industries support collaboration because it can lead to cohesive, efficient production work. Cliff Martinez, composer on ten of Soderbergh's films (though not *The Good German*), observes that:

> [M]onogamy is always a good thing in creative partnerships. . . . [T]here's a kind of ESP that occurs with somebody you've worked with before. You know their likes and dislikes. And the work gets better. . . . [W]hat's changed is we talk less. With *sex, lies, and videotape* we talked a lot, and over the years the dialogue becomes less and less because I guess I know what to do and he trusts me.[9]

Even as Soderbergh works repeatedly with the same small group of collaborators, he has styled himself as a journeyman filmmaker who works in highly disparate modes and whose output bears no specific creative signature. During publicity for *The Good German*, Soderbergh told the *New York Times*'s Dave Kehr, "I would have been so happy to have been Michael Curtiz," referring to the veteran Warners contract director who made over one hundred films for the studio, including *Casablanca*, from the 1920s to the 1960s. Manohla Dargis, also of the *Times*, has noted the disingenuousness of Soderbergh's claim, in that Curtiz had virtually no creative oversight and played no role in decisions about casting, crew, and other production matters.[10] Moreover, Curtiz's authorship has only been assessed retrospectively, whereas Soderbergh's efforts can be assessed alongside his own stated intents and his strong involvement in all aspects of production. Soderbergh's invocation of Curtiz complicates his own status as collaborating artist. The association with a major classical-era director positions Soderbergh as himself a historically notable filmmaker, discounting his collaborators' contributions. At the same time, the connection to the consummate work-for-hire figure Curtiz defines Soderbergh also as part of a team of industrial workers in which no individual agenda predominates.

Creative partnerships occur across U.S. film production. Filmmakers such as Clint Eastwood and Martin Scorsese routinely work with the same cinematographers, editors, sound engineers, and other craftspeople. Soderbergh occupies another, paradoxical position: he not only uses the same crew for different productions but also performs many creative roles himself, in particular those of cinematographer, camera operator, and editor. Filmmaker Robert Rodriguez performs a comparably wide range of duties for capital-intensive productions and often works as screenwriter and composer as well. Similarly, independent veteran David Lynch served as cinematographer and cameraman for the digital-video feature *Inland Empire* (2006) and has played many roles in related video projects circulated online. These cases aside, though, stewardship of multiple, major creative roles for 35mm feature-film production is rare. Still, developments in consumer-grade editing software, in digital-effects technology, and in digital-video camera quality promise to swell the ranks of multi-hyphenate author figures involved in feature production in the global mainstream as well as at its margins. Moreover, though the long-ago breakdown of the studio system has eliminated the streamlined, assembly-line approach to film production, work methods such as Soderbergh's display a mode of production in many ways similar to those of classical studios, with the same teams of craftspeople working together on multiple productions. Soderbergh routinely collaborates with the same people on fully independent productions as well as films shot with studio resources. On studio-supported films, the creative teams exist at a remove from studio oversight, i.e., they work alongside the filmmaker, not the studio. And with Soderbergh in interviews regularly using the pronoun "we" rather than "I" to discuss creative decisions, he repudiates notions of solitary authorship in favor of collaborative ones.

In addition to encouraging collaborative practice, major studios have historically been in the vanguard of experimentation with cinema technology. Studios have bankrolled countless innovations—including deep-focus cinematography, the Steadicam, and rotoscopic animation, to name just a few—though R&D does not emerge as a key component of studios' popular images. *The Good German* allows Soderbergh and his collaborators to conduct retro-experiments, filming with out-of-production camera lenses, with incandescent lighting,[11] and with boom microphones rather than the wireless body microphones common on contemporary studio features. In addition, the production includes simulated rear-projection shots created with digital mattes, as well as archival footage edited and resized to the 1.85:1 aspect ratio but otherwise unmanipulated, with its jerky motion and grainy images marking the artifice of the surrounding fiction. The filmmakers thus merge multiple historical frameworks: the aesthetic of actuality footage, that of classical-Hollywood cinema, and that of the unrepresented 1940s, with sexuality, language, and violence that did exist but did not emerge in popular representation. In one interview, Soderbergh claims to seek a sort of dialectical tension: "a tension between this aesthetic that is very glamorous, very romantic inherently and an approach to narrative and character that is the antithesis of that."[12] Soderbergh tempers his claims of intent with attention to viewer activity, consistent with his authorial strategy of creating dialogues both on- and off-screen. Speculating about responses to the film's tensions, he observes, "[I]t would not be a passive experience to watch a movie in which that battle is taking place."

The Good German's limited release means that few filmgoers have had that experience, passive or otherwise. Even in pre-release publicity, Soderbergh alludes to the possibility of a chilly reception. He told one interviewer that "[m]ixing the modern attitude with the classic aesthetic is a little much for some people. . . . Some people haven't been able to wrap their heads around it."[13] To a *Time Out* reporter, he admitted after a festival screening, "[t]his may have been a way of working, an aesthetic, that may end up being too distancing for too many people—more than we need to make the movie financially successful."[14] Likewise, a short piece in *USA Today* ends with a prophetic Soderbergh quote: "If you are experimenting, some people are definitely going to fall by the wayside."[15] Perhaps ironically, thus far those people have been principally professional film critics and not mass audiences, suggesting ways the critical establishment patrols against certain forms of experimentation on behalf of an abstracted "audience."[16] Amid other criticisms, numerous reviewers faulted *The Good German* for its failure to reproduce exactly the tone and visual style of a 1940s film. Such a critique perhaps says more about critical canons than about the neo-retro experiment overseen by Soderbergh. English-language critics have expressed similar ambivalence about other Soderbergh films that mix historical and contemporary sensibilities. Soderbergh-directed remakes of 1960's *Ocean's Eleven* and 1972's *Solaris*, for example, were critically received with similar combinations of interest and hostility even before their releases. Whatever the studio's response to the film's initial box-office performance, the case of *The Good German* shows that contemporary screen industries offer opportunities for creative industrial practice and for collaboration among corporate, major-studio interests and those of autonomous artist-filmmakers.

We will return shortly to consideration of Soderbergh's collaborative practice on specific films. But first, critical constructions of screen authorship deserve further interrogation. One goal of this book is to rethink the utility of discussions of authorship for understanding industries and production practices, popular-media circulation and reception, and textual artifacts such as individual films. As David Gerstner and Janet Staiger note, "authorship is an enabling tool," organizing critical as well as popular discourse about texts and producers.[17] In academic discourse, the frame of authorship can facilitate analysis of constellations of meaning in groups of films. Filmmakers themselves, seeking to maximize audience interest and interpretive possibilities, frequently do not advance singular interpretations of films on which they play key creative roles. Instead, it is often critics or fans who attribute authorial signatures to works, arranging textual evidence to support particular readings of single films or bodies of films. The limited scholarship on films directed by Soderbergh has principally highlighted politics, gender, and race representation. These readings situate Soderbergh-directed films in social contexts and investigate the degree to which his creative practice foregrounds progressive representation.[18]

Close readings of individual films dominate the existing critical work on Soderbergh. Much director-based criticism, unconcerned with filmmakers' own statements or their documented work practices, is content to find the author in the text. Analyses of Soderbergh-directed films typically use a series of reading strategies to assign meaning to film texts and grant Soderbergh himself, as director, sole responsibility for aspects of representation. Thus, scholars make claims for "Soderbergh's film" or "Soderbergh's films." The director becomes, in the familiar auteurist paradigm, the individual responsible for all textual properties, including a set of meanings, which usually cohere in a preferred reading. Such commentaries rely on what Michel Foucault calls the "author-function" to organize cross-textual systems and enact the disciplining impulse that Foucault associates with this function.[19] These readings celebrate or disparage Soderbergh's films, and by implication the author himself, for their provision of progressive or regressive images and narratives. While framed as political intervention into commercial cinema, this invocation of authorship contributes also to screen taste cultures, as readings of films shape critical canons.

Beyond organizing sets of reading strategies, authorship is a site of, and can be constituted through, various discourses.[20] These include discourses emerging from criticism, industrial practice, reception, textual systems, genres, and cinephilic and other taste cultures. (Regarding the last of these, Soderbergh's continued invocation alongside the construct "independent film" is exemplary.) Staiger cautions that emphasis on authorship as the product of discourses renders the author "a body devoid of agency *and continuity* and, potentially, of significance."[21] Still, particular authors can be understood in terms of reading strategies and surrounding discourses without denying their agency at the level of production. Moreover, we can see that when called upon to speak about their work, filmmakers play key roles in enabling reading formations and contextual discourses. Indeed, many studies of contemporary cinema do draw evidence of authorial agency from interviews conducted after production and preceding or immediately following a film's release. Scholars increasingly rely too on the ancillary texts of DVD commentaries to locate authorial agency (often but not always understood as intent) and textual meaning. What a director says on record about "his films" provides a starting point (or sometimes end point) for critical analysis. In the case of *The Good German*, the frameworks established by Soderbergh himself in ancillary discourse differ markedly from academic reading strategies applied to other "Soderbergh films." (I am content to use this phrase both with and without self-awareness, if such is possible, to designate films on which he plays key creative roles.) Many of us continue to apply academic strategies, emphasizing representation, to popular cinema generally, even as these approaches bear little relation to filmmakers', journalists', and general viewers' framing criteria. Do such readings constitute only "interpretation," valid only if filmmakers articulate complementary ideological sensibilities on record? Soderbergh's political consciousness is not a matter of much public scrutiny. He has been a sometimes public figure, speaking as vice president of the Directors Guild of America (a role held since 2004 and set to end in 2013) on behalf of workers' interests during the 2008 writers' strike, and testifying before Congress in 2009 about film piracy. While contemporaries such as Clooney and Steven Spielberg known for their political advocacy have had their work interrogated accordingly, commentaries on Soderbergh's output have tended not to spotlight his own political sensibilities. Even responses to such controversial films as *Traffic* and *Che* tend to focus on the political content of the films themselves, rather than treating the films as dispatches from Soderbergh's own political consciousness. Soderbergh has been understood as a political filmmaker, and he has occasionally been called to account for his work's content—for example, by detractors of *Che* unhappy with its omissions of the Cuban Revolution's many repressive acts. However, critics and fans have not depended strongly on Soderbergh's authorial claims to legitimate their own responses to his work.

While *The Good German* has been granted little critical attention to date, the case suggests the continued limitations of existing close-reading practices, which routinely produce political readings. Such highly subjective readings tend to demonstrate the agility of the critic rather than indicating collective responses guided by a combination of textual features, promotional discourses, and other reception activity. In contrast to the other Soderbergh-affiliated, Clooney-starring *Good Night, and Good Luck*, which was linked in multiple discourses to outspoken leftist Clooney, *The Good German* was not promoted as topical and political in nature but instead as simultaneously nostalgic, experimental, and realist. Ancillary commentary on the film—trade-press reports and pre-release entertainment journalism pieces, followed by reviews—foregrounds as the film's key creative force director-cinematographer-editor Soderbergh, who in interviews does not emphasize a contemporary political frame. As we have seen, he instead makes claims for the film as a retro experiment and a realist view of 1940s behavior. Thus, Soderbergh's own framing of *The Good German* as its author or part-author is at odds with the interpretive categories on which professional film commentators usually rely.

If insight into authorial sensibilities demands consideration of a corpus of films, Soderbergh's earlier 2006 feature, *Bubble*, provides little continuity.[22] *Bubble* finds Soderbergh working with a much shorter list of collaborators, and the film bears little similarity to *The Good German* in narrative, address, and circulation strategy. Aside from the involvement of the multi-hyphenate Soderbergh, the film bears almost no discernible relationship to *The Good German*, or to most other contemporary U.S. films, for that matter. Regarding *The Good German*, and Soderbergh's larger filmography as director and multi-hyphenate, I have argued thus far for a model of collaborative authorship that tracks the collective and specific contributions of key creative personnel across productions. Soderbergh's penchant for working with the same group of creative technicians on multiple films makes him a figure well suited for such a model. But how do we assess authorship when groups of collaborators change wholly or partly from film to film? *Bubble* shows a filmmaker working in most principal creative roles single-handedly, and with fewer collaborators from previous projects offering continuity. *Bubble* rejoins Soderbergh with longtime producer Greg Jacobs and production coordinator Robin Le Chanu; screenwriter Coleman Hough, who also scripted the 2002 DV effort *Full Frontal*; assistant editor David Kirchner, who as of 2011 has worked with Soderbergh on twelve features and one short;[23] and second AD Trey Batchelor, who has worked on eight films directed by Soderbergh. The film does not include contributions from production designer Philip Messina or sound editor Larry Blake, familiar names on most Soderbergh films. In this case, *Bubble*'s tiny budget dictates their absences, as the film does not credit any production designer or sound editor (merely a property master in the first category and a sound mixer in the second).

In terms of its production financing and budget, and its limited distribution to specialty cinemas, *Bubble* easily fits within the elastic category of "independent film." Still, the "independent" designation quickly loses any meaningful specificity, as nearly all the crew members just noted worked also on Soderbergh productions for Warner Bros., 20th Century Fox, or Universal. If one accepts that these collaborators perform their professional roles similarly irrespective of who finances their work, company banners and related studio/independent binaries need not organize our understandings of creative labor on discrete films. While this might seem an entirely logical proposition, loosely designated production categories routinely underpin discursive claims of authorship. The initial formulations of auteurism hinged on conceptions of filmmakers battling the constraints imposed by studio production, while the more recent "indie auteur" designation implicitly attributes creative autonomy to filmmakers who may face budgetary or other resource limitations. Though execution of an artistic vision necessarily depends on management of available filmmaking resources, production categories such as "studio" and "independent" often serve as shorthand for particular authorial sensibilities, even as screen practitioners regularly cross production scales.

Bubble and *The Good German* do show multiple points of intersection at the levels of production, textuality, and promotional and reception discourses. The films address a range of taste cultures, including informal, self-selecting cultures of Soderbergh or filmmaker connoisseurs. While the two works differ in production scale, financing, and roster of performers, both include contributions from recurring Soderbergh collaborators, and Soderbergh himself serves as creative multi-hyphenate, working from another's commissioned script. Textually, both foreground aesthetic innovation: *The Good German* in terms of re-creation of 1940s aesthetics, *Bubble* through a realist aesthetic facilitated by still-novel digital cinematography. Like *The Good German*, *Bubble* attracted few viewers in theatrical exhibition, partly a consequence of the hostile exhibitors' response noted in the introductory case study. *Bubble*'s distribution could be described with the same sound bite Soderbergh himself offered with regard to *The Good*

German: "If you are experimenting, some people are definitely going to fall by the wayside." This remark, offered with resignation or regret, points to Soderbergh's own artistic investments, necessarily balanced with the desire for the degree of commercial success required to sustain a professional career. As Chapter 4 discusses in more depth, many critics argue that *The Good German* overemphasizes its creators' needs at the expense of viewers'. Still, Soderbergh's willingness to speak at length about his own production processes—and his strongly articulated investments in and borrowings from particular strands of global and historical film cultures—contributes to theorizations of taste and artistry not only outside production cultures but also within them.

Collaborative production activity represents one component of the phenomenon of screen authorship. The fluctuating recognition of collaboration shows how authorship functions as practice and construct, linked to both production work and discursive activities. I turn next to a consideration of international production activity and its contribution to Soderbergh's global artistic profile. Trade discourses, historical accounts, and critical commentaries have linked Soderbergh indelibly to the American independent cinema, perhaps in the process limiting perceptions of him as a filmmaker with interests beyond U.S. culture and film culture. Nonetheless, through collaboration and other efforts, Soderbergh has sought to establish himself as an authorial talent whose works resonate in disparate settings. Soderbergh's efforts and the responses to them show the myriad opportunities for, and barriers to, formation of a distinctive artistic signature across international screen cultures.

Soderbergh Abroad: American Indie or Global Auteur?

Like many filmmakers, Soderbergh has made efforts to secure an international reputation through overseas production work, global circulation of major releases, festival appearances, and other creative and discursive practices. These efforts highlight the relationship between a localized reputation, tied to American independent cinema, and a broader status as a global auteur, capable of securing distribution in, and attracting audiences from, different nations' film cultures. Soderbergh has repeatedly used the capital acquired through his "indie auteur" status to take on production challenges in international contexts. These include films with location shooting in Prague (*Kafka*); Italy, France, and Holland (*Ocean's Twelve*); Mexico (*Che* and *Traffic*); Spain and Bolivia (*Che* again); Ireland (*Haywire* [2012]); and Australia (the unreleased *The Last Time I Saw Michael Gregg*, filmed in 2009). He has also pursued transitive associations with many nations' venerated film cultures. For example, he contributed to the omnibus film *Eros* alongside Italy's Michelangelo Antonioni and Hong Kong's Wong Kar-Wai, and he has articulated investments in the works of filmmakers from France, Italy, Great Britain, and China. These claims appear in interviews, DVD commentaries, and other venues, as well as through particular aesthetic strategies across Soderbergh's filmography. Through their textual qualities and Soderbergh's own declared intent, films such as *Kafka, Schizopolis, The Limey, The Good German, Che,* and *The Girlfriend Experience* show Soderbergh in dialogue with celebrated global filmmakers and with global art-cinema aesthetics. To assess the portability of artistic reputations distinguished by particular national contexts or movements, I concentrate here on the production of *Che* in Latin America and Spain and its appearances at international festivals.

Che offers a biopic of sorts of the Argentinean doctor who participated in the 1959 Cuban Revolution and died in 1967 during a similar but failed insurrection in Bolivia. The film's two parts depict these distinct struggles, with *Che: Part One* released in some markets with the subtitle *The Argentine* and *Che: Part Two* subtitled as *Guerilla. Che's* co-producers include Laura Bickford's small U.S. production company, Soderbergh's own Section Eight (closed as of 2007 and credited only for *Che: Part One*), Spanish producer Telecinco and producer-distributor Morena Films, and French sales agent Wild Bunch. For U.S. distribution, IFC Films acquired theatrical and pay-per-view rights subsequent to the film's debut at the 2008 Cannes Film Festival.

Through the investigation of the film's production context and its initial circulation, we can theorize the phenomenon of what might be called "global auteurism," or the dissemination of an individual filmmaker's creative signature into multiple regions of global film culture. I argue that filmmakers may pursue three broad strategies to achieve a global authorial profile and thus the status of global auteur. First, they may drive or benefit from the international circulation at festivals and in wider release of films strongly branded as authored texts. Second, and relatedly, they may participate in localized art and entertainment discourses. Filmmakers routinely promote their films in local forums such as interviews, press conferences, and newspaper and magazine profiles. With *Che,* for example, Soderbergh appeared at premiere screenings in Miami, Havana, Mexico, and elsewhere, and granted interviews to different regional publications, as is routine industry practice over the course of a tiered international release. Filmmakers can also declare cultural or aesthetic connections between their works and the films, filmmakers, and cultures of particular receiving territories. During 1999 promotion of *The Limey*, for example, Soderbergh's references to British crime films such as *Get Carter*, along with the casting of Terence Stamp in the film's lead role, helped position the film for its UK release. Local receivers may also establish such connections based on inferences from textual evidence. In another case, in 1989 the Cannes festival press reportedly queried Soderbergh about *sex, lies, and videotape*'s apparent debt to the films of Eric Rohmer, though Soderbergh claimed not to know Rohmer's work. Finally, filmmakers may acquire global-auteur status by establishing a global production footprint. Multiple labor and economic activities can comprise such a footprint. These include film production outside the U.S., through location shooting as well as use of international studio facilities or soundstages; collaboration with overseas production teams; employment of transplanted international creative workers on U.S.-based productions (as actors, technicians, or in other capacities); and production financing with a non-U.S. component, such as *Che*'s Spanish and French investment. I focus here on *Che*'s international production and its implications for models of collaborative screen authorship.

The transit of artistic producers, textual affinities, and creative reputations represents a form of intercultural migration, often leading to and from global creative-industry hubs such as Los Angeles. Filmmakers from around the world repeatedly use reputations acquired in the international art cinema as calling cards for transit to Hollywood studio filmmaking. Such filmmakers as Ridley Scott, Peter Weir, Wolfgang Petersen, and Peter Jackson have moved from national-cinema contexts to expensive U.S-based or Hollywood-supported productions. Meanwhile, relatively few American filmmakers follow the reverse trajectory, establishing a reputation in the U.S. and then moving into other production contexts worldwide. Hollywood filmmakers have made use of foreign locations extensively since the 1950s, and in the new millennium, Hollywood studios have increasingly pursued production cofinancing from overseas companies and investors. However, the establishment of a strong creative presence outside the U.S. is rare, usually the province of global-blockbuster directors such as Steven Spielberg, popular auteurs such as Quentin Tarantino, and arthouse figures such as Woody Allen and David Lynch. Both Allen and Lynch have directed numerous films backed by overseas production capital—France's Canal+ and CiBy 2000 have co-funded many of Lynch's films since 1992's *Fire Walk with Me*, and Allen and his producers have turned to numerous overseas companies for financing since 2003's *Anything Else*. Allen's European presence has risen in recent years owing to his venture into UK, Spanish, and French production environments. Among historical cases, a handful of well-known U.S. filmmakers—including Jules Dassin, Joseph Losey, Richard Lester, and Stanley Kubrick—relocated to Europe for personal or political reasons, establishing or building their reputations through Europe-centered productions. The movement of filmmakers from the U.S. to Europe represents a contra-flow of Hollywood talent, in contrast to the familiar pattern of Hollywood absorbing foreign talent such as directors, cinematographers, and stars.

Across his career, Soderbergh has intermittently pursued an international footprint. As we have seen, his debut feature, *sex, lies, and videotape*, premiered impressively at the U.S. Film Festival but gained global recognition as well as U.S. box-office success only after winning the Palme d'Or at Cannes. Soderbergh used this initial success to pursue international production, filming his second feature, *Kafka*, in Prague and on London soundstages. Though working in specifically U.S. production contexts across the rest of the 1990s, Soderbergh returned to cross-border production for *Traffic*, filmed in Mexico as well as the U.S. (though many scenes set in Mexico were filmed in California and New Mexico). Some years later, despite his limited foreign-language fluency, Soderbergh filmed much of the Spanish-language *Che* in Puerto Rico, Mexico, Spain, and Bolivia. *Che*, too, benefitted from Cannes publicity, premiering there to a strongly divided press response but earning the Best Actor award for star Benicio Del Toro. *Che* performed only modestly in theatrical release both domestically and worldwide, and despite his status as a brand-name American auteur, many of Soderbergh's other films have received limited releases, or none at all, outside the U.S. Of Soderbergh's filmography, *Ocean's Eleven* and its sequels have performed strongest by far in international release. Notably, promotion of these films foregrounds marquee stars and generic markers of the comedy caper, with Soderbergh named only in minimal fashion in promotional efforts and reception discourse.

How might an "American indie" filmmaker acquire the status of international auteur? U.S. filmmakers earn such critical designations usually when their films circulate in diverse overseas markets and achieve critical or commercial success. Demonstrated affinities for non-U.S. filmmakers—established through interview discourse, textual borrowings, and elsewhere—can help locate filmmakers in international-auteur pantheons. Martin Scorsese, for example, has articulated cinephilic investments not only in U.S. film traditions such as film noir but also in Italian cinema, in particular the work of designated auteurs such as Roberto Rossellini and Luchino Visconti. Similarly, with films such as *Interiors* (1978) and in numerous interviews, Woody Allen has claimed artistic kinship with Ingmar Bergman's philosophical cinema,[24] and his Expressionist homage *Shadows and Fog*, like Soderbergh's own *Kafka*, pays tribute to a venerated era of European film. U.S. filmmakers may also benefit paradoxically from a lack of commercial or critical success in the domestic market. Domestic esteem may tether filmmakers indelibly to their home screen cultures. Meanwhile, the absence of that esteem permits festival programmers, arts journalists, and other gatekeepers to secure their own cultural capital by championing films and filmmakers seen as unheralded or underappreciated in their home cultures.

The global traffic in forms of symbolic capital such as artistic reputation coincides with the international flow of screen production resources, particularly the resource of human artistry and labor, or what Paul Kerr terms "migrating talent."[25] Talent migrates according to the mandates of globalized film production, with what Ben Goldsmith and Tom O'Regan term a "project logic"[26] motivating the pursuit of inexpensive labor and locations worldwide. Shifts toward project-based, one-off production and location rather than studio shooting are fundamental to Hollywood's move in the 1950s to the package-unit production system, with individual films taking shape in effect, or explicitly, as independent productions that studios distribute.[27] Steve Neale notes that as a consequence of the package system, "the director is more overtly institutionalised in a role analogous to author."[28] Thus, Hollywood's postclassical ecology facilitates both globalized location production and the functional creative autonomy of film directors. These twin developments, and the concomitant expansion of global film festivals, enable the emergence of global auteur figures, directors whose work occurs in different global locations and whose reputations travel as well (if not necessarily as a direct consequence of their location production work).

Meanwhile, whereas the many Hollywood productions filmed in cities such as Toronto, Vancouver, and Sydney rarely engage textually with the cultures of those locales, *Che*'s Spanish-language production indicates a willingness to engage with regional cultures at the fundamental level of language. (While Hollywood's Canadian or Australian productions also engage in terms of language, the worldwide ubiquity of English arguably delimits its use as a marker of cultural authenticity.) Casting of performers from Spanish-speaking and Lusophone countries further the film's regional engagement.[29] Thus, filmmakers such as Soderbergh can acquire symbolic capital from cultural collaborations involving production personnel, language, and location. Even without location filming in Cuba itself, *Che*'s production in Spanish-speaking territories and countries guarantees a certain verisimilitude beneficial to the biopic's textual sensibility and to Soderbergh's extra-textual claims of the film's historical fidelity. Goldsmith and O'Regan note that location production can transform "found places" lacking onscreen exposure into "places with signifying and representational power"[30] associated with notable films, and perhaps with globally recognized filmmakers.

Globalization facilitates the cross-border movement of people, financial resources, technologies, material goods, cultural commodities, and ideas.[31] Such conditions might be expected to enrich opportunities for creative workers, particularly those whose activity does not depend on a fixed location such as a factory, studio, or corporate headquarters. Film directors, for instance, might be seen as precisely the kinds of creative workers best able to take advantage of opportunities for global artistic production. Global production does not raise the profiles of all workers, though. Power dynamics do not cease to operate in globalized creative economies but instead take different configurations according to the needs and resources of mobile production entities and local infrastructures. *Che*'s dispersed production benefits partly from Soderbergh's negotiating power as a filmmaker whose work periodically succeeds in international markets. Its production depends, too, on accommodation of local production conditions, including on the one hand employment of production personnel in each filming region, and on the other the use of the lightweight RED One HD digital camera system for much of the production, limiting the need for local postproduction work. Overall, conditions of *Che*'s production indicate the need to recognize directorial work as not just collaborative but as *negotiated* authorship. This creative activity is simultaneously *mobile*, with the liberating possibilities that term implies, and transitory or *displaced*, with those terms' implied instabilities at work as well.

Soderbergh is of course not a subaltern refugee but an elite film artist. In interviews surrounding *Che*, he identifies both creative and economic considerations for its largely Spanish-language production. Like others involved in the production, he invokes chiefly the criterion of realism prevalent in discourse around prestige cinema: "In the rest of the world, the issue of authenticity was really paramount. . . . You can't make a movie about an anti-imperialist and use the language of the imperialist." More practically, he notes, "[O]nce we decided to shoot in Spanish, we understood that it probably meant there'd be no money from the U.S. to make the film, and it turned out to be not a problem because we got our money out of Europe."[32] One consequence of a move from U.S. to foreign, and especially European, production contexts is the receipt of associations with culturally prestigious art cinema.[33] European and so-called art cinemas have historically been understood as supportive of film directors, or dependent on auteur directors for the organization of textual meaning.[34] Similarly, Paul Kerr identifies as a 1990s trend "the globalizing of national art cinemas—through festivals, co-productions, international distribution networks, and the accelerating movement of diasporic talent,"[35] all of which might unhinge creative producers from specific national contexts. Still, Soderbergh remains principally associated with American rather than European or global cinema. Despite his films' appearances at Cannes and other international festivals, his status as a Cannes jury member in 2003, and his involvement in the international omnibus film *Eros*, Soderbergh's associations with the flourishing of American independent cinema at the end of the 1980s have marked him fundamentally as a domestic rather than global artistic producer, and the U.S. settings of most of his films as director and producer have bolstered these associations across the 1990s and 2000s.

In sharp contrast to this U.S.-centric production mode, the two-part *Che* involves the collaboration of hundreds of actors, technicians, and administrators in four countries on three continents. Both parts were shot entirely on location, though not in Cuba: *Part One* in Mexico, Puerto Rico, and New York City, and *Part Two* in Spain and Bolivia. The logistics of this collaborative project that relate to its standing as international co-production deserve some consideration. *Che: Part Two*, for example, includes credits for five translators, three dialect coaches, three immigration attorneys, and six legal advisors or firms. The two parts' postproduction activities also involved a series of transnational collaborations. For example, Madrid-based effects company El Ranchito created postproduction visual effects for *Che: Part One*'s combat sequences, with other U.S. and Spanish VFX technicians working on both films as well. In production, *Che* was shot not only on HD video (with the RED camera and in both anamorphic and spherical formats) but also on Super 16mm and anamorphic 16mm film, necessitating localized film processing; in addition, the theatrical releases of the film's two parts used different print stocks. The film's color timing and editing included a "workflow across Soderbergh's New York City office and ten Technicolor facilities around the world."[36] Trade commentary on *Che*'s production asserts Soderbergh's involvement in these activities,[37] though the editing credit for both parts goes to Spanish editor Pablo Zumárraga, who has worked exclusively on Spanish productions or co-productions. The film's music also takes shape through mediated transatlantic collaboration. Working from Madrid, Spanish composer Alberto Iglesias wrote the score and consulted by phone with the New York-based Soderbergh. Iglesias later relocated to London to conduct the orchestral recording. The collaboration with Iglesias, composer on numerous films from director Pedro Almodóvar since the mid-1990s, links Soderbergh to another major figure in global cinema and partly positions *Che* for exhibition in Spain, the first country in which it received a wide release. The contributions of other key craftspeople also known for work on Almodóvar's films—including costume designer Bina Daigeler and production designer Antxón Gómez—further build the film's pedigree as an international, and largely Spanish, creative production rather than a U.S. or Hollywood export.

Overall, Soderbergh's creative work on *Che* involves the management of a crew of multiple nationalities, principally Spanish speakers. Much of the supporting cast as well comes from the ranks of native Spanish speakers, with the bilingual Benicio Del Toro again (following his role as a Mexican policeman in *Traffic*) bringing his Puerto Rican Spanish to a different regional context.[38] Additionally, in the manner of so-called "Europudding" films that seek to maximize appeals for discrete national viewerships, *Che* gathers stars—including Matt Damon, Julia Ormond, and Franka Potente—from a range of national and international cinemas, as well as scores of actors from Latin America and the Iberian Peninsula. Finally, the film's subject, comparable to that of the earlier *Traffic*, marks Soderbergh as a filmmaker with investments in politics and cultures beyond the U.S.

Like a shift to foreign production, participation in international film festivals contributes explicitly to filmmakers' international reputations. Festival screenings unfix films from domestic settings or production contexts. Abé Mark Nornes contends that festivals' "basic function is to plug spectators into the internationality of cinema."[39] During autumn 2008, following its wide release in Spain and preceding its December release in the U.S., *Che* appeared at festivals in Toronto; New York; Morelia, Mexico; São Paolo; London; Los Angeles; and Havana.[40] At festivals, directors' national origins can come to define a film's identity irrespective of film content or co-production arrangements.[41] While *Che*'s Spanish dialogue limits its categorization as a specifically American film, the film's associations with Soderbergh and with fellow American Del Toro tie it more strongly to American-cinema contexts than to those of its Spanish- or French-industry co-producers. Soderbergh and Del Toro's activities as the principal spokes-men for the film at festivals and in wider publicity situate *Che* as the work of American creators (if hyphenated Puerto Rican–American for Del Toro) rather than Latin Americans or Europeans.

Auteurism is a discursive phenomenon, linked to but distinct from the practice of authoring, and dependent chiefly on recognition. Festival and other trade and cinephile discourse accounts strongly for "global auteur" designations. Evidence or strong inference of directorial control on particular productions also contributes substantially to the recog-nition of global auteurs. The global-auteur label may better describe figures who collaborate narrowly and locally yet maintain global reputations than those who collaborate internationally. Participation in international creative alliances can signal a relinquishing of the specificity of vision on which auteur status continues to depend. Theorizing collaborative authorship, Berys Gaut identifies "two dimen-sions of variation . . . distinguished in collaborative artistic activities," including "the degree to which creative power is determining the artistic properties of a film is centralized or dispersed" and "the degree to which the different collaborators are in agreement over the aims of their film and their role within its production."[42] *Che*'s principal creative spokesmen are director-cinematographer Soderbergh and producer-star Del Toro, but the film's lengthy gestation and logis-tically complex, transnational production define it as an artistically decentralized effort. Moreover, the language differences among production members and the film's dispersed pre- and post-production activities largely preclude consensus views of its artistic aims or individuals' precise roles within the overall production apparatus.

Global production contexts, and the disseminated film-cultural discourse that accompanies a tiered international release, complicate but enrich understandings of collaborative screen authorship. Filmmakers may bring to foreign location productions the same creative sensibility that motivates them for domestic efforts, but the specifics of location cultures demand a range of engagements that can redefine authorial practice as negotiation and translation. Moreover, *Che*'s international production reminds us that collaborative authorship can include face-to-face engagements in multiple locations as well as mediated management of production activity occurring across geographic space. Cohesive theorization of global authorship requires attention to industry workers' local activities and shifting global affiliations, as well as to the different trajectories of economic and symbolic capital that precede and follow screen production.

Financing and distribution of U.S. independent as well as studio-based productions overwhelmingly configure around the one-off project logic, with new co-production alliances and distribution arrangements for each new film. Global investment-market declines of 2008–2009 notwithstanding, productions increasingly rely on global venture capital, and the closing of U.S. studio specialty divisions such as Paramount Vantage and Warner Independent Pictures will surely accelerate the growth of piecemeal distribution arrangements. Flexible financing schemes such as venture-capital investment may be regarded as largely detrimental to global authorship or global-auteur status. These practices disengage filmmakers from the supporting infrastructures of film studios or their specialty divisions, which come with tacit executive support, first-look options, and other spurs to production. The abundance of global production networks and shifting nodes of influence poses challenges for filmmakers seeking to maintain interpersonal relationships with production executives, erecting barriers of language and geographic distance. Still, with U.S. films increasingly dependent on overseas investors and markets, screen producers and their backers will doubtless seek further opportunities for the global spread of authorial silhouettes. Motivated by economic imperatives, the unfixing of auteur brands from national contexts can further the cross-pollination of film cultures and thus the development of truly global collaborative authorship.

Situating *The Informant!*: Authorship on Location

While one strand of Soderbergh's authorial practice foregrounds international location production, another emphasizes regional American filmmaking in locations unaccustomed to screen-production activity. Between the transatlantic production of *Che* and the filming of *The Girlfriend Experience* mostly in lower Manhattan, Soderbergh shot much of the 2009 whistleblower comedy *The Informant!* in Decatur, Illinois, a small city in the state's agricultural heartland. Some two hundred miles south of Chicago, Decatur is far from any substantial production resources such as equipment-rental houses, soundstages, and film-processing or postproduction facilities. In commentaries on the film, Soderbergh proclaims his desire to recreate the ambiance of its nonfiction source text, also set largely in Decatur. He says of the semi-rural production location that "there is a look to that part of Illinois that you can't fake. You have to be there; you have to go and get it," and that "it's such a great way to lock everybody into the movie."[43] This second claim refers to the securing of a suitable mindset for cast and crew to inhabit the fictionalized version of this stereotypically genial, conservative region of the American Midwest. To achieve this mindset, production workers relocate to unfamiliar, sometimes remote areas, and local residents must accommodate those workers. The circumstances of *The Informant!*'s location production allow us to examine its local impact in some detail. Its filming constitutes a largely routine experience for producers but an exceptional one for many local residents. Location filming entails a range of production considerations including cast accommodation, location access, regional infrastructure and economic conditions, and financiers' support for particular kinds of spatial verisimilitude and thus textual authenticity. Production workers also engage formally and informally with the communities in which filming occurs. Through this engagement, community members themselves build impressions of industrial activity and screen artistry. The location shoot thus manifests a particular creative signature. Local discourse defines the shoot not as an auteurist endeavor but as a collaboration of craftspeople and technicians, an impression formed largely out of residents' interactions with below-the-line production personnel.

While films' status as art depends on judgments of completed works, authorship itself is a process, identified and evaluated differently than film artifacts. To recognize authorship as process, we can look to profilmic events and on-set activity, in which producers combine local resources with imported hardware, technicians, and talent. Location production focalizes the efforts of creative agents and contributes in myriad ways to ensuing screen representations. Julian Stringer notes that screen productions can mobilize "the dramatic and affective possibilities" of particular locations.[44] A specific location, he adds, "generates unique dramatic possibilities and offers highly localised sensory pleasures."[45] Stringer's example is the Hawaiian island Oahu, coincidentally also one of *The Informant!*'s locations, but his formulation can be applied to far less exotic sites such as the midwestern American heartland. Beyond the affective and sensory engagements a location affords, location production creates encounters between members of otherwise disparate sociocultural groups. While not so far afield as *Che*'s rural Bolivian or Spanish locations, Decatur presents a community also largely foreign to its transplanted production team. Location productions necessarily involve interactions, if highly managed ones, between screen producers, representing a form of cultural elites, and people with no industry ties. The relocation of industry professionals from Hollywood to central Illinois thus involves the temporary narrowing of the social and geographic distance separating Hollywood practitioners from Middle America.[46] This contingent engagement entails both producers' creative negotiations and local stakeholders' formation of attitudes about entertainment-industry practices.

Through *The Informant!*'s location production in Decatur, local residents and media build perspectives on screen authorship and production activity independent of textual content. With a comic plot involving audio and video recording of corporate malfeasance in numerous locations, *The Informant!* thematizes the logistical and ethical complications of media practice. Based on business writer Kurt Eichenwald's nonfiction bestseller, the film revisits a 1990s price-fixing scandal in the agribusiness sector, in which executives at agriculture giant Archer Daniels Midland (ADM) colluded with global competitors to set prices on chemical corn derivatives. Two senior ADM executives went to prison as a result of the case, which the FBI and U.S. Justice Department prosecuted with the aid of another ADM executive, Mark Whitacre. Whitacre made the case against ADM possible by recording hundreds of conversations and meetings at ADM and elsewhere, though at the same time as collaborating with the FBI, he was himself embezzling millions of dollars from ADM, and he later served nearly nine years in federal prison. The film portrays the seriocomic behavior of Whitacre (played by Matt Damon) as he both cooperates with and deceives the FBI and his fellow executives. The production was partly filmed in Los Angeles and Phoenix though not set in those cities. With an approximately $21 million budget from Warner Bros.,[47] additional scenes set in Zurich, Paris, and Oahu were filmed on location. Most of the film, though, takes place in the Decatur area and elsewhere in the U.S. Midwest, prompting location filming in Decatur and surrounding towns, as well as in Springfield (fifty miles from Decatur), St. Louis, and Chicago.

Location filming of Hollywood productions far from creative or technological hubs elicits a range of discursive responses in different forums. Location filming disrupts dominant trajectories of what Michael Curtin terms "creative migration"[48]—moves to media capitals such as Los Angeles, for example—in favor of short-term migrations to areas that may be remote from loci of industrial activity or creative talent. Such short-term migration represents routine industry practice, so when it occurs, discourse in production hubs may only passingly address the presence of specific productions. In places unaccustomed to screen-production activity, though, discourse about filmmaking can rise substantially. With Chicago the site of location work for such superproductions as *Batman Begins* (2005), *The Dark Knight* (2008), and *Public Enemies* (2009), the passing presence of the mid-budget feature *The Informant!* merits only a minor notice in one of the city's major daily newspapers.[49] In the Illinois state capital of Springfield, local media skews heavily toward coverage of the state legislature, and *The Informant!*'s location work there earns a single if lengthy article in the city's daily newspaper, focusing on a local resident's experience as a film extra.[50] In Decatur, though—with a metropolitan population of around one hundred thousand, half the size of Springfield's—the film's production generates dozens of stories in the local newspaper, the *Herald & Review*. These stories, many accompanied with unpolished video, say a great deal about local residents' and media's impressions of filmmaking practice.

With Decatur's local-news resources typically devoted to quite routine small-city events, the nearly month-long residence of a Hollywood-studio production affords the local press many opportunities for novel reportage. A banner ad on the newspaper's website proclaims it "Decatur's #1 Source For Local Informant Movie News," and its exhaustive coverage includes reports on the project's long gestation and ADM's possible cooperation with the production, discussions of specific homes and streets used in shooting, local citizens' involvement in or views of the shoot, and the finished film's representation of the city and of local celebrity (but no longer resident) Mark Whitacre. These grassroots accounts provide a rich vein of information about local participation in and responses to location production, information typically excluded from extra-cinematic discourse on films and filmmaking. This exclusion follows from producing entities' and intermediary institutions' perception of such discourse as irrelevant to most viewers' appreciation of a film text or its producers' artistic motivations. Yet local accounts vividly recreate production activity, if in mediated form, at some remove from profilmic spaces or the creative decisions made about those spaces. The accounts speak to the collateral consequences of screen production, portraying a specialized kind of reception activity, that of reception of film *productions* rather than film texts. The accounts further distinguish some of the local stakeholders with whom filmmakers negotiate during productions, and who thus form part of the broader discursive communities with which film artists engage.

The published local response to *The Informant!*'s production takes the form chiefly of small-city boosterism. During and shortly after the production's May 2008 location work there, starstruck Decatur-area residents and merchants speak in glowing terms of production workers' professionalism and friendliness, of Damon and other cast members' willingness to endure lengthy autograph sessions, and of "amazing," "awesome," "unbelievable," and "opportunity of a lifetime" experiences as bystanders or extras.[51] Numerous respondents discuss the production's appearance as a stimulating break from routine. One autograph-seeker observes, "I must say, I have been bored now that the cast and crew are gone. It was certainly something fun, different, and interesting to do in this town."[52] A Decatur police sergeant serving as a liaison to the production waxes existentially that "[w]hen it was over with, it was a sigh of relief. . . . But by the same token, there was kind of an emptiness."[53] Some residents experience different kinds of emptiness upon the film's release, when they see that few recognizable locales appear in the finished work. The *Herald & Review* reports that at the Decatur midnight premiere "the audience applauded when they saw a familiar scene from Decatur, such as the Chinese Tea Garden [restaurant] or the vintage set from [radio station] WAND."[54] Evaluating the finished film later, though, Decatur entertainment reporter Tim Cain observes with resignation that "[t]he setting and local people involved certainly add some color and interest to the final product, but they're far from the main point."[55] Cain, who receives a small screen credit, notes that "for the most part, Decatur is just a location for a film about a person."[56]

Local responses to the production and the film recognize authoring forces in numerous ways. Whitacre himself, relocated to Florida, refers to his telephone conversations with "Warner Bros."[57] though not with specific individuals. Meanwhile many business owners recount face-to-face transactions with unnamed production workers— costumers and set decorators buying vintage clothing and furniture, location managers renting business and residential spaces for filming, extras-casting personnel, and various crew patronizing restaurants and other merchants. Some residents organize their perceptions of the production around sightings of star Damon or supporting actors such as Scott Bakula and Joel McHale (both small-screen stars), and much less often director Soderbergh. Indeed, Soderbergh does not fully acquire authorial status until the film's home-video release. Here, his

Blu-ray commentary remarks about scenes filmed but cut from the finished film mark him as a key decision-maker—and part-villain—from the perspective of Decatur commentator Jayson Albright.[58] Albright and other local witnesses' awareness of numerous scenes filmed in the region, coupled with a misapprehension of location-production activity as a reliable gauge of film content, leads to disappointment over the finished product's scope. Lamenting the scenes' absence even from the disc's deleted-scenes assortment, Albright writes, "All that effort, all that time and money—and all those local extras!—and we don't get to see it."[59] In short, local knowledge of profilmic events colors reception of corresponding textual artifacts. This response in turn coheres around production agents perceived as ultimately responsible for creative decisions. Thus, Soderbergh's home-video commentary performs functions other than the circulation of his authorial signature. His claim of responsibility for a content decision marks him as an outsider working partly at cross-purposes to the local citizenry who are filmed but not finally represented.

The Decatur case attunes us to the intersection of production activity, textual artifacts, and reception phenomena. The local response to a Hollywood production affords us with evidence of *production reception*, which accounts for authorship in novel ways. Notably, too, through such claims as "I may not be in (the movie), but I was there when they filmed it,"[60] some residents specifically anticipate the possible content of the future film. The Decatur responses demonstrate that local awareness of screen authorship follows from interactions with—and sometimes service as—well-below-the-line production workers, with logisticians, technicians and craftspeople at relatively low positions in industrial hierarchies. As a corollary to John Caldwell's research on what he terms *"off-screen* media production work worlds,"[61] attention to impressions left by screen workers in location-shooting environments reveals the many narratives that arise around authorship and specific productions. Caldwell's own production ethnographies of industry's "deep texts"—the stories practitioners tell about their work—show us how workers "'distribute cognition' across segregated craft subspecialties."[62] Corollary attention to what we might call the "shallow texts" of location-shoot eyewitnesses indicates the different kinds of cognition distributed when local residents and visiting production workers interact. These shallow texts derive from the highly contingent experiences and narratives of local agents marginal to the production and the subsequent film. At the same time, they articulate community members' expectations surrounding transitory creative infrastructures. *The Informant!*'s production affords little long-term cultural or economic benefit to its central Illinois locations.[63] However, the production embeds in numerous witnesses and local participants exceptional memories that can enhance local social status. Significantly, too, as witnesses to a professional community's semi-public performance of work practices and rituals, Decatur-area residents acquire positive awareness of screen-industry labor and its satisfactions. Recounting his interactions with numerous cast and crew, excitable commentator Albright asserts that "[t]he one thing I picked up from all of them was how much they were enjoying filming this movie. Their enthusiasm was infectious."[64] Lacking access to private industry activities that might challenge this belief, members of communities far distant from media capitals may circulate such overwhelmingly affirmative accounts of collaborative creative practice.

Location productions based on real events can become staging grounds for conflicts over the narration of history, pitting invested residents against screen producers in search of compelling drama. One might expect a location production that restages the criminal behavior of top executives of a major local employer to engender resistance, or at least to arouse residents' emotions and political sensibilities. However, published local discourse around *The Informant!* is surprisingly inattentive to ADM's status as a major corporate criminal in the 1990s. Despite the ADM case being virtually the only event ever to put Decatur in the spotlight of international news media,[65] in advance of the production, local reporter Cain supplies a "back story" on the case of barely sixty words, "for those who don't remember or have forgotten."[66] Meanwhile, ADM itself crafts a strategically nonchalant response to the production. A spokeswoman promises that ADM will not impede the filming, asserting further, "We understand that this is a film, based on a screenplay, based on a book, based on events that a person is interpreting. . . . Films have their own dramatic needs and intents. We focus on who we are. . . . This was more than a decade ago, and we took action at the time. We have a ten-year-strong track record. People know us and know who we are."[67] To accompany the film's release, ADM also produced a bland corporate webpage asserting, among other claims, "ADM, then and today, is made up of ethical, hardworking people."[68] Local reaction to the film's truth claims focuses on the heroism or villainy of Whitacre in particular rather than on ADM's corporate crimes. Meanwhile, Soderbergh's relatively low profile as a political filmmaker—viewed as such by some critics and scholars, but widely known only for the *Ocean's* films and lacking the controversial reputation of directors such as Oliver Stone—means that he and his artistic intent do not figure strongly in local views of the film's political stance. Star sightings and other impressions of Hollywood glamour feature much more centrally in local discourse about the production. This discourse affords very little sense of popular cinema as a forum for political content or ideological struggle.

At the same time, a vigorous if contained debate in the *Herald & Review*'s letters-to-the-editor forum forcefully articulates a handful of respondents' outrage over ADM's disreputable history and the city's present disregard for that history. In the web comments, one writer asks, "have ya'll [sic] all forgotten that the reason for this movie is due to one of Decatur's major employers being caught doing illegal activity?" Another observes that "[t]his film is portraying one of Decaturs [sic] most shameful acts and scandals yet you all act like its [sic] one big party." Another comment expresses "disgust that ADM will come out looking pretty probably [sic] and all anyone can do there is gush and coo over the big old Hollywood people." This last remark specifically identifies the issues raised or elided by the production and its surrounding commentary. Appearing long before the film's release, though, it makes no explicit reference to the film's creative decision-makers or their perspectives on the ADM case.

Location filming creates spaces where different cultural agents seek to make meaning and assert control with the tools available to them. Our study of this negotiated activity can illuminate processes of authorship as well as discursive investments in artistic practices. Location interactions also highlight power relations among industry professionals and distant onlookers. Film studies has tended to recognize the film text as the principal means of communication between filmmakers and audiences. Consequently, scholars interested in questions of power have long concerned themselves with textual representation, attending more recently as well to the range of paratexts such as trailers, press junkets, and DVD supplements through which industry and its agents also communicate to prospective viewerships. Location productions create further encounters between filmmakers and prospective audiences, encounters in which non-professionals judge artistic and technical achievements on the basis of lived experience rather than through completed screen texts. These judgments involve residents' investments in the local events and institutions the productions may bring to the screen, their perceived access to a production's core artists, and their levels of cultural capital.

Progressive approaches to screen production, attuned to institutional power dynamics and cultural relations, can find in *The Informant!*'s production two distinct areas of local engagement: local responses to the white-collar crimes of price-fixing and embezzlement perpetrated by ADM executives and their collaborators, and residents' interactions with film-production personnel who hold culturally elite status. Local discourse downplays the former while inflating the latter. Both impact views of art and authorship—the first by contributing to debates over textual meaning, the second by circulating accounts of production practice. Interactions between production personnel and residents also periodically bridge what Nick Couldry calls "the media/ordinary boundary"[69] while offering potent reminders of the imbalance between the two groups. As on other studio productions, paid extras sign clauses prohibiting speaking to or making eye contact with performers,[70] though such prohibitions are occasionally relaxed. Meanwhile, locals' engagement with creative agents such as Soderbergh occurs at some distance. Numerous witnesses comment on the Decatur High School jacket they see him wearing and manage to banter with him about it during breaks in filming, but he grants no interviews to local media.[71] Decatur residents enjoy more sustained encounters with personnel very low in the production hierarchy whose roles involve community engagement: with extras-casting director Rich King; with numerous location, costume, and prop supervisors; and repeatedly with Matt Damon's bodyguard. In contrast to the distant snapshots of figures recognized in other contexts as key creative forces, residents form impressions of below-the-line craftspeople and managers as the immediate authoring agents of the production. Meanwhile, star Damon registers as the person seen watching a Boston Celtics game on television at a bar, and Soderbergh earns notice principally for his gone-native attire, not his filmmaking practices. Local discourse around this location production thus transforms a global film star and an internationally acclaimed filmmaker into quotidian, sometimes anonymous figures, while elevating the visible labor of below-the-line workers to high status. The transitory event of the production and local views of it thereby invert the terms of authorship on which film industries and institutions depend to maintain their privileged cultural status. Encounters such as those created by *The Informant!*'s production exemplify dynamic relationships among creative agents, local communities, and the discourses that both bind and distinguish them.

Location production of *The Informant!* (2009) as seen by the *Decatur Herald & Review*'s news video, with Matt Damon, Joel McHale, and Soderbergh all partly obscured.

Collaborative authorship involves multiple economic, industrial, and cultural determinants. Authorial work is a complex phenomenon, and its recognition equally so. As we have seen, *The Informant!*'s filming mobilizes a range of views about production events and the finished film. To investigate authorship's recognition in more detail, we turn next to the contested spaces of critical reception, in which tastemakers and stakeholders of varying influence weigh in on the value of Soderbergh's work in its time and its place in the ongoing legacy of popular screen art.

Chapter 4

Critical Reception and
the Soderbergh Imprint

To better understand the many voices involved in the manufacture of film authorship, this chapter interrogates a sample of critical reception of Soderbergh's directorial efforts, focusing on four features released from 2006 to 2009 that bridge numerous production, textual, and exhibition categories. While film studies has identified the role of discursive formations in constructing film authorship and textual meaning, the tools and goals of mainstream film criticism have received limited scrutiny. Critical discourse plays key roles in the circulation of authorial personas, shaping subsequent reception discourses surrounding authorship and textual meaning. Critical reception of popular cinema responds to prevailing taste hierarchies while contributing to the maintenance and longevity of those hierarchies. Film journalism in particular encourages the manufacture of auteurs to legitimate journalistic discourse as art-critical practice rather than entertainment commentary, to construct narratives of artistic production, and to grant readers access to production environments. For much of the 2000s, reviews of Soderbergh-directed features have repeatedly highlighted Soderbergh's formal experimentation on expensive studio productions as well as low-budget independent efforts, a motif that simultaneously invokes the filmmaker's festival-cinema origins and his diverse filmography.

Critical discourses have granted Soderbergh the status of individual most directly responsible for the textual features and meanings of the films on which he is credited as director. In line with auteurist models persistent since the 1960s, critical commentary on Soderbergh's films has tended to proceed from the premise that directors should be seen as the key creative force in film productions, with the corollary that the totality of a film's artistry should be attributed to the named director. Soderbergh's work across film genres (comedy, social-problem film, political thriller, crime film, and others), modes (blockbuster, star vehicle, experimental film, and television series), and media (film, television, and digital video) might be expected to complicate critical efforts to discern a specific artistic signature. Soderbergh himself has celebrated this apparent lack of artistic identity, telling one interviewer that "[t]he fact that I'm not an identifiable brand is very freeing. . . . I've never had a desire to be out in front of anything."[1] Schooled in auteurist reasoning, though, critics have persisted in attempts to attribute a distinct personal vision to Soderbergh's work, particularly in narrative and thematic terms. Even J. Hoberman's contrary view, cited in Chapter 2, that "Steven Soderbergh has no particular stylistic signature and one of the most uneven oeuvres imaginable"[2] imposes an auteurist model on a body of films made in collaboration with hundreds of creative professionals with wide-ranging artistic sensibilities. Some other commentators on Soderbergh's work have, thoughtfully or reflexively, found it to exhibit compelling thematic continuity, often selectively periodizing the work to establish such a view. For example, Ryan Stewart asserts in a 2009 interview with Soderbergh that "[m]oney is one of your pet subjects—even *Erin Brockovich* was explicitly about money." Soderbergh obligingly agrees, not mentioning his many features—from *sex, lies, and videotape* and *Kafka* to *Solaris* and *Che*—that do not substantively take up questions of economics. Recall, too, that many years previously (as noted in Chapter 1), Soderbergh had offered interviewers the easily apprehensible construct of "main characters that are out of sync with their environment"[3] as an interpretive frame. This claim, made in 1993, fit well for the romantic leads of *sex, lies, and videotape*, the alienated writer of *Kafka*, and the socially awkward preadolescent of *King of the Hill*. Interviews with Soderbergh in the 2000s do not highlight such a figure, even in the many cases where one might be discerned. Soderbergh's subsequent assertions of interests in money (presented in numerous interviews surrounding 2009's *The Girlfriend Experience*), social class, politics, and other subjects occur alongside his own many references to production collaborators including actors, screenwriters, editors, and more. Even as Soderbergh repeatedly name-checks his collaborators and foregrounds their contributions, many commentators, reviewers in particular, reframe this collaborative output as the artistic work of Soderbergh exclusively.

This chapter unpacks the critical production of a Soderbergh aesthetic and accounts for its presence in a collaborative, industrial system.

Though critical assessments of films under Soderbergh's direction have varied substantially, few offer any challenges to his putative ownership of the films, with reviews at most noting the collaborative work of screenwriters and actors. Even Soderbergh himself long ago asserted ownership of a body of work, telling an interviewer in 1999 that "[t]here have been good ones and bad ones, but I look back and think, 'That's an eclectic group of movies that, for better or worse, belong to me.'"[4] Resisting familiar claims of authorial intentionality, I have argued that Soderbergh's stewardship of a collaborative filmmaking process encourages a degree of stylistic continuity in his films. At the same time, the discernment of an authorial signature is in large part another kind of collaborative effort, a collusion of film promotion, criticism, and fan discourses that convincingly abridges the complexities of film production. Robert Kapsis reminds us that an "understanding of how an artistic reputation is socially constructed must take into account the interlocking and self-serving relationships that can emerge between various representatives of the art world and the artist."[5] To tease out such relationships in contemporary media industries, I address the critical reception of a series of Soderbergh's films that differ hugely in production scale, subject matter, and tone. This reception activity further demonstrates the interdependence of practitioner and critical discourse in the global circulation of film texts and their accompanying taste signifiers.

In producing discourse about Soderbergh, film-review journalism shapes not only popular reception but also filmmaking practice. This chapter investigates responses to a pair of Soderbergh's polarized works—the two-part prestige feature *Che* and the low-budget *The Girlfriend Experience*—as well as to previous if equally dissimilar Soderbergh efforts *The Good German* and *Ocean's Thirteen*. This range of texts brings forth critical perspectives on disparate strands of commercial production: mainstream summer blockbusters, prestige star vehicles, art-cinema historical biopics, and outré fare for boutique tastes. Regarding the fabrication of a filmmaker's imprint through material other than film texts specifically, I draw on Kapsis's pioneering reception model, sensitive as it is to the role of entertainment journalists and reviewers in forging perceptions of contemporary popular artists. Correspondingly, to assess film critics' and their readerships' particular cultural investments, I take cues from Pierre Bourdieu's rich models of cultural-production networks, which are strongly attendant to taste cultures, symbolic capital, and the roles of multiple tastemaking agents in consecrating artworks and creative practitioners. Overall,

I consider the interactions among filmmakers and critics as those interactions occur through review discourse, interviews, festival participation, and mutual investments (if from opposite directions) in film texts themselves.

Film Journalism and Taste Capital

The work of film journalism involves a kind of double legitimation, with journalists gaining prestige through their engagements with films and filmmakers, and industrial agents earning status when their names circulate in journalistic discourse. Film journalism includes such varied output as actor, director, writer, or production-executive profiles; reports on industrial organizations such as production companies and distributors, talent agencies and conglomerate-owned studios; prerelease commentaries on specific productions; and capsule or extended reviews of films playing at festivals, in limited or general release, in retrospectives, or appearing on home video. Owing to their need for ongoing access to industry agents and institutions, film journalists work in negotiated relationships with the industries they cover. Journalists continue to fulfill key gatekeeping roles between producing institutions and consumer publics. While ostensibly objective, journalists traffic in discourse with an explicit critical role. This discourse must champion a wide span of quality practice while recoiling against practices and texts that fail to meet shifting criteria of artistic or entertainment value. Film journalism simultaneously serves a range of promotional functions. Entertainment content in newspapers, arts periodicals, and dedicated entertainment magazines exists principally as a backdrop for profitable advertising content, particularly newspaper advertisements for current theatrical releases. In other ways too, journalists depend on the continued existence of film industries for their own professional livelihood, and overly negative commentary on film texts or industry personnel can adversely affect films' market prospects. Film journalists also gain symbolic capital through the production of discourse about artistically and economically rich film industries and cultures.

The delineation of labor roles among film journalists contributes as well to their articulated cultural investments. Notwithstanding the ongoing contraction of newspapers' arts divisions, most major newspapers maintain separate stables of entertainment reporters and film reviewers. Reviewers attend press conferences, festivals, and premieres, and periodically conduct interviews with filmmakers. They regularly produce reviews of current films, supplemented with analyses of particular filmmakers or cycles accompanying local retrospectives, DVD releases and other topical developments. Separate arts-reporting personnel generate profiles of films, filmmakers, and stars in advance of theatrical releases and cover industry business activity (aside from that specifically relegated to newspapers' business rather than arts or culture sections) and other arts and entertainment trends. With their professional roles mandating subjective judgments about films and film culture, reviewers enjoy somewhat more latitude in their written discourse than do reporters. Still, their non-review discourse about entertainment industries, and their access to working filmmakers, depends partly on the tone and content of their reviews and analysis. Reporters secure symbolic capital through their access to screen-industry personnel, while reviewers acquire capital through discursive performances of taste, articulating specialized judgments about industries' output. Overall, reviewers' status as cultural gatekeepers requires that they situate themselves at a remove from the industries they critique, both discursively and in their labor practice. With rare exceptions such as critic Pauline Kael's short tenure as a Paramount consultant, critics shape and participate in film culture but not film-industry culture.

Film journalists and reviewers perform explicit tastemaking functions for their readerships. In practice, these tastemakers become de facto gatekeepers as well. While not explicitly controlling screen texts' distribution, writers and the publications supporting them partly determine texts' cultural reach simply by granting or withholding coverage. At the same time, their own status as legitimate gatekeepers depends on the consensual approval both of industrial bodies and practitioners (such as studio publicity departments, review-conscious production executives, and filmmakers) and of general readerships (which may also include those with economic or other ties to industries). To amass professional credibility and influence, critics must distinguish themselves from each of these groups—from the former to maintain the premise of objectivity, from the latter to maintain claims of expert knowledge and persuasive credentialing. Given the proliferation of film-review forums since the 1990s mass emergence of the Internet, reviewers must labor ever more conscientiously to distinguish their own utterances surrounding films and film culture from those emerging from the general public. Identifying the range of constructors of textual meaning and the associated benefits of meaning-making, Bourdieu argues that an artwork "is made not twice," by one artist and one receiver, "but a hundred times, by all those who are interested in it, who find a material or symbolic profit in reading it, classifying it, deciphering it, commenting on it, combating it, knowing it, possessing it."[6] Film journalists likewise leverage their critical discourse to secure professional and public recognition. Bourdieu argues too that "[f]or the author, the critic [and others], the only legitimate accumulation consists in making a name for oneself, a known, recognized name, a capital of consecration implying a power to consecrate objects . . . or persons . . . and therefore to give value, and to appropriate profits from this operation."[7] While Soderbergh has denied being a brand-name filmmaker, many critics have fashioned a distinct authorial profile for him. These critics, paid to appraise screen artifacts and cultures, quite literally profit from this consecration process.

Review discourse surrounding Soderbergh's multifarious output reveals as much about critical predispositions as about the discernible signs of screen authorship. Because he has worked at the poles of industrial practice, directing star-ensemble spectaculars as well as contained, low-budget experiments, critical discourse about his work often involves efforts to police the boundaries of film culture, betraying the partly taxonomic project of film reviewing. Absorbing auteurist language for numerous reasons, film reviewers work partly to hail into existence particular artistic signatures that they and others can trace across ongoing filmographies (and reviewers' parallel professional careers). They also regularly deploy their own film-historical knowledge to supply relevant contexts to film-literate readers, or in naming historical figures and past films, to encourage readers' acquisition of film literacy.

Contemporary professional film criticism shares allegiances with the most celebrated Western critical models but does not precisely reproduce those models. Appearing principally in advertising-supported forums overseen by publishing conglomerates rather than in specialist journals, mainstream criticism depends on responsiveness to market and audience considerations. Mainstream film journalism thus differs measurably from the highbrow practice of venerated reviewers such as the 1950s *Cahiers du cinéma* critics. Still, contemporary reviewers enjoy the residual status granted them by auteurist discourse and the work of critics such as the *Cahiers* group. Addressing the phenomenon of cinephilia, Christian Keathley argues that a key byproduct of auteurist discourse "was its elevation of the status and autonomy of the critic."[8] Keathley builds on William Routt's discussion of the cultural

critic as an intermediary, meaning-making figure. In Routt's formulation, auteurism:

> paradoxically raised the viewer to a position of creative power. The critic-
> viewer became the auteur's collaborator and double, *semblable, frere*. . . .
> Some critics . . . at the same time moved between the work and its viewer,
> assuming the position of translaters [*sic*] or augurers. Auteurist critics were
> able to add to the commonplace critical claim of embodying the perfect
> spectator the rather more drastic claim of speaking as 'the *cineaste*,' the
> perfected artist (the person who knew better than the artist what the work
> meant).[9]

Auteurist critics produced starkly subjective responses to films largely
irrespective of those films' industrial situation. At the same time, they
modeled the selective, canonizing activity of the connoisseur alongside
the meaning-making activities of all viewers. Following Routt and
likewise attuned to this significant intermediary function, Keathley
argues that "[t]he auteur critic—functioning as a kind of translator,
mediating between work and viewer—enjoyed self-designation as a
viewer who had special knowledge or skill, one who could see and show
to others."[10] Appearing in quotidian venues such as mass-circulation
newspapers and magazines, mainstream criticism downplays the "special" voice of the auteurist critic while retaining the popular-cinephile
perspective of movie love that itself acts as a status marker and source
of discursive power.

Lacking the space or audiences to engage in lengthy exegesis,
newspaper and magazine critics tend to rely on shorthand associations to distinguish films under review and their own critical activity.
Review journalism can distribute signposts of specialized taste and film
literacy through fleeting invocation of canonical films and branded
auteur filmmakers. For example, some newspaper advertisements for
the theatrical release of *The Girlfriend Experience* carried a blurb from
Scott Foundas's *LA Weekly* review that reads, "Scintillating! It strongly
recalls the Godard films of the 1960s."[11] In strictly narrative terms, *The
Girlfriend Experience* depicts the ambient professional and personal
lives of a high-end New York City prostitute and her personal-trainer
boyfriend. Beyond affiliating the film with unspecified precursors,
Foundas's remark assures readers of his own familiarity with 1960s
French films from director Jean-Luc Godard and supplies a rough map
of expectations to readers who might themselves have knowledge of

1960s or Godardian cinema. Even as its appearance in the advertisement denotes its suitability to promote the film in question, it can bestow symbolic capital upon (or activate the symbolic capital of) both the reviewer Foundas and the discerning reader. Similarly, Peter Keough's 2009 review in the *Boston Phoenix* alternative weekly remarks in relation to the RED digital camera used to shoot the film that "it offers the kind of inexpensive naturalistic immediacy and visual quality and freedom to improvise that the Godard of the '60s could only dream of. Not that *The Girlfriend Experience* rises to the level of Godard's *Vivre sa vie* . . . ." Keough taps into precisely the same taste categories as does Foundas, name-checks a specific film as well, and implicitly demonstrates cross-historical awareness of production technologies and practices. Thus, unempirical speculation about the hypothetical historical mindset of the still-living filmmaker Godard functions as connoisseurial discourse joining filmmakers, reviewers, and cinephile readers.

Many other reviews of *The Girlfriend Experience* emphasize the starring role of Sasha Grey, well known within the porn-film subculture if mostly anonymous to that segment of mainstream and arthouse audiences that lacks awareness of contemporary pornography.[12] The film's Magnolia Pictures press kit showcases Grey ahead of and at slightly greater length than director, cinematographer, and editor Soderbergh, and lists among her credentials such novel awards as *Adult Video*

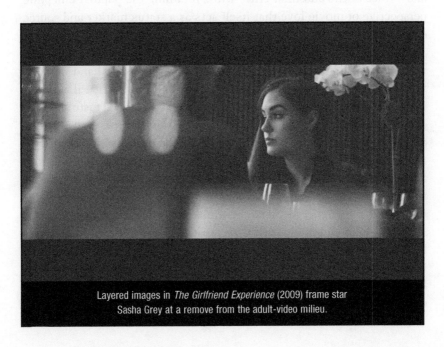

Layered images in *The Girlfriend Experience* (2009) frame star Sasha Grey at a remove from the adult-video milieu.

News' "AVN Award for Best Three-Way Sex Scene." Steered by these publicity materials or by the novelty of reporting on video-porn to arthouse-film crossovers, entertainment reporters and film critics remarked extensively on Grey's casting. This mainstream-media interest could upset understood taste categories, with a celebrated figure in one popular but disreputable category repositioned in a culturally valued category where her own reputation has been negligible or negative. As with the varying attention granted to similar efforts from such stars as Marilyn Chambers, Traci Lords, and Jenna Jameson, though, Grey's appearance in both mainstream and art-cinema discourse suggests the fundamental stability of taste categories. Discussion of Grey's work in a principally dramatic role performs a strategic disavowal function, reminding readers where an actress such as Grey belongs in cultural-legitimation terms. (Never mind that the film sections of tastemaking publications such as *The Village Voice* often give way to many pages of advertisements for phone-sex services and other grey-market erotica.) Despite substantial overlap among reception groups—in that most video-porn viewers watch other films as well—gatekeeping industries such as entertainment journalism maintain strong convictions of the separation between mainstream cinema and so-called "adult" video. With access to a long list of attention-grabbing video titles such as *Anal Acrobats* (2007) and *Gang Bang My Face* (2006), critics' invocation of Grey's extensive filmography can introduce readers to unrecognized realms of stardom and textuality, reinvigorating the cultural or subcultural value of a particular commodity by relocating it in a different taste demographic. *The Girlfriend Experience* itself performs this maneuver as well, gaining its key publicity from the introduction of the enigma "can a porn star act?" into film-critical and other reception discourse.

Some reviews credit Soderbergh's casting of Grey as an act of creative risk-taking, thus marking it as part of a larger construction of him as a boundary-disrespecting filmmaker known for shifts across industrial categories. Though not the credited casting director, Soderbergh is central in the film's genesis narrative, with multiple accounts repeating his claim to have learned of the actress by reading a 2006 profile of her in *Los Angeles* magazine.[13] Curiously, the article in question opens with an extended but mostly superfluous discussion of Soderbergh himself, with a prolific porn director's career arc compared to Soderbergh's. Before turning to the lengthy profile of Grey, the article names director John Stagliano's 1989 debut video feature as analogous to *sex, lies, and videotape* and a 2006 porn-star ensemble piece directed by Stagliano as "the adult film industry's equivalent of *Ocean's Eleven*."[14] One may presume that if the magazine profile did indeed make Soderbergh aware of Grey, it did so partly through its atypical repositioning of Soderbergh's own films. The magazine article provides the creative catalyst as much as the actress Grey does. Hence, Soderbergh's self-constructed trade narrative includes his use of ancillary material that itself portrays his professional trajectory as common knowledge, at least for readers of the regionally focused publication.

Within reviews of *The Girlfriend Experience*, all centrally framed by the question of the film's cultural or entertainment value, the key subthemes include the novelty of Grey's appearance in an art film, alongside the protean nature of filmmaker Soderbergh and this film's situation within his overall output as director. Periodically, as with many of Soderbergh's films, critics argue for the film as a metaphor for Soderbergh's career[15]—in this case, self-aware individual with pretensions to good taste and aspirations to a high public profile in diverse sectors of cultural activity makes living through outright prostitution, which grants autonomy in other creative and commercial work. Responding to an interviewer's question about "whoring out," Soderbergh straightforwardly links the film's narrative to his own professional work:

> I guess it all depends on what your definition is. Mine is doing something you would not ordinarily do for money. I don't see any difference between what Sasha's doing in the movie and what I do for Warner Bros. The character in the movie is doing what she wants to for money, and so am I.[16]

Soderbergh's provocative remark invites scrutiny of his overall filmography as well as consumption of the new release under consideration.

Commentary on Grey and Soderbergh appears as ancillary to or digressive from the larger question of the film's artistic value and viewing pleasure to be gained from it. The persistence of the question "is it worth seeing?" indicates mass-circulation film criticism's explicit role—not to engage readers in discussion of film art but to facilitate choices about commercial consumption. Relatedly, reviews demonstrate some degree of sensitivity to the predispositions of their presumed audiences. For example, the *Village Voice*'s reviews address urbane cinephiles—though those who do not fit into such a category may read the *Voice*'s reviews as well—while *USA Today* presents its reviews to mass audiences with widely varying degrees of film literacy. The review-analysis website Movie Review Intelligence, inaugurated in 2009, divides reviews according to overlapping publication categories, including broad national newspapers, local newspapers, alternative weeklies, the "highbrow press," industry periodicals, and city publications ranked according to city size. Each category underscores particular reader demographics and hints at styles of reviewer address, aiming at systematic evaluation of critical reception in a range of media forums and theatrical markets. The site's own market research claims that "81% of moviegoers follow reviews," and that persistent review readers also patronize cinemas regularly, indicating the substantial tastemaking and consumer-steering functions of critical discourse.[17]

Movie Review Intelligence also measures the print space devoted to film reviews and calculates the advertisement value of reviews based on that space. (The site calculates the reviews for *The Girlfriend Experience* to be worth $775,000—or nearly half the film's $1.6 million budget—if purchased as advertising space.[18]) Thus, whatever their content, reviews literally grant valuable space to promotion of specific films. Reviews' relevance to a film's commercial prospects can thus be understood as roughly proportional to their visibility within a film's overall advertising campaign. The larger a film's advertising budget, the less visible reviews will be in the wide promotional landscape. The well-worn characterizations of independent filmmakers and small distributors as reliant on positive film reviews, compared to large-scale studio productions' dependence on the publicity value of opening-weekend grosses, follow from this logic. Studios often mobilize saturation advertising in anticipation of negative critical response or word of mouth, discounting the impact of reviews except for particular releases such as awards-season contenders. Nonetheless, the abundance of review forums as well as online aggregators such as Rotten Tomatoes and Movie Review Intelligence indicates that reviews remain significant to general moviegoers as well as to industry executives and practitioners.

Disingenuously or not, Soderbergh claims not to read reviews of his own films. In a 2009 interview with Ryan Stewart on SuicideGirls.com, he remarks:

> After *Traffic* I just stopped [reading reviews] completely. . . . After winning the LA and New York film critics awards, I really felt like, this can only get worse. Nothing about reading reviews from here on out is going to enhance my life at all.

While he subsequently acknowledges the commercial impact of poor reviews on arthouse films, Soderbergh's idiosyncratic personal response suggests his own cultural investment. While few filmmakers enjoy consistently favorable reviews across their careers, reviews contribute to canon formation as well as reformation. (Notably, he does not claim to avoid film reviews altogether, and presumably is sometimes prompted, like other industrial actors, to view unfamiliar works based on affirmative critical commentary.) Soderbergh's ambivalence regarding reviews of his own work underscores critical discourse's consecrating function. Investigating what he calls independent film's "value chain," Peter Bloore similarly identifies critics as contributors to film texts' cultural and economic value. While reviews may guide consumers toward films in current release, reviewers' judgments also help determine texts' long-term worth. As Bloore observes, "the long term 'library' value and reputation of the film is highly influenced by the response of both the general audience (box office figures and word of mouth) and critical voices (including both formal 'approved' media critics and informal 'unapproved' critics, for example on internet websites or bulletin boards)."[19] With Soderbergh's films, the myriad comparisons to world-cinema auteurs rather than associations with contemporaneous U.S. releases contribute in particular to a possible future canonical status for films and filmmaker.

Review Discourse: Constructing and Dismantling Auteurs

Reviews of *The Girlfriend Experience*'s U.S. theatrical and video-on-demand releases position both the multi-hyphenate filmmaker Soderbergh and the reviewers themselves. Following its debut as an unadvertised sneak preview at Sundance in January 2009, the film officially premiered at the Tribeca Film Festival in April. Festival reviews, once the province of the trade press, now appear also in second-tier entertainment websites gaining traffic thanks to these reviews' semi-exclusivity. Reviews of the Tribeca screening appeared not only in *Variety* and *The Hollywood Reporter* but also on the websites eFilmCritic.com and Ain't It Cool News,[20] the last reviewing the film in passing before describing a post-screening press conference featuring Soderbergh and Grey. The film went into video-on-demand release eight days after the festival screening, so entertainment blogs and numerous lesser-known websites also posted reviews well in advance of its late-May theatrical release. Reviews in these varying forums could be credited with creating or sustaining moderate buzz about the film. They also effectively put the film in the hands of nonprofessional reviewers, revising the taste markers traditionally on display in review journalism. Rather than flaunting signs of canonical film literacy, for example, the reviewers tend to demonstrate their awareness of Soderbergh's relatively recent, very high-profile films such as the *Ocean's* series.[21] This tactic can indicate a lack of film-historical awareness, but can also serve as part of a strategy to communicate most directly with readerships possessing limited film literacy or with highly contemporary interests. Both professional and nonprofessional reviewers may self-consciously craft critical voices that speak to particular types of film viewers.

Reviews' comparisons to Soderbergh's expensive studio features also contribute to the production of a particular authorial silhouette. Rather than defining the filmmaker through thematic interests or subject matter, the reviews identify Soderbergh in terms of transit between distinct poles. Far more than for any other contemporary filmmaker, reviews define Soderbergh's work not just *by* but *as* this shifting practice, the alternation between expensive, highly commercial projects and low-budget films reviewers often describe as "personal." Thus, taking one of auteurism's structuring absences to its limit, critics' comparisons help define Soderbergh not through specific film output but through the movement among different types of production practice. Publicity for Soderbergh's films tends not to contribute strongly to this construction. A range of unrelated companies distribute Soderbergh's various projects, so particular companies may gain little added value from cross-promotion. And in a routine strategy to maximize immediate interest, advertisements promote each film as a discrete event rather than as part of a series of authorial dispensations. For example, distributor Magnolia did not advertise *The Girlfriend Experience* as a film from the director and writers of *Ocean's Thirteen*, though its press kit did include this information, and some reviews reproduced that connection. In this case and many others, distributors anticipate that critical interventions will draw together bodies of work. Through these interventions, individual films become points on an evolving map of creative activity and movement.

Critics highlight particular films and neglect others to support hypotheses of Soderbergh as bipolar industry agent. With *The Girlfriend Experience*, it is mostly longer reviews in weekly publications that move beyond the film in question to make claims about Soderbergh's larger filmography. For example, Christopher Orr's nearly 1,200-word review in *The New Republic*, David Edelstein's more than five hundred words on the film in an omnibus review in *New York* magazine, and Peter Keough's 560-word *Boston Phoenix* review each comment on

Soderbergh's other films. Most daily newspaper reviews (also usually around five hundred words) mention Soderbergh only in passing, using a phrase or short sentence to contextualize him and the film.[22] The reviews that highlight Soderbergh's transit across filmmaking scales tend to valorize the smaller productions through such descriptors as "experimental," "avant-garde," and "micro-indie," all locating film and filmmaker in principally artistic rather than commercial categories (though "micro-indie" arguably belongs to both). These reviews take as a given that larger productions such as *Ocean's Thirteen* represent the antithesis of authored filmmaking. With the critical validation of reflexive auteurism comes the implication that films such as the *Ocean's* series contribute nothing of value to cinema culture and that readers concur in this assessment, that the films are made only for profit or to give Soderbergh latitude to pursue other, riskier projects.[23]

With *Che*, as with *The Girlfriend Experience*, film reviews and surrounding publicity focus less on the filmmakers than on a charismatic, headline-grabbing central figure. For *The Girlfriend Experience*, that figure is the film's star, hardcore porn actress Grey. For the biopic *Che*, the iconic revolutionary Che Guevara takes center stage in publicity and reviews, with reviewers assessing the film's fealty, or lack thereof, to its historical subject as well as weighing potential viewers' ability to endure its epic running time. (The film was released in two parts but also screened in some cities in a single, 258-minute version.) *Che* premiered at 2008's Cannes Film Festival, where it reportedly received a "lightning-rod" reception, "which saw dozens of journalists flee at intermission."[24] Following the premiere, *Variety*'s Todd McCarthy produced a strongly negative review of more than 1,500 words, asserting in the opening paragraph that "the pic in its current form is a commercial impossibility."

Some months after the film's general release, Soderbergh asserted the reviewing community's role in the film's circulation: "It's a film that, to some extent, needs the support of people who write about films."[25] From the production companies' perspective, though, the film was literally review-proof, with its production budget largely recouped prior to Cannes through international presales.[26] The press response and McCarthy's review instead contributed, according to Soderbergh, to the film's "publicity magnet" status. French co-producer Wild Bunch even reproduced McCarthy's premature eulogy in a full-page advertisement in the trade publication *Screen* during the Toronto Film Festival later that year, contrasting it with news of the film's strong opening-weekend receipts in Spain.[27] During *Che*'s later theatrical release,

Soderbergh claimed that rather than seeking a positive response from journalists or buyers at Cannes, "[w]e just wanted to detonate there."[28] He thus retroactively spins the film's premiere as a strategic use of Cannes's notoriously volatile audiences, reshaping negative festival and trade-press response into provocative publicity. With the film involving four production companies in the U.S., Spain, and France, and at least fifteen companies for its global theatrical distribution, discourse surrounding its Cannes premiere is primarily intra-industrial, calling not on taste markers relevant to general or cinephile viewerships but on status markers involving the ability to predict commercial prospects in discrete exhibition zones.

Festival reception represents only one of many determinants of a film's commercial and critical position. Nonetheless, a festival presence has long been instrumental to the construction of authorial reputations and to accumulation of prestige that distinguishes films in wide release. Festivals connect filmmakers and critics in ostensibly art-driven environments. Even festivals with substantial market sections, such as Cannes, enjoy reputations as staging grounds for artistic achievements. They also play key promotional roles for films their producers wish to identify as prestige works. Soderbergh's career of course received jump starts thanks to *sex, lies, and videotape*'s U.S. Film Festival and Cannes reception, and his films have repeatedly debuted at festivals.

Benicio Del Toro's Che Guevara celebrates with compatriots near the end of *Che: Part One* (2008).

The Good German received a limited U.S. release in December 2006, but its tiered international release followed its appearance at the Berlin Film Festival in February 2007. In similar geographic synchrony, the Manhattan-set *The Girlfriend Experience* officially premiered, as already noted, at Tribeca. His previous micro-indie, *Bubble*, played at multiple festivals, including Venice and Toronto, in the months before its January 2006 U.S. multiplatform release and at other international festivals subsequently. Also making the rounds months after its Cannes "detonation," *Che* appeared at numerous fall 2008 festivals, including Toronto, New York, London, and Havana. Even *Ocean's Thirteen* debuted at Cannes, though playing out of competition and thus for chiefly promotional purposes given its wide global release two weeks after the late-May 2007 screening there. With its red-carpet showcasing of tuxedoed stars, the Cannes premiere facilitated the promotion of the film as itself a playground for a cast of glamorous male icons. The event thus enabled the foregrounding of stars rather than offscreen figures such as Soderbergh. He and producer Jerry Weintraub appear in some group photos at the premiere, though unsurprisingly in far fewer than the film's stars, and Soderbergh in particular remains conspicuously marginal in the red-carpet photo sessions. With out-of-competition films typically not on the receiving end of critics' passionate apprais-als, *Ocean's Thirteen* debuted without controversy, a strong contrast to *Che*'s premiere in competition the following year.

Che's festival response, and the management of that response in trade discourse, suggests ways producing entities navigate critical dis-courses to communicate to potential viewers. Festival screenings and reviews tend to target highly film-literate audiences. Major festivals use directors as a key promotional category, gaining esteem through premieres of works from anointed global-cinema auteurs. Thus, festi-val audiences and readers of festival-screening reviews receive many signals impelling them to organize their tastes around directors, and subsequently to seek out author-driven cinema or to evaluate films according to the criterion of perceptible authorship. Contrastingly, mainstream film exhibition and corresponding reviews of wide theat-rical releases often withhold authorial markers as evaluative criteria, particularly if exploitable elements of genres, stardom, topicality of subject, or others can be brandished instead.

The shifting attention to authorship as an evaluative criterion becomes strongly evident when comparing reviews of Soderbergh's ostensible art films to those of more widely released, studio-produced films under his direction. *Ocean's Thirteen*, which one might intuitively expect to have been poorly received, earned largely positive reviews, with a seventy percent favorable rating on the Rotten Tomatoes aggregator's "Tomatometer" scale (sixty percent and higher indicating on balance positive reviews).[29] Among the close to two hundred reviews that make up that rating, many discuss the film as a diverting if unmemorable entertainment, and reviews usually only name Soderbergh as director and comment on his role no further. A handful make the director's name synonymous with the film itself—phrases in David Denby's brief *New Yorker* review include "Soderbergh assembles the elements of [the] scheme" and "Soderbergh ends the movie with a few jokes"—thus assigning all textual characteristics to the director but withholding commentary on production practice. J. Hoberman remarks near the end of his *Village Voice* review that "[o]stensibly, *Ocean's Thirteen* is that which enables Soderbergh and Clooney to make their personal projects," echoing the many similar claims appearing in reviews of those "personal projects." Also, as might be expected of a sequel, reviews overwhelming cite only the two previous *Ocean's* films for comparison, rarely naming any other films or filmmakers as points of reference. Andrew O'Hehir does acknowledge the discussion of *The Sting* (1973) at the press conference accompanying *Ocean's Thirteen*'s Cannes premiere, and Roger Ebert's review notes the debt that the *Ocean's* series owes to *Bob le Flambeur* (1956). Aside from these references and sporadic mentions of the 1960 *Ocean's Eleven*, review discourse regarding *Ocean's Thirteen* defines it as a discrete contemporary-Hollywood product.

Reviews of *Ocean's Thirteen* largely focus on elements that can be judged without explicit attention to Soderbergh's directing role: plot details, the film's generic situation as heist film and male-ensemble comedy, star performance and chemistry, and its overall glossy look and feel. The intra- and extra-narrative discourses of male play of the *Ocean's* series steer many reviews. As is common for film reviews, screenplay and performances receive credit for such tonal features and the characterizations that contribute to them. The film's overdetermined status as a star-heavy summer blockbuster and CGI-laden studio release further inhibits detailed commentary on offscreen creative agents. Correspondingly, Soderbergh's labor in directing the actors is rendered invisible. Manohla Dargis names Soderbergh as the film's "master of ceremonies" in her own review, and many other reviews internalize this description, implicitly defining the director as the person responsible for a film's total creative effort, but with no demonstrable role in any specific area of onscreen content. Dargis does assess Soderbergh's creative roles in great detail. She not only credits him with construction of the film's "world of visual enchantments" but explicitly references his work with actors: "to watch Mr. Clooney, Mr. Pitt and Mr. Damon in the 'Ocean's' films . . . is to realize that it's a mistake to separate Mr. Soderbergh's personal visions from his professional commitments." Relatedly, O'Hehir's 2007 report on the film's Cannes premiere shows Soderbergh himself crediting the labor of actors, if also his own role as their steward: "Soderbergh said that the main thing his series has inherited from the Sinatra Rat Pack pictures of the early '60s was the 'camaraderie of the cast,' adding that his principal casting rule was 'No jerks.'" On the other hand, receiving the film's male play and luxury surround less generously, some reviewers accuse the film (if no specific members of the production team) of smugness.[30] This critique appears more prominently in earlier commentary on *Ocean's Twelve*, which partly absorbs critical negativity, its poor critical reception leading to more generous responses to the third installment.[31] Favorable reviews that do cite Soderbergh tend to highlight his contributions to the film's imagery in his pseudonymous role as director of photography. Despite using the catch-all phrase "Soderbergh's *Ocean's* franchise" in its opening sentence, the *Austin Chronicle*'s review discusses Soderbergh's contribution solely in terms of cinematography, observing that the project permits Soderbergh "to indulge his passion for saturated color palettes and stylized dissolves."[32] Meanwhile, Mick LaSalle's *San Francisco Chronicle* review manages the feat of both acknowledging and ignoring Soderbergh's input. Leading into praise for the film's compositions, he asserts that Soderbergh "keeps his directorial personality out of 'Ocean's Thirteen,' but his artistry is everywhere."

Overall, reviewers' inattention to Soderbergh's specific behind-the-camera creative roles facilitates the judgment of *Ocean's Thirteen* as superficial and personality-less. This omission also fits a larger pattern of critical response to large-budget studio productions, particularly star- and effects-driven summertime releases perceived as lacking psychological depth. Strongly branded filmmakers such as Steven Spielberg or onetime independent director Christopher Nolan tend to warrant discussion in any case, but in the reviews of his films in widest release, Soderbergh has to date received only sporadic consideration as a creative agent with particular artistic intentions. Retrospective attention may well rewrite existing narratives of Soderbergh's career. For now, if one goal or byproduct of film criticism, particularly auteurist criticism, is to identify and consequently attune viewers to a filmmaker's way of seeing, then the withholding of this view in commentary on each new Soderbergh offering contributes to similar narrowness of perspective for reader-viewers.[33] At the same time, because Soderbergh's name does not carry indelible associations with particular genres—particularly the comedy or thriller categories into which the *Ocean's* films can be located—neither critics nor viewers receive powerful cues to weigh the films strictly in terms of Soderbergh's prior achievements in those generic fields. In a separate case, Robert Kapsis finds in his study of Alfred Hitchcock's reputation that Hitchcock's association with the suspense thriller was so complete that critics judged his late films principally in relation to his earlier work in the genre. Critical suspicion of popular genres such as the thriller long disallowed Hitchcock's entry into the critical canon of artist-directors. The more polyvocal sphere of contemporary film criticism regards genres not as anathematic to artistic endeavor, but instead as platforms for distinct filmmaking proficiencies. With Hitchcock in mind, Kapsis argues that "changing genre conventions can condition the critical vocabulary and frames of reference used by critics."[34] Kapsis also identifies divergent critical frames, one focused on films' satisfaction of genre imperatives and another on their demonstration of auteur ability.[35] The present-day critical climate arguably includes overlapping attention to genre and authorship, with the paradoxical result that critics consecrate as auteurs those filmmakers who work consistently in narrow genre categories. A critical focus on genre/auteur intersections disadvantages multimodal filmmakers as they seek to build and enhance their artistic reputations.

"In the Film Laboratory That Is Mr. Soderbergh's Brain": Artwork vs. Art Work

Turning to a differently contested case, response to 2006's *The Good German* did foreground Soderbergh. Many reviews cite the film's use of 1940s-vintage technology and production methods and attribute this creative decision to Soderbergh himself. The film's largely negative reviews—it earns a "Tomatometer" score of only 33 percent based on nearly 150 reviews—often do name Soderbergh, attributing principal responsibility for the film's perceived artistic failure directly to him. (In an uncharacteristic digression from this tone, *Time*'s Richard Schickel spreads the blame across the film's collaborators, asserting that "[w]atching *The Good German*, you feel the unease, the discontent, of its makers with their basic material."[36]) At the same time, the reviews tend to undermine the predominant critical view of Soderbergh as a practitioner of disparate filmmaking styles with no overlap. Here, mainstream studio features and personal experiments apparently do merge, to critics' dismay. In a sentiment shared by many critics, *Rolling Stone*'s Peter Travers calls the Warner Bros. production "more of an experiment than a movie."[37] Manohla Dargis, prone to lengthy discussions of Soderbergh's production practice in her reviews, identifies his experimental impulses as well, remarking that "[i]n the film laboratory that is Mr. Soderbergh's brain, ideas boil, steam and sputter," and later that "Mr. Soderbergh's penchant for experimentation has become an end in itself rather than a means to aesthetic liberation."[38] While raising the film's taste profile by invoking experimentation, Dargis cannily identifies a limitation of the "process geek" signature elsewhere attributed to Soderbergh.[39] She recognizes that process and product are separate categories, and that even as critical analysis can demystify production processes, criticism's key task is to appraise discrete textual artifacts. We might ask that critical interest in artistic practice involve different evaluative criteria than reviews of finished films. In relocating discussions of film-industrial practice into the film-cultural realm of taste constitution, though, journalists and other commentators can persist in hypothesizing the synonymy of creative work and textual artifact. Dale Hudson and Patricia Zimmermann identify the same narrowness of perspective in cinephilic discourse at large, where "[w]ork as object (art*work*) overshadows work as process (the *work* of conceiving/ producing art)."[40]

Critics have often responded negatively to Soderbergh films they judge to be overly process-oriented or otherwise reflexive. *The Good German* draws out particularly strong responses. The *San Francisco Chronicle*'s Mick LaSalle asserts that Soderbergh's intention "was to go back in time to tussle with the past," unfortunately delivering "a bloodless, academic exercise." His 2006 review's title, "Here's Looking at You, Kid (Nudge, Nudge, Wink, Wink)," explicitly addresses the film's perceived self-reflexivity. Carina Chocano similarly asserts in the *Los Angeles Times* that the film "does get mired in its obsession with its own style." Critics have diagnosed similarly inward preoccupations in aspects of other Soderbergh films, for example in *Che*'s interest in the complexities of a protracted military operation that amounts to a collaborative location production, or in *The Girlfriend Experience*'s depiction of a performance professional seeking to expand her creative profile while coping with the competing agendas of bedmates and critics. The critiques of *Ocean's Twelve*'s Hollywood-celebrity subplot and star cameos, and of *Full Frontal*'s insular film-industry milieu, raise comparable objections, though around explicit industry self-regard rather than around questions of style and cinephilic homage. Critics do not entirely produce a consensus view of Soderbergh as director. None have reconciled the competing claims that a filmmaker who "has no particular stylistic signature," to repeat again J. Hoberman's phrase, can also make multiple style-obsessed films. While critics may understand process as the work of authoring, that same process does not serve as a mark of auteurism.

Soderbergh's own statements help direct critical attention to his filmmaking interests and methods rather than to completed films. He adds fuel to Dargis's critique by telling an interviewer in 2009, "I'm not a results person, I'm a process person."[41] In many other forums, too, Soderbergh emphasizes the pleasure of the creative activities of film production, particularly shooting, while commenting little on editing and other postproduction labor. (With his many credits as film editor, he has actively participated in postproduction, even while working simultaneously on one or more other projects.) Practitioner rhetoric regularly invokes the creative and artisanal satisfactions of the act of filmmaking. Such discourse asserts the artistic dimension of what can appear to be highly regulated, corporatized, undynamic labor—a familiar impression for anyone who has visited a working soundstage or studio production location (as distinct from the impression of bustling, glamorous environments that entertainment news and DVD featurettes depict). At the same time, the "process" emphasis maintains the filmmaker in the hypothetically autonomous, liminal space of creative endeavor. This emphasis can conceal the administrative milieu of production offices, editing rooms, or any space linked to the mainstream marketplace—the focus-group screening room, the publicity department, the travelling press junket, and other sites that denote commerce over artistry. If "results" speak to commercial imperatives, "process" speaks principally to craft, and above all, to continuous work.

Soderbergh's work involves artistic choices judged in a robust, and robustly contested, cultural-historical context. In this respect, reviews of *The Good German* also evidence conflict over legitimate and illegitimate appropriations of the film-historical past. As noted in Chapter 3, *The Good German* explicitly evokes the classical Hollywood standard *Casablanca* at many levels: in its production technology; across textual categories such as narrative, genre, mode of address, and visual style; in promotional discourses such as Soderbergh's interviews; and in the film's marketing campaign, which includes a poster image exactly modeled on *Casablanca*'s. Far from celebrating the revival of a beloved classical text, many reviewers used *Casablanca* as a source of unfavorable comparisons, citing *The Good German*'s inexact reproduction of 1940s Hollywood films' lighting and composition, as well as its inadequate romantic chemistry and overall ambiance, as central to its artistic shortcomings and unsatisfactory audience engagement. Claims of specialized knowledge of film-historical modes—with reviewers arguing in effect, "I know classical Hollywood, and this is not classical Hollywood"—are a repeated undercurrent in review discourse. Through such claims, critics and other invested cinephiles assert ownership over a selection of classical-Hollywood output, and their critical exertions work to patrol that sacrosanct terrain of film history. In interviews, Soderbergh explicitly declares his intent to combine past production methods with contemporary sensibilities, by, for example, flouting Production Code–era taboos regarding sexual activity and profanity. Nonetheless, reviewers invoked specialized understandings of 1940s Hollywood stylistic regimes to counter any residual impressions that the film might faithfully reproduce a 1940s aesthetic. David Bordwell, one of the key shapers of critical understanding of classical-Hollywood style, discussed *The Good German* at length before and after its release in his detailed weblog. As with much of Bordwell's scholarship and commentary, his goal in assessing *The Good German* was to analyze its stylistic tendencies in depth and situate them alongside their historical antecedents, not to judge the film's entertainment value. Reviewers, in fashioning themselves as custodians of the film-historical past, merge the roles of historian of poetics and judge of quality. As such, many reviews of *The Good German* function less as popular criticism per se than as maintenance of a subjectively understood Hollywood canon.

Contemporary film journalists' investment in classical Hollywood and *Casablanca* may be understood as passionate nostalgia for an unexperienced era of film culture. J. Hoberman ends his generous if overall negative review of *The Good German* with the assertion, "In his most fatal re-creation, Soderbergh closes with an homage to *Casablanca*," a film Hoberman describes as "the acme of wartime romanticism."[42] He reserves his strongest critiques for the film's—and particularly Soderbergh's—"simulation" of 1940s Hollywood cinema. Offering his own simulation, Mick LaSalle resurrects a legendary studio chief in his assertion that "Soderbergh has delivered a film that would have made Jack Warner throw him off the lot." Meanwhile, *Salon*'s Stephanie Zacharek proclaims that with the film, Soderbergh "apes a style, and a way of *seeing*, that he clearly doesn't understand."[43] With this critique, Zacharek implies that she *does* understand the style and perspective in question, that her critical view outstrips Soderbergh's execution of his own inadequate vision. In one of the few generally positive reviews of the film, the *Los Angeles Times*'s Carina Chocano does not presume totalizing knowledge of a way of seeing and instead claims that "Soderbergh has made a movie set in 1945 that looks as if it were made in 1945." *Variety*'s Todd McCarthy does not share this judgment of the film's stylistic parallels. Instead, echoing Bordwell's objections to the film's inexact reproduction of 1940s aesthetics though with a comic flourish, he offers that the "[p]ic looks less like a 1942 Warner Bros. melodrama than a 1962 *Twilight Zone* episode intercut with background shots from Rossellini's *Germany Year Zero*."[44] McCarthy also perceptively describes the film's closing *Casablanca* homage as "an ill-advised move in that it forces the inevitable negative comparison." He thus recognizes that debates over the film take place not only in the realm of new artistic achievements but also in the minefields of cinephilic movie love. Soderbergh's overall output grants critics platforms for the parading of their own film-historical knowledge, with *The Good German* igniting particular sentiments surrounding classical-Hollywood aesthetics and tone. Whatever the film's limitations as a revival of 1940s aesthetics, it cannot possibly compete with critics' mental maps of the venerated era, bound up as they are with those critics' entire professional identities.

The Significance of Cultural-Intermediary Practice

Reviewers not only serve as custodians of historical film culture but also play key roles in constructing future historical accounts of contemporary cinema. Their work involves the production of timely, professional discourse about new film releases. Just as film texts represent collaborative efforts among groups of practitioners, so those texts' places in film culture depend in part on reviewers' shaping discourse. Filmmakers' own commentary can steer reception activity as well, particularly in the contained environments of press conferences at festivals and elsewhere. As with other directors, Soderbergh's interviews with entertainment journalists and film critics contribute to critical viewpoints. In turn, dialogues between filmmakers and critics can produce synthetic insights about films and film culture. For example, following the Sundance screening of *The Girlfriend Experience*, Manohla Dargis combines Soderbergh's cited influences with those she discerns herself: "Though Mr. Soderbergh name-dropped Michelangelo Antonioni during the question-and-answer session after the movie, 'The Girlfriend Experience' is very much under the thematic influence of Jean-Luc Godard."[45] Dargis's engagement with Soderbergh's work shows her attunement not just to isolated films but to the wider film culture and Soderbergh's range of activities within it. As with Scott Foundas's *LA Weekly* review, though, a deftly deployed Godard reference can reassert a critic's bona fides, overshadowing declared artistic intentions. In many cases, journalists' need to maintain their own stores of film-historical knowledge and aesthetic preferences can lead them to discount individual filmmakers' perspectives as well as evidence of collaborative production activity.

Appraising the legacy of French New Wave cinema, Geneviève Sellier argues that "[m]ore than aesthetic innovation it is the figure of the auteur that has become the criterion of value in cinema, on the literary model inherited from romanticism, accompanied by a touch of formalism that establishes the connection with contemporary art."[46] In Sellier's formulation, the New Wave filmmaker-critics, and the wider early-1960s critical establishment, fundamentally enshrine the director as auteur and institute auteurism as the "dominant optic" for film criticism. Collaboration consequently receives short shrift, trumped by "a fantasy of absolute mastery that makes of the filmmaker a demiurge rather than the motor of a collective project."[47] On the whole, the reviews discussed in this chapter proceed strongly from an auteurist perspective, in which discrete texts evidence a designated auteur's personal style, partly independent of knowledge of collaborative authorship and even sometimes filmmakers' own testimony about their artistic goals and production activity. Reviews celebrate Soderbergh's personal style as apparent through narrative and thematic proclivities, or lament the absence of a style if they fail to identify consistent subjects and themes across films. According with Sellier's model, too, reviews intermittently comment on Soderbergh's formal ambitions (praised in the case of *Ocean's Thirteen*'s cinematography, for example, and scorned for *The Good German*'s), while regarding aesthetic innovation itself as less relevant to auteur status than particular storytelling methods that lend themselves to categorization as somehow universal. Overall, reviews of this cluster of Soderbergh-directed films show critical discourse still wedded to literary-critical models even as it ostensibly argues for films' entertainment value to broad viewerships. Likewise, even as it provides a major source of public insight into screen production culture, entertainment-press discourse continues to foster myths of individual artists working without collaboration or compromise.

Film reviewers' alternating attention to industrial practice and to artistic output indicates in part their own intermediary status. Film journalists are asked to work simultaneously as objective reporters on industrial activity and as subjective judges of discrete screen texts. While many credentialed journalists represent news organizations, their work constitutes a large portion of entertainment industries' promotional apparatus. Critical negotiation of the diverse practices of filmmakers such as Soderbergh demonstrates a range of affiliations and audiences for film journalists' own output. Soderbergh remains an unusually dynamic figure in contemporary Hollywood, highly active in multiple production activities that inhibit the construction of a fixed industrial profile or authorial silhouette. Still, many high-profile industry agents perform creative labor in numerous capacities and modes, and popular awareness of this labor depends partly on the intervention of mediating agents such as review journalists. Across the late 1990s and 2000s, film culture has witnessed new modes of criticism and reporting, particularly the emergence of online critics who bring professional profiles to their work or enjoy access to film sets, premieres, and other sites. These new agents and voices change the ways industries address the body of film writers and how writers perform their intermediary work, with rhetoric increasingly situated within audience and fan communities rather than within institutions such as journalism itself.

This chapter has begun to interrogate some of the factors involved in the manufacture of authorial imprints through films' reception at festivals, in arthouses, and in wider theatrical and home-video release. Much of this process involves claims made about the content and meaning of individual films. I turn next to film texts themselves, considering how textual elements come to signify authorship. Moreover, just as this chapter has sought to position review discourse in various status hierarchies, I next approach film texts in relation to varying cultural and work contexts that influence the ways we discern textual meanings.

Part Three

Soderbergh and Textuality

Chapter 5

Reading Soderbergh
Textuality and Representation

This book thus far has sought to distinguish responsibilities for particular creative tasks in films directed by Soderbergh and to map the
construction of his wider authorial profile across film texts and
surrounding film-cultural discourses. Many viewers are drawn to
Soderbergh's films for their textual features, particularly those features
recognized not as purely formal but as linked to sociocultural concerns.
According to numerous commentators, many of Soderbergh's features
manifest Hollywood cinema's progressive potential, inclined toward
political questions, power relations, and periodically, narratives attentive to marginal social subjects. Academic film studies, though, regularly
untethers films from their producing agents, circumventing questions
of intent and privileging critical interventions into textual meaning.
The resilient analytical frame of ideological criticism names directors
or other production workers principally to group texts for study rather
than specifically to interrogate authorial practice. Critics identify texts'
ideological functions largely through interpretation, a reading strategy
not beholden to particular production workers' articulated intentions
and sensibilities. But while viewers make *sense of* films, it is filmmakers who *make* those films. I have argued that Soderbergh's films
exemplify transformations in contemporary screen industries and the
opportunities available to creative individuals within those industries.
Relatedly, Soderbergh's work inflects in compelling ways the dynamics
of U.S. cultural relations as mapped through terrains of gender, race,
class, and other contested categories. For a broad and deep understanding of screen authorship, I turn now to questions of representation.

This chapter redirects attention to Soderbergh's films of the late
1990s and early 2000s, including *Out of Sight, Erin Brockovich,* and

Ocean's Eleven, addressing some production and reception conditions but concentrating on textual qualities. Case studies of these three films, with corollary attention to related works, demonstrate the ways the films Soderbergh has directed consistently challenge long-standing patterns of Hollywood representation while often replicating those conservative patterns in problematic ways. Soderbergh's films periodically critique outmoded hierarchies of race, gender, and other social formations, yet they also call upon those hierarchies in ambivalent or uncritical ways for dramatic emphasis. Overall, this chapter argues that cultural formations both familiar and original accompany representations of gender, race, ethnicity, and social class throughout Soderbergh's directorial work. In addition, following Chapter 3's focus on production context, this chapter takes up questions surrounding the utility of textual criticism and interpretation.

Toward a Model of Cosituated Textualities

Representation is a contested category, sometimes designated as the product of authorial intention or other production activity, sometimes assigned wholly to reception contexts, and sometimes understood as an inherent textual property. Farsighted scholars might agree that representation depends on all three categories, on conditions of production and reception as well as textual features. Ella Shohat and Robert Stam argue that "[a] full understanding of media representation . . . requires a comprehensive analysis of the institutions that generate and distribute mass-mediated texts as well as of the audience that receives them."[1] However, the bulk of film-studies scholarship on representation scrutinizes texts alone. Work informed by cultural studies locates films in surrounding cultural contexts, if sometimes advancing straightforward reflection hypotheses in which individual texts come to embody set ideological positions allegedly symptomatic of particular times and places. Meanwhile, sociological criticism makes efforts to account for reception conditions, though collation of empirical data about reception activity limits options for nuanced readings of discrete feature films. Finally, only those approaches perceived as most retrograde address intentionality, crudely marrying textual properties and inferred authorial intent.[2] Nonetheless, screen scholars invested in both texts and contexts have sought to combine textual analysis with research on production and authorship, cultural contexts, and reception activity.

Charles Acland reminds us that "it would be a profound and presumptuous misstep to think that cultural artifacts harbor their own essential meaning effects."[3] Still, we may meaningfully evaluate textual features in terms of their engagement with a range of materially significant frames. I propose here a comprehensive approach to screen representation that accounts for textual features informed by, or situated within, multiple contexts. Such a model, of what I term cosituated textualities, interrogates the textual features of a given screen work alongside a range of significant contexts that each enunciate different rationales for and consequences of representational choices. While the range of possible contexts is vast, I offer the model with three key contexts in mind: those of production, reception, and culture. These three necessarily interrelate but carry sufficient distinction as to be critically useful. Meanwhile, other contexts, particularly that of genre, interact strongly with the three major contexts and could be understood as subcontexts operating within each of those three larger fields. Overall, I propose the model of cosituated textualities as a hedge against critical subjectivity and a means to identify some of the multiple aesthetic, discursive, and social phenomena that comprise screen textuality. The term "cosituation" acknowledges that textual analysis can attend to multiple contextual fields or specify particular focal areas. Criticism that identifies the parameters it puts around particular texts can illuminate not only texts themselves but also interlocking contexts, critical processes, and the relationships among the three. Attention to cosituation challenges academic interventions that serve to fix the strategies and meanings of polyvocal texts.

While the cases that follow flesh out the model and its implications, I begin with some working definitions. To link screen texts to their production contexts, I propose the construct of production-situated textuality. This frame attends to production workers' statements about the representational aims of their creative practice and of specific projects, along with consideration of workers' positions in social and industrial hierarchies. Producers, directors, performers, and other above-the-line creative workers quite literally matter more in industrial hierarchies than do below-the-line or peripheral production agents, so a production-situated textuality considers particularly the activities of major creative workers in determining textual features. Production-situated textuality can attend as well to the market concerns, financing, location requirements, and other logistical determinants that inform textual choices. To give one brief example, the casting in *Ocean's Eleven* of Chinese acrobat Shaobo Qin (in his first film role) over the rumored original choice of Jet Li affects the finished film's representation, circulation, and reception. Qin's untested comic persona takes the place of Li's global star markers, likely limiting the film's visibility in East Asian markets but also shielding Hollywood from further criticism of its poor showcasing of Li's talents.

Consideration of textual elements in terms of production contexts can alert us to another crucial codeterminant of representations: that of location. Location analysis recognizes the pools of labor from which given productions draw, or the situation into which a production transplants creative workers. Such analysis also recognizes the geographic spaces available for filmmaking, whether chosen for purposes of verisimilitude, creative autonomy, convenience, or economics. Location points, too, to cultural imperatives and negotiations, as screen production involves not only what John Caldwell terms "production culture"[4] but also production *within* a culture. As discussed in Chapter 3, productions embed themselves in particular locations' economies and cultures, engaging in expressly temporary, contingent interactions with those cultures but forming relationships of mutual dependency nonetheless.

The second critical category, reception-situated textuality, investigates ways that reception materials such as reviews reshape film texts in their initial theatrical circulation and in film-historical memory. Some film criticism positions film viewers as neutral parties with respect to critical discourses. Critics may acknowledge that viewers' judgments are socially formed but rarely that viewers might respond to films based on cues offered in review discourse (aside from review etiquette surrounding revelations of major plot points and so-called spoilers). Necessarily, though, reviews and other reception phenomena strongly impact subsequent viewers' perspectives on film texts. Reviewers' ideological stances, to the extent that reviews enable their expression, shape widespread understanding of textual meaning. Through the weight of accumulated discourse, then, reviews can create the impression that particular interpretations simply explain inherent textual elements. Reigning interpretations cast films as progressive or conservative, contestatory or reactionary, to such an extent that those meanings adhere powerfully to the texts in question. Critical debates over *Traffic*, for example, showed interpretive lenses linked to critics' own ideological positions. Many critics found the film to endorse their own view of subject matter: critics for progressive publications identified a clear critique of the U.S.'s seemingly futile "war on drugs," while reviewers for conservative publications located in the film a call for individual responsibility and self-reliance. (At the same time, critics of many persuasions took issue with the film's melodramatic family narrative.) Though not cohering into a fixed ideological position, these debates did successfully cast the film as principally "about" the drug war rather than about other subjects such as cross-border relations, class conflict, and so forth.[5]

I offer as a third key category that of culturally situated textuality. While sharing features with production and reception contexts, this third category stresses the degree to which texts articulate connections to (or disconnects from) a surrounding sociocultural reality. Meanwhile, for films with historical or foreign settings (the latter designating settings outside a central producing region or major release market), culturally-situated textuality can illuminate ways texts enunciate proximity to or distance from another time or place. This category also addresses the ways cultural conditions inform viewers' perceptions of contemporary texts. Distinct from viewing cues supplied by specific intermediaries such as reviewers, cultural factors such as dominant views of race or class relations create powerful templates for identification and processing of particular representations. While closest to extant scholarly approaches to filmic representation, this category can remind us further of the highly contingent nature of screen textuality. Sensitive to particular textual features and amenable to close readings, culturally situated textuality can also challenge assertions of fixed meanings for particular representations. If history proves any guide, those films we now convincingly claim as the most enlightened cultural artifacts will someday be unmasked as hopelessly naïve and shortsighted (as inevitably will our readings of them). Film form and content mobilize a host of investments and engagements, and a culturally situated approach to textuality seeks to acknowledge the culturally specific lenses through which all texts reach us.

The three central categories of textual situation could include subcategories such as generically situated textuality, which would cross into the areas above as well. A hybrid of production-situated and generically situated textuality would foreground filmmakers' relationships to particular genres and thus their uses of generic fields as parts of the canvases on which to construct new screen representations. Meanwhile, a subcategory of formally situated textuality could emphasize the image and sound relationships comprising film and television form. Textual form follows principally from production contexts. At the same time, it depends on reception to the extent that reception frames inform stylistic choices—for example, decisions to shoot films such as *Kafka* and *The Good German* in black-and-white contend with the art-cinema associations that such aesthetics invariably create within contemporary screen cultures. Similarly, Warner Bros.'s willing-ness to let Soderbergh serve as his own cinematographer on the *Ocean's* films must account for audiences' tolerance for his largely handheld shooting style and consistent underlighting of faces. The films' merger of Soderbergh's stylistic predilections with an overall unobtrusive visu-al and lighting design represents the management of production and anticipated reception frames. Formal choices contend, too, with cultural preferences. The mostly Spanish dialogue of *Che* may signal authentic-ity, or alternately may render the film unwatchable for those averse to subtitling. *Che*'s shooting mostly on HD video might also have met with executive, critical, or mass-audience resistance at one time, but the widening use of digital rather than film cameras on studio or other major-release productions has normalized it as an accepted industrial practice and exhibition technology, if not yet the standard for capital-intensive productions.

With this array of textualities in mind, we remain free to advance contingent claims about the meanings and possibilities of screen repre-sentation. In so doing, we might meet the challenge offered by Shohat and Stam, who note in their own study of representation that "[a] more nuanced discussion of race and ethnicity in the cinema would empha-size less a one-to-one mimetic adequacy to sociological or historical truth than the interplay of voices, discourses, perspectives, including those operative within the image itself."[6] The voices in the interplay to which Shohat and Stam refer include those of a film's collaborative production team: its authors. While filmmakers may bring personal investments to bear in crafting screen representations, films take shape according to many production decisions and resources. Thus, the first cases covered here look to categories of representation alongside con-siderations arising from films' settings and locations.

Production-Situated Textuality: Locating Women

While Soderbergh's films since *sex, lies, and videotape* have included prominent roles for women, only a few of his works specifically showcase female protagonists rather than presenting women as love interests, adversaries, or other foils for male characters. The HD fea-tures *The Girlfriend Experience* and *Haywire* stand out as the most woman-centered of Soderbergh's more recent films as director, with the former an immersion in the career and personal life of a high-end prostitute, the latter a platform for mixed martial arts star Gina Carano.

Previously, only one Soderbergh-directed film, the mainstream hit and Academy Awards contender *Erin Brockovich*, could be categorized as a "woman's film" or a female-centered narrative. (Indeed, the film's one Oscar victory—Julia Roberts won best actress—helps affirm this classification.) In this section, I survey key women's roles offered in Soderbergh-directed films—*Erin Brockovich* and the metafictional *Full Frontal* in particular—to assess the latitude they afford women characters. In addition, as a point of entry for textual investigation cognizant of production contexts, I begin my analysis in terms of the films' settings and locations.

Production circumstances invariably contribute to textual characteristics, yet studies of representation otherwise scrupulously attentive to questions of culture, power, and subject position often overlook production determinants. One consideration for situated studies of representation is that of literal, geographic situation: of location. Sites for filming present a range of opportunities and limitations for production teams. Coupled with his substantial location activity, Soderbergh has, like many American filmmakers with Hollywood affiliations, repeatedly directed films set and shot in Southern California. *The Limey*, *Erin Brockovich*, and *Full Frontal* all feature principally Los Angeles-area settings; *Traffic* includes a substantial San Diego narrative; and the *Ocean's* films, while largely set and filmed over 250 miles east of Los Angeles, include numerous L.A.-area settings as well as scenes filmed in Los Angeles spaces standing in for Las Vegas or elsewhere. *Solaris* similarly uses Los Angeles spaces, including Warners' Burbank studio facilities and one downtown location; and *The Good German* was filmed on Warners and Universal lots as well as at numerous other Southern California locations. For this section's purposes, I offer location as one means to focus attention to constructions of women characters in Soderbergh films. *Erin Brockovich* and *Full Frontal* offer abundant, strong female presences as well as instrumental uses of particular settings. The locations add not only particular ambiances to the films in question—e.g., by populating *Full Frontal* with film-industry workers and other creative professionals—but also contribute substantively to the films' constructions of femininity altogether. As we will see, different films' uses of similar locations such as greater Los Angeles or Southern California highlight ways production teams build stories around particular places. The varied representations of those places, in turn, impact the types of characters shown to thrive or suffer within them. Linking location and gender as categories for analysis, we can see how women's prospects in narrative fictions are tied to geographic obstacles and opportunities as well as to economic and attitudinal ones.

Erin Brockovich situates itself geographically in its second scene. Following a failed job interview, Julia Roberts's Erin drives away from the interview site and suffers a car accident at a North Hollywood intersection. This event catalyzes Erin's meeting with lawyer Ed Masry (Albert Finney), leading to her investigative work at Masry's law firm and the development of the film's major whistle-blower narrative. Amid scenes at Masry's and other offices and episodes in Erin's domestic space, the film represents repeated transit between metro L.A. and the desert locations northeast of the city where Erin investigates California utility Pacific Gas and Electric's rural water pollution. For her investigation, she amasses corporate and local-government documents and interviews many small-town residents affected by the pollution. These interviews occur in public settings (a bar in one scene, and in another a fire station where a town-hall meeting takes place) as well as private homes. The film thus defines Erin in multiple ways: as a single mother facing financial hardship and inattentive to her own domestic environment, as a professional gathering information in formal settings (e.g., a records office) and the informal ones such as homes in which she can interact compassionately with afflicted townspeople,

In *Erin Brockovich* (2000), Erin goes door-to-door to canvass rural Californians about water-pollution exposure.

and as a worker in transit between these spaces and between her own work sites of office and field.

The film locates Erin through repeated driving scenes as well as extensive location shooting in Hinkley (where the real events that comprise the film's non-L.A. narrative occurred) and other small towns outside Barstow. At the same time, the film dislocates characters and events from specific geographic and cultural spaces through emphasis on Erin's physical display. In work settings, Erin's provocative ensembles contribute to comic-awkward interactions with men and conflicts with women, who Erin repeatedly antagonizes. Thus, amid its depiction of Erin's literal mobility and her symbolic movement from unemployed mother to fulfilled woman professional, the film presents her interactions in public space as colored by her eye-catching personal style. This style not only distinguishes her visually from other women in the workplace but also narratively creates antagonisms that preclude friendships with other women there. Though tipping the scales by presenting her exclusively female detractors as generally sour-minded, the film also narrates Erin's strained interactions with her employer, Ed, as well as with her neighbor and then boyfriend, the easygoing biker George (Aaron Eckhart). Devoting most of its running time to showcasing the unruly Erin's abundant interpersonal conflict and occasional cooperation, the film speaks to contemporary gender politics and workplace dynamics not fixed to particular geographic locations. At the same time, Erin's ability to win over the men and women of Hinkley depends partly on that space's construction as a working-class environment, with scenes set in open spaces or modestly appointed interiors. Travelling mostly alone in her dilapidated car, Erin models a pioneer-woman spirit in this largely daylit western setting, championing populist interests against PG&E's invisible malice. While toxic to its residents, this setting positively inflects Erin's character. Rural San Bernardino County determines Erin's representation in a manner quite distinct from, for example, the way Roberts's star-making role in *Pretty Woman* (1990) depends on her traversal of differently classed zones of urban Los Angeles.

Erin Brockovich's settings, thematic investments, and development history all locate the film in contexts in which women are central. The film's workplace scenes represent substantial female conflict. Following an early courtroom outburst directed at a male lawyer and his client, Erin's profane diatribes target only women. However, scenes of her door-to-door investigation in Hinkley emphasize her measured, sympathetic engagements with families and particularly with women. These interactions help situate the film's narrative in the modality of melodrama, critically understood both as a dominant mode of Hollywood address and a particular platform for female subjectivity.[7] *Erin Brockovich* also presents itself as a woman's film in multiple categories—as star vehicle for Hollywood's dominant female figure of its era, as biopic of a living woman, and through foregrounding of motherhood and family, subjects discursively understood as particularly relevant to women. Notably, Soderbergh did not initiate the project but joined as director following its development at Danny DeVito and Michael Shamberg's Jersey Films, where it took shape from efforts begun by Shamberg's wife, Carla Santos Shamberg. A DVD featurette frames the film as the product of the interaction of three Los Angeles–area women: Shamberg, Brockovich, and the chiropractor who both patronized and whose informal conversations with each led to development meetings between Shamberg and Brockovich.[8] The film's creative pedigree also includes women as three of the film's six credited producers, as well as credits for screenwriter Susannah Grant and editor Anne Coates, making it one of Soderbergh's more woman-centric production collaborations. A *Newsweek* profile of Roberts portrays her career and the forthcoming film strongly in terms of gender, mixing fawning praise for her talent with mildly indignant accusations of Hollywood's "double standard" for compensating her and other female stars with salaries well below those of their male counterparts. The profile also cites the simultaneously scolding and approving comment of an *Erin Brockovich* test-screening participant: "The 100th time I saw Julia Roberts's breasts was too much. The first 99 were OK."[9] Like the film itself, the profile positions Roberts as both a figure through which to address feminist concerns and an ambiguous sex symbol.

As an industrial and cultural phenomenon, *Erin Brockovich* achieves the creative goal of legitimation for both performer and director. The film's popular success demonstrated Soderbergh's ability to deliver a commercially viable studio production in the wake of a diminished public profile across the 1990s. Similarly, though Roberts's industrial profile far exceeded Soderbergh's at the time of *Erin Brockovich*'s production, her star persona remained tied to romantic comedies such as *Notting Hill* and *Runaway Bride* (both 1999) and straightforward genre exercises such as *The Pelican Brief* (1993). Two 1996 films showcasing her dramatic skills, *Mary Reilly* and *Michael Collins*, were substantial box-office failures. *Erin Brockovich* thus represents Roberts's first successful reinvention of her airy star persona. Even as the film relies on

Roberts as its chief marketable asset as well as the motor of its narrative and emotional appeals, it also reconstructs her as a dramatic talent. Moreover, by linking her textually and discursively to the historical Erin Brockovich's investigations on behalf of social justice, the film enables a view of Roberts as politically aware cultural worker (if still entertainment-gossip stalwart, with the *Newsweek* profile referencing her current and past paramours). Soderbergh's work with Roberts represents part of a process through which a onetime indie auteur benefits from work with a mainstream female star, exemplifying a kind of double legitimation process that accords with Hollywood's industrial logic. The female star becomes an asset facilitating the independent filmmaker's mainstream legitimation, while her work with an acclaimed independent filmmaker affords her the film-cultural bona fides often difficult for actresses to acquire. *Erin Brockovich*'s narration of a historical case and its use of rural southern-California locations germane to that account also help legitimate the work, the filmmaker, and the star.

Full Frontal, the low-budget, semi-experimental independent released through Miramax, reteams Soderbergh and Roberts, centrally positioning her alongside other Hollywood film and television veterans. Roberts plays a Hollywood star, Francesca Davis, but her role is only a part of a multi-layered metanarrative that interrogates celebrity culture while experimenting with the boundaries of mainstream narrative form. The film works in the metafictional mode of historical forebears such as *David Holzman's Diary* (1967) and *Symbiopsychotaxiplasm: Take One* and more contemporary films such as the Charlie Kaufman/Spike Jonze collaboration *Being John Malkovich* (1999). *Full Frontal* opened in August 2002, three months before the subsequent Kaufman/Jonze effort *Adaptation*. *Full Frontal* exploited publicity arising from the combination of its title and its marquee star Roberts, begging the question of whether she would appear nude in the film. (She does not, but supporting player David Duchovny does, albeit as a flaccid dead body.)

Partly improvised but with a screenplay by Coleman Hough, *Full Frontal* represents Soderbergh's second collaboration with a female screenwriter.[10] The film stages a series of strongly gendered and raced encounters and conflicts. *Full Frontal* begins with and intermittently returns to a film-within-the-film, *Rendezvous*, in which Roberts's actress character plays a journalist, Catherine, who conducts a lengthy, travelling interview with a black actor, Nicholas (Blair Underwood).

This interior film toys with the possibility of an interracial romance between the two media professionals, while in the narrative world outside this Hollywood-esque fiction, other characters face conflicts or engage in assignations that foreground longstanding taboos in cinematic and other visual representation.[11] Underwood's other character, Calvin—i.e., the actor playing the actor-star of *Rendezvous*—meets an unhappy wife, Lee (Catherine Keener), for a hotel-room tryst. In other scenes, Lee, a corporate executive, holds bizarre and aggressive meetings with male subordinates and job candidates. Meanwhile, she has unceremoniously broken off her marriage by leaving a note for her already emasculated husband, Carl (David Hyde Pierce). Another plotline follows Lee's sister, Linda (Mary McCormack), a masseuse who at one point allows a film-producer client, Gus (Duchovny), to pay her for a so-called "happy ending" to a massage, also occurring in a hotel room. In short, the film proliferates hierarchical encounters that turn on gendered power. In these, the spectres of miscegenation on one hand, of illegitimate matriarchal dominance on another, and the continued privileges afforded by white patriarchy all come into play.

As in the other Soderbergh-directed films noted already, *Full Frontal* links women's power or lack thereof to their professional roles. Roberts's two characters manifest binary oppositions: the actress Francesca's high social status allows her to make petty demands of her male assistant, while the journalist Catherine adopts a persona of professional obsequiousness for her interview with Nicholas. Sisters Lee and Linda also occupy largely opposite roles: the pantsuit-wearing Lee's executive position facilitates her off-kilter workplace behavior as well as her affair with the studly Calvin, while Linda's status as freelance tradeswoman locates her in a compromising position with producer Gus and implicitly determines her own romantic prospect, the bottom-rung playwright she meets through an online-dating forum. Power and influence are the implicit currencies in *Full Frontal*'s media-industry Los Angeles. Class origins receive no particular attention, in distinction to *Erin Brockovich*'s comparatively realist Southern California, where working-class characters repeatedly fall prey to moneyed interests' exploitation or indifference. In both films, though, career roles substantially determine women's agency. Erin's joblessness equates to powerlessness, but once she is employed, her blunt manner evolves into professional poise. Material power follows, both through the literal mobility afforded by the new SUV Masry gives her as a gift, and later in the form of a seven-figure bonus check. *Full Frontal* offers more polarized views of women's work predicaments. Though mischievously embodied by Keener, Lee fits a caricature of the too-powerful female professional. Meanwhile, outside the corporate and film-industry worlds, Linda's masseuse career makes her a literal manual laborer and, in giving Gus the offscreen hand job, a paid sex worker as well. A dispute over payment for this latter act underscores Linda's lack of negotiating power.

Full Frontal and *Erin Brockovich* offer sometimes overlapping, sometimes divergent portraits of female work and agency in contemporary Southern California. These very different treatments complicate straightforward claims about authorial sensibilities. Even accounting for the particular contributions of each film's female screenwriter as well as performers' and other creative workers' input, only the most forced interpretation could cohesively merge the film's sensibilities. Likewise, to introduce *The Girlfriend Experience* and *Haywire* into the Soderbergh corpus further discounts ironclad assessments of ideological intent and consistent textual meanings. What I hope to have accomplished in this section, though, is to offer a comparative frame of reference through which to view groups of films. By highlighting film setting and production location while attending to categories such as gender representation that reward continued interrogation, we can accumulate multiperspectival knowledge about film texts, their creators, and the nature of creative work presented to viewers for meaning-making in diverse social and cultural contexts.

Representation of women and their professional roles creates one organizing principle for textual study, while location supplies another. Both constitute only a fraction of the possible points of entry into individual films or groups of films. Bridging the gap between discrete screen texts and issues of authorship, production contexts point to further pathways of meaning and significance. Viewed in terms of a production-situated textuality, *Full Frontal* in particular benefits from extratextual knowledge of its production process. Through its alternation between grainy digital video (still a relative novelty in 2002) and crisp 35mm film, its cast of familiar industry faces playing either fictional characters (as do Roberts, Duchovny, and others) or themselves (as do A-listers such as Brad Pitt and David Fincher), and its overall metanarrative form, the film strongly cues viewers to bypass its narrative layers and image world to consider production circumstances. Indeed, numerous of the film's generally negative reviews faulted it for a lack of textual coherence but praised its performers' apparent commitment to its narrative and performative experimentation. Reviews thus implicitly distinguished between the fiction text and discernible evidence of production context. In similar fashion, all screen texts acquire different meanings when positioned in relation to their own production histories or linked to their collaborators' other creative endeavors.

Reception-Situated Textuality: *Out of Sight*, *Erin Brockovich*, and the Emerging Popular Soderbergh

With a continued emphasis on the textual features of *Erin Brockovich* and other films, I turn next to a discussion of reception contexts. Chapter 4 looked to film-review journalism to understand ways reception discourse traces an artistic signature for the designated author-figure Soderbergh. I investigate that same discourse here for its attention to categories of representation. When it takes representation into account, reception commentary can consolidate views of authorship as well. At the same time, receivers often judge films without addressing the efforts of offscreen creative personnel, concentrating instead on the artistic and entertainment appeals of a self-contained text. To characterize the relationship between texts and reception, we might begin with the straightforward proposition that textual features contribute to particular horizons of expectation in reception contexts. Reviews of *Full Frontal*, for example, responded strongly (if not often positively) to its narrative structure and its perceived industry-insider tone. Consequently, social categories such as gender and class received little if any commentary, except to the extent that the smugness many critics attributed to the film was seen to emanate from upper middle-class characters or the elite performers who embodied them. In this case, the film's class representation supplies one of the points of origin for a negative critical judgment.

Returning to *Erin Brockovich*, the film's subject matter does apparently compel reviewers to assess the film in terms of gender and class. Todd McCarthy's *Variety* review opens with the phrase "[a]n exhilarating tale about a woman discovering her full potential and running with it." Discounting the film's central legal-investigation plot, McCarthy observes that the "[s]tory is ultimately about how a downtrodden but determined woman fights to make her innate sense of self-worth stick and be acknowledged by the world."[12] A. O. Scott's *New York Times* review responds similarly to the narration of Erin's life, asserting that "[y]ou not only witness the humiliations casually and routinely visited on working-class women; you feel in the pit of your stomach the overwhelming anxiety of impoverished single motherhood." Indeed,

Scott faults the film only when it turns its attention away from Erin's social position to her (historically accurate) battle with a major corporation. Recoiling against the film's perceived narrative clichés, Scott finally derides it as "the feel-good movie of the year." Nonetheless, he maintains an investment in representation, prompted by the narrative, visual, and performative centrality of Roberts's Erin. Following an observation about the absence of other performers of Roberts's star wattage, he suggests that:

> The noncompetition clause seems to have been applied with special rigor to the female characters. Erin's co-workers at the law firm are frumpy, badly dressed and just plain mean. Her nemesis, a lawyer . . . who is actually on the same side of the case, is an uptight snob with no feeling for the ordinary hard-working folks she must represent. In contrast, Erin is a life force, brimming with wholesome sexuality and unpretentious common sense.[13]

Taking his cues from the film's emphasis on female subjectivity, Scott's critique combines description and interpretation. Narrative elements, costuming (he refers to Erin's wardrobe elsewhere in his review), and performance style (which can be implicitly linked to direction of the actors) combine to drive Scott's response. Roger Ebert infers genre connections fostered by the film's narrative and tone, beginning his own review with the assertion that "*Erin Brockovich* is *Silkwood* . . . crossed with *A Civil Action* . . . plus Julia Roberts in a plunging neckline."[14] He bases his final verdict on a design element, claiming boldly that "the costume design sinks this movie" and using this feature as evidence of a lack of narrative complexity and compelling characters. Thus, though drawing intertextual connections based on his own viewing history, he focuses his overall judgment on a visible, recurring textual feature. With his attention focused on women's costuming, though, Ebert's critique of this mise-en-scène element is at root a critique of representation.

We can compare *Erin Brockovich*'s critical reception to that of Soderbergh's previous studio feature, 1998's *Out of Sight*. An adaptation of a 1996 Elmore Leonard novel and a pairing of then-rising stars George Clooney and Jennifer Lopez, the film's marketable elements might be expected to contribute to substantially different reception. *Out of Sight*, a Universal production, represents Soderbergh's first film made wholly under the auspices of a major studio: upon its release, he remarked to one interviewer, "I've never made a movie that had a release date before."[15] Because of Soderbergh's limited commercial footprint across the 1990s, categories such as genre and adaptation overpower attention to his specific creative contributions. Major publications' reviews of the film unsurprisingly foreground its heist plot, its star pairing, and in particular its status as Leonard adaptation. Returning to Ebert's criticism, his *Out of Sight* review begins by framing the film alongside other Leonard adaptations released in the same period—*Get Shorty* (1995), *Touch* (1997), and *Jackie Brown* (1997), the last of which shares some supporting cast and characters with *Out of Sight*. Ebert riffs on genre conventions before favorably assessing the film's narrative elements, particularly its unschematic approach to character, which he links to Leonard's work, writing, "Elmore Leonard is above all the creator of colorful characters."[16] Emanuel Levy's *Variety* review echoes Ebert's approach, observing, too, that "Leonard's forte lies in his sharp, nonjudgmental characterizations" and comparing *Out of Sight* favorably to *Get Shorty* and *Jackie Brown*. Reflecting *Variety*'s industry-focused appraisals of films' commercial prospects, Levy also notes *Out of Sight*'s "intricate format of flashbacks, which enrich the tale but may prove too demanding for mainstream viewers."[17] Ebert likewise cites the film's fractured chronology, which he terms "a time line as complex as *Pulp Fiction*," offering readers a further intertextual frame. Ebert addresses Soderbergh's reputation only at the end of his review, claiming that "it's not what we think of as a Soderbergh film—detached, cold, analytical," then linking it again to *Pulp Fiction*. Levy's review does frame the film initially in terms of Soderbergh and later in terms of the film's other collaborators and technicians. Ebert's review, though, as with his later appraisal of *Erin Brockovich*, highlights particular textual elements—approach to character and editing style—and uses these to build an intertextual frame that determines his judgment.

Distinct from Ebert's and other reviews of *Erin Brockovich*, terms such as gender and class hardly figure in *Out of Sight*'s critical reception, nor does the otherwise prominent category of race. The film depicts male criminals at odds, mostly along racial lines though with casual or uneasy cross-racial alliances in evidence: it sets the close rapport of bank-robbing duo Jack Foley (Clooney) and his partner Buddy Bragg (Ving Rhames) against the precariousness of the mixed-race team led by Don Cheadle's thuggish Maurice. Respecting Hollywood custom, the Latina Jennifer Lopez's federal agent Karen Sisco mediates between white worlds (the dominant complexion of her fellow marshals) and black ones (the color of most of the criminal underclass and its kin, aside from Foley, Steve Zahn's Glenn, and Luis Guzmán's Chino).[18]

Writing in an academic context, Elaine Roth notes of the film's racial and gender politics that "[t]he dynamic between rapacious black men and subsequently heroic white men is crucial to the plot of *Out of Sight*."[19] Mainstream film critics hardly remark on such dynamics. Of those who mention race at all, the *New York Times*'s Janet Maslin observes that "the movie benefits from presenting more of an ethnic mix than the book did."[20] In the *New York Observer*, Andrew Sarris speculates about the commercial prospects of a film with a "conspicuously interracial cast."[21] Still, these and other critics mostly restrict their commentary to matters of plot and character, crediting Leonard, Soderbergh, screenwriter Scott Frank, and individual performers for the crafting and execution of these elements.

Reviewers' varying attention to representation and ideology depends on their presumed audience and the nature of their professional address. Social critiques of films occasionally surface in mainstream commentary pieces, though rarely in release-day reviews. Reviews touching on social concerns tend to do so to supply casual viewing protocols, put forth to improve cinemagoers' consumption experiences. They can provide suitable art-appreciation contexts, and can manage expectations in order to ensure a close fit between viewer attitudes and film content. Relatedly, reviews can warn viewers of potentially objectionable content, usually on the terms dictated by MPAA ratings: sex, violence, drug use, and profanity. For example, writing for the *Boston Phoenix*, Peter Keough calls *Out of Sight* "[a]s coy and unsettling in its violence as in its sex—the carnage is abrupt, ugly, and very funny."[22] Keough's linkage of otherwise incompatible terms alerts viewers to aspects of the film's content (it's unsettling and ugly) while suggesting an interpretive strategy for that content (it can be read as comic).

Keough first describes *Out of Sight* as "quirky," a keyword of esteem for the presumed readership of an urban alternative weekly in the late 1990s. Certainly not all viewers would respond in this way to the film's content. It includes numerous acts of racially motivated violence as well as multiple rape threats, with black men repeatedly posing sexual threats to white women. While not explicitly endorsing these episodes, the film gains comic and dramatic impact from the deployment of pernicious racial constructs. As Roth notes too, the film thus joins, by default or design, a long history of racist representation in Hollywood cinema and U.S. popular culture. Apparently, though, the typologies on which the film draws retain insufficient traction to merit reviewers' commentary. This silence reveals less about professional reviewers' viewing strategies than about the explicit goal of critical discourse: to judge a film's entertainment value, a judgment in practice removed from political or ideological concerns. Film studies, cultural studies, and other disciplines have labored to demonstrate the inseparability of such categories—as after all, to ignore a film's cultural politics is itself an ideological act. Still, mainstream criticism continues to distinguish between quality judgment and social critique, strongly privileging a version of the former. Responding to the presumed interests of undifferentiated viewing groups, popular criticism orbits around categories such as narrative plausibility (sometimes accounting for genre contexts), generally realist character psychology, and interpersonal chemistry, romantic or otherwise. Critics occasionally attend to categories such as those Steve Neale, following Tzvetan Todorov and Jonathan Culler, terms "generic verisimilitude" and "cultural verisimilitude."[23] Reviews manifest these concepts in mostly commonsensical ways rather than according to rigorous academic models. Reviewers in effect validate indistinct belief systems rather than using textual analysis to perform cultural critique. Here we might identify the limitations of a reception-situated textuality. Reviewers respond to a circumscribed set of textual cues, lacking the space, inclination, discursive forum, or institutional support to take on the entirety of a text's content and cultural implications, to say nothing of markers of authorship.

Nonprofessional reception privileges different if overlapping critical languages and viewing protocols. The Internet Movie Database's "User Reviews" and message boards represent a widely used, English-language reception forum, regulated only by site administrators and users for explicitly profane or defamatory content. The less formal nature of such online commentary shows the idiosyncratic investments of individual viewers whose livelihoods do not depend on cordial relations with film-industry personnel. Nonprofessional reviews might thus be expected to convey cultural preferences and viewing strategies more transparently than comparatively restrained professional reviews do. However, IMDb user reviews for *Out of Sight* largely replicate professional reviewers' criteria, remarking on character, narrative, and story structure most prominently, and secondarily on aspects of genre, performance, visual style, and music. (Reviews intermittently name and discuss Soderbergh, but only as a very minor strand of commentary.) The bulk of reviews are highly impressionistic, privileging strongly personal judgments rather than rigorous close readings that reference textual evidence. Most work to manage fellow users' expectations, invoking moral positions as well as genre codes. Numerous user reviews, for example, echo Keough's *Boston Phoenix* review, describing the film as violent but finding this acceptable as a generic convention, and calling for the violence (especially a scene in which a character slips on a staircase and shoots himself in the head) to be read as comic.

Perhaps unsurprisingly, categories of social representation receive virtually no attention in *Out of Sight*'s IMDb user reviews. Of the 279 user reviews posted as of early 2010, only one explicitly addresses the film's gender politics, for example, attributing a "slight anti-feminist slant" to the film.[24] Invoking realism, a handful of reviews take issue with Lopez's costuming, asserting that Sisco wears skirts too short for a law-enforcement professional. Such wardrobe patrolling echoes Ebert's and other professional critics' responses to *Erin Brockovich*. The similar remarks on the two films serve either as critiques of narrative logic or as culturally prescribed scrutiny of women's bodies and appropriate comportment, as well as implicit critiques of costume designers' labor. Race also figures only marginally into reviews—two reviewers use Lopez as a springboard for crude riffs on Latina actresses,[25] and another reviewer and a handful of message-board posters describe Cheadle's performance as a criminal as "just scary as hell" and "extremely frightening."[26] One such post adds commentary on Isaiah Washington's character, Kenneth (who provides the film's rape threats), calling him "very frightening" and a "total psychopath." These latter impressions can be read as signs of racist anxiety, as progressive critiques of racist constructs, or as esteem for convincing performances. The vast majority of commentators, though, do not present explicitly ideological readings of the film. Even those reviews that address particular formal elements— including David Holmes's jazz score; Anne Coates's disjunctive editing; and Elliot Davis's cinematography, with its varied color palette to distinguish settings such as Miami and Detroit—mention form in purely evaluative rather than analytical terms. The vast majority of reviewers argue for the film as worthwhile entertainment (or not) rather than for particular textual meanings.

Both professional and amateur reception contribute to Soderbergh's recognition as a popular filmmaker, periodically judging his artistry and his ability to oversee a genre film suitable for mainstream audiences. For amateur reviewers such as IMDb users, principal evaluative categories include narrative clarity and interest, fulfillment of generic expectations, and the appeals of lead and supporting performances. IMDb reviewers and message-board posters respond to *Out of Sight* extensively in terms of stars Clooney, Lopez, and well-known supporting performers (for example, many users weigh in on the roles of Ving Rhames, Don Cheadle, Albert Brooks, and Steve Zahn, and dozens refer enthusiastically to Samuel L. Jackson's final-scene cameo). With this film and in other manifestations of their personas, Clooney and Lopez in particular elicit polarized responses often not tethered to specific films. Relatedly, nonprofessional reviews tend not to link director and actors; that is, commentators remark on an actor's perceived talent, not on a director or screenwriter's contribution to a strong or weak performance. Still, given the character-centered nature of much nonprofessional reception, candid judgments about lead performers constitute a key site for determinations of a film's popular appeal. By association, judgments about performance become judgments on directors as well.

With studios engaging Soderbergh to work on larger, more commercial projects beginning in the late 1990s, films under his direction increasingly circulate in popular reception contexts rather than among more selective groupings of critics or cinephiles. Compared to *Out of Sight*'s 279 IMDb user reviews, for example, *Erin Brockovich* accumulated 456 reviews, and *Ocean's Eleven* received 803 reviews as of January 2010.[27] The evaluative criteria of professional and amateur reviews make clear that for Soderbergh to be a popular director, films under his direction must be character- and performance-driven, with stylistic flourishes accepted if they do not impede legible plotting. Reviews celebrate performative play but not formalism, responding with hostility or indifference to self-reflexive elements in Soderbergh's work. Intentionally or not, his subsequent studio features respond precisely to these criteria. Character and plot are central to Soderbergh's most elaborate and successful studio productions, the intricately plotted, large-ensemble *Ocean's* caper films. Soderbergh has repeatedly asserted his uninterest in reviews, and reviewers in turn have accused him of showing little interest in audiences. Still, *Ocean's Eleven* and its sequels represent his most substantive dialogue with worldwide audiences and, thanks to the films' saturation releases, with film critics as well. Such measureable cultural circulation makes the films ideal for consideration in terms of culturally situated textuality. If reception discourse around *Out of Sight* and *Erin Brockovich* indicates an emerging popular Soderbergh, then the *Ocean's* films show the expansion of that profile into the global mainstream.

Culturally Situated Textuality: Race and Male Style in the *Ocean's* Series

With cumulative worldwide grosses over $1 billion, the *Ocean's* trilogy represents by far Soderbergh's most commercially successful work as director. Many of Soderbergh's other films indisputably have a lesser cultural impact owing to their minimal visibility. While all screen texts are embedded in the sociohistorical moments of their production and can thus be said to speak *from* a cultural position, only those achieving some commercial success can reasonably be said to speak *to* large groups of viewers. As star-driven, heavily advertised, and widely seen Hollywood studio releases, *Ocean's Eleven* and its sequels can strongly illuminate the cultural situation of Soderbergh's work. I argue for the films as emblematic of a particular cultural sensibility, a "neo-retro" sensibility that takes shape through textual characteristics, engages with generic and cultural codes of past eras, and finds further expression in subsequent popular texts. *Ocean's Eleven* articulates this sensibility particularly through its multiple investments in contemporary formations of masculinity. The film's neo-retro attitudes create a space for the multiracial male group, a group defined by style codes and casual as well as highly formalized homosocial interactions.

My analysis here concentrates on *Ocean's Eleven*, the most critically successful of the series as well as the most straightforward in terms of narrative arcs, intersecting subplots, and overall integration of an ensemble cast into a single storyline. Still, the three films together demonstrate reasonable consistency in their narrative dynamics, characterizations, and overall textual attitudes. In *Ocean's Eleven*, paroled criminal Danny Ocean (Clooney) assembles a team for an elaborate Las Vegas casino robbery, motivated in part by his desire to reclaim his estranged wife, Tess (Julia Roberts), now romantically involved with the casino's owner, Terry Benedict (Andy Garcia). Ocean and his team achieve both goals, setting up *Ocean's Twelve*, in which Benedict tracks them down and demands repayment. The group relocates to Europe for heists, intrigue, romance, and myriad narrative complications amid Dutch, Italian, and other continental scenery. In a narrative overflowing with characters and plots, Ocean's team's adversaries include not only Benedict but also aristocratic robber Francois Touleur, a.k.a. "the Night Fox" (Vincent Cassel), and the film introduces the additional con artists and thieves Gaspar LaMarque (Albert Finney) and Isabel Lahiri (Catherine Zeta-Jones), revealed at the film's denouement as father and daughter. Finally, *Ocean's Thirteen* reassembles the male team to rob and discredit the new casino owned by Willy Bank (Al Pacino), who at the film's outset swindles one of the eleven, Rueben Tishkoff (Elliott Gould), causing his apparent mental breakdown. For this operation, the team enlists Benedict's backing, cons Bank's aide Abigail Sponder

(Ellen Barkin), and again fends off the persistent Touleur. All three films showcase male performance, with arch role-playing and subterfuge in abundance.

Ocean's Eleven crafts an ensemble of playful yet highly professionalized male criminals. Their work involves dressing up, acting up, and going out, usually in each other's company. The film and its sequels negotiate their homosocial, and sometimes homoerotic, spectacle by depicting male activity as performative role-playing. *Ocean's Eleven* presents this performance in highly mediated form, usually viewed through the surveillance cameras and monitors that are central to its narrative world. In his well-known "Masculinity as Spectacle," Steve Neale ponders the consequence of situating the male as the object of the camera's gaze. In films where male interactions are central—in Neale's example, the westerns of Sergio Leone—the viewer's "look is not direct, it is heavily mediated by the looks of the characters involved."[28] Coupled with the emphasis on aggression rather than desire, such films "minimize and displace the eroticism they . . . tend to involve, to disavow any explicitly erotic look at the male body."[29] Yet in *Ocean's Eleven*, this erotic look is strongly present. The male stars—including Clooney, Garcia, Brad Pitt, and Matt Damon—often comport themselves like runway models while other men watch them from different locations. Narratively, these looks verify the execution of parts of the complicated heist. They also serve as mediated views of male performance, with the men's composure, role-playing ability, or sleight of hand under scrutiny. Neale argues that in popular cinema generally, "[w]here women are investigated, men are tested."[30] In *Ocean's Eleven*, men are simultaneously tested—by their compatriots as well as their antagonists—*and* investigated. While linked to this dominant pattern in representation identified in academic film studies, the films' men also stand in close proximity to other contemporary pop-culture configurations, exemplifying so-called metrosexuality and anticipating the much-discussed trendlet of the bromance in ensemble form. More distinctly, all three *Ocean's* films construct a large, multicultural male group that is both available for viewers' looks and resistant to the debilitating male rivalries endemic in genre films. With their many costume changes and disguises, the films give viewers a male ensemble whose interactions occur largely at the level of personal style.

Ocean's Eleven's textual sensibility follows partly from its reworking of the 1960 Rat Pack caper film of the same title. We can position it within a particular subgenre, the contemporary caper film, or what

Heist planning in *Ocean's Eleven* (2001) involves many episodes of men looking at other men.

could be called the neo-retro heist film. The newer *Ocean's Eleven* also initiates a cycle of heist-film remakes. Chapter 6 takes up questions of remaking and adaptation in more detail, but insofar as heist-film remakes constitute a discernible body of early-2000s films, and thus can be said to comprise part of popular cinema's zeitgeist, they merit some discussion here. In the wake of *Ocean's Eleven*'s release, *Welcome to Collinwood* (2002), *The Good Thief* (2002), *The Italian Job* (2003), and *The Ladykillers* (2004) all adapt existing 1950s and 1960s heist films from Italy, France, and the UK. Rather than reviving the specific values of past U.S. or European cultures, the newer films all highlight casual, semiprofessional relations among large male groups. Young, white, American men dominate these groups, but they all include rainbow coalitions of sorts. *Ocean's Eleven* casts African Americans Don Cheadle and Bernie Mac, the young Chinese actor Shaobo Qin, and older Jewish actors Elliott Gould and Carl Reiner. The other neo-retro films similarly replace all-white casts with multiracial groups that variably include African Americans, Latino Americans, East and Southeast Asians, and Arabs. Though "remakes" only in the broadest sense, borrowing titles, characters, and kernels of plot from their predecessors, the films emphasize the camaraderie of men engaged in narrowly defined, extralegal enterprises. Generically, the heist film sets its male protagonists apart from the worlds of corporate work and the law, as well as from social institutions such as marriage and family. In *Ocean's Eleven* in particular, aside from a leading man whose romantic pursuits metonymically assure his teammates' heterosexuality, group members are wholly unencumbered by family or romantic ties.

With heist-film remakes blossoming in the early 2000s and the reworking of historical texts and styles across Soderbergh's filmography, we can locate neo-retro as a specific pop-cultural formation, as part of a generic cycle, and as a distinct feature of a Soderbergh sensibility. "Neo-retro" designates a mode of simultaneous transformation and recuperation. Contemporary heist films foreground in particular neo-retro configurations of masculinity, shaped around male group relationships. The neo-retro combination updates past sensibilities for contemporary tastes, either as a bulwark against perceived losses (i.e., a response to patriarchy's manufactured crises of masculinity) or as an accoutrement to refined social roles (a revival of old masculinities for a postfeminist age, for example). In his work on "new retro" cinema, Philip Drake identifies the retro film as one of multiple film subgenres capable of activating the past. Retro cinema, he argues, fuses past and present iconographies, accentuates "pastness" as a stylistic feature, and exploits that pastness to market films and ancillary products such as soundtracks.[31] *Ocean's Eleven* cohesively embodies each aspect of the retro sensibility Drake describes. The film updates Rat Pack iconography through an ingratiating model of onscreen playfulness that extratextual discourses link to stars' offscreen behavior, but that lacks the racial tokenism and misogynistic undercurrent that characterize the early-1960s Rat Pack films. Like some retro films, the neo-retro *Ocean's Eleven* continually measures its distance from the past—through arch, anti-naturalist performance and narrative emphasis on contemporary security technology—producing a sensibility forward-looking enough to sustain two more films.

The generic heist film uses a crime plot as a backdrop for semi-intimate relations among male professionals. Correspondingly, reception discourse frames the 2001 *Ocean's Eleven* as a vehicle for male group interactions. Major U.S. critics found the newer film relatively insubstantial, either blandly or deliciously superficial. Words such as "suaveness," "flair," and "polish" recur throughout reviews, as does the suggestion that the film is less about the complex heist that drives its narrative than about the easy, familiar interactions among its male principals.[32] Given its Rat Pack origins, one might expect the newer *Ocean's Eleven* to nostalgize the era of its predecessor or retread conservative positions about male bonding. However, its male groups and interactions are ultimately irreducible to such simple schemata. On one level, the cool relations among members of criminal groups in the neo-retro heist film work conservatively, reaffirming sanctioned boundaries of male homosocial interactions. These relationships also function progressively, positing an original configuration of male interaction inclusive of racially and ethnically marginal figures. The *Ocean's* films define their male group not by mutual antagonism and mistrust but by communalism and recognition of specialized abilities. With this group, the films shun the ruthless individualism and fatalism prevalent across thriller and crime-film modes. Fraternal conflicts instead turn on strategy decisions and on codes of male style. These codes, often expressed through clothing and comportment, make the group dynamics legible to viewers and facilitate the men's autonomy within and ultimate victories over inegalitarian institutions. In *Ocean's Eleven*, tycoon Terry Benedict and his casino's operations signify big business, class condescension, and affectlessness. The resourceful criminal group combats this adversary through deception, in particular repeated episodes of implausible, comic role-playing. Clothing and body language stand in for psychological and physical intensity, foregrounding layers of male performance. For example, in one scene Ocean and his second-in-command Rusty Ryan (Pitt) stage an argument for the benefit of one of their teammates. At another point Ocean receives an apparent beating in a camera-free room, but his assailant fakes the blows, exaggerating them through sound. Ocean's wrinkled clothes subsequently attest to his manhandling. Overall, the men's simulation of a range of generic male pursuits both defines their professional method and enables their fundamentally friendly interactions. Reviews' highlighting of such traits as flair and suaveness suggests the broad appeal of this mode of male engagement at the outset of the twenty-first century.

Ocean's Eleven anticipates as well the surveilling tendency that comes to define its cultural moment. Watching and being watched, particularly men watching men, are crucial to both the film's plot and its mise-en-scène. The film acknowledges the perils of visibility—the team must circumvent the many surveillance cameras that could detect their crime—but transforms them into benefits. Popular cinema typically gives viewers sustained visual access to a film's principals, and *Ocean's Eleven* makes stars' playing for the camera essential to its plot. The film renders star performances, and the accompanying performances of characters, as assertions of power, control, and agency. In its narrative construction, the film works to maintain all the characters' screen presences. In their DVD commentary, Soderbergh and screenwriter Ted Griffin note that they tried to construct the film so that each of the eleven would make an appearance at least every ten minutes in screen time.[33] The film still maintains a hierarchy based on stardom and white patriarchy: Ocean clearly leads, with Rusty as a near equal, and supporting actors' relative star power largely determines their centrality. At the same time, the film defines the group as an extralegal, utopian entity, somewhat removed from traditional social hierarchies. This implicit promise of relative equality suits the film's structural goal of maintaining the characters' screen presence. The narrative premise that the men regularly parade themselves in view of surveillance cameras suits this goal, too, and in doing so feeds into arguments about male visibility and display.

My reading of *Ocean's Eleven* positions it firmly within the categories of representation that scholars have routinely brought to bear on contemporary popular cinema. In its manifestations of male bonding and race relations, the film may be said to fulfill academic film critics' desires for progressive, if not outright utopian, representation. *Ocean's Eleven*'s neo-retro sensibility allows men to renew their dominance of the film frame, but only by adopting modified codes of style, performance, and fraternization. The film imagines a world in which self-conscious performance underwrites positive race relations and the transfer of wealth from the very privileged to men of other class positions. Ocean and his team use public performance as a form of subterfuge. This performance fuses classical gentlemanliness, contemporary metrosexual dress and grooming, a professionalism that crosses historical periods, and a leavening of arrested-adolescent antics. For Mac's character, onetime Atlantic City blackjack dealer Frank Catton, a double-consciousness performance of aggrieved blackness contributes as well to control of a contested space. After joining Ocean's team, Catton moves from being a low-level, service-industry worker to playing one, planting himself as a dealer in Benedict's Bellagio as part of the heist plan. (Later, in *Ocean's Thirteen*, he infiltrates Bank's casino by posing as a salesman of novelty slot machines.) In *Ocean's Eleven*, the team exploits Catton's subordinate status through a staged racial showdown. In Benedict's presence, Ocean accomplice Linus Caldwell (Damon) refers to Frank as "colored," producing a commotion during which Linus steals a passkey from Benedict. The film's one racially motivated conflict is thus performed and artificial, with the men using a camouflage of racism to achieve their shared goal. While the racial antagonism is staged, viewers may recognize Frank's outrage as an authentic response, a realist performance akin to Mac's own stand-up-comedy and television persona. In contrast, Rusty's arch caricatures of a federal agent and a local doctor in other scenes do not mobilize tropes of social inequity.

At the same time as *Ocean's Eleven* supports the conservative fantasy of vast wealth on conspicuous display, it challenges a conservative (or any prosocial) agenda by lionizing a criminal group. This mixed-race, mixed-ethnicity, mixed-age, extralegal male ensemble represents an original, vaguely utopian grouping. Still, the film does gesture toward conventional configurations of power. The sixty-something, Jewish Reuben Tishkoff represents property and finance: of all the men, only his home appears, and he funds and presides over the operation without actively participating in it. Moreover, in *Ocean's Thirteen*, Tishkoff's bilking at the hands of the more diabolical mogul Willy Bank mobilizes his old friends to restore his financial welfare (along with his mental health, imperiled by Bank's treachery). Tishkoff's friends rally to his aid, thus aiming to reinstate a more traditional Vegas entrepreneur. This restorative project also leaves out women entirely—"it's not their fight," Danny asserts with regard to Tess and Isabel, both of whom enjoyed more central roles in the con games of *Ocean's Twelve*. Also across the series, the Afro-British Basher Tarr (Cheadle) is less than fully integrated, marked as an outsider by his exaggerated accent and his slang discourse, though visually joining the group at regular intervals in keeping with the film's circulation project. Similarly, Qin's nearly silent role as Yen makes it easy for viewers to regard him as an inscrutable Oriental, though the films make sport of this typage as well. Most of Qin's rare lines of dialogue are delivered in untranslated Mandarin, though in *Ocean's Eleven* he speaks one line in English—"What the fuck?"—to comic effect, showing the film's minimal (if knowing) commitment to cross-cultural dialogue.

Ocean's Eleven uses its locations for multiple showcases and tests of masculinity. The film repeatedly delivers the runway-model spectacle of handsome, carefully attired men striding down well-lit corridors and across casino floors. The overarching remarriage plot mitigates this spectacle's homoeroticism, though that plot is itself a test of masculinity, pitting Ocean against Benedict. Consistent with popular representations generally, the spectacle favors white men. In contrast, Cheadle's role includes scenes of him emerging from a sewer caked in mud, and later, sitting alone in a hotel room. (*Ocean's Thirteen*, meanwhile, repeatedly shows him laboring over a large underground drill.) For his key contribution to the first film's heist, he appears alone in a long shot in an empty parking lot. In his roles as blackjack dealer, Mac is similarly static, standing behind a card table in a casino-issued outfit. He does wear a stylish, brightly colored suit for a scene in which he literally strong-arms a car dealer, but here, too, he remains virtually motionless. Black men provide the foundations for the heist, leaving their white partners free to range about with movie-star panache. The very presence of African Americans (and to a much lesser extent, of the Chinese character Yen) signifies the hip multiculturalism of the otherwise white group, allowing the film to parcel out physical command of space to actors Clooney, Pitt, Damon, and Reiner. As the Bellagio's owner, Benedict also commands physical space, but the film marks this authority as illegitimate, based on tightly wound severity rather than carefully but casually managed style. Ocean's clothes, including the tuxedo he often wears, are modishly rumpled, and Rusty favors inelegantly wide collars and wears a sport coat and tie only in his deliberately clichéd disguises. Benedict's style is more inflexible, his gait purposeful rather than relaxed, and he is ultimately undone by a too-candid performance captured on his hotel's security cameras, in which he reveals his largely mercenary interest in Tess. His loss of command spurs Tess's departure from the casino, filmed in a long tracking shot; prior to this scene, she appears only within the Bellagio interior.

Ocean's Eleven's climactic events depend on performance and masquerade, and in particular on malleable white masculinity. To extricate themselves from the casino vault they penetrate, some of the men don the black jumpsuits and facemasks of SWAT commandos, temporarily hiding their features. Meanwhile, other group members, including the black men Frank and Basher, remain in a hotel suite, watching the staged action on a video monitor. Here the film partly contests the convention of representation in which white men savor the limelight while nonwhites are subjected to a punitive, emasculating gaze. Instead, black men watch from a safe distance. However disguised, white men are central to the film, upholding a racial hierarchy more retro than neo. Despite periodic incursions from black and East Asian men, white men dominate visual and narrative space. They can be chameleon-like in their shifts of identity (as are Rusty, Linus, and Casey Affleck and Scott Caan's clownish Malloy brothers) or fully on display (as is Danny, who plants himself at a casino bar before his role in the heist, and later allows himself to be arrested). In all, they bear out Richard Dyer's observation that white men—despite their apparent racial invisibility and their definition in relation to other races rather than through essential characteristics—remain "at the centre of global representation."[34] Across the *Ocean's* franchise, flexibility of personal style guarantees this centrality, as white men are able to mobilize a range of charismatic personas irrespective of social class while evading the grasp of authoritarian institutions.

We can conclude this textual interrogation with attention to two disparate moments in *Ocean's Eleven* that exemplify the film's treatment of male looking and race-based style. The first is Danny Ocean's release from prison, which actually occurs twice, both at the beginning and end of the film. Both times he wears a tuxedo, indicating a festive situation preceding his internment. The film also takes a casual view of incarceration by not showing the prison itself. The opening scene depicts Danny speaking before his parole board, but the camera remains in a medium-long shot on him, never cutting to his questioners. Thus, *Ocean's Eleven* maintains the genre-film fantasy that repeated prison terms need not encroach measurably on a man's personal style.

White men in the *Ocean's* series respond to social control by dressing up and putting on a show. The films' black men, laboring in popular representation under the legacy of minstrelsy, negotiate social control in different ways. *Ocean's Eleven*'s other notable synthesis of style, race, and the look occurs midway through the film, and accompanies the public spectacle of the destruction of the fictional Xanadu Hotel. While Danny and Rusty stand in a crowd witnessing the demolition, Basher views it from a hotel room. Given his role as the team's explosives expert, professional curiosity could motivate his viewing. Sitting on a couch in an undershirt, he watches the event on television, though one shot shows the hotel fully visible through the window behind him. Aside from its visual irony, the brief scene suggests that this black character prefers the mediated spectacle to the unmediated view; this preference joins him thematically with his surveillance-conscious white teammates. Moreover, the scene hints at the possibilities of black use of media technology, particularly as a means to upset power. The demolition causes a temporary power surge, inspiring Basher's plan to stage the citywide blackout that serves as a diversion for the heist. The viewing of the demolition marks his literal turning away from destruction, as he instead pursues an undamaging use of technology. This insight occurs in an exceedingly casual setting, with Basher lounging on the couch half-dressed, and thus embodying a male style distinct from the upper-class leisure style favored by the white stars.

Though Soderbergh's and others' commentaries do not touch on the racial connotations of the film's style politics, these representations still circulate in a cultural milieu in which race matters a great deal, and in a context of film representation where fictional characters' activities are routinely presented and received in strongly racial terms. Progressively and conservatively, *Ocean's Eleven* merges its inflections of style into a coherent representation of uncompetitive male solidarity. The film and its sequels finally withhold substantive critiques of inegalitarian social institutions and belief systems. Nevertheless, they demonstrate that popular cinema's representation of masculinity need not depend on violence, suffering, misogyny, or racial scapegoating.

We should ask in closing, why does representation matter to authorship, or authorship to representation? Sharon Willis, building on James Naremore's work, observes that investments in auteurs relate in part to:

> anchoring filmic production to a social location through its point of enunciation. Such an anchoring, significantly, allows for and encourages the formation of collective cultural solidarities organized around author figures.[35]

In his preceding piece, Naremore argues specifically that "[m]arginalized social groups can declare solidarity and create a collective identity by adopting authors as cultural heroes."[36] Even if not possessed of marginal status, academics and other readers of films can impose twin frames of authorship and culture onto their viewing experiences as means of discerning coherent artistry as well as coherent understandings of a culture's articulations. Attributing representation to a designated author-filmmaker merges these impulses, in turn fostering additional reading protocols. Popular cinema's familiar, idiomatic language and often-illusionistic style can encourage beliefs that films express the concerns of a given sociocultural moment. Locating films in prescribed cultural terms helps grant them significance, justifying or rewarding responses that involve critical reasoning. Similarly, as argued across this volume, by recognizing authors, viewers position themselves in particular taste cultures. Reception practices attuned to authorship and representation maintain appeal even as idiosyncratic artistic decisions, collaborative compromises, and purely commercial imperatives may more powerfully influence industry practice and film content. U.S. film-industry creative practice bears the legacy of its former Fordist production system, contributing to a stylistic baseline that encourages viewers to identify patterns in representation across films.

Specific efforts to create textual affiliations to diverse demographics also motivate production decisions about film content. Willis reminds us of "representations that strive to accommodate diversity through scripts organized around specific identities and intended to capture new identity-based market segments."[37] These contexts are worth bearing in mind when examining Soderbergh's films or the work of other anointed auteur filmmakers.

The above approaches to the *Ocean's* films, and the preceding perspectives on *Erin Brockovich, Out of Sight,* and other works, demonstrate different ways to process popular texts made under the stewardship of a particular author-director. These approaches show that Soderbergh-directed features reward varying forms of close analysis, and that the significance of collaboratively authored popular films can be mapped in many ways. Some but not all clusters of meaning can be traced back to particular authorial strategies. We can separate representation from other approaches to screen study but should acknowledge its dependence on a breadth of industrial and social phenomena. As we have seen, production resources and cultural norms are powerful determinants of representational choices, as are genre imperatives. Generic parameters for narrative structure, character typology, iconography, and more contribute to codes of representation. In turn, tropes of representation maintain currency thanks to their recurrence in genre cycles. Other industrial phenomena such as remakes and adaptations also enable the persistence of particular treatments of social categories. The next chapter turns to the abundant genre films, remakes, and adaptations among Soderbergh's filmography. These forms bring together diverse intertexts that further inform our understanding of industrial, artistic, and cultural processes.

Chapter 6
Intertextual Conversations
Genre, Adaptations, and Remakes

Soderbergh's many adaptations of novels and other preexisting texts, as well as his direction of numerous remakes of earlier Hollywood and international films, represent a core component of his diffuse artistic imprint. His diverse creative work in screen and print media constitutes a series of dialogues—with collaborators on particular screen projects, with fellow filmmakers past and present, and with numerous eras and movements in U.S. and global film culture. Creative dialogue around existing cultural texts and generic fields demonstrates shared investments in particular artistic expressions, investments motivated by taste and cinephilia as well as by artistic processes involving elaboration on preexisting aesthetic modes. As for other creative artists, Soderbergh's activity in the intertextual spaces of genre, adaptation, and remake reveals the overlapping investments of the filmmaker and the film lover. In reworking existing print, screen, and other source material, Soderbergh joins ongoing conversations about cultural materials in which fellow artists, commentators, active fans, and other receivers also participate. Notably, all of Soderbergh's remakes and adaptations also belong to recognizable genres or cycles. Even *Gray's Anatomy*, the screen version of Spalding Gray's stage production, joins the mini-cycle of film adaptations of Gray's monologues.[1] Industrial, textual, and reception contexts often frame genre films and remakes in comparable terms. In his work on film remakes, Constantine Verevis builds on genre scholarship to articulate the shared features of both categories. For Verevis, remakes and genres both depend on "the existence of audience activity,"[2] including "not only prior knowledge of previous texts and intertextual relationships, but an understanding of broader generic structures and categories."[3] Among their other properties, genres and remakes contribute to industrial, intertextual, intercultural, and reception dialogues. These dialogues broaden networks of film-cultural agents, and in all of them, collaborating authors such as Soderbergh serve as key participants and intermediaries.

This chapter approaches processes of repetition and adaptation as authorial practices, and as forms through which authorial markers arise and circulate in screen cultures. Remaking, adaptation, and genre-film production have been understood as industrial strategies for managing risk through the reliance on standardized production formulas. These formulas can capitalize on preexisting public interest, extending recognizable and thus pre-sold properties such as popular novels, preceding screen texts, or historically successful genres. Remaking and adaptation further activate reception discourses, particularly around issues of perceived originality or fidelity to source text. Verevis notes that discourse such as film reviews can "stabilise the point of origin,"[4] thus fixing intertexts in particular cultural positions. In the various framings of remade or adapted texts, intertextual relays manage textual relationships but also attributions of authorship. Critical and other reception discourses position directors (and less often, screenwriters) as intermediary figures in intertextual relays. If the newer filmmakers enjoy an existing authorial profile such as a persistent designation as an auteur, they can receive attention as key creative agents motivating remake or adaptation activity and responsible for some portion of a newer text's content.

Genres, adaptations, and remakes participate in different kinds of standardized systems. In the spaces they create, terms of authorship can be deployed to attribute creative origins and recraftings, and to lend symbolic value that distinguishes individual films. For genre films that are also remakes, authorial markings become one of many features distinguishing the multiple versions of a text. Rick Altman observes that not only genre films but also genres themselves arise and persist thanks to the efforts of particular agents and groups. In his formulation, "[a]ll genre terms are implicitly authored; that is, they are always the product of a specific user group."[5] While these groups include film viewers as well as producers, I will concentrate here on ways filmmakers, in films under their collaborative control and in extratextual discourses, explicitly articulate interest in and stimulate activity around genre films and other precursor texts. For Soderbergh in particular, genres and other adaptable source material become crucial to an authorial profile, not subordinated to a persona framed around individual artistic genius or otherwise disengaged from industries, cultures, and precursor texts. He told an interviewer in 1993, "I don't consider myself an artist or a visionary. [Unlike those] who push the film language, who bend and twist the medium to suit their vision . . . I'm a chameleon. Style is secondary to me."[6] By labeling himself a "chameleon," he promotes elasticity and awareness of surrounding terrain as key features of his authorial style. Like many other contemporary screen authors, Soderbergh presents an authorial silhouette defined not in isolation but specifically in relation to other films, intertexts, and aesthetic strategies. He also participates actively in the circulation of this silhouette. Genres provide screen authors a means for self-promotion. They also facilitate the development of collaborative and dialogic authorial signatures. As they evolve, these signatures can refer not only to particular films' elaboration on preexisting texts and contexts but also to the overarching explication of an authoring persona initially called into existence through discourse around a successful film. (In Soderbergh's case, the debut feature *sex, lies, and videotape* sets this discourse in motion.) As genre work, remakes, and adaptations constitute the majority of Soderbergh's filmmaking output over time, intertextual dialogues and contexts may be seen not as extensions of his authorial signature but as its very core.

Artistic production within the spaces of genres and adaptations can represent a form of cross-historical or cross-media collaboration. Contemporary filmmakers engage with generic and discursive fields delineated by prior generations of artists and by continuously active cultural agents such as fans, reviewers, and historians. Soderbergh's work within generic fields links him in numerous ways to the New Hollywood forebears with whom he has expressed creative kinship. David Cook argues that "[t]he return to genre production [in the 1970s] grew out of the preoccupation of New Hollywood auteurs with film history and film form."[7] Cook further argues that the 1970s films and filmmakers lay the foundations for contemporary Hollywood's genre films, particularly generically hybridized ones. In all, Soderbergh's work in genres and his penchant for remakes and adaptations exemplify routine practice in contemporary Hollywood. At the same time, Soderbergh's films' intertextual properties and chosen source texts display an idiosyncratic sensibility unique to contemporary cinema. His reworking of existing material constitutes neither romantic homage nor ironic postmodern inversion, but a use of historically significant texts and movements in filmmaking and other art forms as raw materials for experiments with film form, narrative, and audience expectations. Soderbergh has repeatedly stressed the collaborative nature of his own screen practice.

His experimentation takes a similarly collaborative form, proceeding through dialogue with preexisting works of Hollywood and global cinema, popular literature, and popular film genres. His generic works, adaptations, and remakes represent interventions into global film history and film culture. These activities mark him as an artistic interlocutor, a creative artist in dialogue with diverse collaborators and a breadth of preexisting artworks. Soderbergh's remakes and adaptations position him alongside corpuses of filmmakers working in different and varied traditions: classical studio workers such as Michael Curtiz, art-cinema figures such as Andrei Tarkovsky, the British television producers of the prestige miniseries *Traffik*, and the legions of contemporary documentarians, directors of literary and theatrical adaptations, and more.

Altman reminds us that genres emerge and develop through a series of dialogues involving producing institutions, textual artifacts and surrounding promotional ephemera, institutional intermediaries such as reviewers, and viewers. For Altman, screen genres can spur the emergence of "generic communities" composed of invested viewers. In practice, these groups operate as "constellated communities" whose "members cohere only through repeated acts of imagination."[8] Constellated communities exist through their members' direct or imagined dialogues with one another. Dialogues around particular texts, generic corpuses, and filmmakers both designate participants as cinephiles (or at least as viewers with particular taste investments) and hail into being the communities themselves. Though filmmakers do not feature specifically in Altman's formulation, they belong to constellated, generic communities as well, as creative workers engaging productively with generic material and as themselves viewers of genre texts. Like other members of generic communities, filmmakers such as Soderbergh contribute to various constellations through discursive investments in individual screen artifacts, production cycles, and genres. More significantly, as a screen author, Soderbergh shares with the constellated community his material output of highly intertextual, cinephilic genre films. Filmmakers' participation in generic communities as both producers and consumers of generically affiliated texts underscores the thoroughly dialogic nature of screen authorship. Authorial dialogues can incorporate transhistorical, interpersonal, and international dimensions, linking films and filmmakers across historical periods and geographical spaces.

To account for the intersection of generic registers and adaptation methods in Soderbergh's filmography, the following two sections draw conclusions about groups of Soderbergh-directed films organized into generic or modal clusters. These clusters, broadly defined, take in Expressionism and film noir (*Kafka, The Underneath,* and *The Good German*) and crime and corporate-whistleblower films (*Out of Sight, The Limey,* and the *Ocean's* trilogy in the former category, and *Erin Brockovich* and *The Informant!* in the latter). Even these large categories overlap in some instances: *The Underneath,* for example, is both a heist film and a remake of a 1949 film noir; the revenge drama *The Limey* can be framed as a crime film and an update of styles and motifs from the 1967 neo-noir *Point Blank;* and *The Informant!* could itself be categorized as a species of crime film, as its protagonist is both whistle-blower and criminal. I use these groupings, though, to draw attention to the range of artistic maneuvers possible within the broad categories of adaptation, remaking, and intertextuality. After remarking on Soderbergh's authorial strategies in these works, I turn to sustained discussion of a film marked as both adaptation and remake, the science-fiction romance *Solaris.* I emphasize Soderbergh's collaborative authorship of the 2002 film, focusing on industrial context, textual features, and its relationship to its precursor texts. Like the other genre-film adaptations interrogated in this chapter, *Solaris* showcases a range of textual, intertextual, and authorial strategies. *Solaris* and other works demonstrate how acts of adaptation and generic production can also be acts of authorship. For Soderbergh, these acts constitute dialogues with and interventions into multiple realms of film culture. They exemplify further an authorial strategy distinguished by continuous engagement with film history and wider spheres of popular-culture production.

Soderbergh's Intertextual Activity 1: Expressionism and Film Noir

Expressionism encapsulates a broad current of artistic pursuits: from 1910s and 1920s German visual art, theatre, and then film; to its later American variants in 1940s film noir; to various revivals and reimaginings across media and art forms. In cinema, Expressionist works have long served as points of entry, gateway drugs of a sort, combining bold images and classical storytelling. As staples of university and film-school curricula, such films as *The Cabinet of Dr. Caligari* (1920), *Nosferatu,* and *Metropolis* (1927) have alerted countless viewers to cinema's expressive possibilities, permitting recognition of distinctive styles not necessarily tethered to major studios' assembly-line practices (notwithstanding the fact of Expressionist films' production by studios such as UFA, Nero-Film, and Decla-Bioscop). A discrete artistic movement that contributed to the long-lived mode of film noir, Expressionism remains, with early-Hollywood narrative in the classical-continuity style and Soviet montage, one of the major artistic legacies of global cinema's first mass-production era of the 1910s and 1920s.

With Soderbergh's own film education occurring largely outside academia, his sophomore feature *Kafka* arguably represents his first sustained engagement with a specific, canonized era of film history. *Kafka* positions Soderbergh in relation to multiple European artistic contexts. In cinema, it connects him to Expressionism as well as what might be termed European noir, with the British film *The Third Man* a particular stylistic reference point; and in literature, to German-language modernism, among other contexts to which the Prague-born Kafka might be assigned. The film also acquaints him with European talent pools, its cast including British stars Jeremy Irons and Alec Guinness, Holland's Jeroen Krabbé, and Germany's Armin Mueller-Stahl. In addition, it brings him to European production sites, with shooting in Prague and London. *Kafka* occupies too the generic field of the artist biopic, a loose constellation of texts institutionalized in myriad ways in different national cinemas. In sum, *Kafka* evidences Soderbergh in a creative dialogue that spans continents, media, historical epochs, and genres and modes. *Kafka*'s relationship to Expressionism and to its literary subject are explicit in visual, biographical, and geographical terms: it uses the black-and-white photography and chiaroscuro lighting characteristic of Expressionist film, and it merges elements of Franz Kafka's fictions with an embellished narrative of the writer's actual time working at an insurance company in Prague.

As *Kafka* explicitly engages with 1920s Expressionist film style, Soderbergh's later investment in the post-Expressionist tradition of film noir indicates a consistent artistic trajectory. Film noir enjoys a beloved status among cinephiles, filmmakers, and historians and has amassed a voluminous critical and popular literature. The category includes, formatively, a set of 1940s and 1950s U.S. films, augmented from the mid-1960s onward by numerous remakes, homages, and reworkings (including such films as *The Killers* [1964], *Chinatown* [1974], *Body Heat* [1981], and legions more). Creative screen work in the space of noir or neo-noir now involves participation in not only a genre or mode but also a group of discourses. Writing on noir remakes, Verevis argues that "the 'idea' of *film noir* is sustained through specific discursive formations," and thus "an understanding of *film noir* and its 1980s remakes (and beyond) resides primarily in the determination

of a discursive structure, in issues of cultural history and memory."[9]
For Verevis, *Body Heat*, as part-remake of *Double Indemnity* (1944)
and borrower of other noir devices, "does not recreate a (pseudo)
period setting but rather *reinvents* the *film noir*, plundering a *critical*
genre to promulgate a stylised, *industrial* cycle of neo-*noir*."[10] While
less self-conscious in its appropriations than *Body Heat*, Soderbergh's
The Underneath participates in this industrial cycle as well as in the
expanded noir discourse.

As mentioned in Chapter 1, *The Underneath* remakes the 1949 film
noir *Criss Cross*, or from another vantage point, both films adapt Don
Tracy's 1934 novel *Criss Cross*. The Soderbergh-directed film borrows
considerably more from its 1949 screen predecessor than from Tracy's
novel, and the development narrative for the Soderbergh version frames
it also as a film remake rather than a literary adaptation. Soderbergh
reports anecdotally in a 1995 interview, "Universal called me to say
they were thinking about remaking *Criss Cross*."[11] He observes in the
same interview, "I had written the script based on Don Tracy's novel
and on Daniel Fuchs's script for the first version of the film,"[12] but
makes no further reference to Tracy's source text. *The Underneath*'s
writing credits include both Tracy and Fuchs, while Soderbergh, owing
to a Writers Guild dispute, receives screenplay credit under the pseudonym Sam Lowry.[13] All three texts narrate a luckless protagonist's
efforts to revive his relationship with his ex-lover by helping execute an
armored-car heist alongside her new, criminal paramour.[14] (Character
names vary across the three versions.) In all of them, the protagonist tries to double-cross the criminal, and vice versa. In the Robert
Siodmak-directed 1949 film, in fatalist but Production Code–respecting
fashion, the criminal kills the couple but then faces imminent arrest.
In the 1934 and 1995 versions, the protagonist manages to kill his
rival, but the ex-wife double-crosses them both. In Tracy's novel, she
last appears *in flagrante delicto* with the protagonist's younger brother.
In Soderbergh's film, she passes her ex the gun that allows him to kill
the criminal, but then leaves her immobilized ex to face the messy
consequences of the shooting. She absconds with the remaining spoils
of the heist, and the final scene shows this de facto femme fatale being
tracked by the armored-car company boss, now revealed as a ruthless
criminal himself.

Beyond tracking the three texts' plot permutations, we can address
The Underneath's participation in the extended dialogue that con-
stitutes the film-noir mode. *The Underneath* tells us something of
Soderbergh's artistic choices—both in accepting Universal's offer to

revive its property *Criss Cross* and in the production work of screen-writing and directing—as well as demonstrating the highly inter- and transtextual nature of his evolving artistic voice. In Gérard Genette's formulation, transtextuality designates "all that sets the text in a relationship, whether obvious or concealed, with other texts,"[15] including explicit, acknowledged adaptations as well as intertextual homages, metatextual connections based on critics' or other receivers' inferences, and myriad other correspondences across textual and discursive fields. *The Underneath* engages with film noir through multiple registers: through the reconstitution of Tracy's hard-boiled novel and its initial film-noir adaptation, through a thematic emphasis on fatalism, and through noir narrative staples such as the ordinary man drawn into underworld activity and the alluring, scheming femme fatale.

While tethered to film noir through numerous transtextual relationships, *The Underneath* displaces itself from canonical noir (as well as much neo-noir) through geographic relocation, narrative idiosyncrasies, and an updated toolkit for formal expressiveness. Bypassing the stock noir setting of the nocturnal metropolis such as *Criss Cross*'s Los Angeles, *The Underneath* is set and filmed in the medium-sized city of Austin, Texas, including scenes filmed at the music venue Emo's (renamed "Embers" in the film) in the city's popular Sixth Street district and another in the Town Lake Park area, locations that do not evoke the hopelessness and cynicism motoring traditional noir. Despite its Texas setting, Soderbergh's film does not portray the region as desolate, arid, and lawless, tropes informing such southwestern noirs as *Border Incident* (1949) and neo-noirs such as *Blood Simple* (1984). Instead, *The Underneath*'s setting allows the presentation of sun-dappled, atmospherically warm exteriors, taking advantage of the region's climate and lighting effects. At the same time, the film revisits classical noir's stylization, using (as noted in Chapter 1) an anti-realist color palette that emphasizes artificial greens and cobalt blues. Thus, the film displays Soderbergh's evolving authorial style through reworking of source material, variation on classical noir settings and thematics, and fabrication (abetted by cinematographer Elliot Davis) of a novel color world. An updated character motivation furthers the film's elaboration on classical noir templates: the protagonist's relationship has failed because of his compulsive sports gambling, and this original backstory explains his reckless decisions in the present-tense narrative as well as the pleasures he derives from risk-taking. *The Underneath* also offers a familial subtext, with the protagonist's mother playing the lottery, and, like her son, desiring material gratification in the form of a giant-screen television. In a slight departure from classical noir's pervasive cynicism, then, Soderbergh's screenplay attributes corrosive tendencies to particular characters rather than to an entire social milieu.

Following *The Underneath*, Soderbergh directed numerous crime films—*Out of Sight* and the *Ocean's* films in particular—but did not return to strongly noir-inflected territory until 2006's *The Good German*. As discussed in Chapter 3, *The Good German* shows Soderbergh in dialogue with the European noir *The Third Man* as well as with the classical-Hollywood wartime romance *Casablanca*. In combining these diverse traditions, *The Good German* underscores the transhistorical and global nature of intertextual conversations. The film also showcases technology and craftspeople as agents of intertextual dialogues. Its participation in a transatlantic film-historical dialogue occurs not only through textual and generic attributes but also in the use of archival footage and vintage filmmaking equipment. The film's visual and sonic language explicitly engages with historical material, which it positions amid contemporary cinema's codes and practices. The film does not use 1940s cameras or film stock, for example, and while initially released in 35mm prints, it has circulated most widely in the DVD format of course unavailable to 1940s distributors (though the 1940s films it mimics also now circulate principally in DVD rather than 35mm format as well). The earlier *The Underneath* finds Soderbergh and his collaborators working to contemporize the visual field of classical noir, substituting stylized color contrasts for the historical mode's high-contrast black and white. *The Good German*, meanwhile, seeks to replicate a historical mode, albeit with the creative contributions of present-day artists and performers.

While framed by critics and by Soderbergh in interviews as a work indebted to previous films and filmmakers, *The Good German* is also a literary adaptation, bringing to the screen Joseph Kanon's 2001 novel of the same title. Kanon's historical thriller itself bears comparisons to the works of earlier writers such as Eric Ambler and Graham Greene. Owing to its past setting and imperiled-journalist plot, it may be regarded as a nostalgic production, reviving past narrative modes and tones to craft appeals to twenty-first-century readerships. Kanon's novel narrates the return of a U.S. journalist, Jake Geismar, to Berlin at the end of World War II, where he rekindles a relationship with Lena Brandt, with whom he had had a romantic entanglement before the war. The novel thematizes journalistic ethics as well as the complexities of wartime collaboration. In pursuing Lena anew, Geismar becomes embroiled in political and military intrigue involving Nazi war crimes and U.S.

and Soviet plots to export and employ German scientists, including Lena's fugitive husband. The Lena of Soderbergh's film, based on Paul Attanasio's screenplay, absorbs key aspects of two of the novel's other female characters: Lena's prostitute roommate, Hannelore; and Renate, a Jewish worker at Geismar's office before the war who turns informant to protect herself.[16] The film's Lena is herself a cold-hearted prostitute and, as revealed in the final scene, a Jewish informant reporting fellow Jews to the Nazis. Also diverging from the novel, the film makes Lena the perpetrator of the murder that sets both versions' thriller plots in motion. In another departure, in the film Lena's husband is killed in a climactic scene, so her efforts on his behalf are rendered entirely futile. Screenplay and film transform Lena from the bruised innocent of the novel into a complex (if confused) embodiment of the situational ethics practiced by some Germans seeking to survive Nazism. Meanwhile, the profiteering young soldier, Tully, who appears briefly in the novel before turning up dead becomes in the film a central character, still a minor criminal out of his depth but also a violent adversary to Geismar and a cruel sugar daddy to Lena.

Overall, Kanon's 500-page novel shows strong investments in the moral history of civilians and governments during and after World War II, building its interrogation of this subject around a murder narrative whose resolution implicates American politicians and American and Russian military officers (though placing specific blame on a high-ranking American officer). The sprawling novel also narrates a renewed romantic and erotic relationship between Lena and Geismar. The film condenses the multiple narrative strands but also eliminates the novel's sunnier elements, including many warm scenes between Lena and Geismar, who remain coupled at the end; and the optimistic symbol of Renate's young child entrusted to the care of a German-Jewish camp survivor who manages to leave the country thanks to Geismar's intervention. The film's Geismar is far less resourceful than the novel's, and Lena becomes an overdetermined fallen woman: a murderer and informant, but also a rape victim and a survivor who risks her life in vain for her husband. In this the film accords with the Hollywood convention of making characters vessels for multiple ideologies and historical conditions, but it also retains the novel's emphasis on moral ambiguity. Framed as a product of Soderbergh's sensibilities, the film continues a pattern across his work of foregrounding doomed romances. His and Attanasio's version of the story focuses on interpersonal conflict rather than larger historical forces, and intervenes much more strongly into intertextual film dialogues than into historical ones concerning the volatile aftermath of the war.

To view adaptation in terms of authorship, we must consider artistic motivations alongside textual evidence. Robert Stam observes that "[f]ilm adaptations can be seen as a kind of multileveled negotiation of intertexts."[17] Situated in the spheres of World War II–themed fiction and popular-literature thrillers more broadly, Kanon's novel engages with a far different range of intertexts and contexts than does the Soderbergh-directed film. Both works participate in processes Stam terms "intertextual dialogism," or "the infinite and open-ended possibilities generated by all the discursive practices of a culture, the entire matrix of communicative utterances within which the artistic text is situated, which read the text not only through recognizable influences, but also through a subtle process of dissemination."[18] In his involvement with the adaptation of Kanon's novel, Soderbergh brings to bear his own artistic influences and predilections, steering the intertextual dialogue toward areas of film style and technology and largely away from questions of politics and historical understanding. As with *The Underneath*, and to an extent *Kafka* as well, Soderbergh's formal engagements occur through narratives that combine crime-thriller plotlines with troubled romances. These three films thus operate in terrain long demarcated by Expressionism and film noir: expressive imagery not strongly fixed to historical reality, and psychological states with real-world corollaries but realized onscreen with a marked degree of ambivalence and unease.

Soderbergh's Intertextual Activity 2: Crime and Crimestoppers

A second discernible generic strand in Soderbergh's adaptation activity encompasses a range of crime narratives. These include numerous comic caper films (*Out of Sight* and the three *Ocean's* films), stylized dramas with lawbreakers as vengeful protagonists (*The Limey*) or profit-minded antagonists (*Traffic*), and two corporate-whistleblower biopics (*Erin Brockovich* and *The Informant!*).[19] To varying degrees, each extends Soderbergh's interest in film language and genre, engaging with a range of filmmaking styles and generic discourses as well as often adapting preexisting literary, film, or television texts. Each of the films also deepens Soderbergh's investment in character and interpersonal relationships, with romantic entanglements and family conflicts intensifying the films' crime and crime-detection narratives. If considered together for their positions regarding individuals and institutions, or regarding law, the state, and extralegal activity, we can identify across the texts a coherent artistic worldview, a set of creative concerns that animates Soderbergh's diverse production activity.

To frame Soderbergh's crime-related films, we might look, perhaps counterintuitively, to the 2008 epic *Che* as a map of the filmmaker's social and political consciousness. With Che Guevara's published diaries forming the basis for a screenplay by Peter Buchman (co-credited to Benjamin A. van der Veen for *Che: Part Two*), *Che* evidences Soderbergh's major commitment to global geopolitical issues in historical context. The film portrays the charismatic but aloof revolutionary leader whose explicit Marxist ideology supplies a catalyst for discussion of social inequality, exploitation, and the ethics of violence. Soderbergh's earlier *Traffic*, adapted from the 1989 British Channel 4 miniseries *Traffik*, poses similar questions about political violence in the Americas, if containing these in the more generically familiar forms of family melodrama, political film, and police-investigation narrative. While *Che* and *Traffic* deliver a far more realist textuality than the antic *Out of Sight* or the *Ocean's* films, the dramas show Soderbergh's capacity to render a combination of law-breaking and law-abiding characters drawn from preexisting texts. Even the more fanciful crime films articulate Soderbergh's abiding interest in questions of power and inequity, though members of subordinate groups receive far different treatment in the glossy *Ocean's* films than in the guerrilla undertaking *Che*. Ultimately, each of the Soderbergh-directed films involving crime or anti-state violence depicts creative responses to economic and technological challenges, whether those challenges involve executing high-risk heists, moving cocaine across national borders, or mounting a socialist revolution.

Nearly all of Soderbergh's features dealing with violent crime or other illegal activity derive from preexisting source material, and most operate within clear genre parameters for crime, caper, or corporate-whistleblower films. Of the last category, *Erin Brockovich* merges whistleblower-biopic and melodrama sensibilities, locating it alongside such films as *Silkwood* (1983), *A Civil Action* (1998), and *The Insider* (1999). The later *The Informant!* mines the latent humor of its nonfiction source, creating a curious hybrid of serious nonfiction and film comedy. The crime and caper films revisit existing print or film texts, enabling Soderbergh to participate in widely or subculturally venerated realms of pop-culture production. With *Out of Sight*, as already noted, he joins the ranks of major filmmakers adapting Leonard's novels; and with *Ocean's Eleven* and its sequels, he engages with the buddy-ensemble tradition emblematized by the 1960 *Ocean's Eleven* and its Rat Pack cast. Soderbergh's work on these studio-produced crime films represents a commercial decision as well, albeit one he couched in artistic terms before production of the 2001 film: "*Ocean's Eleven* will be the apex of my yielding to whatever populist instincts I might have. This will be potentially the most indulgent I'll ever be toward that side of my personality."[20] Through crime films, such populist impulses have repeatedly earned filmmakers critical acclaim as well. Long after the *Cahiers du cinéma* critics' championing of filmmakers such as *Scarface* (1932) director Howard Hawks and international acclaim in the 1960s for French New Wave crime films such as *A bout de souffle* (1960), crime films have provided sites for myriad artistic dialogues, even as they speak, too, to mass audiences through generic attributes. As discussed in Chapter 2, *The Limey* stages an intertextual dialogue with such films as Ken Loach's *Poor Cow* and the John Boorman-directed *Point Blank*. However, it is principally the film's genre-affiliated revenge plot, rather than its nonlinear structure or intertextual links to 1960s films, that encourages its release by genre-film producer-distributor Artisan and its moderate box-office success. Overall, crime films in diverse forms constitute a set of genres (gangster, detective, and police films, and more) that have served as the staging ground for countless commercially viable as well as critically esteemed films across the medium's history. In turning repeatedly to this category, Soderbergh demonstrates to producing industries, critical institutions, and filmgoing communities his capacity for creative work that bridges categories of elite and popular taste.

Moreover, in both working in a generic mode and adapting or remaking preexisting texts, Soderbergh's creative practice depends strongly on collaborations—with writers and filmmakers across cultural eras and with the multiple individuals, groups, and institutions that make up generic communities. His authoring role involves the orchestration of intertexts and collaborators into discrete new works. Linda Hutcheon, writing on "multilaminated" adaptations involving multiple sources, argues that such texts "are directly and openly connected to recognizable other works, and that connection is part of their formal identity, but also of what we might call their hermeneutic identity."[21] Presiding over adaptations of novels such as Leonard's *Out of Sight* or nonfiction works such as Kurt Eichenwald's 2000 business exposé *The Informant*, Soderbergh articulates a shaping sensibility yet does not radically reinvent the precursor texts. Both films maintain the narrative events, overall formal structure, and much dialogue of the texts they adapt while adding stylistic and tonal embellishments that situate the films in particular screen-art constellations. The adapted *Out of Sight*, for example, includes virtually every scene and line of dialogue from Leonard's screenplay-ready novel but adds nonlinear flashbacks and freeze frames, devices later used in *The Limey* and *Ocean's Eleven* as well. (It also adds an optimistic, audience-friendly coda, suggesting the possibility of its protagonist's future escape from prison and continuation of a romance with the comely federal marshal who has captured him.)

The Informant!, meanwhile, by adding a telling exclamation point to the book's title, hints at both the streamlining of the 650-page book to feature length and the molding of a narrative of colossal corporate crime, personal hubris, and investigatory missteps into a brisk, semi-absurdist comedy. Working from the largely transcribed dialogues of Eichenwald's book, Scott Burns's screenplay lends whimsical voice-overs to the delusional protagonist, Mark Whitacre, and generates a Keystone Kops atmosphere for the FBI and Justice Department agents pursuing the case. In his Blu-ray disc commentary with Burns for the film, Soderbergh identifies numerous ways Eichenwald's book grounds the production. Regarding the actors' and crew's preparations, he notes, "We all had our copies of the book, and it was a great way, if you needed it, to get some instant context for the scene that you were doing."[22] Soderbergh notes, too, the book's suitability for film comedy. He observes that its narrative structure features "a classic building block of comedy, the escalating lie," and asserts later that "the way [Eichenwald] wrote that book is really cinematic—the way he releases information is really smart." In this respect, the film follows the book's method of disclosure. Eichenwald's *The Informant* is more a chronology of revelations than a linear recounting of events. For example, readers learn late in the text of Whitacre's victimization in an e-mail scam that had begun years before the events that open the book. Whitacre himself divulges this information to his FBI contacts and to Eichenwald long after their initial conversations as well. The structures of both book and film thus chart the mutations of narrative that can occur in discourse among differently empowered historical actors.

The retention and manipulation of source material across a series of collaborations reinforces Hutcheon's further claim that "[a]daptation is not only a formal entity . . . it is also a process."[23] Soderbergh's collaborations with fellow film artists and technicians have distilled crime narratives into screen forms appropriate to the crimes' gravity. Adapting previous works of fiction, *Out of Sight* and the *Ocean's* films take relatively light views of such otherwise disturbing subjects as armed robbery, rape and death threats, and outright murder. At the same time, as argued in Chapter 5, these films show keen awareness of the power dynamics of race, gender, and class. Within their generic worlds, the films also recognize the transgressive, antisocial pleasures of illegal activity, along with its ability to forge temporary professional communities. Whether defined as protagonists or antagonists, the criminals of *Out of Sight* and the *Ocean's* films enjoy their work or at least recognize its satisfactions, and the films narrate the maintenance (and in *Ocean's Thirteen*, resuscitation) of their identities as men and professionals. The whistleblower films, meanwhile, measure their rousing or cautionary stories against historical realities. Both show a prosocial Soderbergh interested in crime-*stopping* as well as in mainstream narrative pleasures. *Erin Brockovich* and *The Informant!* both present white-collar crime narratives, with dueling populist-hero and family plotlines. *Erin Brockovich* respects the personal hardships and hard-won triumphs of its titular heroine as well as the historically real health consequences of California groundwater contamination it depicts. *The Informant!* maintains Eichenwald's incredulous response to massive but nonlethal corporate crime as well as its sympathetic treatment of a conflicted protagonist and the resource-scrounging investigators following the case. Both films are animated by the key issue of how individuals work to patrol institutions, and how institutions seek to thwart oversight—highly topical concerns in the era of corporate malfeasance that has given the world the Enron, Arthur Andersen, Tyco, and WorldCom accounting scandals of 2001 and 2002; the banking and mortgage-loan debacle of 2007 and beyond involving companies such as AIG, Lehman Brothers, and Goldman Sachs; the BP Deepwater Horizon oil-spill disaster of 2010; and additional follies of unregulation. Soderbergh contributes to popular interrogation of this pressing subject through collaboration with a range of historical agents and entertainment-industry workers, their varying motivations cohering around discrete screen texts.

Intertexts and Authorships: Lem's, Tarkovsky's, and Soderbergh's *Solaris*

This chapter has thus far looked to a range of generic categories and to multiple theorizations of adaptations, remakes, and other intertextual processes. I turn finally to an interrogation of authorship around the multiple iterations of *Solaris*, with Soderbergh's 2002 film the most recent screen feature. Hutcheon's work on adaptation addresses briefly the question of authorship, noting among other motivations for adaptation that of elevated cultural capital. For creative workers in commercial-entertainment contexts, "one way to gain respectability or increase cultural capital is for an adaptation to be upwardly mobile," with producers or texts able to "benefit from their adapted works' cultural cachet."[24] *Kafka* and *Solaris* enjoy substantial old-Europe pedigrees, but the source texts for numerous other adaptations directed by Soderbergh carry either neutral or negative cultural cachet. Mainstream global awareness of A. E. Hotchner's 1972 memoir *King of the Hill* (adapted for Soderbergh's 1993 film), the novel and film *Criss Cross*, or the *Traffik* mini-series is sufficiently modest as to offer no substantial leveraging of cultural capital. Comparatively, with *Ocean's Eleven*, Soderbergh's own description of the 1960 film as "more notorious than good"[25] indicates a need to manage understandings of the adapted work. Star George Clooney's similarly uncomplimentary appraisal of the earlier *Ocean's Eleven* as "a film that doesn't work at any level"[26] suggests a conscious, coordinated anticipation of the tenor of entertainment-press inquiry. Less problematically, adaptations of popular novels and nonfiction carry commercial appeals if not high-cultural cachet: adapting a crime novel such as Leonard's or a business potboiler such as Eichenwald's represents customary practice in contemporary Hollywood, promising generic innovation at best and assembly-line over-standardization at worst. Even adaptations of acclaimed past films contend with omnipresent perceptions of Hollywood's unoriginality and risk aversion. Film remakes are routinely understood as the lazy maneuvers of a cynical industry rather than as challenges for contemporary artists, and adaptations of popular literature must contend, too, with the critical stigma of their pre-sold qualities. Paradoxically, efforts to raise filmmakers' or industries' cultural cachet through adaptation of esteemed works often feed impressions of philistinism or overreach, as the response to such remakes as the U.S. *Breathless* (1983) demonstrates.[27]

Still, for screen authors, adapted materials continue to provide creative risks and satisfactions independent of market or reception conditions. The complex iterations of *Solaris* reveal the interplay of generic frameworks, adaptation considerations, and a range of artists' worldviews and creative methods. To address these concerns, I offer a primarily textual comparison of the two film versions, Andrei Tarkovsky's from 1972 and Soderbergh's from 2002, with periodic attention to Stanislaw Lem's 1961 novel and to respective cultural and industrial contexts. The Soviet *Solaris* was co-written and directed by Tarkovsky and produced by Russia's Mosfilm studio, while the U.S. version is a product of 20th Century Fox and James Cameron's Lightstorm Entertainment production company. With authorship and adaptation in mind, this section interrogates Soderbergh's film in particular in terms of industrial situation, film style, and gender representation. Uncommonly for a major U.S. production, the newer *Solaris* merges the styles and appeals of popular genre cinema, international art cinema, and U.S. independent film, while itself fully occupying none of those categories.[28] It represents an admittedly rare form of adaptation: a major U.S. studio and brand-name filmmakers remaking a well-regarded film of the Eastern European art cinema. What emerges is a film with an art-cinema aesthetic, generic iconography, and a neoclassical heterosexual romance at its center. The film manages these disparate modes through emphasis on mediation, artifice, and subjectivity. Evidencing a sensibility discernible in many other works in his filmography, Soderbergh's *Solaris* foregrounds the mediated nature of its images, sounds, and events; its status as Hollywood genre fiction; and its relationship to classical narratives of romance and redemption.

At some level, shared sensibilities underpin the two *Solaris* films. In the third act of the 1972 *Solaris*, the film's most rational character, the cyberneticist Dr. Snaut (Jüri Järvet), advises the protagonist Chris Kelvin (Donatos Banionis), "Don't turn a scientific problem into a common love story."[29] Ostensibly the advice (which does not appear in Lem's novel) is directed to Kelvin, whose guilt over his complicity in his wife's suicide years before manifests itself as a full-blown moral crisis when she mysteriously reappears on the space station orbiting the planetary mass known as Solaris. In the scientific vocabulary in which the film takes marginal interest, the reanimated wife, Hari (Natalya Bondarchuk), is not human but an "unstable neutrino system." From Kelvin's and the filmmakers' perspectives, though, Hari represents the complexity of love and human relationships. In this respect, Snaut's statement may be read as a winking allusion to viewers from director and co-screenwriter Tarkovsky, as the film is more "common love story" than "scientific problem." It uses its science-fiction premise and iconography to explore moral dilemmas far more than it takes up the scientific questions about the limits of human inquiry on which the science-fiction film genre thrives. The advice may serve, too, as a prophetic warning to screenwriter and director Soderbergh, whose latter-day *Solaris* also stresses romantic and interpersonal questions over science-fictional ones. Repeatedly in interviews, Soderbergh claims to make a second adaptation of Lem's novel, not a remake of Tarkovsky's film. Nonetheless, a preponderance of industry and reception discourse frames Soderbergh's version as a film remake.[30] In cinephile circles in particular, the reputation of Tarkovsky's film far exceeds that of Lem's novel. Questions of intent aside, then, the 2002 *Solaris* demands consideration as a film remake and not only a literary adaptation. Indeed, the two films depart from the novel in similar ways—both films omit most of the novel's long scientific discussions, and both include many original scenes taking place on Earth and highlighting romantic or family relationships. And despite Soderbergh's claim to adapt Lem's novel, his film stages far fewer scenes from the novel than Tarkovsky's does (partly a consequence of their differing running times: ninety-nine minutes for the newer film, compared to a languid 165 minutes for its precursor).

A curious market position and Soderbergh's multiple creative roles also distinguish the newer *Solaris*. Of his numerous remakes and adaptations, *Solaris* is arguably the most audacious. It transforms the slow, dense philosophical inquiry of Tarkovsky's film into Hollywood material worthy of a holiday-season release (opening in the U.S. on November 27, 2002, the day before Thanksgiving). Fox marketed *Solaris* as a science-fiction romance as well as a star vehicle for the bankable Clooney, and featured producer Cameron's name in advertising ahead of Soderbergh's.[31] On the other hand, Soderbergh enjoyed substantial creative autonomy, working at nearly all levels of production: in addition to writing and directing, he served as the film's director of photography, principal camera operator, and editor. Still, he brings to the project a collaborative as well as an autonomous-author mindset. The film continues his work with Clooney (though in this case, not as part of their Section Eight production company) as well as with regular below-the-line collaborators such as production designer Philip Messina and set decorator Kristen Toscana Messina, composer Cliff Martinez, sound editor Larry Blake, and assistant director Gregory Jacobs. As to Cameron's role, John Rockwell reports in the *New York Times* that "as producer, Mr. Cameron was content to serve as Mr. Soderbergh's sounding board through endless conversations and many script revisions." Cameron also tells Rockwell that:

> My own take was very different from what Steven saw in it. . . . My version would probably have been much, much further afield. I had so many ideas that they may reappear through the cracks of other projects.[32]

Notably, *Solaris* is the lone feature on which Cameron receives a producing credit between *Titanic* (1997) and *Avatar* (2009), so his work with Soderbergh can be said to constitute a key part of the authorial and intertextual dialogue that results in the phenomenally successful *Avatar*. *Solaris*'s manufactured consciousnesses arguably inform *Avatar*'s manufactured bodies, and Cameron's discussions with Soderbergh represent part of the creative gestation of both films. These conversations do not mean that Soderbergh merits any kind of conceptual credit for *Avatar*. But they do remind us that processes of creativity crucial to authorial production may extend beyond the understood pre-production phases of discrete films. The completed *Solaris* fits far more readily into Soderbergh's perceived oeuvre than Cameron's. Soderbergh had not worked extensively with science-fiction material before, though *Kafka* treads into mad-science territory at its climax. This lack of genre proficiency, and the emphasis instead on romantic discord across Soderbergh's filmography, partly explains *Solaris*'s elevation of relationship matters over cosmic ones. Framed as a product of Soderbergh's creative signature, the film is more *sex, lies, and videotape* in outer space than the epic CGI showcase that Cameron's credit might imply.

Even if Cameron's actual production role exceeds the conversations and revisions that Rockwell cites, the fact remains that Soderbergh is singly responsible for more aspects of the film's production than was Tarkovsky on the critically acclaimed, Criterion-enshrined *Solaris* of 1972. Discourse surrounding the 1972 film positions it as a resolutely auteurist work, the realities of its production notwithstanding. Mosfilm was itself a commercial studio, though subject to state oversight. Tarkovsky worked on development of *Solaris*, then allegedly proposed to direct it because he could not secure funding for other, more personal projects, while the science-fiction genre and Polish author Lem were both popular in Russia.[33] Tarkovsky collaborated with writer Fridrikh Gorenshtein on multiple screenplay drafts, with numerous changes requested or demanded by both the Mosfilm studio committee and by Lem. (The Soviet/Mosfilm committee's requests were apparently commercial as well as ideological: Tarkovsky was asked to cut "lengthy discussions about the problem of knowledge and science"[34] as well as to "remove the concept of God."[35]) Despite Tarkovsky's involvement in many facets of the film's production, then, he is singly responsible only for its direction. Comparing the two versions of *Solaris*, we see that a contemporary Hollywood studio, a property of the multinational

News Corporation, affords a single filmmaker demonstrably more control over production than did a European studio known for stewardship of auteurist, art-cinema texts. Industrial and market conditions rather than issues of collaboration and control may have determined the films' prospects. The first *Solaris* film received the Grand Jury Prize at Cannes; the second opened to largely indifferent reviews and was a substantial commercial failure.

The substantive differences in the films' receptions and modes of production make their textual affinities all the more remarkable. Both *Solaris* films are distinguished by narrative ambiguity, limited interest in genre iconography, and manipulation of film-romance conventions. Like the 1972 film, the remake compellingly interrogates cerebral masculinity, though its premise inhibits a comprehensive view of femininity. At many levels in both films, femininity is a male construct, the byproduct of men's restless memories. Soderbergh's film does introduce questions of male and female agency and interiority not germane to Tarkovsky's film or to Lem's novel. Soderbergh's *Solaris* uses genre backdrops and a doomed-romance narrative to explore a compromised masculinity, further developing the theme of failed interpersonal communication visible since *sex, lies, and videotape*. Like *sex, lies* as well, both versions of *Solaris* manifest and then interrogate mediated male fantasies. In each film men have power over, and derive sexual gratification from, representations of women that they create but which cause them deep anxiety and finally catalyze their transformation into more sensitive, unselfish, and fully aware men. As it happens, when men create fantasy images of women for their own use, personal growth ensues. Yet rather than appearing as a transparent exercise in ego gratification, Soderbergh's *Solaris* traces this premise's unreality, its dubious appeal, and its psychological pitfalls.

Soderbergh also uses the raw material of Lem's *Solaris*—its premise of a sentient technology that gives material form to subconscious desires—to explore the dynamics of film narrative and screen recording technology. In this respect, Soderbergh's film can be located within science fiction's generic field, but the film also revisits his previous work's preoccupation with media technology. (To recall other examples, *sex, lies, and videotape* uses video footage within the film to investigate mediated desire, and *Ocean's Eleven* and *The Informant!* extensively depict audio and video recording and surveillance.) *Solaris* includes repeated shots of video displays, including two scenes in which Kelvin (Clooney) watches video messages addressed to him by characters who have subsequently committed suicide. Tarkovsky's *Solaris* also features many mediated images and screens within the screen, which in part provide evidence of human estrangement from nature. At Kelvin's father's home on Earth, for example, people watch video but rarely venture forth into the picturesque countryside. The video mediations also connote people's estrangement from each other, with video communications aboard the space station replacing face-to-face interaction.

The newer *Solaris* offers a particularly suggestive use of mediated imagery in a fragmented video image that appears early in the film, just as its narrative conflict is introduced. Corporate messengers visit Kelvin at home to show him a video message from the scientist Gibarian (Ulrich Tukur), who viewers never encounter in an unmediated, present, living form. In the video, Gibarian looks directly into a camera and in somewhat cryptic language beckons Kelvin to the space station orbiting Solaris. At the end of his message, Gibarian reaches out of frame and the video freezes, with the image becoming largely pixelated but with parts of the close-up of his face still visible. In the subsequent shot of Kelvin speaking to the looming messengers, the large-screen video image fills nearly half the background space over Kelvin's shoulder, though the shot's shallow focus blurs this background. Following a brief reverse-shot, an extreme-close up of the pixelated image appears, then a lap dissolve connects it to the film's first CGI image, of a blue plane viewers can identify as the surface of Solaris. Beyond its expository function, the scene presents multiple layers of film and digital technology: the filmed or videotaped shot of Gibarian, a shot which is then copied and manipulated digitally, presented within a filmed shot of Kelvin's apartment, then printed over the next image, the digitally generated view of the psychedelic planet Solaris. Created by a confluence of production and post-production technologies, the scene presents viewers with a legible, moving image of Gibarian; then a still, blurred one; and finally a mostly frozen but haltingly pixelating one. The digital static preceding the otherworldly CGI shot attests to the faltering, incomplete nature of communication in the near-future environment.

Beyond giving viewers this momentary layering of Hollywood's then-current technologies, Soderbergh's *Solaris* offers a protagonist who willingly immerses himself in a conventional Hollywood redemption narrative. Embracing the planet Solaris's ability to revive a dead past, Kelvin finally chooses to live within its artificial world alongside his reanimated wife, Rheya (her name also in Lem's novel, but not in the 1972 film). Reunited with Kelvin in this fantasy space, Rheya

The frozen, pixelated image of scientist Gibarian concludes his cryptic video message in *Solaris* (2002).

(Natascha McElhone) contributes the film's final line of dialogue: "Everything we've done is forgiven." The line echoes a project of mainstream cinema, to offer calculated redemption through the *deus ex machina* of fiction narrative. Philip Lopate writes that Tarkovsky's *Solaris* "helped initiate a genre that has become an art-house staple: the drama of grief and partial recovery."[36] Soderbergh's film massages the grief-and-recovery subgenre into more mainstream form, rendering grief in shorthand. This emotion appears connotatively via Kelvin's averted gaze, his isolation from other characters in frame compositions, and repeated shots of the back of his head that discourage empathy. The off-casting of Clooney magnifies this tone, with the actor relocated from his gregarious persona into a character who is depressed, withdrawn, and silent for most of his screen time. Through its overall story arc and the construction of Kelvin as glibly charismatic in flashbacks, then silently contented at the film's hopeful denouement, Soderbergh's film simultaneously celebrates and interrogates the Hollywood redemption narrative. The planet Solaris grows ever larger as it animates the nostalgic, fantastic desires of those in its orbit. Ultimately, Kelvin's goal is revealed as regressive—with the space station's destruction imminent, he returns to the warmly lit domestic world of an artificial Earth, while the other remaining human character, Gordon (Viola Davis), climbs into her space suit and a waiting sci-fi shuttlecraft. Like his predecessor in Tarkovsky's film, this Kelvin, too, prefers the "common love story" over the "scientific problem," as apparently does Soderbergh. Still, his *Solaris* is unequivocal in depicting all-encompassing redemptive love as a regressive fantasy.

The newer *Solaris*'s merger of memory and fantasy corresponds to a thematic emphasis on narratives and recollections of intimacy. Accordingly, the film presents gendered agency, or the struggle for control within a heterosexual relationship, as its primary psychological conflict. Male-female relationships, and particularly the taming of an iconoclastic male temperament to accommodate a relationship, have been central to nearly all Soderbergh's films as director. Soderbergh's *Solaris* begins by emphasizing its woman protagonist's simultaneous presence and absence. Rheya's dialogue opens the film as well as closes it. The opening lines—a woman's voice saying, "Chris, what's wrong? I love you so much, don't you love me anymore?"—first registers as offscreen, disembodied sound. Rheya does not appear until the first-act climax, and the line is repeated just thereafter, by which point we recognize the opening dialogue to have been a sound flashforward. Tarkovsky's *Solaris* delays Hari's appearance a bit longer, though in both films she is an explicit manifestation of male memory. In the Soderbergh version, Rheya enters the film's acoustic and visual space through the exercise of a male character's subjectivity rather than her own, hailed into being by Chris's flashbacks or via the planet Solaris's revival of her from Chris's memory. In Lem's and Tarkovsky's flashback-free versions, Rheya/Hari is entirely an apparition, never a real person in narrative terms.

While Soderbergh's *Solaris* first constructs the reanimated Rheya as a product of male memory, the film then represents her growing interiority. After her initial appearance, Chris acts decisively to send her away, guiding her into a podcraft that he sends into space. This brief scene features a pair of direct-address close-ups of the two characters linked by an eyeline match, then a shot of Chris averting his gaze from the departing craft. The scene indicates Chris's raw rejection of the new Rheya, as does his inability to respond to questions she poses in the preceding scene: "Why are you sitting over there? Can I come and sit with you?" Just as with the film's first dialogue, Rheya asks a pair of questions that leave Chris speechless. Tarkovsky's *Solaris* depicts Kelvin as similarly incapable of giving explanations to his reanimated wife, but the initial scene of him loading her into a spacecraft does not allow her a reaction shot or a match cut linking the characters' gazes. Kelvin's pain does not register on his face, either; the scene of the rocket's departure shows him rolling under a fire-retardant blanket, and his charred clothing stands in for his psychological distress.

The two films' structures contribute to their depictions of gendered subjectivity. Limiting Hari's perspective (and the viewer's), Tarkovsky's film does not return to the past to illustrate Chris and Hari's marriage. This withholding of the characters' histories pointedly closes off viewers' understanding of the relationship: sharing Hari's mystification, viewers can recognize the couple's mutual love only as an abstraction. The newer film, on the other hand, provides numerous flashbacks to Chris and Rheya's romance and marriage, flashbacks that unfold chronologically if episodically across the film. The initial two flashbacks are cued by Chris's subconscious, with shots of him sleeping introducing the flashback scenes. Later in the film, though, two long flashbacks are apportioned to Rheya as well, as she stares out a space-station window at the planet Solaris. The flashbacks throughout are triangulated. In narrative terms, the flashbacks represent Solaris studying Kelvin's memories; but in terms of editing, the film offers a relay among views of Chris, Rheya, and digital compositions of Solaris. Initially, Rheya is forced to occupy the subjectivity through which the flashbacks appear: she claims the memories we see, but adds, "I don't remember experiencing those things." Thus the film calls attention to its own restricted narration, its privileging of a male perspective toward narrative space, a space in which Rheya is first a presence but not an agent. The second pair of flashbacks highlights her perspective, showing events for which Chris is not present or those foregrounding her gaze and subjectivity. As the flashbacks progress, they depict both an unstable Rheya and a frustrated, closed-off Chris. As Rheya's death has been forecast, though, the flashbacks particularly accentuate her tragic trajectory. In the film's present, Rheya duels with Chris for control of those incidents, or agency within them, accusing him of misremembering her and asserting, "In your memory you get to control everything." Yet the final flashback occurs embedded within a nightmare sequence, and it depicts the aftermath of Rheya's suicide, an event Chris explicitly does not control.

Soderbergh's Solaris stages its gender conflict through film style as well as through narrative. As already noted, the film long denies Chris visual and vocal authority. Also, like numerous other Soderbergh films, Solaris unfolds nonlinearly—not only with its flashback structure, but also with its opening scene featuring images that could be located at the beginning or end of the film's chronology and sound that occurs diegetically in the middle. In Soderbergh's Solaris, nonlinear editing is the key formal device used to represent the conflict between Chris's and Rheya's subjectivities. Contrastingly, the long-take aesthetic of Tarkovsky's *Solaris* largely shores up its male protagonist's subjectivity. Even its one ostensibly nonlinear or nondiegetic episode—a dream featuring Kelvin's mother as a young woman, but with him as an adult—powerfully represents Kelvin's interiority. Hari is not present in the episode, but is referenced visually there. In the dream, the mother first appears shot from behind, dressed like Hari and with a similar hairstyle. Preceding the dream, a panning shot on the space station features three Haris and the young mother dispersed around the set.[37] The film's psychological conflation of women accords with Tarkovsky's own perspective, into which women per se do not figure at all. In an interview about the film, he says, "the story of [Hari's] relationship with Kelvin is the story of the relationship between man and his own conscience. It's about man's concern with his own spirit."[38] Soderbergh's version of *Solaris* shares an interest in Kelvin's guilt and transformation, but the film's fantasy redemption is collaborative: Chris wills it only after the reanimated Rheya challenges his earlier outlook, and only after she rejects his plan for a static life aboard the space station. The final redemption belongs to her as well—it is co-authored, and the film concludes with a series of close-up shot-reverse shots of the couple embracing.

The Hollywood *Solaris*'s metacommentaries on cinematic redemption and mediated communication take shape in both narrative and formal terms. The Russian *Solaris* engages viewers in profound ways but does not foreground a critical perspective on cinematic storytelling or production practice. When Soderbergh's film does so, it metaphorically acknowledges its debt to the two previous versions of *Solaris*. In its narrative manipulation through editing and its emphasis on mediated images and memories, the newer *Solaris* emulates the reshaping processes of textual adaptation and film remakes. Many of Soderbergh's other films, adaptations or not, have been understood as self-reflexive exercises, as ruminations on Hollywood celebrity culture, production logistics, and the narrative possibilities of layered fictions. Jonathan Romney approaches *Solaris* as a self-reflexive commentary on genres and movements: for him, Soderbergh is "pastiching 1960s art cinema's own pastiche appropriations of the genre."[39] Though with its circulation curtailed by poor commercial results, *Solaris* allows its viewers to consider its position, and their own, relative to transnational screen industries and regimes of popular narrative. Additionally, the film uses its generic affiliations and Hollywood resources to work through questions about human communication, communication mediated by gendered subjectivities and by audio-visual technologies represented onscreen. These questions arise from the finished film and Soderbergh's screenplay as well as the intertexts they adapt. The extratextual discourse of Soderbergh's interviews and DVD co-commentary with Cameron reveals further creative negotiations in the complex adaptation process.

Productive study of film texts in industrial, generic, and adaptation contexts requires not only theoretical models but also recognition of individual creative roles and sensibilities. Addressing the role of screenplays in adaptation, Jack Boozer writes:

> An adapted film begins as a screenplay transformation of a source, and eventually becomes a film derivation from that screenplay. Recognizing this specificity of textual stages not only confirms adaptation's intertextual status but can also point more precisely to the contributions of key individuals and their most significant impact along the way. Tracing generic, institutional, ideological, and cultural influences need not entirely displace considerations of key creative decisions by individuals most directly responsible for a film.[40]

Boozer identifies numerous contexts into which adaptation studies may take us, and the richly synthetic critical perspectives that can ensue. In a related vein that Boozer also mines, Robert Stam observes that studies of film authorship "now tend to see a director's work not as the expression of individual genius but rather as the site of encounter of a biography, an intertext, an institutional context, and a historical moment."[41] This chapter has articulated some of the encounters, intertexts, and contexts involved in Soderbergh's genre-film, remaking, and adaptation work. I turn next to Soderbergh's work in a production sector, television, long seen as disengaged from the nexus of creative work that constitutes film authorship. Soderbergh's television work nonetheless evidences an artistic signature that meshes with his feature-filmmaking efforts. This creative work remains distinct, however, in terms of production workflow, thematic engagements, and the particular surround of prestige serial television, all of which influence our understanding of professional collaboration and recognizable screen authorship.

Part Four

Soderbergh and Screen Industries

Chapter 7

Soderbergh and Television

Following on from the intertextual contexts of Soderbergh-directed feature films, this chapter examines his limited work on television series, a format routinely distinguished from cinema in its textual characteristics and mode of authorship. Soderbergh's work in television affords the opportunity to consider a different range of critical issues. The television programs Soderbergh has directed or produced merit scrutiny in particular for their narrative appeals, stylistic experimentation, and improvisational performances. Eschewing artificial distinctions between media forms, however, I wish to emphasize the continuity of style, content, and address among Soderbergh's projects in film and television, as well as his consistent role as producer across the two media. Central to this chapter is a case study of the 2003 HBO series *K Street*, an experiment in rapid television production. Remarkably for prestige television, episodes of the part-reality, part-fiction series were aired the same week they were filmed, and they incorporated within their plotlines breaking national news and the ongoing primary campaigns for the 2004 U.S. presidency. *K Street* embodies what I term the parafictional form, identifiable also in other Soderbergh efforts such as *Traffic* and *Bubble*, though to a lesser degree. Relying on television's more intimate address and serial-narrative possibilities, *K Street* generates a semi-fictional commentary on Washington, D.C., political culture while participating in curious ways with that culture. The portability of the parafiction mode is evidenced by the production of a subsequent HBO series, *Unscripted*, executive-produced by Soderbergh and directed by his Section Eight partner George Clooney and Clooney's other producing partner, Grant Heslov. Substituting L.A.'s entertainment culture for D.C.'s political milieu,

Unscripted follows the staged but partly improvised activities of a real group of aspiring Los Angeles actors. In addition to demonstrating Soderbergh and Clooney's cross-media investments, the two series further showcase the hybridized narrative modes that form part of both men's creative signatures as directors and producers. As such, this television work highlights continuities of authorial activity as well as distinct provisions of the television medium.

Soderbergh and Clooney both began their professional media work in television. The son of a longtime broadcast host, Clooney enjoys a professional profile that owes much to television. His five seasons on the NBC television series *ER* (1994–2009, with Clooney starring from 1994–1999) refine his performance style and, viewed retrospectively, position him for feature-film stardom. Soderbergh, meanwhile, worked during the 1980s in well-below-the-line television production. In the 1990s, his television work consisted only of two episodes of Showtime's noir-inspired series *Fallen Angels* (1993, 1995), which imported a range of creative talent from independent-cinema as well as studio-filmmaking sectors. For both Clooney and Soderbergh, the return to prestige television via HBO series represents an expansion of their respective creative profiles. Feature-film work continues to carry the greatest cultural cachet of screen-media forms. However, affiliations with prestige television offer opportunities for experimentation with serial narrative, clearly of interest to Soderbergh, whose penchant for long-form and multi-protagonist narratives becomes evident with *Traffic* and continues with the *Ocean's* series and *Che*. Specialized television production, and *K Street* in particular, enables production practices not available to feature filmmakers, most prominently a condensed work flow that allows a narrow window between filming and release. Significantly, too, the return to television profitably extends both Soderbergh's and Clooney's industrial reputations. Allen Scott argues that contemporary Hollywood labor practice privileges a model of advancement based not on "firm-specific human capital and seniority" (i.e., rising up an organization's ranks over time) but on "reputation as the main currency of worker evaluation." Consequently, he continues, "[w]orkers adopted as far as possible the strategic imperative of planning their credits and experiences across the entire entertainment industry in the quest to mold their reputations."[1] Soderbergh's and Clooney's reestablishment of cross-media creative profiles accords fully with the imperative Scott identifies. Meanwhile, the specific production methods and formal strategies of the HBO series enhance their creators' artistic signatures. In terms of arcs of creative practice and authorship, *K Street* in particular demonstrates collaboration and experimentation around narratives of politics and interpersonal relations, features strongly evident in much other screen-media work with which Soderbergh has been affiliated.

K Street's Parafictions

Each episode of *K Street* concludes with a written disclaimer that reads: "The events and characters depicted in this motion picture are fictional, excluding only those persons portraying themselves."[2] Whatever legal standing this statement grants the series, one might still ask what it could possibly mean. Scenes from the program itself, which follows the mingled professional and personal lives of employees of a fictional Washington, D.C., lobbying firm, provide examples if not explanation. In the series' third episode, political consultant Mary Matalin and journalist and bestselling novelist Joe Klein (identified in dialogue only in passing as "Joe") have an impromptu discussion on a busy Capitol Hill street as a single, handheld digital-video camera films them from a distance in surveillance-video style. The meeting is staged for filming, and while Matalin and Klein improvise their dialogue, it relates loosely to a fictional plotline constructed by writer Henry Bean and director Soderbergh as well as to real events in the U.S. political world in the week prior to the scene's filming and telecast. The dialogue is not particularly memorable, and the brief encounter contributes little to the series' immediate or overarching storylines. The scene's chief appeal is the fact of the staged encounter itself, though only a narrow subset of viewers would immediately recognize the people involved. In the series, shown on HBO over ten weeks from September to November 2003, a small group of professional actors interact with real politicians, political consultants, and other public figures within improvised narratives that mix real and fictional events. Television critics praised the show's premise but not its execution, calling it "shapeless," "oddly flat," and "a parlor game for insiders."[3] By its fourth episode, viewership had fallen nearly 40 percent.[4] The critical and popular failure of the series is easily explained: it accurately represents the business of Washington lobbying and political consulting as mystifying and tedious. *New York Times* television critic Virginia Heffernan notes of the program, "As much as people claim to want Wiseman or Warhol versions of reality, it's pretty unwatchable."[5]

In line with this book's overall approach, the goal of this chapter is not to measure *K Street*'s relationship to documentary or experimental

A surveillance-style shot from *K Street* (2003) captures an encounter between political consultant Mary Matalin and journalist Joe Klein.

film, nor even to dispute the assertion that many people actually claim to want Wiseman or Warhol-style texts. Instead, I wish to consider *K Street*'s articulation of what I define as the parafictional mode, a liminal mode of narrative that foregrounds screen texts' proximity to historical reality. *K Street*'s parafictions further accentuate Soderbergh's authorial sensibility, deepening his association with innovative narrative address and structure. The series depends also upon his simultaneously collaborative and multi-hyphenated work method. Soderbergh receives credits for all episodes as director, cinematographer (supervising two camera teams), and lead editor (with four assistants or associates). He receives no writing credit but works closely with Bean and the performers on each episode's plot and actions. Unusually for him, the other technical personnel include none of his regular collaborators on feature-film work, attesting to continued industrial demarcation of film and television industries as well as to the different time commitments required of television workers. Though *K Street*'s intense production schedule ultimately involves not much more time than a studio-feature shoot, the possibility of the series continuing beyond its initial season precludes the participation of those committed to feature work. The program's cast does include three veterans of previous Soderbergh features: John Slattery (a supporting player in *Traffic*), Mary McCormack (among the leads of *Full Frontal*), and Elliott Gould (one of *Ocean's Eleven*). The overall creative team thus shows Soderbergh's interest in collaborative continuity across media forms, even as the program assembles an original group of collaborating technicians for its staging of a narrative fiction in the midst of Washington's living political-corporate ecosystem.

Parafictional texts establish connections between their own characters and events and those that appear and occur simultaneously in historical reality. The Greek root "para" designates a multitude of relationships: it can mean alongside (as in parallel), subsidiary to (as in paramilitary), closely resembling, related to, beyond, contrary to (as in paradox), faulty or disordered (as in paranoia), and more. Parafiction itself relates to fiction in each of these ways: it sits alongside fiction, resembles fiction, moves outside fiction, and disorders fiction. Parafictional screen texts include historical films such as *Bloody Sunday* (2002) and *Munich* (2005) that adopt a realist aesthetic of hand-held cameras, unflattering figure lighting, and so forth; docudramas such as *The Battle of Algiers* (1966), *The Road to Guantanamo* (2006), and *United 93* (2006) that emphasize realist formal and narrative codes while still shaping events into character-driven docufictions; fiction films with public figures playing themselves, including the numerous films with appearances from former New York mayor Rudy Giuliani or talk-show host Larry King, for example; and texts that incorporate actuality footage into fictional narratives, which I will discuss below. Because many loosely topical texts draw part of their appeal from their proximity to current political events, an exhaustive list would have to encompass all forms of cultural verisimilitude. Many film and television fictions connect their events to other historical realities, not just to contemporary political discourses. Moreover, audiences can read texts according to nonfiction codes however divorced texts themselves might appear from contemporary reality. I note here those elements most relevant to the examination of *K Street*, whose significance lies primarily in its collapsing of fictional and nonfictional worlds. Contemporary television has produced such intersections principally for comic rather than dramatic effect, as in HBO's many successful comedy series set within the entertainment industry, including *The Larry Sanders Show* (1992–1998), *Curb Your Enthusiasm* (2000–), and *Entourage* (2004–2011).

One might argue that texts such as *K Street* that release professional performers into unstaged events in the historical world belong instead to the category of paradocumentary, gaining power from their relationship to documentary modes and their attendant truth claims. Such a category would include mockumentaries such as *The*

War Game (1965), *David Holzman's Diary* (1967), or *Incident at Loch Ness* (2004), which approximate historical reality in sometimes convincing ways. Paradocumentary extends documentary address, making truth claims (or deliberately advancing false ones) and marshaling supporting evidence through interviews and fabrication of the world of lived experience, often using the vérité staple of footage of informal or dead time. Parafiction, on the other hand, extends existing modes of fiction-narrative address, embellishing them with the presence of historical actors appearing as themselves or parallel versions of themselves, but always with the historical world as an index for narrative content and viewer reception.

John Caldwell uses the term "docu-real" to designate a televisual mode in which (usually) fiction texts borrow the conventions of screen documentary: "episodes in entertainment programs that self-consciously showcase documentary units or modes as part of their narrative and plot and/or documentary looks and imaging as part of their mise-en-scène."[6] *K Street*, in comparison, does not pretend to be documentary; its aim is not the *illusion of* authenticity or truth but rather the *proximity to* truth. It does not say "this is really happening" but instead "things like this are really happening" (along with "many of the people you see and hear are presently doing things just like this"). The program's benchmarks are fiction rather than nonfiction narratives. It requires its principal cast members to perform within broad parameters established by a writer, director, and technical crew. Appearances by figures who have power and visibility in the public world—i.e., the politicians, journalists, and lawyers who appear in person or whose voices carry over the speakerphones prominent in many episodes—are not serendipitous but staged, even as their specific dialogue is improvised. Cameras may appear strategically or haphazardly placed but are not concealed from their filmed subjects. The program often adopts a cinema-vérité visual style, as with episode seven's moving, handheld shot following a political candidate through a crowd of supporters that recalls the iconic shot of John F. Kennedy in the 1960 documentary *Primary*. Still, *K Street* puts its form in service of fictional narratives, not to documentation and interrogation of events in the historical world.[7] Also, the program aired in HBO's prestigious Sunday-night timeslot, a longtime home for an expensive, multi-camera fiction series. While HBO does produce much documentary programming—including such socially conscious fare as *Real Sex* (1992–2009), *Taxicab Confessions* (1995–2006), and *G String Divas* (2000)—*K Street* addresses viewers anticipating the channel's brand of mature dramatic series (although one episode does reference the pornographic magazine *Oui*). While *K Street*'s narrative and Soderbergh's creative pedigree tie it more powerfully to fiction than to nonfiction, it engages viewers similarly to the docu-real category, which in Caldwell's view "offers a dense, complicated, responsive meditation on viewership, programming, and cultural taste."[8]

K Street's narrative concerns the fictional lobbying firm Bergstrom Lowell and its partners' efforts to cultivate new clients, including a recording-industry trade group, a commercial trucking firm, and an energy-policy institute, all real organizations whose representatives appear in episodes. The series' principal cast consists of three professional actors—Slattery, McCormack, and Roger Guenveur Smith—playing fictional characters, alongside celebrity political consultants Matalin and James Carville, playing displaced versions of themselves (that is, performing according to their trademark personas, but transplanted to a different, fictitious workplace).[9] These five interact in each episode with real U.S. politicians and other newsworthy figures, who are also relocated into the program's fictional plotlines. In the sixth episode, former CIA Director James Woolsey gives advice via speakerphone to Matalin about one of her firm's fictional clients. In episode eight, Carville appears on the set of the real CNN program *Crossfire* conversing with his co-host Tucker Carlson, and the men have a conversation about a fictional federal investigation of the consulting firm. The former scene stages the Woolsey-Matalin encounter, while the latter injects a semi-scripted, fictional moment into a nonfictional event, the debate-show telecast that occurs subsequently, but which does not appear in the *K Street* episode. (That is, the scene was filmed on the *Crossfire* set, but no part of the actual *Crossfire* taping appears in the *K Street* episode.)

K Street frequently recontextualizes real events by referencing them in characters' dialogue and actions, by positioning actors amid real, public events (such as a Kennedy Center opening reception and a Washington Wizards basketball game), and by editing these events to fit the series' fictional storylines. Episode six begins with Roger Guenveur Smith speaking at a charity awards dinner. Outside the fiction of *K Street*, Smith, an actor perhaps recognizable from his supporting roles in many Spike Lee–directed films of the 1980s and 1990s, was an actual presenter at the dinner.[10] The episode, though, presents the scene as if Smith's fictional character, Francisco Dupré, is the invited speaker. Within the series, the scene helps establish Dupré as well connected in D.C. political circles. In other words, the episode films a nonfiction event and transforms it into parafiction, recontextualizing the awards dinner as a part of the *K Street* narrative universe. Such repositionings are not fundamentally new to popular media. They often take the form of reedited footage: many 1940s and 1950s war films repurpose combat footage shot by documentary cameramen, and countless texts borrow U.S. Army footage of mushroom clouds from nuclear tests for various ends. As already discussed, too, Soderbergh's later *The Good German* interweaves archival footage of postwar Berlin into its self-consciously fictional narrative. Periodically such sampling, as we might call it, promotes texts' putative engagement with the historical world, as with war films' uses of stock footage or the provocative deployment of the Zapruder film in *JFK* (1991). Other texts transport their fictions into the "live" historical world. *Medium Cool* (1969), for example, films its fictional protagonist, a television cameraman, at Chicago's 1968 Democratic convention and follows its female lead through the demonstrations that surrounded the convention. Similar moments in *K Street* not only destabilize the relationship between documentary and fiction, but also underscore the performativity and staginess of political discourse and public life.

It is no revelation that politicians adopt personas, perform, and dissemble to gain and retain power. We know, as do Soderbergh and his collaborators, that life in the public eye demands self-conscious performance. Yet *K Street* prevents its viewers from making precise judgments about who onscreen acts from a script, who improvises, and who might be speaking with conviction (these categories not being mutually exclusive, of course). Such distinctions fail to apply within the parafictional frame, though they remain crucial as we consider, for example, the real legislative and advisory duties many of the figures perform offscreen. Overall, *K Street* suggests the degree to which many representations, fiction and nonfiction, bear signs of parafiction. Notably, though, the voluntary entry into the semifiction of *K Street* results in framing distinct from such formats as press conferences and television news, formats that are differently managed by producers and participants. Public figures appear in *K Street* in ways not solely legible as self-aggrandizing. Roger Guenveur Smith's charity-dinner appearance cements his fictional character's construction as a devious networker, Carville's actions in both fictionalized and nonfictional scenarios in the program show him as ideologically confused and fundamentally profit-minded, and in their cameos, members of Congress appear both rigidly partisan and strikingly undynamic, particularly when judged on the terms of prime-time, prestige cable-television drama. *K Street*'s parafictional merger of the fictive and the real thus demystifies the political process and its participants, arguably to the point of uninterest. The program highlights the relationship between staged representation and historical reality, between profilmic events and what we might term the post-filmic world.

The program's aesthetic of liveness or near-liveness demands a rapid production and postproduction schedule. In its ten-week run, episodes were written and filmed Monday through Wednesday, edited by Soderbergh on Thursday and Friday, and aired on Sunday night.[11] Consequently, the series regularly invoked recent news developments and the ongoing campaigns for the 2004 presidential election. The program's liveness and topicality contribute to its immediate appeal but limited shelf life. Viewed years after its original airing, *K Street* becomes a time capsule, similar to an archived news broadcast. Substantially time-shifted viewing illuminates the program's dependence on temporal proximity to the real events it follows and invokes. Because it includes fictional plots and characters, it does not evoke the more straightforward historical memories of political documentaries to which it bears comparison, such as *The War Room* (1993) or Robert Greenwald's film critiques of the George W. Bush administration. In this respect, near-liveness becomes an aesthetic prerequisite for blended fictional and nonfictional narratives. Soderbergh's later parafictional feature *The Girlfriend Experience* adopts this strategy as well. Its own tight production and postproduction schedule—it was filmed in October 2008 and premiered in rough-cut form in January 2009—allows its characters to refer to still-topical U.S. political and financial news. As for other parafictions, this contingency represents a key feature of the film's address. The predilection for time-sensitive narratives then forms a subtheme of Soderbergh's creative endeavors.

Soderbergh has described *K Street* with the suggestive if imprecise label "real-time fiction."[12] While series such as 24 slavishly mimic real clock-time while locating their overall events in a vague near-present, *K Street* instead tethers its fictions specifically to the week of its shooting and telecast. In practice this involves the weaving of fictional storylines into ongoing, real-world political discourse, and vice versa. The program supplies Slattery and McCormack's characters in particular with fictional personal narratives that achieve at least partial resolution by the final episode. Almost none of the characters ever appear in their homes, but their activities outside the workplace do appear.[13]

Since characters' work involves being visible and contacting politicians and other public figures in informal or semi-formal settings (at social functions, in office corridors, or on the street), the program emphasizes the blurring of personal and professional activities. The separate romantic misadventures of Tommy Flannegan (Slattery) and Maggie Morris (McCormack) both intrude into their work environments, through phone calls and other women's real or imagined appearances in the firm's office. These personal narratives, along with a workplace-intrigue storyline involving Carville, Matalin, and Smith's Dupré character, progress sporadically in each episode. At the same time, each episode incorporates events from the nonfiction world of 2003—the California recall election and Arnold Schwarzenegger's candidacy for governor, the exposure of CIA operative Valerie Plame (which the program develops into a key fictional subplot involving an investigation of Matalin and the firm), the political campaigns of Howard Dean and Philadelphia mayor John Street, and others.

In some respects *K Street* intertwines its fictional and nonfictional narratives so thoroughly as to obscure their boundaries. Soderbergh says of the program in interviews that it should leave viewers "asking whether it's documentary or fiction."[14] Indeed, after viewing episode five, in which Matalin becomes the possible target of a Justice Department investigation, one must consult other sources to determine whether such an investigation actually occurred or was an embellishment from Soderbergh and Bean. (Muddying the subject further, the truth was somewhere in the middle.[15]) Moreover, the program does not engage in "breaking the fourth wall" tactics such as dollying out to reveal the presence of boom microphones and production crew, as occurs at the end of *Medium Cool* and in Soderbergh's earlier *Schizopolis* and *Full Frontal*. Likewise, *K Street* does not represent its celebrity politicians and public figures in ironic ways (in the manner, for example, of a subplot in *Ocean's Twelve* in which Julia Roberts's fictional character, Tess, impersonates the star Julia Roberts). In the program, too, realist sound predominates, with much ambient noise and no nondiegetic music until the final scene of the last episode. Sound mixing is subtly evident, as when dialogue carries across cuts and is heard at the same volume independent of camera position (in one episode, characters in dialogue first appear shot from outside a glass-enclosed office, then from within the office, but the sound quality does not change from shot to shot). Still, this process does not markedly unveil the workings of the cinematographic apparatus.

However, *K Street* does sabotage its connections to realist representation in many ways, using subjective imagery, jump cuts and dissolves, and other stylistic and narrative obtrusions. Episodes four and nine take the form of flashbacks, airing in October and November but set in July and August, and with copies of past newspapers (as well as intertitles beginning the episodes) used to situate the episodes in time. Events in these episodes partly explain incidents that occur later in the series chronology, but which have appeared in previous episodes. Such a break from linearity in order to create and then resolve enigmas is characteristic of fictional narrative. The flashbacks enable a knowing irony as well. In episode nine, filmed and aired in November but set in August, Flannegan bets his father's young wife $1,000 that Schwarzenegger will not be elected governor; in real time, the bodybuilder-turned-film-star had won the election some weeks before. Acting flaws also undermine the series' potential unobtrusiveness: many of the featured politicians glance self-consciously at the camera as if unwilling to maintain the pretense that they are unaware of being filmed. In the third episode, though, both McCormack and Matalin glance at the camera during one scene, indicating that such self-consciousness is not restricted to the program's nonprofessional actors. This moment suggests, too, that such glances are not mistakes but a managed component of the series' distinct address. Since *K Street* does not pretend to be a documentary, in which subjects' looks at the camera would be expected, such glances here contribute to a particularly parafictional address.

Other episodes apply formalist devices not common to realist texts or to documentary. In a long scene in episode eight of Justice Department agents questioning Carville, a series of lap dissolves denotes the passage of time. Other episodes include subjective camerawork—slow-motion pans, step-printing, and out-of-focus shots—to illustrate characters' perspectives or the overall mood of a situation. Throughout the series, jump cuts occur regularly, and nearly every episode begins with a series of close-ups of objects or parts of settings— a pair of shoes, a car interior—insignificant to key plots and subplots. The program also deliberately undercuts its realist posturing through the casting of 1970s misfit icon Elliott Gould as paranoid agoraphobic Richard Bergstrom, the lobbying firm's co-principal. In his appearances in the program's two flashback episodes, Bergstrom appears in a cluttered Brooklyn apartment, where he views and comments obsessively on the film *Mildred Pierce* (directed by Michael Curtiz, who Soderbergh in another context later name-checks as a model of filmmaking versatility). In the final episode, in which the firm dissolves, Carville questions Dupré about his knowledge of Bergstrom, and Dupré reveals their employer's fixation on the film, linking that mania to a disconnect from the firm's troubles: "For him this is all just a movie he can replay again and again." Not only, then, does *K Street* recast Gould as the nefarious alter ego of the shambling losers he played in films such as *M*A*S*H* (1970) and *The Long Goodbye*, it also deploys a Hollywood film with cultish appeal to signify excess attention to film fiction. One might regard this as a radical assertion of television authorship from a filmmaker who had at this point in his career directed remakes of two classical-Hollywood films (*Criss Cross* and *Ocean's Eleven*) and some of whose works bear similarities to the Robert Altman-directed films that made a star of Gould. *K Street*'s authors thus reject the hermeticism of the film-historical world in favor of the openness and immediacy of parafictional television. Soderbergh would of course later intervene further into parafiction with *Bubble* and other digital-video projects, and into film history through the Curtiz-emulating *The Good German*.

Despite this apparent textual openness, *K Street* erects substantial barriers to comprehension, likely hastening its commercial failure. With the premise of fictional and nonfictional figures intersecting in Washington, it presumes no specific knowledge base among its viewers. At the same time, it rewards detailed knowledge of contemporary politics, and indeed each episode includes numerous fleeting references virtually unintelligible to those not conversant in the period's daily political developments. Such knowledge is in principle available to all, but is most often pursued by members of elite groups: educated professionals, those whose corporate or legal work demands attention to political affairs, and above all those whose economic position affords them the time and inclination to pursue such subjects.[16] Even with such knowledge, *K Street*'s narrative appears not so much complex as complicated, developing inconsistently and ambiguously. Episodes do not balance personal and political narratives, or fictional and nonfictional ones. The series rewards careful viewers with substantial doses of confusion and tedium, and yet, these elements contribute almost inadvertently to an uncanny replication of the political process. They contribute, too, to Soderbergh's authorial interest in textual experimentation with form and content, and to his declared enthusiasm for process over product.

K Street's difficulty in fashioning a riveting narrative from the activities of influential Washington lobbyists reminds us that power brokers succeed in part by rendering their efforts unremarkable and uncompelling, thus mystifying those who would seek to challenge the exercise of power. (The Soderbergh-produced film *Syriana*, about Middle East power brokers, arguably points viewers toward the same conclusion.) *K Street* itself risks mystifying its audiences by withholding accessible narrative markers such as morally and psychologically legible characters, clear exposition, redundancy for key plot points, and consistent story arcs both within and across episodes. Coupled with its part-erasure of discrete boundaries between reality and fiction, the program's address can exacerbate taste and class disparities evident elsewhere in screen-media reception. Legibility is popular, opacity is not, and so the program's narrow taste profile becomes a mechanism for disengagement. To dismiss *K Street* as "a parlor game for insiders" is to scorn not just the parlor game but also the insider, although logically all citizens should aspire to the status of well-informed insider. *K Street* arouses taste judgments akin to those routinely mobilized around Soderbergh's work, with narrative experimentation sometimes seen to obstruct viewers' engagement with politically charged narratives such as *The Good German* and *Che*.

K Street uses the parafictional mode to demonstrate that politics is enacted by people with shifting and sometimes arbitrarily chosen interests, people who are charismatic or withdrawn, people whose behavior is by turns pragmatic, illogical, off-putting, and objectively boring, but above all people who engage consequentially with public affairs at key sites where power circulates. *K Street*'s political parafiction invites us to care about this essential subject even as it reminds us why most choose not to. Framed alongside Soderbergh's prior and subsequent screen practice in feature films, the series articulates his abiding interest in narratively complex explorations of political realities, evident in particular in *Traffic* and *Che*. While Soderbergh's specifically televisual work is limited, the medium rewards his investment in large narrative tapestries. Soderbergh's *Traffic*, as already noted, evolves from the UK television miniseries *Traffik*, and reflecting on *Che*, he suggests its narrative would have been best suited to the miniseries format as well.[17] Soderbergh remains most recognized as a filmmaker, but this core artistic identity includes parallel work in television, short films, essay nonfiction, theatre directing, and most recently painting. This diverse activity further defines a creative sensibility alternately timely and historical, but always premised on dialogue with artists and art forms across taste categories and modes of engagement.

Before returning to consideration of Soderbergh's overall artistic profile, we should attend briefly to his producing partner Clooney's experiment in series television authorship. Continuing in the parafictional mode established by *K Street*, the HBO series *Unscripted*, airing for ten episodes in early 2005, focuses on a loose group of young actors enmeshed in narratives on the border of fiction and nonfiction. During its run, the series earned generally unfavorable comparisons to another HBO series, *Entourage*, which also combines a fictionalized insider view of Hollywood with appearances from industry figures (including Mark Wahlberg, James Cameron, Martin Scorsese, and scores of others) playing themselves.[18] *Unscripted*, like *K Street*, does not substantially exploit the celebrities (such as actress Meryl Streep and screenwriter and producer Akiva Goldsman) who appear in cameo roles. Instead, the series integrates them into the fabric of episodes as incidental figures, with expository clarity reserved (if at all evident) for the three principals, Krista Allen, Bryan Greenberg, and Jennifer Hall. Like most of the series' cast—aside from Frank Langella, who takes on a wholly fictional role as an imperious acting teacher—these three play themselves, if in necessarily self-conscious fashion. While *Unscripted* includes staged scenes and fictional plotlines, it remains true to its title in granting no writing credits.

Even more than *K Street*, *Unscripted* depends for its dramatic value on its protagonists' career activities in the historical world. Episode plots detail their apparently nonfictional successes and failures at casting calls for films, television series, and commercials. The program's continuing narrative arc meshes the three leads' career progressions with fictionalized narratives of their social and romantic relationships with each other and with their acting teacher Goddard Fulton (Langella), in whose class they meet and to which they return each episode. In foregrounding the craft of screen performance, *Unscripted* explicitly narrates Clooney and Heslov's own creative interests. (Clooney directed the series' first five episodes, Heslov the next five.) Heslov worked as a comic and dramatic character actor for decades—with key roles as comic accomplices in *True Lies* (1994) and *The Scorpion King* (2002), among other films—before moving into producing and directing roles on projects with Clooney. Clooney's own work as both producer and performer has been well documented, as have his roles in two experiments in live television drama: a 1997 episode of *ER* broadcast as two live performances (one for each coast, staged three hours apart), and a 2000 adaptation of *Fail Safe* also broadcast as a live performance.[19] Thus, *Unscripted* continues Clooney's interest in convergences of historical and narrative time, as well as his and Heslov's investments in acting as craft and industry.

Both *K Street* and *Unscripted* exemplify the narrative, aesthetic, and cultural investments of Soderbergh and Clooney during their partnership in the Section Eight production company. Both series emphasize the fostering of performers' creative practice through improvisation and through novel engagements among professional and nonprofessional actors occurring at the boundary of reality and fiction. In exploring this liminal terrain and in other mixtures of narrative forms, both series demonstrate high-visibility experimentation within Hollywood, which Soderbergh and Clooney would continue in films such as *Good Night, and Good Luck* (co-scripted by Clooney and Heslov, partners in the post-Section Eight production company Smoke House) and *The Good German*. Both series illuminate, too, their creators' investments in particular kinds of self-reflexivity. *Unscripted*'s focus on screen acting continues Clooney's interrogation of people's relationships to media discourses. His first three films as director—*Confessions of a Dangerous Mind* (2002), *Good Night, and Good Luck,* and *Leatherheads* (2008), each developed in some fashion with Soderbergh—all showcase men negotiating their own media celebrity. (His fourth, *The Ides of March* [2011], not involving Soderbergh, continues this thematic trajectory.) Meanwhile, *K Street* merges Soderbergh's competing interests in political-historical subjects and in forms of intertextual screen culture. *K Street* and *Unscripted* work in narrative modes specific to television—i.e., the episodic serial with an overarching narrative arc—and *K Street*'s condensed production-to-airtime schedule adheres to a television-production ecology. Nonetheless, both Soderbergh and Clooney's creative efforts indicate the porousness of media categories and production roles. They take on a multitude of administrative, creative, and technical roles in film and television production. While contemporary screen industries involve high degrees of craft specialization, professional profiles such as Soderbergh's and Clooney's indicate the dynamism of Hollywood's production world at the top tier of industrial hierarchies.

Soderbergh and Clooney began developing a third series for HBO, to be based on the exploits of an NBA expansion team and thus presumably also in the parafictional mode. This project ceased development in 2006, with both men engaged in many other producing and directing projects instead. Clooney's interest in television led to the well-received historical film *Good Night, and Good Luck*, focused on 1950s television journalism. On their shared DVD commentary for that film, co-producers Clooney and Heslov assert that *Unscripted* was an essential precursor.[20] Despite the substantial differences between the two projects, both investigate historical agents who precariously balance on- and offscreen lives, and both merge fictional or staged scenes with television footage drawn from the historical record.

Soderbergh also departed from series television production, though he retained interest in television as distribution platform for new feature films as well as site for consumption of ancillary material such as DVD commentaries. (*Bubble*, *Che*, and *The Girlfriend Experience* all played simultaneously in theatrical and pay-television release, as discussed in other chapters; and HBO serves as producer and platform for the Liberace biopic *Behind the Candelabra*, in pre-production as of this writing.[21]) The two HBO series, and surrounding Soderbergh/Clooney efforts developed and produced by the pair's Section Eight production company, represent components of diverse professional portfolios. Each creative agent circulates through industrial affiliations, textual artifacts, and discourses of art and authorship across a range of media platforms. The next chapter considers further Section Eight's production activity and industrial position, alongside a range of artistic affiliations cultivated by Soderbergh as part of a polyvalent cross-media profile.

Chapter 8

Boutique Cinema, Section Eight, and DVD

As argued in the previous chapter, Soderbergh's television work further exemplifies a creative practice attuned to topical discourses such as politics and current events as well as to formal experimentation in the parafictional mode. The execution of this creative sensibility involves a range of practitioners across different projects. The output, meanwhile, addresses different groups of viewers based on subject matter, tone, genre, exhibition venue, and other distinguishing characteristics. While no precise pattern connects Soderbergh's multifarious output to the diverse communities drawn to that work, we might characterize this relationship as that of a boutique sensibility catering to boutique tastes, and with boutique exhibition spaces a frequent site of mutual encounter.

In his own late-1990s work on authorship, James Naremore argues that directors circulate as markers of distinction in contemporary film culture partly because of "the presence of a well-organized boutique cinema, geared to an up-market audience,"[1] promoted by film festivals, film-review journalism, and advertising such as Miramax's in the 1990s that hails film connoisseurs. Though not elaborating on this suggestive label, Naremore's points about festivals, mini-major distributors, and cineliterate viewers implicitly define boutique cinema as a conjunction of aesthetic predispositions and consumption sites. Through its positioning of directors and other figures, the category can link the efforts and interests of a range of specialized groups. Indeed, another name for "boutique" is "specialty," the term used to categorize particular industrial units and markets to circumvent the presumed intellectual demands made of viewers by the more polarizing "arthouse" label. A vague industrial descriptor, "specialty" denotes only something narrower than an abstracted mainstream. Meanwhile, the "arthouse" label not only carries negative industrial connotations but also remains strongly tied to a perceived high-water mark of cinemagoing in the 1960s and 1970s, when particular exhibition venues did function explicitly as arthouses. Among other developments, the rise of multiplex cinemas in the 1980s and 1990s, the proliferating screens of the new century, and the myriad services to which all these screens are put render the "arthouse" construct a crude marker of conditions of film culture today. As Section Eight's output demonstrates, boutique cinema can include not only traditional "arthouse films" but also popular star vehicles and offbeat genre films aimed at niche audiences. This latter category includes films labeled as "indie films" or "smart films" (among other industrial and critical designations), films often exhibited at venues that in the past showcased foreign-language films.[2]

The concept of boutique cinema joins industrial agendas with those of a range of taste cultures. Production entities utilize directors, A-list or otherwise, as essential components of project development and financing.[3] Existing arthouse cinemas and franchises such as Landmark Theatres and the Angelika Film Center, both of which have screened and promoted Soderbergh's features, identify directors prominently in their own promotional material as they reach out to selective potential audiences. Specialty home-video distributors such as the Criterion Collection, New Yorker Films, and Home Vision Entertainment cater to similar constituencies and likewise employ auteurist, director-centric framing; Soderbergh has been involved in the output of each of these companies as well. Print-media advocates such as the *New York Times* and the *New Yorker* and culturati or specialist websites such as *Salon* and *indieWIRE* promote these cinemas and distributors through their own reviews and feature stories, again with directors as a frequent currency. Finally, educated or film-literate audiences may read reviews, patronize specialty venues, and consume the output of boutique companies and divisions. Following Naremore, I offer "boutique" as an overarching construct uniting creative personnel, producing infrastructures, distributors of special-interest works, and cinephile reception frames. These reception milieus include both physical spaces (specialty cinema and domestic viewing surrounds) and the more abstracted, mutable cartographies of personal, institutional, and collective taste. In this chapter, I examine boutique cinema from two vantage points, studying Soderbergh and Clooney's production company Section Eight as well as Soderbergh's discursive performances on specialty DVD releases. These categories might initially be regarded as polar opposites—the before- and aftermarkets of film culture—but can be better understood as imbricated sectors in extended fields of artistic engagement.

One way to apprehend boutique cinema is to consider the operations and output of Hollywood's many small production companies. Even when supported through major-studio production deals and infrastructure provision, these companies can function literally as boutiques, contained physical spaces where creative craftsmanship may flourish before wares pass into larger commercial markets. "Boutique" can designate both the small offices in which ideas incubate and screen projects develop, and the specialty distribution networks and exhibition venues that present completed projects. The term can also refer principally to a creative sensibility cultivated in particular atelier spaces, and articulated textually at varying production scales. While boutique productions tend to be low- to medium-budget works with niche appeal, boutiques can also develop or co-develop wide mainstream releases such as the *Ocean's* films or works of other directors affiliated with small production companies. The activities of the Los Angeles-based production company Section Eight enrich the view of Soderbergh as a boutique filmmaker in the multiple senses of the term. Soderbergh and Clooney first worked together on the 1998 film *Out of Sight*, which saw Soderbergh seeking to reestablish his commercial prospects alongside the then still-rising film star Clooney. They formed Section Eight in 2000, and it operated until 2006, though with its last developed films released in 2009. Its seven-year run was relatively short for a company with two Hollywood A-list figures as principals, but the company was prolific in its output. During its existence, Section Eight produced or co-produced most but not all of Soderbergh's films as director from 2001 onward, Clooney's first two films as director, features from other longtime Soderbergh collaborators and newcomers, two HBO television series produced and directed by Soderbergh or Clooney, and one short film—24 projects in total.[4]

Overlapping with but also distinct from his production labor, Soderbergh has been remarkably active in the milieu of DVD commentary. As extensions of or complements to production activity, DVD supplements such as commentary tracks reanimate the production process and sometimes literally replay it (if in idealized, anecdotal form) for home viewers' edification. Challenging notions of discrete film texts wholly separate from contexts, DVD extras link texts to the conditions of their production, or at least to an agreed industrial narrative of a production. DVD playback subsequently restages production contexts in domestic reception spaces. Designated industrial spokesmen such as directors serve as key intermediaries rehearsing production activities for interested DVD viewers. Authoring figures occupy key positions in boutique cinemas, as the category bridges spheres of production and consumption. In keeping with the overall aims of this book, this chapter considers how Soderbergh's boutique efforts help outline a particular authorial signature. Section Eight's industrial situation, its film and television output, and Soderbergh's discursive strategies in DVD commentaries (for Section Eight films as well as many other releases) demonstrate additional ways that discourses of authorship take shape and circulate in contemporary Hollywood.

Section Eight and Collaborative Production

Section Eight's activities represent one site for the manufacture of a coherent creative identity within the larger Hollywood industrial apparatus. Section Eight's identity is directed both inward, to the industry, and outward, to media consumers. For the industry, Section Eight's principals carry networking and dealmaking power, with Soderbergh's and Clooney's names helping secure production capital and sometimes distribution arrangements, if not guaranteeing audience interest. In consumption contexts, meanwhile, the Section Eight name may stir recognition among interested cinephiles. Bridging the two realms, the production imprint helps create awareness for particular properties among influential constituencies of film critics. For example, with a limited release in ten U.S. cities, the Section Eight–produced *Wind Chill* (2007) merited only a 200-word review in the *New York Times*, but that brief review included the claim that "the production values display the finesse fitting a movie counting George Clooney and Steven Soderbergh among its producers."[5]

As an industrial brand, Section Eight speaks principally to other production entities and only secondarily to exhibitors or viewers. As with many other small production companies, Section Eight attaches only its name and no graphical logo to its completed projects. Its films and television programs appear under the company logos of Warner Bros. and Warner Independent Pictures, Miramax, HBO Films and its Picturehouse joint venture with New Line, HBO television, TriStar, Focus Features, and the independent Magnolia Pictures (these all in the U.S. alone—many other distributors, such as Germany's Constantin Films and the UK's Optimum Releasing, secured distribution rights outside the U.S.). Warner Bros. provided Section Eight's offices on the

Warners studio lot and paid the company's operating expenses, but did not finance or distribute all Section Eight productions. Thus, while co-principals Soderbergh and Clooney have worked repeatedly with Warner Bros. and Warner Independent Pictures—the latter shut down, along with Picturehouse and other specialty divisions, in 2008's industry belt-tightening—their production company represents no exclusive affiliation with a studio producer or distributor. Nor does Section Eight facilitate packaging by talent agencies—Soderbergh and Clooney themselves are represented by different agencies (Soderbergh by the management company Anonymous Content, Clooney by CAA).[6] In short, the Section Eight enterprise affords no comprehensive advantage to its executives or to the participants in its projects, guaranteeing neither production financing nor distribution deals. Conversely, Section Eight's productions are not more or less free of studio oversight. The company's first completed project was the Warners production *Ocean's Eleven*, produced under studio oversight, and a later Warners/Section Eight production, *Rumor Has It* (2005), received negative industry publicity when Warners replaced first-time director Ted Griffin owing to on-set conflicts. Moreover, post-Section Eight, Soderbergh and Clooney maintained intermittent but not exclusive relationships with Warner Bros. After *Ocean's Thirteen*, Soderbergh made multiple films, including *The Girlfriend Experience* and the Spalding Gray documentary *And Everything is Going Fine* (2010), without Warners' involvement, but did work with the studio on *The Informant!*, *Contagion*, and further projects. As for Clooney, while WIP co-produced and distributed his well-received *Good Night, and Good Luck*, he worked with Universal for his next directorial effort, *Leatherheads*, the first completed feature from his subsequent production company, Smoke House.[7] Soderbergh had spoken in interviews throughout the 1990s about the *Leatherheads* project, so its completion through a separate production company— and with his involvement not acknowledged in the film's credits— represents the rare case in which a Soderbergh-affiliated project did not finally carry his name.

I articulate these industrial relationships, or lack thereof, to suggest the ways Section Eight operates not so much as a powerful industrial unit but rather as a creative clearinghouse. The term "section eight" has two origins. In one usage, it refers to a U.S. government program offering subsidized housing to low-income Americans. The other is a U.S. military designation (no longer in use) for personnel psychologically unfit for service and thus discharged, and U.S. popular culture is

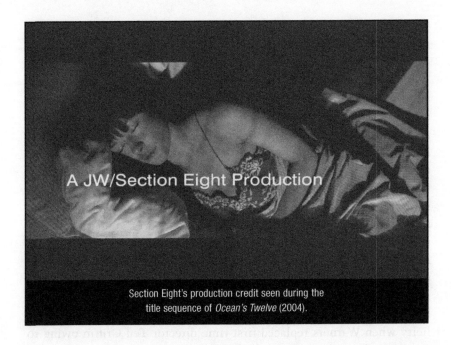

Section Eight's production credit seen during the
title sequence of *Ocean's Twelve* (2004).

littered with film and television characters feigning insanity or homosexuality to qualify for a Section 8 discharge. The diverse efforts of the Soderbergh/Clooney production company arguably stay true to both promises—shelter for the underprivileged and principled madness—with glossy studio productions, familiar as well as idiosyncratic genre pictures, and low-budget semi-experimental fare all appearing under the Section Eight banner. This varied output suggests that the company facilitates screen craftsmanship, that works released under its name represent particular artistic sensibilities and collaborating craftspeople, distinct from homogenous corporate product (some reviews of the *Ocean's* sequels notwithstanding). Soderbergh's diverse production roles characterize him as a screen-industry entrepreneur, providing creative input and logistical support for sometimes risky artistic ventures. As part of Soderbergh's myriad artistic labor, Section Eight represents a distinctive strategy to manage and channel creative U.S.-based filmmaking. Section Eight enables Soderbergh to create material and symbolic affiliations with a substantial body of filmmakers across a range of modes, genres, and sensibilities. Consequently, through this production company and through other industrial maneuvers, Soderbergh constructs a dispersed, transmedia industrial signature, one defined by what I would term benign colonization of creative screen practice.

Filmmaker-founded production companies often only manage the efforts of single filmmakers, serving less frequently as sites for development and stewardship of multiple, distinct screen productions. Clint Eastwood's Malpaso Productions has worked almost exclusively to produce Eastwood's own films as director. Francis Ford Coppola's American Zoetrope has produced Coppola's own directorial efforts as well as those of his children Sofia and Roman, in addition to other film and television projects with different creative teams. More widely active production companies such as Ridley and Tony Scott's Scott Free, and Matt Damon and Ben Affleck's Live Planet, have been associated with dozens of independent and studio features and television series. Beyond serving as development units, these companies organize their principals' own filmmaking labor and maintain those men's presence in production credits, contributing to their own industrial signatures visible to industry and audiences. For example, Ridley Scott's recurring television credit as executive producer of *NUMB3RS* (2005–2010) and Jerry Bruckheimer's for *CSI* (2000–), *Cold Case* (2003–2010), and other series and features contribute to their reputations as high-concept producers, just as Damon and Affleck's involvement with the *Project Greenlight* series (2001–2005) burnished their standing as champions of independent film.

No single model effectively accounts for the disparate efforts of independent production companies. Their profiles tend to disinvite scrutiny. Trade presses do not report or investigate their operations in depth, calling attention to them only at their inception or when particular deals are struck. With little need for recognition beyond industrial circles, many maintain no websites or other public-relations presence. But rather than being shadowy cabals operating through subterfuge, many are of course tiny entities housed in small offices, with output limited enough that wider visibility would not facilitate their activity. Production companies can afford business-tax status to their principals, and they create geographic presence in the form of physical office space where discrete production work can occur. A production company may afford its executives few industrial advantages. However, with company principals often earning on-screen producer credits, companies' affiliation with diverse screen projects contributes to the transmission of creative signatures in multiple contexts. Section Eight broadens the circulation of Soderbergh's authorial signature across industrial, textual, and reception contexts. Distinct from his producing partner Clooney, Soderbergh has worked to affiliate himself with many other strands of media discourse, particularly in the form of prestige-DVD releases and DVD commentary tracks. Combined with his prolific output as director, these efforts fashion a comprehensive authorial signature characterized by investments in and relationships to particular modes of production, aesthetic strategies, and creative sensibilities.

Considered as a corpus of film and television texts, Section Eight's productions form a fairly cohesive orbit of taste categories, all in proximity to successful or recurrently visible modes and genres in contemporary Hollywood production or specialty exhibition. At the most prestigious end of the scale, Section Eight's productions include the Clooney-affiliated political dramas or thrillers *Michael Clayton*, *Good Night, and Good Luck*, and *Syriana*. Meanwhile, Section Eight's highest-profile productions in popular terms, the *Ocean's* films, all star Clooney and allow a degree of creative autonomy still uncommon for Hollywood productions, with Soderbergh serving as director, cinematographer, editor, and often camera operator on all three films. Section Eight has also produced projects from well-regarded directors in independent cinema. For example, in 2002 these included Todd Haynes's *Far From Heaven* and Christopher Nolan's *Insomnia* (the former co-produced and distributed by Universal imprint Focus Features, the latter by Warner Bros.). *Insomnia* remakes the 1997 Norwegian film of the same title, and Section Eight has produced other transnational remakes: the comic thriller *Criminal* (2004) revises the Argentinean film *Nine Queens* (2000), and the similar *Welcome to Collinwood* updates the Italian caper film *Big Deal on Madonna Street* (1958). (Soderbergh developed the *Solaris* remake through Fox and James Cameron's Lightstorm Entertainment rather than Section Eight.) In genre-film output, Section Eight also produced the science-fiction films *The Jacket* (2005) and *A Scanner Darkly*, the latter distinguished as a Philip K. Dick adaptation and a rotoscopic-animation work from longtime indie filmmaker Richard Linklater. Meanwhile, *Wind Chill* stakes out the generic terrain of the supernatural thriller, and *The Half Life of Timofey Berezin* (2006), released on HBO television (in 2007) under the title *Pu-239*, mixes science-fiction, crime, black-comedy, and dramatic-thriller elements.

These projects, representing some but not all of Section Eight's output, occupy safely commercial territory in the contemporary Hollywood landscape—comic thrillers, other genre films, ensemble star vehicles such as the *Ocean's* films, and prestige films positioned for Academy Awards contention such as *Syriana* and *Good Night, and Good Luck*. These last two films, like many of Section Eight's productions, foreground arguably progressive political content. Numerous other features—*Confessions of a Dangerous Mind* (based on game-show host Chuck Barris's fictionalized memoir), *A Scanner Darkly*, and *The Good German*—adapt cult and popular novels. Some Section Eight productions can also be defined by different strains of formal experimentation, evident in Soderbergh's *The Good German* and *Bubble* as well as the intensely subjective *Keane*. Taken as a whole, all exemplify constellations of filmmaking at the intersection of independent cinema and Hollywood. Most focus on the exploits of middle-class, heterosexual white men, many venture into crime narratives, and few pose particular viewing challenges for educated, urban cinephiles. This designation need not dampen the body of work's creative achievement, but it bears noting that the Section Eight shingle does not promote overtly noncommercial efforts or enable the circulation of determinedly radical works of cinema.

Perhaps to expand his creative signature into these other areas (and as noted in previous chapters), Soderbergh has received executive-producer credits for his role in securing the theatrical and DVD releases or re-releases of such works as *Naqoyqatsi*, from experimental documentarian Godfrey Reggio; *Killer of Sheep*, from black independent filmmaker Charles Burnett; and *Symbiopsychotaxiplasm: Take 2 1/2*, from black independent and experimental filmmaker William Greaves. Whereas the Section Eight efforts construct Soderbergh as a steward of narratively stimulating or semi-adventurous contemporary commercial production, these separate affiliations distinguish him as a patron or preservationist for key works of American film history and experimental cinema. Soderbergh's constitution as discerning cinephile-patron creates particular heuristics for reception of his own filmmaking efforts, with the filmmaker not defined solely by his own works as director but by a span of aesthetic and industrial affiliations. Among other effects, such affiliations contribute to critical discourses that frame Soderbergh's films not only in terms of their entertainment value but also their fulfillment, or lack thereof, of his potential as a boundary-pushing film artist.

Both Soderbergh's idiosyncratic solo promotions and his Section Eight collaborations exhibit a form of benign colonization. I use the term to designate a creative or discursive practice involving claims of kinship to an artist or text or even part-ownership of a work. The colonizer does not seek to profit directly from this association but to establish his or her position in a continuum of or dialogue about screen art. I offer "benign colonization" as a concept distinct from, if not wholly opposite to, textual strategies of creative appropriation. Soderbergh's practice involves not so much ironic textual quotation or pastiche as material or symbolic collaboration. For example, interviewed in 1996 for a documentary on the Sundance Film Festival, Soderbergh remarks less on his own current directing efforts than on his role as producer of festival entry *The Daytrippers*, from first-time feature director Greg Mottola. Recalling his response to a short film of Mottola's, Soderbergh comments, "I thought, 'Who is this guy? Maybe I can attach myself to him.'" Also in an enthusiastically ironic tone, he notes that "I saw a short film of his and said, 'Give me some of that,'" and just as directly, "I just wanted to glom onto him."[8] Though Soderbergh and Mottola did not collaborate again, Soderbergh's off-the-cuff remarks at the festival highlight the relationships of patronage, affiliation, and collaboration that define his filmmaking practice across his long career.

As a component or byproduct of his colonizing activity, Soderbergh has earned producer or executive-producer credits for projects completed with his thoroughgoing or virtual stewardship. This latter term "stewardship" might partly situate the notoriously hazy executive-producer credit, often granted as a courtesy or industrial genuflection to personnel with no specific production role. With Section Eight, Soderbergh's executive production has included forms of creative oversight and control associated with executive work roles. He reportedly has had final-cut privileges over numerous productions, including *Far From Heaven*, contracted as a condition of the film's financing.[9] The credit conversely can aid circulation of films with limited commercial prospects, as Soderbergh's executive-producer title does in promotion of the experimental, largely non-narrative *Naqoyqatsi* and *Symbiopsychotaxiplasm: Take 2 1/2*. Soderbergh's name also accompanied the theatrical and DVD release of the 2004 independent and Section Eight co-production *Keane*, the latter version demonstrating that the executive-producer credit can reflect creative activity. *Keane*'s DVD release includes as a supplement a re-edited, longer version of the film labeled the "Steven Soderbergh Alternate Cut," which Soderbergh claims he prepared for writer-director Lodge Kerrigan as a creative brainstorming device, or as Soderbergh writes, "in case it jogged anything (it didn't)."[10] Contrasting with perceptions of producers as mercenary executives, Soderbergh in his leadership position at Section Eight speaks of industry economics with a candor unusual for a de facto company head. He observes of films perceived as commercial risks, "If it ends up being a wash, we win because we got some interesting stuff made," adding the part-disclaimer, "Maybe that's not what you want to hear from a producer, but we can't lie."[11] Producers routinely invoke risk-taking to distinguish their successful stewardship of unconventional hits, or to counterbalance negative commentary on films perceived as commercial failures. However, they tend not to showcase their art-over-commerce bona fides while seeking financing for future projects. Soderbergh's consistent invocation of filmmaking's artistic satisfactions distinguishes him as an entrepreneurial producer, possessed of creative integrity if not of any particular Midas touch.

Executive-producer credits, supplemental creative activities such as the *Keane* edit, and the more concrete producer role all craft an industrial signature deployed across media forms, discourses, and textual and extratextual categories. Soderbergh's unhyphenated producer credits signify explicit logistical and creative labor on behalf of particular films. Matthew Bernstein, looking across Hollywood history at divisions of labor in studio and independent production, argues that producers' activities do not qualify them for authorial status, that they function principally "to facilitate contemporary auteurs' work."[12] While the retention of the auteur label can cloud understandings of production practice, Bernstein also claims usefully that a "fruitful way to think about producers and their creative work is as a brand name," a framing that he suggests "places producers at some remove from . . . artistic creativity."[13] Bernstein implicitly defines creativity in terms of particular textual outputs rather than demonstrable creative production activity. These outputs ascend to the status of art only through the intervention of the discerning critic, making artistic production itself fairly inconsequential. But we may instead mobilize the claim offered by Producers Guild of America president Marshall Herskovitz that "the producer is the driving force behind the film from the beginning all the way to the end,"[14] a definition that emphasizes the stewardship work required for the execution of collaborative artworks such as motion pictures.[15] Soderbergh's colonizing impulses and his relationships in multiple categories to diverse screen-media productions further expand the boundaries of artistic creativity. Producer-branding such as Soderbergh's through Section Eight and other projects that bear his name for production and marketing purposes locates the producer within categories of artistry and authorship. The circulation of a broad artistic sensibility complicates distinctions between armchair connoisseurship and verifiable creative labor.

Section Eight's productions locate Soderbergh (and less so Clooney, whose public face is as actor and sometime director, not as producer despite his efforts in this regard) not only as a steward or patron but also as a collaborator. Many Section Eight productions showcase creative workers who fill secondary roles on Soderbergh's own films as director. *Ocean's Eleven* screenwriter Ted Griffin was poised to earn his first studio-feature directing credit for the star-driven *Rumor Has It*, before being replaced midway through its troubled production. Soderbergh's longtime assistant director, Gregory Jacobs, debuted as director with *Criminal* and despite its commercial failure followed up with *Wind Chill*. Thus, Section Eight productions allowed Jacobs to move to a more artistically central role on projects similar to the other works he had done with Soderbergh. *Criminal*, for example, mixes a complicated heist plot with casually deceptive interactions among men, linking it tonally to *Ocean's Eleven* and other Soderbergh-directed crime films (an infrequent screenwriter, Soderbergh pseudonymously co-wrote *Criminal*'s adapted screenplay with Jacobs). Meanwhile, *Wind Chill* features a steel-blue palette and other compositional elements promi- nent, too, in such Soderbergh-directed films as *Traffic*, *Out of Sight*, and *The Underneath*. Beyond enabling Soderbergh's collaborators to rise in stature, Section Eight has operated partly like a scaled-down version of a classical studio operation or a contemporary talent agency, supplying writers, performers, and technicians for work on different productions. Another longtime Soderbergh collaborator, sound editor Larry Blake, has worked on multiple Section Eight productions as well, as have pro- duction designer Philip Messina, editor Stephen Mirrione, and many others. Section Eight thus fosters creative collaboration across work categories, drawing from a deep roster of above- and below-the-line workers. It also nurtures collaboration across modes of production, in particular cutting across economic categories with output ranging from the $1.5 million budget for *Keane* to $119 million for *Ocean's Twelve*. Section Eight depends on economically and creatively interdependent artistic networks, and its productions show creative workers moving up, down, and across production scales. Such movement indicates the porousness of particular industrial categories, or at least the ability of the Soderbergh/Clooney partnership specifically to facilitate the flow of creative-industry workers across such categories.

Transitive and Domesticated Authorship: Soderbergh and DVD

Section Eight builds on existing industrial relationships among Soderbergh, Clooney, and their collaborators. Practices of collaborative authorship apparent on Soderbergh-directed films carry over into the production company's practice as well, facilitating the creative work of Soderbergh collaborators and cross-pollinating diverse productions crafted by individuals and groups both within contemporary Hollywood and at its margins. Soderbergh's dispersed presence in other kinds of texts—including short films, documentaries, books, interviews, and DVD audio commentaries—evidences further creative dialogue and cross-pollination. This next section considers the ways DVD commentaries in particular, part of what Timothy Corrigan calls "semi-textual strategies" for engaging and dispersing authorial agency,[16] can deepen understandings of the forms and functions of authorial discourse.

Showing self-awareness about the generic format and pitfalls of audio commentary tracks, Soderbergh has single-handedly parodied the form. For the 2003 Criterion DVD of his very-limited release 1996 film *Schizopolis*, one audio commentary track features Soderbergh interviewing himself (to discuss the film in which, of course, he also plays the lead). For the commentary, he adopts twin personas of fatuous interviewer and pompous director, with the latter issuing vaporous pontifications—such as his attempts to "break down the fifth wall"—and at one point taking a cell-phone call during the commentary.[17] Beyond satirizing the easy targets of egotistical filmmakers and sycophantic commentators, Soderbergh's performance caricatures the multiple work roles that partly define his filmmaking practice: this Soderbergh is so thoroughly engaged in film culture that he can be on both ends of an interview at once. The commentary's split nature also links it to *Schizopolis*'s thematics and narrative; one of the film's conceits is that Soderbergh plays two identical characters romantically involved with the same woman. The DVD includes a second audio commentary track featuring other production personnel, ensuring that Soderbergh's comic track does not undermine the premise of professional insight and critical analysis inscribed into the Criterion brand. This second track offers co-commentary from four members of the production team, thus reasserting the centrality of the collaboration that also defines Soderbergh's creative practice.

DVD commentaries can promote works of anointed auteur directors. They can also create auteurs, by authorizing single individuals to account for film production and textual meaning and thus to claim author status for small- or large-scale media texts. Writing before the advent of DVD on "the commerce of auteurism," Corrigan labels auteurism "a commercial strategy for organizing audience reception."[18] Building on Corrigan's discussion, Robert Alan Brookey and Robert Westerfelhaus observe that "[m]edia conglomerates have a vested interest in maintaining the ideology of the auteur because it facilitates the promotion of their products."[19] Corrigan himself notes that discourses such as director interviews contribute to marketing initiatives, creating brand awareness of filmmakers. Participation in interviews and commentaries does not itself guarantee authorial, let alone auteur, status. Performers and technicians routinely recount their production experiences without asserting creative oversight. But multiple discourses in film culture—promotion and publicity, highbrow press and academic writing, and popular reception—work to encourage views of *all* film directors as distinct creators whose works contain interior meanings, on which they are routinely asked to expound. Particularly in the landscape of popular-entertainment writing and reception, the parlorgame debates over auteurs, metteurs-en-scène, and technicians are well behind us. Promotional and other foregrounding of directors constructs them as auteurs, and granted this sacrosanct status, they become key mediating presences between films and viewers. For Corrigan, this relationship of mediation means that "the auteur can be described according to the conditions of a cultural and commercial *intersubjectivity*."[20] Corrigan's formulation reminds us that discourses of authorship depend on and interpellate consuming subjects.

Building on claims such as Corrigan's about auteurism as commercial strategy, Barbara Klinger notes that "DVD acts literally as an ambassador of context, entering the home complete with its own armada of discourses meant to influence reception"[21] and that "DVD provides ample opportunity for affirming authorship."[22] Most discussions of DVD and authorship consider directors' commentary tracks on films they have directed, obviously the principal form of director commentaries. Film directors also contribute periodically to extratextual material on home-video releases of films for which they play no production role—e.g., Todd Haynes's 2006 DVD introductions to Max Ophuls-directed films such as *The Reckless Moment* (1949) and *Le Plaisir* (1952),[23] or William Friedkin's interview on the 2004 DVD box set of the Kinji Fukasaku-directed *Yakuza Papers* series of the 1970s. And in select cases, directors participate in DVD commentaries on such films. For example, Allison Anders shares commentary with Monte Hellman on Criterion's 2007 DVD of *Two-Lane Blacktop* (1971), and music video and feature director Mark Romanek interviews Soderbergh on the *Bubble* DVD. Soderbergh also appears on co-commentaries on DVDs of numerous films he claims as influences, including a shared commentary with director John Boorman for the 2005 DVD release of *Point Blank*, another with writer-director James Gray for the 2005 DVD of *The Yards*, and interviews or co-commentaries with director Mike

Nichols on three DVDs to date of Nichols-directed films of the late 1960s and early 1970s.

These latter-day interviews construct the original director and the interviewer as co-authors of the overarching text that combines film and commentary track. As Catherine Grant observes, the combination of narrative film and audio commentary transforms a text into a "re-directed" documentary about the initial film, "in which the film's existing visual track is employed as a graphic illustration of a teleological story of its production."[24] Shared commentaries enlist a new co-author to help tell this production story. As this new figure does not claim original authorship or intent, his or her (usually his) enunciations differ from those that define commercial auteurism. This process returns us to Corrigan's work on auteurism, where he notes the conventional function of the director interview as "the promotion of a certain intentional self" or as "the commercial dramatization of self."[25] Modes such as the co-interviews in which Soderbergh repeatedly participates involve no less an authorial performance. But rather than ascribing total authority to one person, they promote a form of transitive or associative authorship, with the new interlocutor positioning himself artistically alongside the initial text and its designated creative spokesman.

Co-commentaries usually do not serve explicit commercial functions as promotions of the interviewing directors' own films. They can be produced for DVD distributors, such as Criterion, with no economic stake in theatrical releases of any filmmakers' work. Similarly, such DVD releases often do not coincide with releases of the interviewers' own films, even when creative links are apparent. For example, Soderbergh interviews screenwriter Tony Gilroy for a commentary on *The Third Man*'s Criterion DVD, released in May 2007. During interviews in late 2006 surrounding the release of *The Good German*, Soderbergh cites *The Third Man* as a stylistic point of reference. *The Good German* received a tiered international release during winter 2007 but was no longer in theatrical exhibition at the time of the Criterion DVD release. While the commentary track offers no specific cross-promotional value, then, it does discursively promote the creative signature and collaborative work of Soderbergh and Gilroy. Gilroy in particular stood to gain from this discourse; the screenwriter of the popular *Bourne Identity* films (2002, 2004, 2007), his debut as writer-director, *Michael Clayton*, premiered in September 2007. Criterion positions its releases for a selective grouping of connoisseur-consumers, so despite their modest commercial impacts, these releases carry weight in film culture. Soderbergh and Gilroy's discussion links them creatively to a canonical text in world cinema and acts as a guarantor of the artistry of Gilroy's Hollywood feature debut, which as already noted is also a Section Eight production. Soderbergh and Section Eight have worked with many of Gilroy's other collaborators as well. *The Bourne Ultimatum* (2007)'s script credits go to three men: Tony Gilroy; George Nolfi, screenwriter of *Ocean's Twelve*; and Scott Burns, who as noted previously debuted as feature director with *Pu-239*, and who later wrote *The Informant!*'s adapted screenplay. Thus, the dialogue with Gilroy exemplifies the collaborative networks that link Soderbergh and Section Eight to other productive, high-profile industry workers.

Both the Section Eight collaborations and the DVD commentaries align Soderbergh with critically or commercially lauded figures of the present and with venerated films and filmmakers across cinema history. Section Eight's productions represent behind-the-scenes creative partnerships made visible to public film cultures through the circulation of films in theatrical and domestic exhibition (with Section Eight's two HBO television series furthering the company's presence in homes). But as artifacts circulating primarily to home viewers, the DVD commentaries exist mostly as private, domestic commodities. Like many other filmmakers, Soderbergh participates in conversations replayed mostly in private consumption environments. In this forum, Soderbergh becomes a domesticated artist, his authorial voice literally most audible in the homes of interested viewers. The phenomenon of domesticated authorship accords with a pattern identified much earlier by Klinger, also in the pre-DVD era. Writing on 1980s film promotion and reception, she argues that "the success of commodification relies on a personalization or privatization of what are originally public discourses; the further a text can be extended into the social and individual realm by promotional discourses, the better its commercial destiny."[26] Building on related claims, Grant argues that "the kinds of enunciatory performances taking place in DVD commentaries . . . often attempt to interpellate a connoisseur community or a community that may construct itself as connoisseur."[27] The mediated, private DVD commentaries accord with a range of industrial logics. These performances show creative networks across time, for example in connecting contemporary filmmakers to 1940s films or to still-working figures such as Nichols and Boorman who began directing in the 1960s. They also transport creativity across space, from the audio-recording site to domestic or other personal-consumption spheres. Finally they link creators across industrial categories, such as 1940s British production and contemporary Hollywood as in the case of *The Third Man;* or contemporary Hollywood and micro-indies, as with Soderbergh's Criterion co-commentary for the ultra-low-budget feature *Clean, Shaven* (1993).

We can frame the concept of the domesticated author in still another way, returning to the concept of the boutique cinema. While boutique cinema exists in the physical spaces of boutique exhibition sites—such as specialty miniplexes favoring limited-release or ostensibly non-Hollywood films—it also occupies the domestic spaces where cinephiles engage with film texts and culture through such practices as reading reviews and consuming DVD commentaries. In domestic contexts, intersubjective balances arguably shift in favor of the consumer, who has some greater claim over the space than he or she does over the boutique theater. Playback of commentaries can transform the private home into a ciné-salon where cultivated observers drink in the insights of artists and intellectuals. James Kendrick argues that specialty home-video distributors such as Criterion depend on this formulation, observing that "the foundation of the Criterion Collection rests on the legitimacy of the home theater as an important alternative space for film spectatorship and analysis."[28] In this environment, consumers further their senses of ownership of or participation in screen culture by acting as audiences for dialogues among filmmakers. The recruitment of interviewers with no privileged relationship to the original production, such as that of Soderbergh to co-commentate on films made during his childhood or earlier, further erodes boundaries between cinephiles and screen texts. (I confess that here I am tempted, like the joking Soderbergh, to invoke the concept of the "fifth wall.")

DVD materials deserve our close attention because of their centrality in telling stories about the production process and defining the terms of authorship. Critiquing the commercial imperatives of DVDs, Dale Hudson and Patricia Zimmermann argue that "[w]ith their special 'behind the scenes' and 'making of' features, DVDs draw [the] new generation of cinephiles into an illusory identification with the industry."[29] This identification, however, may be no more nefarious than that which ensues when someone not employed in media industries reads a *Variety* headline. DVD materials address viewers in sometimes personal ways but, like trade-press stories, do not promise absolute, unrestricted access to the material in question. Seen from another vantage point, DVD extras facilitate their users' legitimate participation in film culture, merging commercial, aesthetic, and sociocultural concerns. Craig Hight, for example, writes of making-of documentaries or "MODs" that the form can explore "the influences on a film's creative personnel, the nature of actors' performances, and the often innovative filmmaking techniques employed," adding that "the MOD subgenre also has the potential to open a space for debate over the overall social, political, and cultural value of the film in question."[30] John Caldwell, scrutinizing a different set of intermediary discourses linking the general public to industry professionals, argues that "producer-as-audience initiatives work to merge audience identification with industrial identity."[31] Caldwell refers to intra-industry promotional efforts very different from those Soderbergh undertakes, but Soderbergh's professional-connoisseurial discourse forms part of the larger constellation of industry dialogue. As Caldwell argues further, "industry professionals know a great deal about the industry, the screen and screen culture, and spend considerable time, money and effort complicating, elaborating and commoditizing that industry knowledge for the trade and public."[32] Soderbergh's own discursive efforts interweave cinephilic and industrial sensibilities. At the same time, he speaks regularly from a specific position as an industry leader. As DGA vice president, for example, he has been a vocal advocate for anti-piracy initiatives. In this and other cases, his legacy of cinephile discourse and his patronage of myriad substrata of world cinema legitimate his industrial stances in ways unavailable to figures such as MPAA executives, who lack broad-based connoisseurial profiles.

Soderbergh's specific practice on DVD interviews shows various ways in which connections among filmmakers, films, and domestic viewing subjects are made. In the Soderbergh/Mike Nichols commentaries such as that for *Catch-22*, Soderbergh shapes discussion around particular ideals of filmmaking and film connoisseurship. As informed interviewer as well as discerning film lover, Soderbergh foregrounds his own knowledge of and enthusiasm for playful, experimental aspects of the filmmaking process, irrespective of cost or commercial considerations. He prompts Nichols to celebrate specific collaborators' efforts, and together the men portray studio filmmaking as a well-resourced laboratory for artistic risk-taking and collaboration. Their conversations define cinema's value in terms of process rather than output. The pleasure or complication of filmmaking itself dominates the discussion, aesthetic considerations take on secondary significance, and commercial outcomes receive only passing commentary, usually in relation to aesthetic questions. (With *Catch-22* for example, Soderbergh repeatedly praises the film's formalism, but Nichols calls the film "too cold" and suggests that its formalist tone limits viewer engagement and thus may account for the film's commercial failure.) Soderbergh also brings to his conversations with Nichols a range of other filmmakers' anecdotes and epigrams, culled from his own apparently voracious reading. Beyond their playback in the home environment, the co-commentaries domesticate Soderbergh through these proclaimed associations with sources such as biographies and memoirs, popular resources available to the general public. At times, Soderbergh's knowledge attests to his privileged industry situation, as he recounts, for example, his own conversations with screenwriter Buck Henry. Overall, though, his merger of this material with knowledge harvested from books and news accounts further presents him as a liminal figure, drawing on industrial resources as well as resources available to fellow cinephiles.

DVD commentaries also involve consumers in the domestic circulation of authorship by transforming the viewing space into a salon in which consumers eavesdrop on privileged but semi-casual interactions among filmmakers or other screen-culture professionals. The official dialogue between original filmmaker and interlocutor involves the new domestic receiver in discussion of the film at hand and a wider body of films and film cultures. Filmmakers' intertextual dialogues reward the cinephilic impulse that brings a consumer to play an audio commentary. In alluding to other films, commentators invoke groupings of texts and their surrounding institutions, all useful in securing cultural or artistic capital. The ways home viewers and industry professionals secure that capital, and the uses to which they put it, can differ substantially. On the *Catch-22* commentary, Nichols recounts what he now deems a crude attempt to recycle a shot from *Triumph of the Will* (1934) to depict a character's growing authoritarianism. Soderbergh matches him with an aside about his own pilfering of shots from *The Battle of Algiers* for use in *Traffic*. In other Soderbergh commentaries and interviews, he admits to further borrowing, claiming to reproduce shots from such films as *Klute* (1971) and *All the President's Men* for other films on which he serves as cinematographer. Such pronouncements cast Soderbergh as intertextual plunderer engaged in selective acts of appropriation, further defining him as author by association. They join him, too, with like-minded filmmakers such as Nichols in defining cinema in terms of shared ideas and images from which film artists and viewers may gain pleasure, and from which they may draw to augment their own cultural capital. Filmmakers such as Soderbergh put these discourses in service of contemporary, synthetic film art but also in service of their own authorial brands. And just as lifestyle brands such as sportswear and personal-electronics companies enlist consumers in the manufacture of brand identities, so the technologies and practices of domesticated authorship involve viewers as co-constitutors of fields of intertextual association.

The domestic space becomes the boutique or salon in which viewers' own tastes are cultivated and rewarded. Here, screen professionals serve as expert curators, and their very participation in the system creates feedback loops that burnish their own credentials. On *Catch-22*'s audio commentary, for example, Soderbergh repeatedly alludes to his participation in the film's transfer from celluloid to DVD. Thus he defines his own collaboration as material and not merely discursive. Since he receives no screen credit for this labor, he earns public acknowledgment only by declaring the work on the audio commentary. Soderbergh's uncredited re-authoring work becomes part of the larger narrative of *Catch-22*'s circulation, further asserting his productive and custodial relations to film culture. The audio commentary provides a pretense for associative authorship as well as a site for its recognition.

Boutique Authors and Screen-Industry Architecture

Another facet of the boutiquing of film culture is the increasing prevalence of films, independent and otherwise, bypassing theaters in favor of domestic viewing spaces. Home and private consumption formats such as DVD, video-on-demand, digital downloads, and streaming online video contribute to a range of transformations in the nature of creative practice, the situation of film texts, and the activities that constitute film reception. Amid this climate of transformation, Soderbergh's production company and his activities in DVD and related forums foreground discrete pleasures for collaborative filmmakers and for connoisseur viewers who help maintain and disseminate Soderbergh's creative brands. In one of the few lengthy news articles on Section Eight, Soderbergh repeats the rationale he claims he supplied to Clooney for starting the production company, saying, "If we can keep it lean and mean and it's fun, I'm in."[33] Soderbergh here makes a case for filmmaking as dynamic, festive work performed by enthusiasts. The same sentiment emerges in his discussions with Nichols, who on the *Catch-22* interview track muses to Soderbergh about his own idealized filmmaking practice: "make it on the cheap, make it fast, make everybody work hard—that's the excitement of doing something that is not trying to be a mass movie."[34] The rhetorical flouting of commercial imperatives also links the venerated Nichols's model of authorship (or at least the model advanced on the DVD) to the practices of Section Eight, and both help define the boutique Soderbergh brand. Indeed, such rhetoric helps define Soderbergh *as* a boutique brand, linked to scaled-down artistry rather than mass circulation, and to promises of quality independent of economics.

A final case—one of Section Eight's productions, the 2004 omnibus film *Eros*—demonstrates clearly the principles of boutique and associative authorship. *Eros* compiles three distinct shorts, scripted and directed in turn by contemporary arthouse star Wong Kar-Wai, Soderbergh, and the elderly Michelangelo Antonioni. It screened at 2004's Toronto and Venice film festivals and received limited U.S. theatrical distribution from Warner Independent Pictures the following year. Soderbergh's participation links him (via Antonioni) to the critical high-water period of 1960s European art cinema as well as (via Wong) to the presently esteemed categories of world cinema and Hong Kong or East Asian art cinema. Though a product of multiple production companies and co-financiers in seven different territories, *Eros* includes the Section Eight title and circulates partly through WIP, indicating Soderbergh's connection to the project. Moreover, Soderbergh's segment of the film stars Alan Arkin, a performer closely associated with comic and dramatic eccentricity in 1970s Hollywood, particularly through his roles in such films as *The In-Laws* (1979), *Freebie and the Bean* (1974), and of course *Catch-22*. *Eros* nurtures Soderbergh's authorial brand through associations with key filmmakers and performers across time frames, cultures, and industrial contexts. And given the film's limited theatrical release (like that of numerous Soderbergh or Section Eight projects), its consumption occurs principally in domestic environments.

We need not see "domesticated authorship" as a circular process by which a filmmaker's work and voice are consigned to home video after being shut out of theatrical release and promotion. Indeed, connoisseur viewers and the filmmakers they support may claim selective distribution as a mark of positive distinction rather than a symptom of commercial failure. Domesticated authorial discourse invites viewers to join film cultures at a remove from commercial or economic imperatives. Discourses surrounding authorship have explicit commercial functions but also help constitute taste publics. To unpack these discourses, I have offered the terms domesticated, transitive, and associative authorship, along with the concept of benign colonization. These categories denote industrial and cultural relationships that are both discursive and material. Production companies' unpublicized creative labor, such as that Soderbergh performed with Section Eight, involves the same kinds of collaborative associations that underpin the public construction of directors' and producers' authorial brands. These relationships highlight the intersubjective processes involved in the constitution and circulation of artistic authorship. In his efforts to locate screen-industry activity, Caldwell writes of "the seemingly endless layers of cultural and institutional mediations that manage movement from the 'outside' to the 'centre,'" concluding that "arguably, the mediating layers *are* the industry."[35] Such layers certainly make up the virtual architecture of boutique cinema. Like the phenomena of screen authorship to which it contributes, boutique cinema engages a range of discourses, texts, technologies, and institutions operating in global screen cultures.

Conclusion

Between 2009 and 2011, interviews with Soderbergh and some collaborators suggested that he would soon retire from filmmaking. "I feel like I'll hit the ceiling of my imagination," he told the *San Francisco Chronicle* in 2009, on the eve of the release of *The Girlfriend Experience*.[1] At the end of 2010, interviewed during production of the Soderbergh-directed *Contagion*, Matt Damon discussed Soderbergh's plans for retirement, noting that "[h]e's kind of exhausted with everything that interested him in terms of form. He's not interested in telling stories."[2] But while Soderbergh confirmed his interests in turning away from filmmaking and toward painting, he also signed on to direct a screen adaptation of the 1960s television series *The Man from U.N.C.L.E.* with longtime collaborator Clooney as star (both later left the project);[3] and later, to direct the male-stripper biopic *Magic Mike* (2012), based on the early career of *Haywire* co-star Channing Tatum. Amid this activity, he also worked, in a fairly unprecedented move for an A-list filmmaker, as second-unit director for *The Hunger Games* (2012), directed by his friend and earlier collaborator Gary Ross (Soderbergh acted as one of multiple producers on Ross's directorial debut, *Pleasantville*).[4] With these and multiple other projects brewing, Soderbergh's creative activity showed few signs of losing speed. He also maintained a presence in other surprising areas of pop culture. In early 2011, he participated in a lengthy NFL Network podcast[5] that included his detailed handicapping of U.S. television networks' HD football coverage. Not long after, to accompany an interview with Soderbergh, WNYC Radio's "Studio 360" program published on its website a list he had compiled of his entire past year's media consumption, including movies, books, and television series.[6] (As readers might surmise by this point, Soderbergh's "Daily Diet," as the site titled the list, is bountiful and wide-ranging.) These conversations and disclosures, while unusual for any major filmmaker let alone one claiming an imminent retirement, are entirely consistent with Soderbergh's creative profile. As the interview that follows also demonstrates, amid prolific filmmaking activity, Soderbergh shows himself in deep, enthusiastic dialogue with many modes of cultural production.

Throughout this book, I have emphasized Soderbergh's creative collaborations and his material and discursive affiliations across screen culture. I have argued that these complex artistic and professional relationships indeed constitute significant elements *of* that culture. The maintenance of artistic and professional profiles depends on networks of work activity, patronage, and also taste. Public and private reputations, and the circulation of these reputations, are central to artistic practice and its wider recognition. The phenomena that comprise what technology evangelist Chris Anderson terms the "reputation economy"[7] operate not only within industrial circles but in wider connoisseur and consumer activity as well. While I have interrogated artistic reputation-building and critical reception throughout this book, in closing I wish to consider the specifics of a Soderbergh-directed film's circulation through emergent discursive channels increasingly significant to screen industries. This final case identifies new agents involved in the formation of contemporary author personas, the stakes and rewards of this cultural activity, and above all the continued importance of recognizing authorship as the convergence of production, textual, and reception activities.

Guerilla Hunters: The Precirculation of *Che*

This concluding case study investigates the embryonic and subsequent half-life of a prestige independent release. As noted in Chapter 3, the over-four-hour feature *Che* debuted at the 2008 Cannes Film Festival, where it earned the Best Actor award for star Benicio Del Toro. Despite this accolade and Soderbergh's name recognition, the film did not find a U.S. distributor until four months after its festival debut. During and after this period, print periodicals and online forums reported on or reproduced abundant promotional material for the film—set photos, film stills, and eventually moving-image teasers, trailers, and video clips. The circulation of *Che* material shows how official and unofficial discourses can converge in prefiguration of theatrical film releases.[8] In most markets in which it played theatrically, the film was released in two parts, and in some advertising with the subtitles *Guerilla* and *The Argentine*. The first part follows Del Toro's Che Guevara mostly in the run-up to the 1959 Cuban Revolution; the second covers his attempts to coordinate similar activity in Bolivia beginning in 1966. Select markets also included a roadshow-style screening of the full 258-minute film. In addition, *Che* appeared on video-on-demand services in the U.S., in some cities coterminous with its theatrical release.

With the eventual U.S. distributor, IFC Films, advertising the film in remarkably limited fashion, most advance promotion of *Che* occurs through unofficial channels—YouTube postings of festival and interview footage, entertainment websites and blogs, and fan sites devoted to Soderbergh or to cinema more broadly. *Che*'s precirculation thus illustrates a larger digital-era trend in which distinctions between *promotion* and *publicity* increasingly blur. Studies of film marketing have tended to regard promotion as producers' official, paid efforts to market and advertise products, while defining publicity as the activities of journalists, entertainment commentators, and the like to circulate information about screen industries, workers, and texts to the public.[9] In these usages, promotion follows from a vested interest in a commodity, while publicity does not. The origins of *Che*'s advance materials complicate these categories. New-media publicity organs do not profit directly from films' box-office or other receipts but from page views and associated advertising sales. As a film's climate of anticipation and later box-office success can produce communities of interested viewers, specialty websites maintain indirect investments in the films and other media they cover. Serving multiple interests, these outlets merge publicity and promotion. With *Che*, pre-release clips of the finished film in particular acquire value as time-sensitive ephemera. Often lacking narrative context or subtitles for the all-Spanish dialogue, the clips grant prestige to the sites in which they are embedded through their apparent exclusivity. Conversely, the sites gain value through their associations with the highly anticipated (at least in select circles) prestige release.

Che's advance circulation involves numerous discourses surrounding cinemagoing, cinephilia, entertainment, and film authorship. The discourses help maintain particular taste cultures even as they promote online destinations for entertainment news and cinephilic commentary. In *Che*'s precirculation, sanctioned and unsanctioned video footage promotes the film in many spaces, ranging from commercial entertainment-news sites to pirate forums streaming bootleg copies of complete features. By interfering with official distribution practices, these latter grey-market venues, and the related phenomenon of peer-to-peer file-sharing networks, also affect the ways films are seen as commodities and artworks in screen culture. With *Che* and countless other films, online forums privileging timeliness and ephemerality reshape discourses of authorship. Theorists of artistic practice, and of mass and elite taste more broadly, have recognized the fluid nature of authorship and artistic reputation. Not only do critical judgments of artists shift over time according to dominant intellectual traditions and cultural preferences, but definitions of artistic achievement shift as well. Craftsmen become artists, and vice versa, and changing views of artistic production and collaboration periodically transform our conceptions of artistry altogether. As I have argued throughout this book, production practice, textual and extratextual artifacts, and a range of reception discourses including popular/amateur and elite/professional film criticism all contribute to the production of contemporary screen authorship.[10] Thus, I ask in this concluding case how we might understand authorship as a discursive phenomenon constructed around video ephemera. Increasingly in the digital age, ephemeral-media spaces such as specialist entertainment websites arise around textual fragments including images, clips, and trailers. The uses of these fragments contribute to cohesive articulations of authorial imprints.

Discourse surrounding film authorship has always been fluid, expressing contributors' multiple cultural and economic investments. Nonetheless, the 1990s mass emergence of online forums for entertainment commentary has enabled the wide circulation of a range of previously marginal critical voices. Less dependent on press credentials to gain access to new or venerated film texts, many participants in contemporary critical discourse have achieved a correspondingly elevated cultural status not only for their novel judgments but also for their ability to reproduce and circulate textual ephemera. These include practitioner interviews (particularly those on video), marketing materials such as poster images and trailers, and production footage such as on-set video, workprint segments, and scenes from completed or nearly completed films. The emergent class of website hosts, bloggers, and uncredentialed critics acquires status not through indiscriminate circulation of novel media fragments, but by providing material resonant to particular taste cultures. Some of those cultures articulate specific investments in mainstream or cult auteur figures. This class destabilizes hierarchies of journalistic access, exclusivity, and privilege (to say nothing of verifiability, empiricism, and discretion). It also relies partly on preexisting constructions of individual screen artists to establish its own new-media presence and to gain further symbolic capital. Adopting novel discursive strategies while retaining some existing understandings of film art, the new critical class has quickly become instrumental to films' promotional efforts.

Producers of *Che*'s precirculatory material, and of ancillary material appearing subsequent to its release, include agents both new and old. I have emphasized so far the discursive apparatus composed of non- or semi-professional critics and the specialty websites they represent (which include in my survey ShowbizCafe.com, RopeOfSilicon.com and JustPressPlay.net). Old-media stalwarts also compete to offer novel precirculatory content. The *New York Times* website, for example, routinely accompanies film reviews with trailers, and some of its advance feature stories include production-design sketches, short audio and video interviews with practitioners, film clips, and other multimedia content that facilitates descriptive, analytical, and promotional activity. While its May 2008 review of *Che*'s Cannes premiere had no accompanying video (no trailer had yet appeared in any public forum, online or otherwise), its review of the theatrical release in December included a nearly two-minute trailer. Among other post-release promotion, Amazon's UK website accompanied its listing of the film's Region 2 DVD release with "exclusive" video, a four-minute Soderbergh interview that also appears as one of the DVD's extras. Meanwhile, the official websites for the film's U.S. and UK theatrical releases included film trailers but no other video content, and neither website actually promoted the home-video release. Distributor Optimum Releasing holds rights to *Che*'s UK theatrical and home-video releases. In summer 2009, Optimum's website listed the recent DVD release, but *Che*'s official UK site, also maintained by Optimum, showed only the long-past theatrical-release dates. Official U.S. sites offered even less information. IFC Films acquired rights to the film's U.S. theatrical, video-on-demand, and DVD releases, but until late July 2009, IFC Entertainment's website did not include *Che* among its future DVD releases and did not provide information about video-on-demand availability, but did include an inactive "official website" link. These conditions belie IFC's claims of robust promotion, with *Video Business* reporting, "IFC wanted to comprehensively push the film to audiences because of [its] pedigree as well as because of its unique story structure."[11] The trade publication also writes of the Blockbuster video chain's exclusive sixty-day distribution window for *Che*'s U.S. DVD rentals during summer 2009, though online searches for the DVD during that time did not show Blockbuster's listing among the first few hundred results (unless the terms "rent" or "Blockbuster" were included in the search). Meanwhile, IFC's own updated listing for the film, including a "now available on DVD" icon but no links or vendor information, did not enable users to locate the DVD.

How can we contextualize the surprisingly poor promotional efforts of the film's official distributors? At one level, they highlight the shoe-string nature of independent distribution. While superficially polished, websites of non-multinational media corporations are routinely far out of date. In summer 2009, IFC's "Now on DVD" listings advertised the 2006 film *This Is England*, released by IFC on DVD in November 2007 in the U.S. Another U.S. independent, 2929 Entertainment, producer and distributor of two of Soderbergh's smaller, specialty films in col-laboration with its Magnolia Pictures, HDNet Films, and Landmark Theatres divisions, shows similar fraying. During summer 2009, while Magnolia's website received regular updates, the 2929 website listed numerous 2007 releases as "coming soon," and the front page of the HDNet Films website promoted films set to screen at the Sundance Film Festival—eighteen months earlier, in January 2008.[12]

More significantly, then, these poorly updated promotional forums reveal that film consumers and web users cannot rely substantively on producers' or distributors' official or corporate websites for information about consumption choices. Instead, potential viewers increasingly gather information from the websites of local and national theater chains, from online retailers such as Amazon, and from entertain-ment sites that amass economic capital through advertising sales and symbolic capital through the circulation of timely news and video con-tent of mass or specialist interest. Specialty websites' content related to Soderbergh and *Che* reveals emerging strategies for circulation of authorial markers. While online forums have markedly transformed discourse about screen creative workers such as stars, recognition of film directors depends strongly on formal education and other incuba-tors of cultural capital. Many online film writers present themselves as enthusiastic film fans and industry watchers rather than as cultural elites, though directors remain a key reference point. In its varying attention to film directors or other designated authors, the popular-critical discourse that proliferates on new-media platforms reconfigures screen creativity and contemporary film culture.

One specialty entertainment website, ShowbizCafe.com, supplies by far the most video content from *Che* of all sites I researched in the months preceding the film's staggered releases in late 2008 and early 2009. The site bills itself as a destination for Hispanic American filmgoers,[13] and so gives particular attention to Latino actors and Latino-themed films, though most of its content appears to cover contemporary Hollywood releases indiscriminately. (The site is bilingual, however, and showcases interviews with Hispanic American stars.) Its feature on *Che* includes eight short videos (none culled from YouTube or other video-hosting sites) totaling just over 16 minutes of the film, accompanied with just over 160 words of descriptive text.[14] The text names Benicio Del Toro in its first sentence and other actors later. Soderbergh is noted in the second sentence, which claims, "These clips are in Spanish without English subtitles, just the way director Steven Soderbergh intended them to be."[15] The writer gives no evidence for this claim of intentionality, which is incorrect in any event, as the film was, unsurprisingly, released with subtitles outside Spanish-speaking countries. No other attention to Soderbergh appears, and the page's tagline includes only the film's title, with no other keywords or links to related material on the film or its makers. Thus, numerous contexts recede in favor of discrete, fragmented textual artifacts.

The ShowbizCafe clips have considerable short-term value but lose their novelty appeal once the film is in release and thus available in full to desiring viewers. At the same time, whenever accessed, these clips reconfigure the film in ways replicating the viewpoint of production and postproduction workers. Lacking narrative context and postproduction graphics such as subtitles, the clips resemble film dailies (though not reproducing multiple takes), a somewhat ironic parallel given that the actual production, using HD video, did not require printed dailies. Like a compilation of dailies as well, the isolated, fragmented clips do not strongly indicate a shaping, authorial presence. The clips succeed more in mimicking (if inadvertently) an industry-insider viewing of a work in progress than in promoting *Che* as an authored work or a quality viewing experience. Language barriers aside, the clips suggest the film's tone and address but offer few guides to its scope or narrative structure, nor of course to its aesthetic achievement given the small size of the streaming-video frame and the low resolution of the video transfer.

Other websites, lacking the film footage that ShowbizCafe hosts, foreground different distribution and reception contexts to lure web traffic. In his work on film trailers, Keith Johnston explores "how new digital technologies allow . . . online fan audiences to partially commandeer and interact with a trailer text."[16] Such interaction is apparent in recirculation of *Che* trailers on particular sites. One of these, RopeOfSilicon.com, a self-proclaimed "one stop shop for everything movie related on the Internet," enjoys advertising revenue from the familiar ranks of discount weight-loss vendors as well as mainstream corporations such as Budget Rent-a-Car and the UK's Three mobile network.[17] RopeOfSilicon contributes to the discourse surrounding *Che* and Soderbergh its news of an alleged "bootleg trailer release."[18] Given the haphazard nature of official promotion for the film, the notion of the "bootleg" becomes particularly amorphous in this case. As trailers serve explicit promotional functions, their online circulation expands the film's potential viewership, particularly in the absence of official promotion to undercut or supplement. The posting's accompanying text replicates trade-press–style discourse and emphasizes topicality. The news item references Soderbergh in its headline and in passing in the text, and comments at length on the film's industrial position, its reception at Cannes, and its apparently limited commercial prospects (with a subhead asserting, "Oscar chances seem to have dwindled if not altogether vanished"). The trailer in question derives from a YouTube source so is not exclusive, and it features unsubtitled Spanish dialogue. Thus, the video is doubly discounted—not exclusive and not in the chosen language of the website and its presumed audience—but nonetheless indicates the site's efforts to catalog industry ephemera in comprehensive and timely fashion. Almost a month after the initial posting, the site added links to official trailers and posted a short, subtitled scene from the film, with Cannes the attributed source.[19] This newer posting includes a link to the film's supposed "international website"—a site entirely in Spanish, and thus only narrowly "international"—and misspells Soderbergh's first name in one of two references to him. These errors undermine the site's claims of authority and accuracy, and a subsequent review of the film includes further minor errors alongside celebratory remarks regarding Soderbergh's intent, evidenced by quotations of material from the film's Cannes press kit (an electronic press kit, or EPK, easily locatable online). Overall, the site's content merges trade-press–style discourse with the enthusiastic, highly personal claims that exemplify the uncomplex auteurist viewpoint of much online criticism.

A third site, JustPressPlay.net, presents impassioned audience responses alongside Soderbergh as the film's auteur-spokesman. A December 2008 news item on the site, titled "Soderbergh Heckled by Anti-Che Audience," introduces an amateur video clip showing Soderbergh during a New York City post-screening Q&A.[20] This video originates on YouTube as well, so the posting carries no exclusivity and only the novelty of its writer's judgments of the historical figure Che and of Soderbergh's possible intent. (The writer does not claim to have seen the film.) The site's staff page promises "down to earth, easy to understand reviews on games, music and movies" and "no fancy language that requires a PhD to read,"[21] positioning its amateur discourse as useful and accessible. The *Che* item showcases a disgruntled viewer who, from offscreen in the video, shouts numerous remarks about Guevara's ostensible villainy ("He was a murderer!" and more) directed at Soderbergh. In the video and the accompanying text, critical biography of a historical figure sets the terms of the debate, a debate staged through the multiply designated author figure Soderbergh. The video grants Soderbergh visual and verbal authority— he is the only person clearly visible in camera view, and the one who speaks at greatest length and with a microphone. Both the video and the accompanying text thus make Soderbergh the film's (if not its revolutionary subject's) spokesman and advocate. Like other examples discussed here, the page depends on straightforward assumptions of authorship and eschews empirical data or theoretical commentary on the nature of production activity.

By circulating advance or coterminous releases of anticipated films, peer-to-peer file-sharing tools such as BitTorrent also participate in the informal economy of screen-text promotion. Well before *Che's* December 2008 U.S. theatrical release, *Part One* of the film—a.k.a. *The Argentine* or *El Argentino*—was available in numerous video-camera–produced copies of varying grade; some lacked English subtitles, though separate subtitle files were easily accessible on other websites, as is true for most popular file-shared releases. (The film entered theatrical release in Spain in September 2008, so Spanish-language copies circulated abundantly.[22]) Though many web users' quest to see *Che* doubtless ended with the acquisition of this subpar pirated release, for others it expands the scope of the film's recognition and prompts further circulation of the text in various forms. Similar versions of *Che: Part Two* followed in January and February 2009, just preceding that part's international theatrical release. Over the months of their greatest demand, these file-shared copies reach viewing communities that may have no access to the film in theatrical or on-demand release. By spring 2009, still during *Che's* cascading theatrical run in major territories,[23] higher-quality DVD transfers of both parts of the film circulated on peer-to-peer networks. Uploaders of these versions of *Che* reference the author at most via the tag "Soderbergh" in file names or descriptions.

Thus, the shared film file can include a minimal inscription of authorship, but as with the video clips streamed on ShowbizCafe, authorial and many other markers fall away in favor of recontextualized video fragments.

Che flourishes in multiple online forums as discursive object, as series of video fragments, and as complete if for some time aesthetically compromised text. These all contribute to the embryonic and infant life of the haphazardly advertised release (and to the film's continued online presence, its discursive half-life, to the extent the pages remain active). Relatedly, Soderbergh's advocacy of multiplatform releases—simultaneous day-and-date availability of films across theatrical, video-on-demand, and DVD platforms—represents action to limit unauthorized spread of copies of complete films as well as to gain access to underserved groups of viewers. Such anti-piracy and audience-reaching initiatives do not attempt specifically to stall the proliferation of discourse and data that consolidate criteria of authorship. With filmmakers such as Soderbergh involved in multiple projects that can be construed as high-profile in some respects but have limited visibility outside major urban film markets, a tangible if diffuse web presence as an auteur brand remains instrumental in maintaining a status as a major creative agent.

Soderbergh's advocacy of simultaneous cross-platform releases extends to other alternative distribution models targeting specialized viewerships. He has supported efforts for simultaneous festival and video-on-demand release of films, an initiative begun in 2009 with IFC's "Festival Direct" video-on-demand platform, which offers VOD releases of select films around the time of their festival premieres (*Che*'s VOD release came from IFC, but not as part of this scheme).[24] As *Variety* reports, "Soderbergh explained that since theater chains have locked out movies like *Che*, VOD becomes a natural option."[25] Soderbergh further asserts that filmmakers should "change their thinking in the way they expect revenue to be generated,"[26] implicitly challenging long-standing biases in film culture about theatrical versus small-screen releases.

Changing distribution practices can also revise understandings of what constitutes a film's core iteration. Soderbergh's partnership, for films other than *Che*, with 2929 Entertainment and its linked operations includes an innovative revenue-sharing model in which the theater chain receives a portion of DVD sales revenue.[27] This arrangement acknowledges that theatrical runs serve key promotional functions for future (or simultaneous) home-video releases. Theatrical releases of feature films still occupy a privileged cultural and industrial space. Major releases earn intensive and expensive official promotion, supplemented with ancillary promotion from diverse professional, semi-professional, and amateur forums, and received with anticipation and associated viewing rituals that do not yet widely accompany such events as video-on-demand or DVD releases. At the same time, cinemagoers increasingly regard theatrical releases as ephemeral events, with "wait for the DVD" now a stock phrase in lukewarm reviews. Theatrical releases become simply one of a series of opportunities to engage with a desired screen text, and not necessarily the one privileged by emerging industrial practices, critical discourse, and audience activity.

New modes of official, intermediate, and underground circulation continuously reshape attitudes about the ontology of film and the constitutive agents of production and distribution. Further transformations of discourse surrounding authorship—whether that authorship is material, ephemeral, or invisible—will surely continue. Future discourses will consolidate particular understandings of individual agency in commercial screen production, for better or worse. At one level we might lament the decline of professional discourse that systematically investigates production practices and gives rigorous attention to the specifics of industrial creativity. At another we might, following Bourdieu's attention to the unequal distribution of cultural capital, celebrate the dismantling of what he calls "the whole corporation of critics mandated . . . to produce legitimate classifications and the discourse necessarily accompanying any artistic enjoyment worthy of the name."[28] As I have argued elsewhere in this book, professional critics gravitate overwhelmingly toward empirically unverifiable, auteurist claims regarding the film output they survey. These claims classify films into discrete quality-based categories while rehearsing critics' own professionalized aesthetic knowledge. Taste markers surrounding artistic production historically have been put to highly inegalitarian ends, and so we might view film culture's evolving discourses and distribution practices as productive efforts to expand global dialogues about popular art forms.

Polyvocality does not, however, guarantee a pluralistic utopia in which artists are fêted by sympathetic taste publics. Marginal critical voices can easily be put in service of conglomerate interests. Official promotion of major Hollywood releases now routinely includes avowed pull quotes from online entertainment sites that maintain no pretense of professionalism.[29] An industrial rhetoric privileging audience choices over professional critical voices can limit journalistic film criticism's positive gatekeeping function. In August 2009, when Paramount Pictures declined to hold preview screenings of *G.I. Joe: The Rise of Cobra* (2009), which was rumored to have been a troubled production, Paramount vice chairman Rob Moore told an interviewer, "After the chasm we experienced with *Transformers 2* [2009] between the response of audiences and critics, we chose to forgo opening-day print and broadcast reviews. . . . We want audiences to define this film."[30] The strategy of withholding press screenings is common for mid-tier genre films anticipated to receive poor reviews, but rare for high-profile summer releases. Eliminating professional reviewers in the name of abstracted audiences, studios gain the ability to claim opening-weekend grosses as evidence of popular acclaim. If professional discourses may be said to contribute in some way to film culture and the recognition and circulation of artistry, the circumvention of professional critics shifts industrial power balances toward purely commercial imperatives, and away from the artistic investments of classes of creative workers.

The Limits of the Soderbergh Imprint

Che's globally divergent promotion and publicity follow in part from the sale of distribution rights to more than fifteen separate companies at different times. As suggested above, fragmented publicity contributes to a reconfiguration of the text itself. A prominent auteur figure might stabilize the film's circulation efforts, its prefigured meanings, and its overall brand or package as a prestige release. The case of *Che* shows that Soderbergh remains insufficiently valued in promotional discourses to anchor the film in disparate release contexts. Unofficial publicity surrounding *Che* both responds to and magnifies the uneven official promotion. Overall, the fractional narratives of Soderbergh's activity vis-à-vis *Che* follow from decentralized promotional efforts (Spanish promotion offers one story, U.S. promotion another) as well as from the idiosyncrasies of publicity generated by differently situated social agents (the *New York Times*, for example, versus ShowbizCafe). In the varying promotional and publicity discourses, the multi-hyphenate creator Soderbergh is often a marginal figure, named as director and thus explicitly designated as an (or *the*) author but otherwise diminished, his specific creative labor unexplored. Soderbergh's diverse creative portfolio and his substantial collaborative investments in global filmmaking culture carry tangible and intangible benefits for him and the industries that support him. Nonetheless, the sheer diversity of his creative labor arguably works against the fabrication of a coherent, easily discernible artistic persona. We saw in Chapter 3 how *Che*'s status as international co-production entailed contingent engagements with disparate groups of financiers and executives. Echoing these transitory relationships, the marketing efforts and publicity discourse surrounding *Che* suggest that outside narrow connoisseur circles, Soderbergh lacks a substantial footprint as a global auteur brand.

We might ask in closing whether collaborative creative practices across media forms necessarily impede the elaboration of a flexible but legible authorial persona. In contemporary Hollywood, artistic practice such as Soderbergh's is both typical and exceptional. His activities represent virtually all possible modes of contemporary practitioner agency, yet he remains distinct from even his closest contemporaries, fellow multi-hyphenate experimentalists such as the U.S.'s David Lynch or the UK's Michael Winterbottom. Indeed, Soderbergh's experimentation led Columbia in 2009 to halt production on a Soderbergh-helmed adaptation of Michael Lewis's 2003 baseball-themed bestseller *Moneyball*, owing to the company's uneasiness with Soderbergh's revised screenplay, which merged a reality-based narrative with intercut documentary interviews with players.[31] More significantly then, the fluctuating industrial support for and public interest in Soderbergh's work attest to the challenges of crafting an artistic persona legible to industrial and reception communities. Surprisingly or not, the 1950s and 1960s auteur critics' inability to recognize authors whose works did not manifest obvious thematic and stylistic consistencies maps well onto conditions of contemporary screen culture. A substantial grouping of critics and cinephiles lauds Soderbergh's diverse cross-media efforts, but his admitted chameleonism has likely inhibited the recognition and transmission of a coherent Soderbergh imprint. Nonetheless, in engaging so dynamically with collaborative production practices, with emerging modes of distribution and exhibition, and with multiple levels of screen-cultural discourse, Soderbergh can remind us what kinds of cultural work constitute authorship and why this work matters.

The tools we use to conceptualize authorship, and the opportunities we have to experience it and to participate in its construction at different magnitudes, are more diverse than ever before. Today's ecology of authorship is far more complex than that of the 1950s film culture that cemented auteurist discourse. Yet the stakes remain fundamentally the same: cultural capital engaged with globalized art forms, class-bound taste positionings, symbolic and material currencies; in short, social power. Terms used throughout this book—collaboration, negotiation, and affiliation; transitivity and association; discursive constructions and industrial framings; cultural intermediaries and boutique sensibilities—represent different pathways for the articulation of creative stances and the exercise of social power. In the interview that follows, Soderbergh addresses the challenges and satisfactions of creative work within global entertainment industries. This book has shown, I hope, how Soderbergh models exemplary practice at all levels of industrial activity to make meaningful contributions to production culture and film culture.

Appendix

Interview with Steven Soderbergh
New York City, Saturday, July 23, 2011

Mark Gallagher: I have a bunch of questions about art and authorship and filmmaking. I have a big question to start off, but if you don't mind me asking a more basic one to begin with—is this a workday for you, in effect?

Steven Soderbergh: Yeah.

MG: So can you tell me what you've been doing today?

SS: Interviews. [And] I did some editing this morning on a short documentary that I'm making about a film called *End of the Road*, which came out in 1970, and which Warner Bros. has remastered and is going to release this fall. And I agreed to make something about it for them to put on the DVD to help drive sales. So that's a project I've been working on for the last four months.

MG: And what have you been doing with that? Do you mean getting ready a voice recording, or actually shooting?

SS: I shot interviews with everybody that's still around that was involved with the film, so I'm just cutting now. I have a portable drive that I carry with me everywhere so I can cut on the plane or whatever.

MG: Is that a Wim Wenders film, *End of the Road*?

SS: No, it's based on the John Barth novel.

MG: Yeah, OK. They made a film of that?

SS: Yeah, they did. It's become sort of a cult film. It's not available, and it's pretty interesting. Gordon Willis's first feature as a director of photography, Stacy Keach, James Earl Jones, co-written and co-produced by Terry Southern. It's an interesting movie.

MG: And Warners released it back in the day?

SS: No, Allied Artists released it, and Warners obviously picked it up in some kind of yard sale. I've been bugging them about it for years, so now it's happening.

MG: I'm curious about that kind of leveraging. You wanted them to release it, and did you say [to Warners] you would do some ancillary thing?

SS: Yeah, I said if you guys do this, I'll create a special piece of material to go with it, to help sell it.

MG: OK. Is that something you've done in the past? I know you've done a lot of these DVD supplements, been involved in commentary tracks. Is that something you've done with a particular mind toward getting things out there?

SS: Not in this way. I've never gone to somebody and tried to force them to restore or re-release a movie that I thought should be out there. And as such, I felt some obligation to sweeten the pot a little bit. But honestly, the film itself is intriguing enough that I wanted to know more about it, and this was a great way to do that. And it's been really interesting because the descriptions of the experience on the part of the people making the film have really brought home the idea that movies, and the act of making movies, don't matter the way they used to.

MG: Based on having conversations with the people who were involved in the production, you get that sense? What is the language they're using to talk about cinema that is different than what you find today?

SS: I don't know that anybody would necessarily say that that's what they said in the interviews directly. What's clear to me is that in cultural terms, the experience for them of making this movie, which has a lot on its mind, was viewed as both special and at the same time a necessary part of living in this culture. There was a sense of artistic duty, in a way, to use your energy to make something that *meant* something, and that they, in this case, were successful in creating a really unique environment. And I really was struck by that. Certainly I try to create an environment that's conducive to good solutions. But this sounded like a really special circumstance the way everybody was talking about it. And it made me realize, wow, in the late '60s and the early '70s in America, movies meant something in cultural terms. People were looking to movies for not necessarily answers but for clues, at least, about what was going on and how we should be interacting with each

other and the world. And that just for the most part isn't true anymore, certainly isn't the default mode of American film.

MG: Yeah.

SS: So it made me sad.

MG: Well, I think a lot of us in film have the same response and feel
like there's this particular period that was offering that up. You
can see the way that films were being made and the way that
they're being talked about, the kind of criticism around them, that
kind of excitement, as a golden age that we don't have [now]. But I
wonder—I feel that either we have a nostalgia for that, or particular filmmakers like you might try to do things, not to say in the
spirit of that age, but . . .

SS: Well, yeah, I do in the sense that my—when I'm on set, yeah, I
pretend it's 1971, and that I can do whatever I want, and that anything that I can appreciate the audience can appreciate, that I'm
the audience. Absolutely, I put myself in that mindset and draw
inspiration. That happened to be a particularly good year in cinema all over the world, so absolutely. It remains to be seen, since
I'm the generation after that, what the generation after me will be
using as their Rosetta stone, I don't know.

MG: Right, I'm curious about that. And in being the generation after
that, do you feel like you missed out? One of the questions I have
is, do you feel like your career has been well timed, in the sense
that, did you come up at a moment when there was support for the
type of things that you wanted to do?

SS: Yeah. I feel generally that I came up at a very, very good time, that
a few years either side of that, of *sex, lies,* and maybe that doesn't
work out the way it worked out. I would really not want to be
coming up now. I feel that filmmakers starting out now trying to
make features have a much more difficult time than I did.

MG: Is that because of just the sheer number of people that are doing it,
as opposed to the structure of the industry?

SS: Yeah, it's really hard to break through. The democratization of
technology has been good in the sense that you can make a really
good-looking movie for not a lot of money now. The problem is
that's what everyone is doing, and the odds of it getting shown
have dropped. Back then, the hard part was getting it made, but if
you got it made, you had a pretty good chance of getting it released
somehow, and now that's not true. And I was allowed to make
mistakes. This was still at a time when I was allowed to make *sex,*

lies, and then five movies in a row that nobody saw, and not be put in movie jail. You can't do that now; you just can't.

MG: I haven't seen—I've looked at a lot of filmmakers of your generation just to see anybody who's had that experience like you, where the movies are not commercially successful yet you're still given support. Did you feel during that time that the clock was ticking on you to do more commercial things? Or did you just feel, this is my career, and if it goes this way, it goes this way?

SS: Yeah, I was learning. I was trying to figure out what kind of filmmaker I was, or should be. I was trying to figure out what my strengths and weaknesses were. It was a very important period, even though some of the work I wish was better. But I didn't feel in a hurry. I guess it would seem strange from the outside, for someone with my professional history to say I've never been in a hurry. But no, there's never a sense of, things are passing me by, it's always been entirely self—the clock is internal in the sense of, how do I get better at my job? What experiences do I need to have that will make me better at my job? And there's not really a clock on that.

MG: And do you feel you've peaked in terms of your skills, and then are on a decline? Or your enthusiasm is not what it used to be?

SS: I think I'm better than I was ten years ago at a lot of the things that—I'm better at filtering. That's all you're doing every day, you're filtering. You're reducing from an infinite number of films down to one film in every moment, every time you make a decision. And I'm better at filtering, I'm faster than I was ten years ago. I'm not better at any of the things that I think are really important, or that would enable me to make something transcendent. In that regard, I don't feel I'm any closer to anything than I was when I was seventeen. Maybe even further away.

MG: And what are those things, if you can see those things? It's not skill, it's . . .

SS: If I knew what they were—it's something new, something that hasn't been done.

MG: OK. So let me back up a little. I hope this doesn't sound too strait-laced, the way these things are framed. You've read some of the book so maybe you see how this works.

SS: Yeah.

MG: The first stuff is about artistry, and I believe you said this in congressional testimony a couple of years ago. One of the lines was, "I'm a filmmaker, and so by some loose definition I'm an artist."

Based on that, do you think of yourself as an artist, and if so, what does that term mean to you? In what way are you an artist?

SS: If you define art as an expression, a personal expression that is designed to be experienced by other people, in an attempt to transmit some sense of what it is to be here, then yeah, then technically I'm an artist. It's easy to fall into the idea of, well, an artist *paints*. But I think film is an art form, I think cinema is an art form. It was the dominant art form of the last century. I don't know what's going to happen to it in this century. But there's no question in my mind that cinema was the dominant art form of the twentieth century, and that, you know, *2001* was one of the most significant pieces of visual art that anybody's ever created. I know that for a fact. So it's hard to—it never feels comfortable to place yourself in the company of the artists that have come before you and say, "Yeah, I'm with that group." When we had *sex, lies* at Cannes and that all played out, I remember I did an interview on television, and the first question was, "Fellini, Altman, Coppola, Martin Scorsese—these people have all won Palme d'Ors. Are you in that company?" And I just sort of laughed, like that's a trick question. What am I supposed to say to that? Because you never—nobody, filmmakers that are in my sort of generation, that I know, none of us—we're our own thing, and it's up to time to figure out what we mean, or what we meant. So none of us think of them, of the greats that we admired, as being contemporaries or peers or anything like that. So, that's a long-winded answer to that question. It's a qualified yes.

MG: You had immediately brought film into the equation when I asked you that question. And you've worked in a lot of different media. But if you said to yourself what the key aspects of your artistic practice were, what would they be? What does your work as an artist entail? Do you think of it in terms of output, or in terms of particular tools that you're using to create?

SS: I guess I start from the premise of, you should make things, you should make as many things as you can. Perhaps what I admire most in other artists is being prolific, is working. I probably got that from my father. My father was a workaholic. My father went to work, and then after dinner, he would be at the dining-room table for hours, continuing to work. And I guess I kind of swallowed that a little bit. If I'm awake, there's a very strong chance that I'm working on something. So I probably place the scale and breadth of a body of work first, before even quality.

MG: I'm sure some critics would agree with that assessment. But scale and breadth is what a lot of artists, particularly film artists, seem not to be invested in, in favor of being more specialized.

SS: Well, there's no part of the business that encourages you to do anything but what you've done successfully before. If you're someone who's interested in exploring your abilities, you're swimming upstream. I'm not trying to make myself sound heroic, because this is not a choice for me. I can't not want to try things. That's just part of my DNA. I'm not choosing to do that. It's what I have to do to stay engaged. So I have to find a way to navigate through the business that allows me to satisfy my need to try things.

MG: OK. Relatedly, my next set of questions has to do with collaboration. It seems to me if you want to be prolific in any mode of art, you should just go it alone, and paint, or shoot video yourself and do all the recording and editing. And yet, for the most part, you have chosen not to do that, you've worked with different scales and crews. But when you conceptualize your work as an artist, do you think of yourself as someone who has a personal vision, who is a solitary artist and then brings people into projects? Or do you think of yourself as a collaborator, someone who conceptualizes these works in terms of, "I will work on this with this group of people"?

SS: I understood from the beginning, when I started making films, that the only version of a film that you can make alone is probably not that interesting. You look at, say, a Godfrey Reggio movie, and you would think, "Oh, he just goes out with a camera over the course of several years, and just shoots this thing and then he cuts it, and that's really kind of a one-man band." And having worked with Godfrey on one of his films, I can tell you, he has a core creative team that works very hard, and that he relies on to sort of analyze the film as it's being made, and it's very collaborative. And I take advantage of the people around me, both in literal terms by just sucking their brains out and using them, and delegating. To me, the great thing about having a core group of people that move from project to project is it enables us to, while we're shooting one, be prepping the next one, because it's all the same people. So, at lunchtime, you have a mini production meeting about the next movie while you're shooting another movie. But also, one of the reasons I've been able to do a lot of stuff is I delegate. I give people a lot of responsibility. I'll say, "Here's what I need *you* to do." In that regard, there's the famous joke, what is the sentence that Stanley Kubrick never said? The punch line is, "Use your own judgment, don't bother me with the details." I give people a lot of freedom to bring something of their own to this. If I say I'm looking for a certain kind of location, for example. I hope and expect that they will do the parts of my work for me that are not going to be any better if I did it, you know what I mean? I would never delegate something to someone that I felt was absolutely reliant upon a specific decision or action on my part, that was too important to be given over to somebody. But I'm also very good at determining what stuff doesn't fit that definition, and I give it to people to do. That's the only way you can have multiple films happening at the same time.

MG: So, would you describe your pre-production process as somewhat more open-ended, things aren't locked down, and, say, you mentioned the location example—if you let someone choose a location, then you'd kind of build things around that, rather than having something storyboarded in advance?

SS: Oh yeah, absolutely. And when I'm working with the writers, it's a very fluid situation. I may take a run at certain things and say, "I'm thinking of something like this—make this better," in order to just help. I may say, "Why don't you work on that sequence, and I'll take a run at this sequence," just so that we're getting somewhere quicker. But at the end of the day, I'm relying on them to write the thing. I have no interest in being the writer on it, having credit as a writer. My job is just to tell someone what I want to shoot, what kind of thing I would like to see. I guess you'd call it macro-managing.

MG: OK, you're at the other level, all right. The thing about writing, it seems to raise a similar question. You used to be a screenwriter, or co-screenwriter, co-credited. You seem not to do that more recently. Is that something where you feel someone else can do it better than you, and then you can step in and direct it?

SS: Yeah. I wrote to get in, I wrote as a way of getting in. I *have written*, but I don't think of myself as a writer. With one possible exception, all of my best work has been written by other people. And I enjoy that process a lot. Perhaps the three most pleasurable weeks I've ever had in the business were when Scott Frank and I met in his office every day to create what became the shooting draft of *Out of Sight*. That was really fun. That was just pure fun, just sitting in a room trying to top each other, and make this thing as good as we wanted it to be. But it was just us. *You* know, sitting alone, trying to generate something, it's horrible.

MG: There's a lot of blank page.

SS: Yeah, it's just horrible. I don't enjoy it. What I think I did when I started, and I see this in a lot of other directors, I think when I started I was of the mistaken belief that I should be writing and directing. And as soon as I got out of that way of thinking, everything started to improve. And I've had conversations with other filmmakers, young filmmakers who aren't as busy as they should be because they only want to direct what they've written, and some of the things they've written they haven't been able to get financed. And I keep saying, you gotta shoot. If you're a director, you have to be making things. You can't tell me that there's nothing out there that you want to make other than what you wrote. You just can't convince me of that. A couple of them have listened to me and gone off and directed stuff and been very successful doing it, a couple of them still haven't worked.

MG: If I think of the old creative-writing adage, "You have to write what you know," I've never heard a similar thing about shooting what you know. But certainly a lot of filmmaking privileges shooting things that are closer to your experience. When you're working with other writers, do you have a sense that you're taking someone else's vision and then transforming it into yours?

SS: It depends. It depends on at what stage I got involved. Was this an idea of mine? Was it a script of theirs that already existed? If it's an idea of mine, then it's much more, the dynamic is going to shift a little bit to them trying to give me what I want in a more obvious way. Because I may have walked in with a certain construction and a certain style that I want to see. If I've read a script that's already been written, if we're moving forward now and this thing's getting made, then obviously they did something that hooked me already. I'm not going to come in and rip the engine out of this thing. So all I'm doing at that point is trying to—the best analogy I can use is, I've stepped onto the rear car of a moving train, and I'm working my way up to the cabin so that I can be out in front of it. It's a process, and by the time I get to the front of this train, I feel like I'm driving it, too.

MG: Who's the conductor on this train? You're the co-conductor?

SS: I'm ultimately training myself to be the conductor.

MG: But it can start before you; you can hop on.

SS: Yeah, if that's a script that's already been written, I chased it down and got on the back, and I'm trying to get up to the front.

MG: I don't know what's most present for you right now, but where would you say with something like *Contagion*, where did you come into that?

SS: That was Scott [Burns] saying, "I want to make an ultrarealistic movie about a pandemic," and I said, "Great, let's do that." So it was his idea that we kind of explored together. He did all the research, and then we would have conversations about the characters. Who are we following? That's the question you always ask, who are we following? And then we'd agree, we have this many characters, here are the various narrative threads we're going to set up and pay off. And then he would go off and do a draft.

MG: And then would you say things like, "I want to see more of these characters, less of these," or, "I want them to be over here," or, "We need to balance how often these characters are appearing." You would participate in that?

SS: Yeah, sure, absolutely.

MG: Then at the end of the day, that movie exists for us. Do you think of that then as a—maybe you don't conceptualize these things this way at all, but certainly on our side, we always do—do you think of that as, "This is my film," or, this is this collaborative product, that comes from Warner Bros., and you directed it, and that Scott wrote, with your input?

SS: I think we all look at it as our film. The clearest way I can put it is that I directed it. To me that says exactly what I want it to say, and it doesn't have to be any larger than that. It's absolutely appropriate for me to refer to it as my film, in the same way it would be absolutely appropriate for Scott to refer to it as his film, or anyone who worked on it, frankly. I tend to like to refer to things as "ours," you know, "we."

MG: Yeah, I've seen that. And not everybody does that.

SS: I think it's unfair to sort of act as though there wasn't a lot of help around. But, in this medium, I think the best results come from the director having the final word. And that's not true in every other medium, but I think it is true in movies. When I look at the movies that I think are great, 98 percent of them were controlled creatively, ultimately, by the director. Not the producer or the writer. There are exceptions, but most of the time it's the filmmaker.

MG: I guess that's one of the other arguments for [also] being the writer, is having more control.

SS: If you're a writer and you want control, you should not be in the movie business. You should be in television, or writing plays.

MG: Is that why you didn't do more work in TV, because it's more of a writer-based medium?

SS: No, it's—there's a version of "for hire" that I'm comfortable with, and then there's a version of "for hire" that I'm not comfortable with. And it has to do with, ultimately, the edit and sort of the final version of the piece, the edit and the scoring and things like that. I wouldn't want to be in a situation, if I'm directing a pilot for a series or whatever, where I can't have control over the final product. I wouldn't be happy. So the answer is, if I were going to be in TV, it sounds like I would have to create something from scratch, come up with an idea, and execute it the way that I would like to see it done. And then at that point you're hiring other people to kind of follow in your footsteps. But the couple of TV things that I did, the two *Fallen Angels* pieces and *K Street*, I had the cut. I contractually had final cut. Each of us [directors] did on *Fallen Angels*, we all had final cut. That's what made it kind of unique. I'm sorry it didn't go on for longer, because they had a really interesting group of people, and it was fun. But that's not normal. That was Showtime and Propaganda being kind of progressive.

MG: In a way, I think those were the infant stages of cable channels developing that original content, and if it had been ten or fifteen years later, there would be a buzz about those. I remember those were way under the radar.

SS: Yeah, they really were, even then. Now I think they'd be generating a lot more buzz, if you got a group of directors like that to do stuff like this, there'd be a lot more talk about it.

MG: Yes, I concur. OK, should I move on? I know you read around a lot. Maybe you stay away from academic film studies, which is perfectly fine. But one of the things we do is we spend a lot of time scrutinizing film content for its meaning and its significance, either in isolation or as part of some larger cultural moment. And then sometimes we think about those things just completely removed from who created them, and sometimes we'll actually try to look at particular individuals or groups we think of as the authors of those films, however designated. So the question in this relationship is, when you direct a film, whether from a screenplay you did have involvement in, or where you hopped onto this moving train, do you feel that you as a director seek to convey any particular meanings to viewers, about the world at large, about institutions or politics, about human relations, cultures, and peoples? Or do you think of yourself as a storyteller, who tells stories about people and places that someone else will put into some kind of context?

SS: Well, I think that is personal, in the sense that directors are their films, to an extent that's almost comical sometimes. Every decision you make is an expression of what you want to see or what you believe. Even for someone who by all definitions may be pedestrian or middle-of-the-road—that is their worldview, in a way. And it's every bit as legitimate or complete as someone whom we consider to be a great filmmaker. And in that sense, they don't feel like choices to me, in the same way I talked about, I need to be engaged and free to explore stuff because I can't work any other way. It's not a decision, it just has to be that way. Whatever the ultimate take-away is from the body of work that has my name on it, we can be sure that it is a manifestation of what I think, what I feel, what I believe. And that if it isn't coherent or clear, it's not necessarily a failing, in the sense that people are complicated and contradictory sometimes. It's going to be as funky as the world is, it's going to have all the sort of sloppiness and energy hopefully that the world has. I've been in it enough to realize that I don't have to think of it in those terms while I'm in it, you know what I mean? I know there's no way for it not to be a part of me, and to be a part of what I am. That's just not possible, it's not possible for anyone. And it really does become, then, somebody else's job to kind of organize it or try and figure it out.

MG: All right. It seems to me that, maybe during press-junket time, you're asked to participate in the organization of that material. And so I'm curious how you respond when people—viewers, for example, or maybe critics—look for a connection among your films, not to say impose but to bring to the table a view of them as "about" something in particular.

SS: I look at it as, if I'm asked about these kinds of things, I kind of treat it, depending on the question and the context, I look at it as having veto power. If somebody proposes something that I just feel isn't true, a premise or an intent, then I'll say, "Well, that may be the way it came across. I can only tell you that's not what I meant." So maybe that's a failing on my part because I didn't com-municate clearly enough within the film. But I've seen too often that—it's like a fan watching a basketball game. Their experience of that basketball game and their belief of what it meant to the players involved is never going to line up with what the players experienced. It's just different to be on the floor. At the end of the day, it's not really my job and probably isn't even really necessary for me to correct people. It is a piece of art. And what I know for sure is that nothing anybody says is going to rearrange those pixels. It is what it is. And hating it doesn't improve it, or diminish it, or change it in any way. Those pixels or grain, whatever you want to call it, that is the form they are going to take forever. That's why at a certain point, I feel lucky in that I've never really cared what people have said, because it doesn't change anything.

MG: So it wouldn't bother you if someone got something out of watching one of your movies that you had said, "That wasn't my intent, but oh, it came out this way, that was part of the communication."

SS: Yeah, I think that's just part of life. That's analogous to somebody being at a dinner, and making a comment that somebody thinks is a joke, and they laugh at it, not realizing that it wasn't really a joke. Those kinds of misinterpretations happen all the time in life. Why shouldn't they happen when somebody is looking at something as complex as a movie? So that stuff doesn't bother me. It can be frustrating when somebody doesn't know what they're talking about, in either direction. I don't read reviews, but occasionally something might be written that's sort of an overview that I'll take a look at, or somebody will send me something to look at. And it can be frustrating to see. Anybody who says that I don't understand the visual grammar of, say, Michael Curtiz and '40s studio filmmaking, I can tell you does not know what they're talking about.

MG: I know a particular piece . . .

SS: Yeah, I've heard about it. I've had friends angry on my behalf—"You've gotta see this thing." No, I don't have to see this thing. I can tell you my understanding of that particular language is very deep, deeper than what they are seeing. It's axiomatic: if they knew what I knew, they then would be writing about what I knew. And I can tell that they don't. There are huge swaths of influences, inferences, references, connections that are wound into, for instance, that film [The Good German], that are completely going over their heads. Now, that's not saying, oh, I'm smarter than them. I'm just saying that stuff has been swallowed and regurgitated by me in a way that, by making it, can't be duplicated by writing about something. So that can be frustrating, where you feel like, they never are wrong, as far as the public is concerned. I'm wrong all the time. When I make a movie that nobody goes to see or gets shitty reviews, the sort of take-away is that oh, I screwed up, I'm wrong. They are, by virtue of having their last word, sort of infallible. I remember somebody asked Pauline Kael once, "Do you ever go back and see things twice?" And she said, "Why would I want to do that? Why would I want to find out that I was wrong?" So it's a small price to pay.

MG: That's an interesting case, where you said everything you do in the creative process, the output becomes part of you. It seems there's a critical stance where we look at the output, and that has to stand for all the decision-making around it. So you can look at *The Good German* and say, "Soderbergh doesn't know this, this, and this." And in a way, it's really saying, "Based on the evidence on screen in front of me, I can infer that this person has this knowledge," or not that knowledge. So it's a matter of, the film text itself is the way that critics communicate with the filmmaker, for better or worse. And yet, as critics all we produce is criticism.

SS: And you know, it was ever thus. And it's only relevant to me in the sense of its impact potentially on the commercial performance of the movie. Bad reviews don't bother me in the sense that I feel bad or I think the film is bad or anything. But in certain cases, *The Good German* being one of them, getting negative, in some cases virulently negative, reviews killed that movie. We didn't have a chance. We had nothing to build on. That was a movie that really needed critical support to move out into the world, and people needed a lens to view it through. Critical support could've been that lens. We didn't get it, and the thing was DOA. It was just viewed as a disaster. That's where it's relevant to me, it was like, shit, we got really crushed, and the movie tanked.

MG: I seem to recall you said that in interviews before it was released, that this was a film that would need critical support to take off. My sense is that the choice to talk about the movie in terms of technique and the classical-Hollywood stuff is the thing that critics then ran with and really scrutinized almost exclusively.

SS: Yeah, obviously, I threw down the gauntlet, and what we got into was a situation where people were going to say, "How dare you pretend to know more about this than we do." That was the tone of a lot of the feedback, which is, "Nobody knows the visual language of *Casablanca* better than we do—how dare you." And that's just absurd, that's just crazy.

MG: That takes me to another, similar line of questioning. It seems to me that you've kind of limned this divide between speaking in the voice of the filmmaker and speaking in the voice of the film lover. You used that analogy about being a basketball fan and trying to experience the players' point of view. Obviously you've been on both sides of that. In the conversations I listen to with you and other filmmakers, to some extent you seem to be attaching yourselves to the filmmakers themselves, and thinking about films in terms of the production process and decisions being made. And in other cases you seem to be thinking about them as a viewer, in terms of the pleasure that stories and images give you. Do you ever have to separate those? Do you feel like you move one way or another, depending on whether you're actually having a conversation with someone who was involved in it? When you watch a film, do you think, "This is a great film," or, "I wonder how they did that"?

SS: I think all that's happening all the time. It's not possible for me to detach one of those trains of thought. And I don't see it as a problem, because it doesn't reduce my pleasure or impair my ability to sort of immerse myself in a film. In fact, it increases it. Being able to watch a great movie, and to experience it as a filmgoer and as a filmmaker, is really exciting. When you see something that's really great, I get an added boost out of it because I'm watching it through a couple of different prisms.

MG: So you get a boost in terms of the pleasure of artistic experience, and the possibility of channeling that into your work?

SS: Sure.

MG: I don't know if you put things into a comparative dimension, but do you ever look at particular filmmakers as makers of individual works or overall bodies of works, and say, "There's a career trajectory that I really recognize as somewhat similar to mine," or "There's an artistic mode—that person seems to be trying to get at the same things with art that I am"? Or do you just think about it in this larger sphere of, "There is great work"?

SS: Yeah, I think so. I do my own—you get a bunch of directors together, and eventually they're going to start talking about other directors that they like or don't like, or rate or don't rate. Obviously, none of us would ever do that for publication. But there's one game we like to play. We play the pantheon game a lot, which is, you have to have made three great movies to get into the pantheon. So it's fun to sort of go down the list. There are a lot of people who are in easily, and then there are some very good people who are kind of on the cusp. That's a fun game to play. But in general, I'm not a comparative person in the sense that, nothing makes me happier than seeing something good by somebody else. I want that. I draw inspiration from that. I don't want movies to be bad. I want to see really great stuff. I don't view art as a zero-sum game, and that if the Coen brothers make a great movie somehow they've stolen a piece of the great-movie pie from me.

MG: There's a parallel universe where all that bad-movie energy is going.

SS: Yeah, I've never looked at it that way. But I do believe that there is, within a certain, say, calendar period, a finite amount of great art that can exist. If you made 50 movies a year or 450 movies a year, there are still only a handful of them that are going to be great. This doesn't work on a linear scale. It doesn't scale from 50 to 450 with a proportional number of great films being produced. That's not how art works. So I'm rooting for the good stuff. To the point where, there can be a film by a good filmmaker, and I may have issues with that particular film, I may not like that particular film. But let's say for the sake of argument that it's someone who's acknowledged as being worthy of attention, and skilled, and not someone who does stuff that's down the middle. And let's say it was an original screenplay, and it's not a comic book and it's not a sequel. Whether or not I like the film personally, I'm rooting for the film. Its success helps me and other filmmakers like me. I don't look at it and go, "I hated that. I'm so mad that it made a hundred million dollars." It making a hundred million dollars makes it easier the next day for me to go in and go, "I've got an original screenplay, and it's kind of odd, it's not really down the middle," and everybody's more receptive to that because of what this filmmaker did. So I'm aware of how closely the people who pay for things are tracking the performance of certain films and certain filmmakers. And the bottom line is, clearly I'm still a sort of wild card. People don't know exactly what they're going to get when they say yes to me. They could be getting one thing; they could be getting another. I try to tell them what it is. When all the *Moneyball* stuff happened, people said, "Wow, you must be really pissed off." I said no, not really; it means I'm still capable of scaring people. That's a good thing. That means I'm still enough of a crazy person to make somebody pull the plug.

MG: So you value the risks you were taking there?

SS: Absolutely.

MG: There was no Monday-morning quarterbacking on your part?

SS: It really was a sort of irresistible force, immovable object situation. Because this thing was on a certain path, I was taking it on a certain path, and it clearly became a path that nobody was comfortable with. And this is what has to happen. There's no other result that can happen. I get it. The next day, I'm like, "What else have we got?" That's how *Haywire* happened, and I'm really happy with *Haywire*. I would never have made that movie otherwise.

MG: You walked into that after the *Moneyball* thing?

SS: Yeah, I looked around, found that, got it together quickly. I don't look back.

MG: Out of *Moneyball*, did you shoot documentary material that you would repurpose?

SS: I don't know what you would do with it. I shot about two-thirds of the interviews that I needed, and I don't think there's any use for them. It's in a vault somewhere.

MG: The things that you said anticipated my next question, which was about where you saw yourself in contemporary film culture, and whether you see yourself as part of a community of like-minded artists. You seem to be discussing that now, with the idea that "if good films get made, that's good for me," in terms of creative energy and influencing you to continue to work.

SS: Yeah. If I've played any part in getting more independent-minded filmmakers working in the studio system, I'd be really happy. Because I think that's what should be going on. I want to see Gus Van Sant given money to make movies, as much money as other people who aren't as good as Gus Van Sant. I grew up on studio movies that were really good, that were made by really good filmmakers. So I never had that prejudice that a lot of filmmakers did have and do have, or a lot of critics and people who write about movies had or do have, about who's writing the check. I don't give a shit. The delineation I make is between good movie, bad movie, not who financed it. To have the opportunity—I waited longer than a lot of people in my position, nine years, before I made a full-on studio movie with movie stars in it, which would be *Out of Sight*. Because I wanted to make sure that it was going to be the right choice for me. But doing that and doing *Erin* and doing *Ocean's*, I really hoped someone was going to follow me, and that there were going to be other filmmakers of my generation and my taste who were going to follow me and go make movies for Warners and Fox and everybody. This is what should be happening. This is good for everybody.

MG: Do you feel proud that to some extent that has happened? Do you feel responsible, without taking credit for that?

SS: Well, it's an evolving, living thing. It's hard for me to judge if my desire has been fulfilled or not. I don't know. You could look at it and go, "Well, it was for awhile, but not anymore." I don't know. I just know that I hoped that other people would follow me through that door and see that you can work in this arena and still have control. It can still be yours. There's nothing wrong with popular entertainment. There's just something wrong when it's stupid. I watch everything. I'll go from *Red Desert* to *Old School* in the same night. I just want it to be good.

MG: From reading interviews, it seems your tastes are very catholic.

SS: Yeah.

MG: At the same time, maybe I can move back to the historical, '60s-and-'70s–type question. You have repeatedly gravitated toward that area, as something that you invoke as the type of films and filmmakers that inspired you, particularly in the U.S. but also European art cinema, to use that phrase. And as you mentioned, other filmmakers of your generation were inspired in the same way. In a lot of cases, it seems to be people like you, who grew up a little bit after those films were being released, or coming up in the late period of it, and you rediscovered them some other way. So it's not the films of your youth, really, but something you had to re-experience in a different category. What is it about that era that speaks particularly to you? Would you say you have a strategy to embody a similar sensibility? How can you mix old and new to do something original? Is it, as you say, you walk onto the set and it's 1971? How does it work?

SS: First, I would put forth the premise that the way things imprint on you when you're between the ages of thirteen and seventeen is unique. I don't know why. Maybe a brain person could tell me whether I'm talking out of my other hole. But my experience of it is that between the ages of thirteen and seventeen, when I was seeing all those films and others, they had an impact that was very different than when I was quote-unquote an adult. So in my case, it's a function of circumstance. I'm in Baton Rouge, Louisiana, I'm going to high school on the campus of Louisiana State University, which happened to have a significant and well-curated repertory cinema program going on every night. And I was hanging around with these college students who were also interested in making films, and we were seeing everything. And that's really lucky. I was really lucky to be in that time at that place, and to have access to those works. And everything has sort of flowed from that. Had I grown up somewhere else, at another time, then it might be another era of filmmaking or it might be a type of film from another part of the world that would've influenced me. This is just how the planets lined up. And it syncs up, like you were saying. I was thirteen in 1976, so '76 to '80, the movie brats are at their peak at the beginning of that, and then by the end of it, most of them have self-destructed. Then comes the '80s, the worst decade in American cinema. And I'm then feeling, as the corporations have taken control of the movies again, I want to do what those people did. So it's largely a function of circumstance, a lot of that.

MG: So it's that combination of abundance amid scarcity that a lot of people seem to have an experience of, not all from living in small towns with universities.

SS: Well, it's what makes—if you're coming up now and you have access to everything, what is your filter? I was lucky in that I had this filter that happened to be these people that were programming this theater at LSU that turned out to be really good. Because you can't see everything, you do need a filter at a certain point. Especially if you're going to make films, you need to decide what to look at, you need to be looking at good stuff. But who is your filter for that? Like you're saying, the abundance now turns out to potentially be a problem. Your best weapon is your specificity, and you can't cultivate the kind of specificity that you need to distinguish yourself as a filmmaker without identifying a certain kind of thing that you watch over and over again. Because it's important not just to watch a lot of films. There are certain films that you need to watch repeatedly. And I did. Again, this is at a period where I'm a teenager, I can see *Jaws* twenty-nine times, I can see *Apocalypse* [*Now*] sixteen times, I can see *The Shining* eighteen times, *American Graffiti* in re-release thirteen times, *The Last Detail* twelve times. I'm a kid, I'm not really paying attention in school, and the matinees are cheap. I would go on a Sunday and sit through all five shows. I don't think people are doing that anymore. And that was a really important part of my education. And I loved it. I looked forward to it. It wasn't a chore. My dad would drop me off at 11 a.m. and he'd come get me at 10 p.m.

MG: So you are doing the repeat-viewing thing. In a way that does anticipate the way people started viewing things in the '80s. When I first started teaching, I realized all my students were watching the *Back to the Future* films on constant repeat on TNT, and had lost all grasp of world cinema or classical Hollywood, the kind of things that we would get on late-night or daytime television back in the day. Those had ceased to exist for these people, black-and-white had ceased to be anything young people could look at. They'd go back to the same early-1980s films. In a way, maybe that was those people's way of creating scarcity and distinction amid all this other stuff.

SS: Right. Which is fine if you want to grow up to be Robert Zemeckis. Then that's what you should be doing. I was watching the stuff over and over again that was the stuff I wanted to do. There's this evolving lecture that I have whenever I'm asked to speak to a film class that I've been working on for a couple years. It keeps changing. I'm trying to download everything that I feel I've learned in like an hour about directing. It's been hard. But I talk about stuff like that.

MG: Is one of the things you tell people to specialize?

SS: Yeah, you've got to have a thing. "What's your thing?" Even if your thing is that you don't have a thing. What are you bringing to the table? What is distinguishing you from the next person?

MG: You're describing this kind of self-curation process. Then that's something you feed into an artistic profile.

SS: Yeah.

MG: Great. And if you're willing to be reflective about this, I want to ask about the idea of auteurs. As I said before, you seem to read a lot about film, even if you're not looking at reviews as such. But not just film reviews, but other kinds of critical discussions about filmmaking and filmmakers tend, particularly to give it artistic legitimation, to talk about filmmakers as authors or as auteurs, as people whose strong directorial personality or strong artistic vision informs the film released under their name. Does that concept match your own experience of filmmaking? Or does it seem like an imposition on the part of those people in the stands?

SS: For someone like me, I don't know that it matters. In my life and my work, I'm a process person. As a viewer, I'm a results person. Either on a macro level or on a micro level, the delineation of responsibility doesn't really matter to me, because I'm just looking at the result and trying to get out of it something I can use. It seems, like I said, pretty self-evident to me that there are certain people that clearly have a very strong signature that carries across everything they do. But that also happens to be true for people who make things that aren't good. I guess I'm a sort of mixture, because I've never taken a possessory credit, I don't take writing credit on things even when I've done writing. And I've never taken a producer credit on a movie that I've directed, even when I've performed producing duties. You look at that and say, "What does that mean?" I guess it means that, like I said, "directed by"—I don't know what else you need to say. I guess I find all that other stuff kind of redundant. My whole thing is, I want my name up there once. I just want it up there once. I think you reduce the power of it every time you repeat it. "Directed by"—to me, that's a great credit. And I don't view it as the most important credit, just, for me doing what I do, it's sufficient. So I don't know, the auteur thing, it's kind of funny. You have to remember that the people that created it were kind of provocateurs. I guarantee you that half of them would argue for it or would propose it just to get an argument going, not out of any real sense of "we need to order the world in this way, and things need to be looked at this way." You're talking about Truffaut and Godard and Bazin, these French people writing about movies, they liked to say, "Let's stir it up a little bit. Let's say, you've been looking at this all wrong, this is the way it is." We can't assume that these ideas were created in a vacuum. These were ambitious, combative young guys, and they were trying to make a name for themselves.

MG: And they were experiencing movies in a way that nobody ever did before or since, that sense in the postwar period of, suddenly things come flooding over across the Atlantic to them. But that construct has just stuck and become the default mode of film writing, even when it has no real basis.

SS: Yeah, that's what I mean. It's sort of like saying, "Everyone is either blond or brunette." When in point of fact, there are many more possibilities than that. So I guess, again, I don't have to really participate in it because I'm in it. Let me put it to you this way. I have never heard another filmmaker, or been present when other filmmakers, were ever talking about this issue.

MG: Yeah, that's my sense as well.

SS: Nobody who actually does it gives a shit and has any interest in that argument.

MG: But people still want to be remembered as artists to some extent, right? Or they want their work to be taken seriously.

SS: I don't know. I can only speak for me. But I've never heard another director even bring this up. Like you said, when we have the pantheon discussion, you'd certainly like to be somebody that, ten or fifteen years from now, somebody goes, "Yeah, he's in the pantheon. He's made three great movies."

MG: You need the critics to do the legwork so people can have that conversation without starting it from scratch.

SS: Well, it gets into this issue of authorless texts. I think there are a couple movies that I've made, that if they were thought to have been made by a young filmmaker or had been the first film of another filmmaker, especially from another part of the world, that they would've been viewed very differently. Have I benefitted on occasion from being me? Sure. I'm sure it works both ways. But I guarantee you, a couple of my movies, if you stuck somebody else's name on it and said, "Oh, that's a female director who just graduated from the Lodz film school," that there'd be a very different reaction to the film.

MG: In a way, for better or worse, you're watching people connect the dots from your previous work. This can get to a useful question, particularly as you say that filmmakers don't talk about films in these terms. This can go in your lecture to film students. A lot of us as arts researchers want to illuminate the artistic practices and work roles of contemporary filmmakers, not just perform art appreciation about the films themselves. But maybe, as is apparent, we really don't have much access to production activity. And even if we don't "get it wrong" per se, we're just asking really different questions about the type of work, the type of output. As a piece of advice, I would ask, what might we as researchers do to gain insight into the challenges filmmakers face and the way you create works for the screen? Is there a way for us to write about things that really speaks to the way you guys are doing it?

SS: It'd be really difficult. You really have to be a fly on a wall from beginning to end to get a sense of what the issues are and how decisions get made. Because there are so many of them. So many questions have to be answered all the time under so many sets of circumstances. You would really have to be attached at the hip to get a sense of it. If you care at all, it can be like standing in the exhaust of a jet engine. It can be very intense, and it really tests your ability to remain calm. The physicality of it I think would surprise people. It's physically demanding, just the amount of energy it requires day to day over a long period of time I think would surprise people who've only written about films. It crushes people. It's physically intense, and it's obviously psychologically intense. I remember Frank Marshall once gave an interview, and he said, "I think everybody that finishes a film should get some kind of award." I remember laughing and thinking, "Yeah, it's kind of true." There are times when you think it's a miracle that somehow this thing ended up being done. And Warren Beatty said, "Films aren't finished, they're abandoned." And that's partially true, too. The problem is that, as I was saying, these making-of's or even the commentaries or whatever, you're reducing in some cases years of experience into a couple minutes. And there's no shortcut to understanding what those years were like. I'm not saying people should be patting us on the back all the time. You could say that it's not even relevant, when I was saying, the way I look at a movie, I don't care who did what. I'm just looking at the movie. So you could say, "I don't have to know how hard it was, or how easy it was, or who you had to please or who you had to argue with. The movie is what it is." And that's legitimate. You could probably make that fly in a court of law. But if you're going to write about the business at all and why movies are the way they are without being in the rooms where those decisions are made, then I think you're kind of flying a little bit blind. I wish—just for historical purposes, not because I think it would make me look good or make Sony look bad—I wish there was a transcript of the 90-minute conversation between me and Amy Pascal and Matt Tolmach the day before I was fired [from *Moneyball*]. That was a fascinating meeting. I found it fascinating, and I was not in a bad mood when I left. I said to Matt Tolmach, "June 18, remember that day." I was able to look at this and go, this is a really interesting moment in this business, in terms of two forces trying to figure out where to go. It was fascinating to me.

MG: I'm sure a lot of us, on the other side, would be interested.

SS: Yeah, to see what that conversation was.

MG: Is it the art-versus-entertainment conversation? Does it involve those trajectories?

SS: Yeah, people would realize it's not what it seems necessarily from the outside. So, I don't know. Like you said, it's all about access, and nobody wants to give access anymore. People are too scared. And I'd be too self-conscious. I just wouldn't want somebody around because it's like having somebody hang out in my bedroom. It's just not appropriate to me. To me, this is a very intimate situation.

MG: Aside from all those cameras. But they're not facing you.

SS: No, they're not.

MG: Interesting. Well, when you've done the thing for *End of the Road*, do you have a sense that you are trying to illuminate something about the way that film was made or what was going on in people's heads?

SS: Well, currently—we'll see how it ends up—I came up with a new rule recently that has helped me get my arms around it. My rule is that they never talk about what they think of the movie. I only use material in which they're talking about someone else, or they're talking about their experience of working on it. And it's resulted in this really interesting kind of conversation about what it felt like to work on that movie. Not what the movie means or what they think of the movie, but just what that summer was like working on that movie. So it's turned into something that's interesting to me, because I believe that is an important part of the process that doesn't really get discussed, which is the experience itself. These things represent years of my life. I want the experience to be useful and fun and not wasted. The sum of it to me is not the DVD in the shelf. It's the time, all that time. I want to come away feeling like that was a good use of everybody's time. That's what this piece has sort of become about, in a way.

MG: But then you feel that, say with things like DVD commentaries, that that also gives you a forum to discuss how your time was spent on particular films, or to talk to other filmmakers like Mike Nichols about how his time was spent?

SS: Yeah, my reasons for doing those other commentaries are purely selfish. I'm looking for information, I'm panning for gold. I want to know more about how something good got made. What was your filtering process, John Boorman, when you made *Point Blank*? So that's just me being kind of greedy. But that's appropriate. If some filmmaker fifteen, twenty years younger than me said, "Oh, I want to do the commentary with you on *King of the Hill*, because I have a lot of questions about that film," I'd be happy to do that, to hand down whatever I feel is relevant or useful. That's why I try to not do those alone, because I think they're really boring if it's not some sort of conversation.

MG: If you were just walking through your own narrative of it, that would be insufficient? You want to have other people asking you questions, driving the direction of that?

SS: Yeah. I did it once, obviously in a joking way on *Schizopolis*, but yeah, I would never do that alone. It seems pointless.

MG: Maybe I can ask you about working in different art forms. You've hinted in different interviews—correct me if I'm wrong—that you're mostly a formalist, interested in visual challenges, less so in being a writer. But at the same time you've worked in virtually every art-making mode parallel to feature films— television, documentary, experimental video, with acting yourself and playwriting and theatrical directing, and now painting as well. And in film, you've played virtually every creative role aside from composing soundtracks. Do these different modes connect up in your mind in a particular way? Do you think of them as different expressions of an artistic temperament? Or is it just that you want to try different things out of interest? You're trying to find a mode that streamlines art-making for you?

SS: My experience of it is very fluid, that making things—making stuff is making stuff, no matter whatever the medium is. I don't make any distinctions based on medium or job description. You're either creating or you're not. And a lot of the way I work is a result of how I started, in which you had to do a lot of things yourself, because there were only two or three of you. So you had to learn everybody's job. And that's a great way to learn. I guess I didn't see any reason why that shouldn't continue in the professional realm. And I viewed myself as a formalist early, and then I felt like I got out of that, I think. It felt like it. It felt like there was something going on in the first four films that I obviously wanted to blow up when I made *Schizopolis* and *Gray's Anatomy*. But I'm surprised more people, who are in a position to, aren't doing more things in more media. When somebody says to me, "So why are you making all these movies right on top of each other?," I go, "Well, because I can." Why wouldn't I? If I'm in a position to be able to make that happen, why wouldn't I make that happen? What am I waiting for? And that was another thing that I learned from the people that I started making films with—don't wait for permission. People who wait for permission end up not doing anything.

MG: So you've just taken it in stride that you say to yourself, "To get the shots I want to shoot, I should be the director of photography, and then that's going to entail learning the technology around that," or learning how to use the RED One [camera]. Rather than saying, "We need a soundtrack. Here's a guitar. Wait, I don't play the guitar. I can't do this." You just jumped into that?

SS: Yeah. Again, because of the way I started, every aspect of this has been interesting to me. All the jobs are interesting to me. I'd be happy with any job on a movie. I just think it's all really fun and interesting. I guess that's part of the reason that I've never felt compelled to be sort of obvious about trying to take possession of something that I've worked on and make it clear to everyone that this is mine. That's not my experience of it. I've worked as a crew member on movies in which the director—or on commercials and videos, sorry—in which the director was a kind of pasha. And I just really didn't like the vibe that that put off, and the reaction that I saw it creating in the crew. I just thought, "Wow, that's just not cool." And not what I was sort of taught. And that finds its way into the work, that belief. Like I said, directors really are their movies. If you see a director whose movies have a lot of screaming and crying in them, or people throwing plates, I guarantee you hang out with that director, at some point he's going to throw a plate. They can't help it.

MG: We thought it was fiction. "It's pretending," like Olivier said about acting.

SS: No, this is the thing, ultimately we all make what we like. We make what we like, we make what we want to see. And so it makes perfect sense that you'd meet a filmmaker and go, "Wow, you dress like a pimp because all your movies have hookers in them." That makes sense.

MG: We should all give a wide berth to horror directors.

SS: Yes, yes.

MG: But now you're a horror director, since you've described *Contagion* that way.

SS: Sort of, yeah. A little bit horror, Irwin Allen movie.

MG: Let me ask a related question about things that you'd like to do, and as you see yourself, by your definition, having your career wind down. Do you feel you've done everything you wanted to try, worked in every genre you wanted to try, or every art form you wanted to try to this point? Are there things where you say, "If I had more energy, I could be convinced to do this project"?

SS: I don't think so. There's a very strong sensation on my part right now that it's just time to switch horses. It's strong enough to make me sacrifice doing a couple of things that I still have, like *Cleo* and

[The] Sot-Weed Factor. I don't want to add any more stuff onto the end of this train, I just don't. I just feel ready to make a switch. And I've learned to pay attention to that instinct.

MG: So you've said with things like 3-D, you had an interest in it, but it's not strong enough now to go whole hog with that?

SS: I just found that—I shot this 3-D test for *Contagion*, because I thought that at some point, somebody's going to make a drama in 3-D. Somebody must. So I shot this little test, and I was kind of alarmed to find that two of the elements in your drama toolkit, probably the two most important elements in your drama toolkit, the over-the-shoulder and the clean single, were really weird in 3-D. That really concerned me, because those are go-to angles when you're making a drama. The over looked really weird because you had this huge blob sitting on one side of the screen in your lap. And then if you didn't, if you adjusted the stereoscopy or whatever you call it, the relation between the two cameras, the ocularity—interocularity, that's what it's called—so that the over did not move off of the screen. You can determine by adjusting how far out something moves past the plane of the screen, so you can have it sort of closer to you, or you can have it at the plane of the screen. So when you move the shoulder, the blurry shoulder, when you moved it off the plane of the screen toward you, it felt really weird, because it was this blob in your face. But then when you moved it to the plane of the screen, it made everything seem really small and far away. And then the clean single made it just look like you'd taken the actor, cut them out and stuck them onto a background. And I just decided, that's distracting. That's not good. And I'm really curious to see if anyone is ever going to be able to make an audience cry in 3-D. Because I'm not sure you can.

MG: Until they look at their ticket stubs, and see what they paid for that 2-D to 3-D conversion.

SS: I don't think it's going to go away. I think it's going to find its plateau pretty soon, and then it'll be that. It'll be another tool. If I were going to make *Cleo*, I would make it in 3-D. I think a Ken Russell musical essentially in 3-D would be awesome. But I still think—a buddy of mine, when we were talking about this issue, said, "*Avatar* in 2-D is still the biggest movie in the world." And I agree. I don't think that piece of technology is transformative in any meaningful way in terms of the audience experience. I don't. I think it can be cool, but I don't think it's—I think people would trade anything in the world for characters that they're interested in.

MG: Over the long haul.

SS: Yeah.

MG: So can I ask you about painting? I don't really have a segue here except, does painting represent a parallel artistic strand for you? Or is it at the complete opposite pole from what you've been doing?

SS: No, there are obviously connections. I'm bringing to it a certain amount of knowledge regarding composition and tonality and things like that. What I have to learn the same way that I did when I started making films is, I now have to learn how to achieve certain effects. When you're starting out and you're trying to learn, you're imitating things that you've seen in movies so that you can figure out how they did them. So that's sort of where I am now. I'm at the very, very beginning of that process, of having an idea of something that I like, and having to figure out how to create it on a canvas. As simple as learning how to—when you make a painting, you've got to start with the thing that's furthest away, and build. If I'm painting a painting of the street, I've got to start painting the stuff that's in the distance first and work my way forward, so that I'm layering on top of that, so that it has the correct feeling of depth. That's just something I'm starting to get into. If I've got three objects in the frame that one is in front of the other is in front of the other, I've got to paint the furthest one away first, right, and then the one that's second, and then the one that's closest.

MG: And then would you say this is something you realized upon coming to painting, or you said to yourself, "Oh, I've had to do this in my filmmaking, I can just port this right over"?

SS: No that was something that, as soon as I started to actually try and paint, I very quickly—I did not understand the sort of hierarchy of depth on a canvas until I actually started trying to paint on a canvas.

MG: And the things you bring to painting, do you say, "This is an extension of this skill I've developed," like about composition and tonality?

SS: I hope so. I hope that there are both ideas and techniques that I can appropriate from filmmaking that will help me distinguish myself in another visual medium. Certainly I'm not yet thinking like a painter. One of the things I've been doing as an experiment is painting frames from movies, pulling stills from movies and recreating them on a canvas. That's a good toe in the water for me. It feels safe, and yet I'm learning technical things about how to achieve certain effects and make things look a certain way. So that's been fun.

MG: Are you trying to paint in a realist way, or in the way that the film image looked?

SS: For now, I'm trying to recreate the film image.

MG: So is it things that you've been particularly invested in before? What kind of frames?

SS: It varies. I'm working on a frame from *Klute* right now that I like a lot, just an image that I think is really arresting. I'm pretty sure I can reproduce that on a canvas. I'm going to try. So it's stuff like that.

MG: Some of the same things that you borrow for film shots.

SS: Yeah.

MG: Do you plan to make a living there? Do you see yourself as a professional, or just as an amateur?

SS: I don't know. I think it depends. It'll be a couple of years before I can even answer that. There's also probably going to be some photography. I have some ideas for—not just pure photography like, "Oh, here are some pictures I've taken"—but something along— I don't know if you're familiar with this photographer, Duane Michals, but he shoots series, they're stories. They're frames, and there's clearly a narrative in there. So I'm interested in building on that idea. I'm fascinated by the idea of, in still frames, shooting a sequence of somebody chasing somebody in New York. If I were going to do that in six still frames, what would they be? So I think for a while there's just going to be a lot of stuff coming out, and then I'll figure out what to do with it.

MG: Alright. What's the most generous way to ask this? Are you at all self-conscious about the potentially clichéd nature of the trajectory of the filmmaker turning to fine art in the twilight of his career?

SS: No. I just don't care. I'm just trying to stay excited. It doesn't really matter.

MG: And are you interested in staying involved in film industries as a patron, or an activist, or a preservationist like you have been?

SS: No. My sense right now is that it's really going to be kind of a closed door. That's the way it feels right now. I've got two more years being national vice president of the Directors Guild. This'll be my last term. I'm hoping by then that all this stuff will be wound up. It's feeling right now like I really need to step away from all of it for a while. The degree to which somebody may call me and ask me to look at something and help with an edit, I don't know. But I feel like sort of just being away from it for a while.

MG: Well, on behalf of the film culture at large, we're going to miss you. Who will we choose to take your place?

SS: Oh, there's always a Johnny-come-lately. No, look, shit, I've got it great. The only frustrating thing about talking about it—other than, in this economy it's terrible to be talking about giving up a well-paying job—is that I don't want it to seem like a complaint. It's really not. It just feels like time for a change, a radical change. And I love it too much not to love it, you know what I mean? If I can't go to work every day excited and loving it and loving all of it—I have too much respect for the art form than to go to work. That should be your attitude. There's a point where that isn't true for me anymore, where I won't be looking forward to it. I just think it's out of respect that I need to then switch off.

MG: Based on our discussions, is there anything else people should know about you and about your work? Do you feel like we're getting it right, asking the right questions? Do you feel you've had the career that speaks to how you saw yourself or have seen yourself as an artist?

SS: I'm really happy with how things have turned out. If during *sex, lies*, you flash-forward and said, "This is what you're going to do over the next twenty-two years," then I'd go, "Wow, cool." I'm really happy with all the opportunities I had, and I really wouldn't change anything about it. I would change things about the movies, maybe. But I feel, like I said, that the timing of when I came up was good, and that I've benefitted from being in the right place at the right time a lot. And I've also taken advantage of that. I feel I've been sensitive to every potential opportunity that has been in front of me, and I feel that I've taken advantage of those opportunities or tried very hard. I don't feel like anything really slipped by me that I missed because I wasn't paying attention. I've tried to maximize whatever juice I might have to make things happen both for me and for other people. So I'm happy about that. As much as I didn't enjoy producing, for the period that we had Section Eight up and running, we did a lot of shit in a very short period of time. That was an extremely productive entity. It ended up being almost too productive. I think the workload really got crazy for both of us.

MG: Considering how much other work you were doing.

SS: Yeah, we both had day jobs, and it was becoming really overwhelming. And I just don't like producing. It's a terrible job. But I'm happy about that. It's a good list of things to have been associated with.

Notes

Introduction

1. *Bubble* debuted at the Venice, Toronto, and New York film festivals, all in September 2005.

2. Cieply, "Independent Filmmakers Distribute on Their Own," 2009.

3. *Bubble*'s aesthetic is hardly the result of technological determinism, though. The Sony HDW-F900 camera and Panavision lenses used for *Bubble* also captured the images of George Lucas's *Star Wars* trilogy of 1999–2004.

4. The film's official website details the simultaneous-release outlets and includes a promotional interview with Soderbergh (http://www.bubblethefilm .com/about.html [accessed November 10, 2007]).

5. Zimmermann, "Digital Deployment(s)," 246.

6. In 2005, Skoll founded Participant Productions, whose co-productions include *An Inconvenient Truth* (2006), *Good Night, and Good Luck*, and *Syriana*. Jarecki first earned creative acclaim as director of the Magnolia-distributed *Capturing the Friedmans* (2003).

7. Weiner, "Shyamalan's Hollywood Horror Story, With Twist."

8. Caldwell, "Welcome to the Viral Future of Cinema (Television)," 95; see also Caldwell, *Production Culture*.

9. See, for example, Silverman, "*Bubble* Fails to Rock Tinseltown."

10. On the weekend of the film's release, for example, *Variety*'s Gabriel Snyder and Stephen Zeitchik ("Movie Biz on the 'Bubble'") wrote that "the pic has become the totem for those advocating a distribution model that would put films everywhere all at the same time."

11. In a conference call with industry analysts, Iger had hinted at the inevitability of day-and-date releases, prompting Fithian's later claim that such notions were a "death threat" against exhibitors (see Kirsner, "Maverick Mogul").

12. Klinger, *Beyond the Multiplex*, 241.

13. Zimmermann, "Digital Deployment(s)," 251.

14. Prominent director-auteurs or producer-auteurs include, for example, Jerry Bruckheimer (film/television), J.J. Abrams (television/film), Joss Whedon (television/internet/film), David Lynch (film/television/internet), and Edward Zwick (film/television/internet).

15. Caldwell, "Welcome to the Viral Future of Cinema (Television)," 93.

16. This inversion corresponds with Caldwell's mischievous but fundamentally serious claim that "feature film is rapidly approaching the aesthetic significance, cultural stature, and industrial condition of television" ("Welcome to the Viral Future of Cinema (Television)," 92).

17. "The Steven Soderbergh Experience Vidcast," *Bubble: The Movie*, http ://www.bubblethefilm.com/ssexp.html (accessed November 10, 2007).

18. Hozic, *Hollyworld*.

19. Following its initial release on standard DVD, *Bubble* has appeared on Blu-ray (in Region A format, for North and South American release) and in the now-obsolete HD-DVD format.

20. Reaching U.S. audiences is another issue. News accounts invoked theater chains' long-standing policies of not showing films already available on home-video formats, though such a policy is routinely violated for holiday screenings or rereleases. *Bubble* remains inarguably a text with no specific commercial appeal—absent multiplatforming, it would likely have remained a small niche release.

21. No DVD or pay-TV returns have been publicized, but it did not appear on top rental or sale lists. In its theatrical run, it grossed just under $262,000, including $145,000 in the U.S. ("Bubble," http://www.boxofficemojo.com /movies/?id=bubble.htm [accessed July 8, 2010]).

Chapter 1

1. Malcolm, "Back in Sight," 111.

2. Waxman, *Rebels on the Backlot*, 104.

3. Mottram, *The Sundance Kids*, 174–175.

4. For more on changes in film content resulting from the rise of independent producers in the 1950s, see Mann, *Hollywood Independents*.

5. For an interrogation of the "commercial/independent text" as understood during the 1980s, see Palmer, *"Blood Simple*: Defining the Commercial/ Independent Text."

6. Warner Independent Pictures was rumored to have been created partly to maintain Soderbergh and Clooney's relationship with Warner Bros. Warners announced in May 2008 the decision to shutter WIP and its other boutique division, Picturehouse, claiming that the remaining New Line division could absorb its independent-minded projects. See Kit and Goldstein, "Warners Axes Picturehouse, WIP."

7. Minsky, "Hot Phenom," 9.

8. Kelleher, "Out of Sight," 106. *Kafka* relied on a similar if more structured compromise, with a color version prepared for release in some European

television markets. (In its U.S. theatrical release, *Kafka* was in black and white, with a small number of expressive color sequences.)

9. In Soderbergh's recounting, he deliberated with financiers over the absence of female nudity, seemingly promised in the script and the film's title, and regarded as an asset in home-video circulation. Reviewing production dailies, RCA/Columbia Home Video executive Larry Estes told Soderbergh, "I'm not seeing any flesh. . . . We may have a problem" (Soderbergh, *sex, lies, and videotape*, 207; cited in Biskind, *Down and Dirty Pictures*, 31).

10. Tzioumakis, *American Independent Cinema*, 11.

11. See Sundance's timeline at http://www.festival.sundance.org/2010 /history (accessed August 11, 2010).

12. See "Film Independent: Our History," http://www.filmindependent .org/about/our-history, and "Spirit Awards History," http://www.spiritawards .com/about/spirit-awards-history (both accessed April 12, 2012).

13. Prince, *A New Pot of Gold*, 45.

14. Prince, *A New Pot of Gold*, and Wyatt (in Prince) map the varying fortunes of independent and "mini-major" producers and distributors in impressive detail, so I provide this snapshot principally as context for the creative-industrial relationships experienced by Soderbergh and others from the end of the 1980s onward.

15. See in particular Tzioumakis (*American Independent Cinema*, 273), Biskind (*Down and Dirty Pictures*, 27–33, 39–43, 63–66), and Mottram (*The Sundance Kids*, 7–10).

16. The joint venture's financing of Soderbergh's film preceded Sony's acquisition of Columbia, which occurred in November 1989 (Prince, *A New Pot of Gold*, 58).

17. Ciment and Niogret, "Interview with Steven Soderbergh," 17. TriStar began as a partnership of Columbia, HBO, and CBS, so Soderbergh's work with them links *sex, lies, and videotape* to Columbia Pictures' conglomerate efforts from multiple directions.

18. King, *Indiewood, USA*, 8–9.

19. As Peter Kramer notes, writers have used the term "New Hollywood" to designate a group of late-1960s and early-1970s films, the entire late-1960s/ early-1970s era, or the period from the mid-1970s onward. Like him, I use the term synonymously with "Hollywood Renaissance," that is, to indicate all Hollywood film and film culture from the late 1960s through the mid-1970s. See Kramer, *The New Hollywood*, 2.

20. King, *Indiewood, USA*, 12.

21. For more on the formation of taste cultures and different groups' investments in particular taste categories, see Gans, *Popular Culture and High Culture*.

22. Mottram, *The Sundance Kids*, xxi.

23. Ibid., x.

24. Longtime Fine Line president Ira Deutchman asserts 1990 as the year "when suddenly the festival became a feeding frenzy, inundated with agents,

executives, and deal makers." Even Soderbergh joined this dissent, noting that in 1989 the festival "wasn't overrun by agents and wasn't a deal market or sales place" (both quoted in Levy, *Cinema of Outsiders*, 40; no date given for their assertions). Soderbergh has of course benefitted from dealmaking both at festivals and in other venues.

25. See Palmer, "*Blood Simple*: Defining the Commercial/Independent Text," for a discussion of Sayles's directorial debut, *Return of the Secaucus Seven* (1979), as a prospective "calling card" for subsequent larger projects.

26. Biskind, *Down and Dirty Pictures*, 1.

27. Waxman, *Rebels on the Backlot*, x.

28. Mottram, *The Sundance Kids*, xxvii.

29. Dieckmann, "Liar, Liar, Pants on Fire," 40–41; Ciment and Niogret, "Interview with Steven Soderbergh," 22.

30. Johnston, "David O. Russell's Folks Saw *Spanking the Monkey*," cited in Mottram, *The Sundance Kids*, 44.

31. See Anderson, "My Private Screening With Pauline Kael."

32. Prince, *A New Pot of Gold*, 273.

33. Buckland, *Directed by Steven Spielberg*, 21.

34. Scott, *On Hollywood*, 5.

35. Caldwell, *Production Culture*, 244.

36. Ibid., 272.

37. For example, the first choice for director of *Out of Sight* was Cameron Crowe (Mottram, *The Sundance Kids*, 229–230), whose most recent effort had been the huge hit *Jerry Maguire* (1996).

38. King, *Indiewood, USA*, 31.

39. Bart, "Beware Falling Stars!"

40. Ciment and Niogret, "Interview with Steven Soderbergh," 23.

41. Jacobson, "Steven Soderbergh, King of Cannes," 29–30.

42. Ciment and Niogret, "Interview with Steven Soderbergh," 23.

43. Jacobson, "Steven Soderbergh, King of Cannes," 30.

44. See Soderbergh, *sex, lies, and videotape*, 57–65.

45. Mottram, *The Sundance Kids*, 53.

46. Dollard also bridged other roles in sensational fashion. A longtime alcohol and drug abuser, he stopped working as Soderbergh's agent in 2005 and reinvented himself as a far-right military supporter, travelling to Iraq to film a self-described "pro-war documentary" (Wright, "Pat Dollard's War on Hollywood"). See also Waxman, *Rebels on the Backlot*.

47. Wright, "Pat Dollard's War on Hollywood."

48. Ibid. Elsewhere, Christine Vachon credits USA Films's Scott Greenstein with a key role in *Traffic*'s execution and its eventual high profile within the industry, saying "Scott delivered for Steven. . . . He got *Traffic* made for him, he got him the nominations, and he got him the director award" (Biskind, *Down and Dirty Pictures*, 447).

49. Kaufman, "Man of the Year," 164.

50. Waxman, *Rebels on the Backlot*, 108; Mottram, *The Sundance Kids*, 53; King, *Indiewood, USA*, 201.

51. Ciment and Niogret, "Interview with Steven Soderbergh," 76.

52. Soderbergh and Lester, *Getting Away With It*, 190; Waxman, *Rebels on the Backlot*, 108; Mottram, *The Sundance Kids*, 229–230.

53. Soderbergh and Lester, *Getting Away With It*.

54. Mottram, *The Sundance Kids*, xxiv–xxv.

55. Soderbergh and Lester, *Getting Away With It*; Hyman, "The Development Hell of *A Confederacy of Dunces*."

56. Soderbergh and Lester, *Getting Away With It*; Mottram, *The Sundance Kids*, 321.

57. Mottram, *The Sundance Kids*, 63.

58. Much later, in 2002, Miramax co-produced and distributed Soderbergh's first foray into digital video, *Full Frontal*.

59. Cellini, "Mac, Lies, and DV Tape."

60. Ciment and Niogret, "Interview with Steven Soderbergh," 76.

61. "Even Stevens."

62. See "Sold Out: Soderbergh Schizopolis Screening in NYC," http://www .slamdance.com/blog/permalink/2008/9/10/191601.html (accessed April 16, 2009).

63. Ciment and Niogret, "Interview with Steven Soderbergh," 60.

64. Biskind, *Down and Dirty Pictures*, 79.

65. Ciment and Niogret, "Interview with Steven Soderbergh," 61.

66. Chanko, "Steven Soderbergh Hopes," 66.

67. For release data, see the film's entry at Box Office Mojo, http://www .boxofficemojo.com/movies/?id=thisboyslife.htm (accessed April 18, 2009).

68. Around the same time, Soderbergh worked further in neo-noir terrain by directing two episodes (airing in August 1993 and October 1995) of Showtime's television series *Fallen Angels*, an anthology series with historical Los Angeles settings, contributions from emerging directors such as John Dahl and Alfonso Cuarón and actors-turned-directors such as Tom Hanks and Tom Cruise, and adapted stories from Raymond Chandler, Dashiel Hammett, and others.

69. McCarthy, "*The Underneath*."

70. For release data, see the film's entry at Box Office Mojo, http://www .boxofficemojo.com/movies/?id=underneath.htm (accessed April 18, 2009).

71. Richardson, "The Very Boring Life of Steven Soderbergh."

72. See http://www.bfi.org.uk/lff/indiewood_dead_long_live_new_true _indies (accessed March 10, 2009).

Chapter 2

1. Staiger, "Authorship Approaches," 4.

2. Though Henry Jenkins regards historical poetics as "primarily descriptive and explanatory" ("Historical Poetics," 101), it can also be put in service of evaluative projects such as intertextual analysis. In accord with this chapter's project, Jenkins notes, too, that a historical poetics can supply necessary contexts, investigating "the institutions which shape the reception of popularly circulating films" ("Historical Poetics," 109).

3. Ibid., 105.

4. Klinger, *Beyond the Multiplex*, 92.

5. Ibid., 86.

6. Box-office rankings in this section are gathered from the online Box Office Report Revenue Database, www.boxofficereport.com/ybon/rental.shtml, cross-referenced with data from IMDb Pro, pro.imdb.com, both accessed April 27, 2009. Kramer, *The New Hollywood*, produces a slightly different list, though his dollar figures coincide with Box Office Report's.

7. In *The New Hollywood* (108–109), Kramer lists *The Devil in Miss Jones* at number ten, while Box Office Report puts it at number eleven, adding the animated *Robin Hood* (1973) at number seven, though *Robin Hood*'s ranking may include its post-1973 revenues.

8. Klinger, *Beyond the Multiplex*, 114.

9. Hoberman, "Behold the Man."

10. Likewise, *Full Frontal*'s metacinematic approach, indebted to works such as William Greaves' *Symbiopsychotaxiplasm: Take One* and Jim McBride's *David Holzman's Diary*, led many reviewers to proclaim it tedious. Even the film's admirers champion it for its articulation of its director's process— "[t]he fun comes in watching Soderbergh wing it," writes *Rolling Stone*'s Peter Travers—rather than for its intrinsic appeal.

11. Gabriel, "Steven Soderbergh: The Sequel."

12. Ibid.

13. Klinger, *Beyond the Multiplex*, 100.

14. See, for example, Siskel, "Candid Camera"; Gabriel, "Steven Soderbergh: The Sequel"; Chanko, "Steven Soderbergh Hopes"; and Lee, "*Jaws* Hooked Soderbergh on Filmmaking."

15. Jenkins, "Historical Poetics," 115.

16. Bordwell, "Cutting Remarks."

17. See, for example, Goss, "Steven Soderbergh's *The Limey*"; Parker and Parker, "Directors and DVD Commentary"; Carruthers, "Biding Our Time"; King, *Indiewood, USA*; and Baker, *Steven Soderbergh*.

18. The release in question is *Symbiopsychotaxiplasm: Two Takes* (Criterion Collection DVD, 2006).

19. Patterson, "Invasion of the Movie Snatchers."

20. Steven Soderbergh and Lem Dobbs commentary, *The Limey* DVD (Artisan Home Entertainment, 2000).

21. Parker and Parker, "Directors and DVD Commentary," 17.

22. Ibid.

23. John Boorman and Steven Soderbergh commentary, *Point Blank* DVD (Warner Home Video/Turner Entertainment, 2005).

24. Soderbergh and Dobbs commentary, *The Limey* DVD.

25. Levy, "*The Limey*." To be fair to the scope of the review, Levy identifies a network of intertexts, not just those dating to the 1960s. He references Fonda's then-recent role in the independent *Ulee's Gold* (1997), along with the 1979 film *Hardcore*, Soderbergh's own *Kafka* and *Out of Sight*, and this last film's use of "stylistic devices associated with 1970s cinema."

26. Bourdieu, *Distinction*, 270.

27. *Traffic* in particular received criticism for its treatment of race from numerous mainstream reviewers as well as academic commentators. See, for example, Roth, "Black and White Masculinity," and Shaw, "'You are Alright, But . . .'"

28. On this subject, see Lipton, "Weapons of Mass Instruction." Soderbergh's support of Reggio links him to other Hollywood auteur-patrons. While *Naqoyqatsi* was "presented by" Soderbergh and Miramax, Reggio's earlier *Koyaanisqatsi* circulated with benefit of a similar presentation from director Francis Ford Coppola, and its follow-up *Powaaqatsi* (1988) was "presented by" Coppola and George Lucas.

29. Hoberman, "Soderbergh's *Girlfriend Experience*."

30. Thomson makes the same assertion years earlier, noting, "Soderbergh likes to pick and choose (one for them, one for me)" (*The Whole Equation*, 368).

31. Elaborating on this subject, Bourdieu argues that "[t]he sense of distinction . . . is affirmed . . . in the innumerable stylistic or thematic choices which, being based on the concern to underline difference, exclude all forms of intellectual (or artistic) activity regarded at a given moment as inferior," forms including "vulgar objects, unworthy references," and more (*Distinction*, 499).

32. Kramer, *The New Hollywood*, 114.

33. Child, "Winstone to Play Caesar." Following a flurry of attention in 2008 and 2009, the project remains ostensibly in development as of this writing, though with Soderbergh as producer and not director.

34. *Viva Las Vegas* ranks eleventh in theatrical rentals for 1964 (http://www.boxofficereport.com/database/1964.shtml, accessed May 2, 2009), while *Tommy* earned the U.S.'s number-ten spot in 1975 releases (Kramer, *The New Hollywood*, 109).

35. Klinger, *Beyond the Multiplex*, 132.

Chapter 3

1. Directors Guild of America, "Statement of Steven Soderbergh."

2. See Sellors, *Film Authorship*, for a theorization of the relationship between creative activity and authorship.

3. For more on Soderbergh's appropriation of the 1940s aesthetic, see Bordwell, "Not Back to the Future, but Ahead to the Past."

4. Some critics accused the film of taking this film-school approach too far. In a 2006 review, Mick LaSalle calls the film a "bloodless, academic exercise." Even Bordwell, in a January 25, 2007, postscript to his blog essay on the film, derides it as a "film-school exercise."

5. One might have expected the film to gain ground on home video. However, with a DVD release in May 2007, nearly six months later it was not among the top 5,000 sellers in Amazon's U.S. DVD sales.

6. My research has turned up a scant few interviews with co-stars Cate Blanchett and Tobey Maguire, and a single quotation from production designer Philip Messina.

7. Carringer, "Collaboration and Concepts of Authorship," 377.

8. The film credits Chris Lombardi as "A" camera operator, working on his third film with Soderbergh. Cameraman Duane Manwiller has also received "A" camera operator credits on nine films with Soderbergh, though production photos for many films show Soderbergh himself operating a handheld camera.

9. Taylor, "Composer Cliff Martinez Talks Score."

10. In her review of the film, Dargis writes: "The idea that the extremely self-motivated Mr. Soderbergh might be satisfied with a career like Curtiz's is rich nonsense. Curtiz had next to no say on the personnel who worked on 'Casablanca.' By contrast, for 'The Good German' Mr. Soderbergh persuaded the same studio, now owned by a media conglomerate for which movies represent only a thin slice of the pie chart, to cough up millions for what is essentially a pet art project."

11. The production could not use the high-intensity arc lights employed on such features as *Citizen Kane* (1941), as working models could not be sourced.

12. Topel, "Interview: Soderbergh Talks Positions."

13. Whipp, "Nothing Clear-Cut in Noir-Style 'Good German.'"

14. Calhoun, "The Directors: Steven Soderbergh."

15. Wloszczyna, "'German' Takes Hard Look."

16. Numerous reviews of the film invoked the construct of the audience. For example, Dargis's review calls Soderbergh "a filmmaker far more interested in his own handicraft . . . than in the audience for whom he's ostensibly creating that work." Bordwell's blog postscript on the film (also cited above) also opines about limited opportunities for "audience involvement."

17. Gerstner and Staiger, *Authorship and Film*, xi.

18. See, for example, Shaw, "'You are Alright, But . . .'"; Roth, "Black and White Masculinity"; Baker, *Steven Soderbergh*; and Palmer and Sanders, *The Philosophy of Steven Soderbergh*.

19. See Foucault, "What Is an Author?," in particular pp. 124–131.

20. Staiger presses this point as well in *Authorship and Film*.

21. Staiger, "Authorship Approaches," 46; emphasis in original.

22. *Bubble* debuted at festivals in September 2005, but as noted in the introduction, had its national, multiplatform release in January 2006.

23. For all of those except *Full Frontal*, he worked directly alongside Soderbergh, who served as lead editor. In some of these cases, Kirchner received a credit as postproduction supervisor.

24. See, for example, Corliss, "Woody Allen on Ingmar Bergman."

25. Kerr, "Babel's Network Narrative," 48.

26. Goldsmith and O'Regan, *The Film Studio*, 19.

27. See Staiger, "The Hollywood Mode of Production, 1930–1960," 330, cited in Goldsmith and O'Regan, *The Film Studio*, 6.

28. Neale, "'New Hollywood Cinema,'" 118.

29. However, the film's casting does not strongly respect linguistic or national specificity. Aside from casting the Puerto Rico–born Del Toro as the Argentinean Che Guevara, the film casts Portuguese native Joaquim de Almeida as Bolivian president René Barrientos, and Brazilian actor Rodrigo Santoro as the Cuban Raul Castro, among others.

30. Goldsmith and O'Regan, *The Film Studio*, 8.

31. See, for example, Appadurai's theorization of the distinctive categories that he argues inform and shape global cultural processes: ethnoscapes, mediascapes, technoscapes, financescapes, and ideoscapes.

32. See "Interview with Steven Soderbergh," *Che* UK/Region 2 DVD (Optimum Releasing, 2009). Elsewhere, Soderbergh claims: "The language decision we made for two reasons. . . . One, authenticity; and the other thing was that most of our audience is probably going to be outside the U.S. For those people, doing it in Spanish was going to get us a better result commercially. But it meant no American money. So it's a trade-off" (Jeffries, "Rebel Without a Pause").

33. As Mark Betz argues, numerous factors encourage the conflation of the categories "art cinema" and "European cinema." Betz writes that "art cinema overwhelmingly refers to a volume of narrative films produced in Europe from the late 1950s through the mid-1970s" (*Beyond the Subtitle*, 10) and notes that English-language scholarship on broadly formulated "European cinema" tends to theorize it specifically as art cinema.

34. For example, in "The Art Cinema as a Mode of Film Practice"—which as Betz observes, attends principally to European films—David Bordwell asserts that the art film "uses a concept of authorship to unify the text" (Bordwell, "The Art Cinema as a Mode of Film Practice," 59; cited in Betz, *Beyond the Subtitle*, 11).

35. Kerr, "Babel's Network Narrative," 46.

36. Chris, "New Frontier."

37. Ibid.

38. In his *Hollywood Reporter* review, Peter Brunette notes anecdotally that Del Toro does not attempt to replicate Guevara's Argentinean accent.

39. Nornes, *Cinema Babel*, 57.

40. The film played later at additional festivals as well: in December 2008 in Dubai, and in 2009 in Budapest, Hong Kong, Algeria, and Melbourne.

41. On this point, see Betz, *Beyond the Subtitle*, 82.

42. Gaut, "Film Authorship and Collaboration," 164.

43. Soderbergh's first statement appears in the film's press kit (2009), while the second appears on the film's Blu-ray commentary track (*The Informant!* Blu-ray disc, Warner Home Video, 2010).

44. Stringer, "The Gathering Place," 74.

45. Ibid., 76.

46. On this subject, see Zafirau, "Audience Knowledge and the Everyday Lives of Cultural Producers in Hollywood," 194.

47. Budget figures appear on the film's IMDb Pro listing (http://pro.imdb .com/title/tt1130080/business, accessed June 14, 2010).

48. Curtin, "Thinking Globally," 113.

49. Elder, "Screen Scene."

50. Saunders, "Damon Watch."

51. One anonymous day player recounts his experience as "amazing" and "unbelievable" (Albright, "Sun Shines on 'The Informant'"), while a set visitor and sometime reporter observes that "it was an awesome time" ("Professional Profiles: Jayson Albright"). Similarly, an extra filmed in a diner scene says of the episode, "It's a lifetime opportunity you'd never thought would happen to you" (Spates, "Singing the Informant Blues").

52. Spates, "Singing the Informant Blues."

53. Ibid.

54. Rueff, "'The Informant' Debuts to Hollywood Hoopla."

55. Cain, "You May Be a Little Blurry."

56. Ibid.

57. Interviewing Whitacre, Ashley Rueff reports that "[h]e lent his memory throughout the filming process and said he feels Warner Bros. handled the retelling of that part of his life with sensitivity" (Rueff, "Upcoming 'Informant!' Showing").

58. Albright ("Decatur Again Set Aside in 'Informant!'") writes: "Tuesday saw the release of Steven Soderbergh's 'The Informant!' on DVD and Blu-ray with the promise of deleted scenes. Finally! Our chance to see scenes shot in Decatur that were left on the cutting room floor! The Mall! Firestone! That guy I know who was an extra! Sadly, those scenes remain on the cutting room floor, and it appears to be the work of Soderbergh himself. . . . Soderbergh mentions that it was he who decided what deleted scenes to include."

59. Albright, "Decatur Again Set Aside in 'Informant!'"

60. Spates, "Singing the Informant Blues"; parentheses in original.

61. Caldwell, "Cultures of Production," 200; italics in original.

62. Ibid., 202.

63. During production, some Decatur commentaries suggested that the film would boost local tourism, but its unremarkable box-office performance dampens that prospect.

64. "Professional Profiles: Jayson Albright."

65. The city later earned notoriety as part of the Firestone tire-recall case of 2000, which resulted the following year in the closing of a Decatur-area plant cited as the producer of defective tires.

66. Cain, "'Informant' Still Lost in Decatur."

67. Cain, "ADM Working with Filmmakers." This assertion of a "ten-year-strong track record" evades ADM's much longer history—founders George Archer and John Daniels started their business together in 1902, and ADM was formed in 1923. The film's own press kit exonerates the company as well, with Soderbergh quoted there saying that "everybody, including the new brass at ADM, got that this movie is about a specific time and not about ADM or the city of Decatur today."

68. Archer Daniels Midland Company, "About ADM and 'The Informant!'"

69. Couldry, *Media Rituals*, 120.

70. Saunders, "Damon Watch"; Cain, "Extra, Extra."

71. References to this jacket appear in Albright, "'The Informant' Comes Back Downtown"; Albright, "Sun Shines on 'The Informant'"; "Professional Profiles: Jayson Albright"; and Spates, "Singing the Informant Blues."

Chapter 4

1. Stewart, "Steven Soderbergh."

2. Hoberman, "Soderbergh's *Girlfriend Experience*."

3. Ciment and Niogret, "Interview With Steven Soderbergh," 60.

4. Johnston, "The Flashback Kid," 117.

5. Kapsis, *Hitchcock: The Making of a Reputation*, 114.

6. Bourdieu, *The Field of Cultural Production*, 111.

7. Ibid., 75.

8. Keathley, *Cinephilia and History*, 95.

9. Routt, "L'Evidence."

10. Keathley, *Cinephilia and History*, 95.

11. Foundas, "The Sundance Experience." An HDNet Films press release also cites Foundas's review; see "Steven Soderbergh's 'The Girlfriend Experience' Starring Sasha Grey To Premiere As a Sneak Preview on HDNet Movies," May 18, 2009 (http://www.hd.net/pressrelease.html?2009-05-18-02.html, accessed June 20, 2009). The pull quote also appeared in print advertising for the film; for example, in Seattle's weekly *The Stranger*, May 28, 2009, p. 61.

12. Immediately after the film's May 22 theatrical release, Grey ranked as high as #63 on IMDb's "StarMeter," putting her somewhere between Will Smith and Bruce Willis based on numbers of IMDb user searches during that period. See IMDb Pro, "Sasha Grey: StarMeter," http://pro.imdb.com/name/nm2340248/graph (accessed June 22, 2009).

13. See, for example, Associated Press, "Porn Star Headlines."

14. Gardetta, "The Teenager and the Porn Star."

15. For example, during promotion of *Che*, Soderbergh himself discussed its narrative as akin to a film production. Interviewed by the *LA Weekly*'s Scott Foundas in an article titled "Che, Cannes and Hi-Def Video," he remarks, "There are so many metaphors for making a film in what we were trying to do, and that was at least part of my way in. . . . The group of people getting together to accomplish a certain task in imperfect surroundings." Apprehending this logic, A. O. Scott observes in "Saluting the Rebel Underneath the T-Shirt," his review of *Che*, that "its military operations are, like the capers in the 'Ocean's' pictures, at once formal challenges and allegorical stand-ins for the act of filmmaking itself."

16. Hillis, "Steven Soderbergh's *The Girlfriend Experience*."

17. See "About Movie Review Intelligence," http://moviereviewintelligence.com/movie-reviews/about_this_site/ (accessed August 30, 2010).

18. See "The Girlfriend Experience, Very Good Reviews, Also Very Mixed," http://moviereviewintelligence.com/index.aspx?BID=27&RID=314&CID=0 (accessed July 6, 2009).

19. Bloore, "Re-Defining the Independent Film Value Chain," 11.

20. See, respectively, Thompson, "Sundance"; Honeycutt, *"The Girlfriend Experience"*; Orndorf, *"The Girlfriend Experience"*; and "Tribeca '09."

21. These comparisons are sometimes motivated by further creative overlap, as David Levien and Brian Koppelman, the credited writers of the partly improvised *The Girlfriend Experience*, also received screenplay credit for *Ocean's Thirteen*. Numerous reviews also make comparisons to *sex, lies, and videotape*, partly owing to thematic similarities between the 1989 and 2009 films.

22. The sample under study here includes the seventy-one reviews collected on the Rotten Tomatoes website as of June 2009, mostly English-language and most from U.S. or UK publications or websites (see http://www.rottentomatoes.com/m/girlfriend_experience/ [accessed June 21, 2009]). Overlapping with this group are the thirty-seven reviews collected by the Movie Review Intelligence website, representing a selection of English-language U.S. and Canadian print publications (see http://moviereviewintelligence.com/index.aspx?BID=27&RID=314&CID=0 [accessed June 20, 2009]).

23. Soderbergh's record of making expensive independent films (the independently produced *Che* had a $70 million production cost for its two parts) as well as relatively inexpensive studio productions (Warner Bros.'s *The Good German* cost $32 million) further complicates the claim for him as a filmmaker who sells out to studios so he can do small-scale independent work.

24. Foundas, "Che, Cannes and Hi-Def Video."

25. Barnes, "Steven Soderbergh."

26. For a fuller account, see Foundas, "Che, Cannes and Hi-Def Video."

27. *Che's* North American premiere was at the Toronto festival, in September 2008. Regarding the advertisement, see Dwyer, "'Unreleasable' *Che* Finally Goes on Release."

28. Foundas, "Che, Cannes and Hi-Def Video."

29. Because it includes a substantial percentage of uncredentialed, online reviews in addition to professional journalists' reviews, the Tomatometer rating tends to exaggerate favorable reviews and overall provides a mixture of fan and critical responses rather than a scientific survey of critical attitudes.

30. For example, Kenneth Turan's June 8, 2007, *Los Angeles Times* review generally praises the film but notes in closing, "Also a difficulty is the smugness that is one of the defining characteristics of Ocean's team. These guys are awfully stuck on themselves, and though they have reason to be content, it is hard to completely share in their happiness."

31. Reviewing *Ocean's Thirteen* in 2007, Todd McCarthy remarks on the sight of "some of Hollywood's biggest stars brandishing a we-know-we-have-it-and-you-don't unflappable cool that stops short of the arrogance some detected in 'Ocean's Twelve.'"

32. Rosenblatt, *"Ocean's Thirteen."*

33. See Routt, "L'Evidence," and Keathley, *Cinephilia and History*, especially pp. 94–96, for further discussion of auteurism's manufacture of such "ways of seeing," always attributed to directors.

34. Kapsis, *Hitchcock: The Making of a Reputation*, 99.

35. Ibid., 154.

36. Schickel, "In the Heat of the Noir."

37. Travers, "*The Good German.*"

38. Dargis, "Spies, Lies and Noir in Berlin."

39. Dargis's fellow *New York Times* critic A. O. Scott offers the term in his 2008 review of *Che*, in which he writes of Soderbergh, "[H]e's more of a process geek, fascinated by logistics and the intricacies of how stuff gets done" ("Saluting the Rebel Underneath the T-Shirt").

40. Hudson and Zimmermann, "Cinephilia," 136; emphasis in original.

41. Stewart, "Steven Soderbergh."

42. Hoberman, "Nostalgia Trip."

43. Zacharek, "*The Good German*"; emphasis in original.

44. McCarthy, "*The Good German.*"

45. Dargis, "In the Snows of Sundance."

46. Sellier, *Masculine Singular*, 222–223.

47. Ibid., 223.

Chapter 5

1. Shohat and Stam, *Unthinking Eurocentrism*, 184.

2. I do not mean to suggest that intent is a fiction, only that the lack of clear theorization and analysis of authorial intent is a major limitation of much director-based scholarship.

3. Acland, *Screen Traffic*, 234.

4. Caldwell, *Production Culture*.

5. Notably, academic criticism of *Traffic* has focused almost exclusively on its race representation, partly because of its prestige-film status and its relative prominence as a Hollywood production attentive to Mexico and Mexican Americans.

6. Shohat and Stam, *Unthinking Eurocentrism*, 214.

7. On melodrama as modality, see Williams, "Melodrama Revised," and Gledhill, "Rethinking Genre." See Roth, "'I Just Want to Be a Decent Citizen,'" for a detailed analysis of *Erin Brockovich* in terms of melodrama.

8. See "Spotlight on Location: The Making of *Erin Brockovich*," *Erin Brockovich* DVD (Columbia TriStar Home Video, 2000).

9. Giles, "The 20 Million Dollar Woman."

10. In spite of the film's poor critical and commercial results, Soderbergh teamed with Hough again for *Bubble*, which gives still more latitude to performers' improvisations.

11. See Roth, "Black and White Masculinity," for a thorough analysis of the film's race representation.

12. McCarthy, "*Erin Brockovich.*"

13. Scott, "'Erin Brockovich.'"

14. Ebert, "*Erin Brockovich.*"

15. Baumgarten, "*Out of Sight.*"

16. Ebert, *"Out of Sight."*

17. Levy, *"Out of Sight."*

18. Elaine Roth ("Black and White Masculinity," paragraphs 20 and 21) observes that the film does not explicitly code Lopez as Latina, beyond casting as her father Italian American actor Dennis Farina, who has elsewhere appeared in both ethnically marked and unmarked roles. One scene, though, does at least allude to her offscreen heritage. While waiting for Foley in a Detroit hotel bar, Sisco deflects a series of clumsy come-ons from advertising account executives, one of whom describes to her a Mexican bandito mascot they have created for a campaign. The scene demonstrates their lack of self-awareness; if viewers read Sisco as Latina, it also demonstrates the men's cultural insensitivity.

19. Roth, "Black and White Masculinity," paragraph 12.

20. Maslin, "'Out of Sight.'"

21. Sarris, "Sleeping With the Enemy."

22. Keough, *"Out of Sight."*

23. Neale, *Genre and Hollywood,* 28–30.

24. My commentary sample derives from IMDb's "User Reviews" for *Out of Sight,* http://www.imdb.com/title/tto120780/usercomments, and from the message board for the film, http://www.imdb.com/title/tto120780/board (both accessed January 23, 2010). (Notably, Amazon's website offers nearly as many user reviews of the film.) The reviewer in question, "johnnyboyz," argues that Lopez's Karen Sisco "begins as this strong and independent hard bodied female . . . and by the end becomes a seduced abetter of crime."

25. An anonymous reviewer derides Lopez along with Rosie Perez in a post dated January 8, 1999, and in a post dated September 30, 2008, reviewer "robert-temple-1" compares the Latinoness of Mexicans and Puerto Ricans and offers a *West Side Story* reference intended as comic.

26. Reviewer "composer_mike" remarks in a June 23, 2006, post, "In real life Cheadle is a very nice person but in the movie he's just scary as hell." On the message board, user "Senator_Corleone" commences the "Don Cheadle is extremely scary in this" thread on November 2, 2007, eliciting nine responses, including two deleted ones.

27. IMDb user reviews of *Erin Brockovich* appear at http://www.imdb.com /title/tto195685/usercomments; *Ocean's Eleven* reviews appear at http://www .imdb.com/title/tto240772/usercomments (both accessed January 24, 2010). To put review quantities in perspective, as of the same date, *Pulp Fiction's* entry includes 1,475 reviews, *Kill Bill: Vol. 1* has generated 1,963 reviews, and the first *Lord of the Rings* film (2001) has accumulated 4,800 reviews.

28. Neale, "Masculinity as Spectacle," 18.

29. Ibid.

30. Ibid., 19.

31. Drake, "'Mortgaged to Music,'" 187.

32. *Salon's* Stephanie Zacharek calls the film "sharply creased and polished." The *New York Times's* Elvis Mitchell describes it as "an elating blaze of flair and pride" and argues that its chief interest is "manicured, superbly outfitted

masculinity." Roger Ebert calls it "not a movie about suspense but about suavity" and describes Andy Garcia's character as "groomed, polished, and tailored." Similarly, in *The Village Voice*, J. Hoberman describes George Clooney's character as a "suave mastermind."

33. Commentary track, *Ocean's Eleven* DVD (Warner Home Video, 2002).

34. Dyer, *White*, 39.

35. Willis, *High Contrast*, 7.

36. Naremore, "Authorship," 21.

37. Willis, *High Contrast*, 3.

Chapter 6

1. These include *Swimming to Cambodia* (1987), *Terrors of Pleasure* (a 1988 production for HBO television), and *Monster in a Box* (1992).

2. Verevis, *Film Remakes*, 2; citing Neale, "Questions of Genre," 51.

3. Ibid.; citing Altman, *Film/Genre*, 83–84.

4. Verevis, *Film Remakes*, 86.

5. Altman, *Film/Genre*, 99.

6. Chanko, "Steven Soderbergh Hopes," 69.

7. Cook, *Lost Illusions*, 159.

8. Altman, *Film/Genre*, 161.

9. Verevis, *Film Remakes*, 123; italics in original.

10. Ibid., 117; italics in original.

11. Ciment and Niogret, "Interview With Steven Soderbergh," 70.

12. Ibid., 71.

13. The Writers Guild of America required that Fuchs be co-credited on the new screenplay, and rather than be forced to explain how he could collaborate with the late screenwriter, Soderbergh opted for the "screenplay by Sam Lowry and Daniel Fuchs" credit, taking the name of the protagonist of *Brazil* (1985).

14. In Tracy's novel, the couple are not married, but they are in the 1949 film. Soderbergh's film includes no verbal reference to a marriage, and the ex, Rachel (Alison Elliott), is named only by her first name. But in the film's present-day sequences, protagonist Michael Chambers (Peter Gallagher) wears a wedding band on a chain around his neck.

15. Genette, *Palimpsests*, 1.

16. The character of Hannelore does appear in the film in a close approximation of her counterpart in the novel, but Renate's character is entirely subsumed into Lena's.

17. Stam, "Beyond Fidelity," 67.

18. Ibid., 64.

19. I have written extensively on the *Traffik*-to-*Traffic* adaptation (Gallagher, "*Traffic/Traffik*") so will not revisit that case in detail here. For more on the whistleblower subgenre, see Boozer, *Career Movies*.

20. Lim, "Having Your Way with Hollywood," 154.

21. Hutcheon, *A Theory of Adaptation*, 21.

22. Commentary track, *The Informant!* Blu-ray Disc (Warner Home Video, 2010).

23. Hutcheon, *A Theory of Adaptation*, xv.

24. Ibid., 91.

25. Lim, "Having Your Way with Hollywood," 154.

26. "Clooney Predicts New Ocean's Eleven Will Attract Heat."

27. For example, Vincent Canby observes in his 1983 review of the *Breathless* remake, "It's less a film maker's journey of discovery than the film maker's testimony to his awareness of 'cinema,' and sometimes it's just too much."

28. Though I do not address in detail the 2002 *Solaris*'s links to independent film here, I would point to its casting of actors such as Jeremy Davies and Viola Davis, known chiefly for indie-film roles, along with its production by Soderbergh's repeat collaborators on multiple independent as well as studio projects.

29. Dialogue translations derive from the Criterion Collection's subtitled 2002 DVD. The film's translated screenplay gives the line as "Don't turn a scientific problem into a love story" (Tarkovsky, *Collected Screenplays*, 177).

30. See, for example, Rockwell ("On an Odyssey to Love's Outer Limit") and Romney ("Future Soul"). Relatedly, Verevis (*Film Remakes*, 136–137) notes the ways the 2002 *Solaris*'s DVD supplements frame the film in relation to Lem's novel, even as the DVD also reproduces the new screenplay, which includes attributions to both the Gorenshtein/Tarkovsky screenplay and the novel.

31. The U.S. *Solaris* DVD release (20th Century Fox Home Entertainment, 2003) includes the caption "James Cameron and Steven Soderbergh present." Theatrical-release posters used similar phrases: one reads "From the filmmaker that brought you *The Abyss* and the Academy Award winning director of *Traffic*," while another reads, "From Academy Award winners James Cameron and Steven Soderbergh." The film was a notable box-office failure, budgeted at $47 million and opening on over 2,400 U.S. screens but earning just under $15 million (http://www.boxofficemojo.com/movies/?id=solaris.htm [accessed June 9, 2011]).

32. Rockwell, "On an Odyssey to Love's Outer Limit."

33. See Philip Lopate, *Solaris* DVD insert (Criterion Collection) and Natasha Synessios, "Introduction" to the *Solaris* screenplay (Tarkovsky, *Collected Screenplays*, 129).

34. See Synessios, "Introduction" (Tarkovsky, *Collected Screenplays*, 132).

35. Quoted in Lopate, *Solaris* DVD insert.

36. Lopate, *Solaris* DVD insert.

37. Soderbergh's *Solaris* repeats the shot with three versions of Rheya, but no mother.

38. Tarkovsky, *Time Within Time*, 363.

39. Romney, "Future Soul."

40. Boozer, "Introduction," 21.

41. Stam, "The Author," 6.

Chapter 7

1. Scott, *On Hollywood*, 120.

2. Caryn James calls attention to this curious disclaimer in the 2003 *New York Times* article " 'Party Monster' to Pekar."

3. Reviewers commented as follows: "*K Street*'s character and dramatic arcs often feel shapeless and half-formed" (Rubin, "*K Street: The Complete Series*"); " '*K Street*' tried to update [*Tanner '88*'s] improvisational style, but fell oddly flat" (Nussbaum, "Reruns"); and "It is a new reality hybrid that's insidious and potentially dangerous, even if it only serves as a parlor game for insiders and as a vanity series for Mary Matalin and James Carville" (Gilbert, " 'K Street' Is Stranger Than Fiction").

4. Carter, "Media Talk." Bill Carter notes that the program "started out with just over three million viewers and has since dropped to fewer than two million."

5. Stanley and Heffernan, "The Lows."

6. Caldwell, "Prime-Time Fiction Theorizes the Docu-Real," 259.

7. The shot in question occurs in the program's seventh episode, during which Carville becomes a consultant for Philadelphia mayor John Street's re-election campaign. Near the end of the episode, a camera follows Carville and Street into a campaign rally, a nonfiction event woven into the program's fictional storylines.

8. Caldwell, "Prime-Time Fiction Theorizes the Docu-Real," 289.

9. Carville was campaign manager for Bill Clinton's 1992 presidential run, and later consulted for British Prime Minister Tony Blair and Israeli Prime Minister Ehud Barak; he also co-hosted CNN's *Crossfire* (representing the left) from 2002 until its cancellation in 2005. Matalin served in the second Bush White House until 2003 and also served as counselor to Vice President Dick Cheney; she also co-hosted *Crossfire* (representing the right) from 1999 to 2001.

10. Children's Defense Fund, "Children's Defense Fund."

11. Abramson, "Hyperreality TV."

12. Ibid.

13. Matalin does appear at home in one episode, watching a Democratic presidential candidates' debate on television with a group of women whose status (are they Matalin's real friends, or actors?) is ambiguous.

14. Abramson, "Hyperreality TV."

15. Matalin was not investigated but did testify before a federal grand jury in January 2004 (Allen and Schmidt, "Bush Aides Testify in Leak Probe").

16. *K Street* arguably arrived one national election cycle too early. Leading into the 2008 election, it might have capitalized on the burgeoning interest in timely political commentaries following the emergence of the blogosphere, not an influential phenomenon in autumn 2003.

17. See "Making *Che*" DVD supplement, *Che* DVD (Criterion Collection).

18. The two series did not run simultaneously in HBO's lineup. *Unscripted* aired in January and February 2005, midway through the nearly nine-month interval between *Entourage*'s first and second seasons.

19. See Caldwell ("Prime-Time Fiction Theorizes the Docu-Real," 277–280) for analysis of the *ER* episode and related television "docu-stunts."

20. DVD commentary, *Good Night, and Good Luck* DVD (Warner Home Video, 2006).

21. On HBO's acquisition of the Liberace project, see Rosen, "Steven Soderbergh's Liberace Movie."

Chapter 8

1. Naremore, "Authorship," 21.

2. On "smart film," see Sconce, "Irony, Nihilism, and the New American 'Smart' Film"; on "indie film," see Newman, *Indie*. Though I focus here on feature films released theatrically and on home video, the boutique category extends across media, as with the boutique television of *K Street* and *Unscripted*.

3. Relatedly, Edward Jay Epstein observes that "talent agencies [promote] the concept of directorial authorship, [using] their director clients as the building blocks of 'packages' that can include their stars, literary properties, writers, and other talent" (*The Big Picture*, 271).

4. The Internet Movie Database (http://www.imdb.com/company/coo013 349, accessed November 12, 2011) lists *Che: Part One* as an uncredited Section Eight production as well, but Soderbergh confirms that the company "has no involvement whatsoever with *Che*" (author correspondence, June 20, 2011).

5. Webster, "Secrets in the Snow."

6. The Directors Guild of America's website lists Clooney's representation as CAA (http://webapps.dga.org/directory/search_details.cfm?DGAKey=17848, accessed November 16, 2008). Soderbergh in 2008 signed a management agreement with Michael Sugar of management agency Anonymous Content. In a 2008 article in *The Hollywood Reporter*, Borys Kit details Soderbergh's adventures in representation: "Steven Soderbergh's rep-less days are over. The director, notorious for being choosy about who represents him, has signed with Anonymous Content for representation. Soderbergh began his career repped by Anne Dollard at Leading Artists in the late 1980s and then was famously repped by her brother Pat after she died in a freak horse-riding accident in 1988. Soderbergh . . . followed Dollard to WMA. After Dollard was fired from the agency, Soderbergh stuck with him, even as the director hit a new peak with the films *Out of Sight* and *Traffic*. Soderbergh has been without an agent and manager since parting ways with Dollard in 2005."

7. From its launch in 2006 through mid-2009, Smoke House operated as a subsidiary of Warner Bros., and in partnership with India's Reliance Big Entertainment as well. In June 2009, Clooney and the company gave up the Warner Bros. affiliation after negotiating a new partnership with Sony. See IMDb Pro's listing for "Smoke House: Company Affiliations" (http://pro.imdb

.com/company/c00184096/affiliations, accessed November 16, 2008). Regarding the move to Sony, see Kit, "Smokehouse Defecting to Sony."

8. Soderbergh's remarks here appear in interview footage in the documentary *Independent's Day* (dir. Marina Zenovich; Grateful Pictures 1997, New Video/ Medium Inc., 1999).

9. Holson, "Trying to Combine Art and Box Office."

10. Submenu text, *Keane* DVD (Magnolia Home Entertainment, 2006). See also O'Sullivan, "Take Two."

11. Holson, "Trying to Combine Art and Box Office."

12. Bernstein, "The Producer as Auteur," 188.

13. Ibid.

14. Weiss, "When the Producer Comes to Town."

15. Herskovitz was also one of three credited producers on *Traffic*, though the finished film merged two projects in development, one shepherded by Herskovitz and Edward Zwick, the other by Soderbergh collaborator Laura Bickford. Like many films, *Traffic* demonstrated a kind of tag-team collaboration rather than one person's oversight across the length of a production.

16. Corrigan, *A Cinema Without Walls*, 107.

17. *Schizopolis* DVD (Criterion Collection, 2003).

18. Corrigan, *A Cinema Without Walls*, 103.

19. Brookey and Westerfelhaus, "Hiding Homoeroticism in Plain View," 24.

20. Corrigan, *A Cinema Without Walls*, 104; emphasis Corrigan's.

21. Klinger, "The DVD Cinephile," 21.

22. Ibid., 39.

23. Haynes's *Le Plaisir* introduction appears on the 2006 UK DVD from Second Sight Films as well as on Criterion's 2008 U.S. release.

24. Grant, "Auteur Machines?," 111.

25. Corrigan, *A Cinema Without Walls*, 108.

26. Klinger, "Digressions at the Cinema," 16–17.

27. Grant, "Auteur Machines?," 112.

28. Kendrick, "What Is the Criterion?," 126.

29. Hudson and Zimmermann, "Cinephilia, Technophilia, and Collaborative Remix Zones," 138.

30. Hight, "Making-of Documentaries on DVD," 7.

31. Caldwell, "Screen Studies and Industrial 'Theorizing,'" 178.

32. Ibid.

33. Holson, "Trying to Combine Art and Box Office."

34. Audio commentary track, *Catch-22* DVD (Paramount Home Entertainment, 2002).

35. Caldwell, "Screen Studies and Industrial 'Theorizing,'" 179; emphasis Caldwell's.

Conclusion

1. Johnson, "Q&A with Steven Soderbergh."

2. Boucher, "Matt Damon."

3. See "Steven Soderbergh Spies Other Plans, Won't Direct 'The Man from U.N.C.L.E.'" (*The Playlist*, November 18, 2011, http://blogs.indiewire.com/theplaylist/exclusive-steven-soderbergh-opts-out-of-directing-warners-the-man-from-u-n-c-l-e, accessed November 20, 2011).

4. See Jagernauth, "Steven Soderbergh Is Doing Second Unit Shooting."

5. Eisen, "Wild Card Podcast."

6. Dooe, "Steven Soderbergh's Daily Diet."

7. Anderson, *The Long Tail*, 73.

8. On prefigurative materials, see Barker, "News, Reviews, Clues, Interviews and Other Ancillary Materials."

9. In practice—i.e., in popular, industrial, and academic usage—the terms promotion and publicity can become synonyms, perhaps because of the difficulty in distinguishing where one ends and the other begins. For example, studios circulate *publicity* stills as part of *promotional* efforts, and these stills can later appear in forums such as magazines and newspapers.

10. These terms are not precisely synonymous, but for the purposes of the work at hand, the distinction between popular and elite, or amateur and professional, remains useful.

11. Ault, "IFC's *Che* Gets Close Theater."

12. See, for example, "IFC Entertainment—Now on DVD" (http://www.ifcfilms.com/nowOnDvd.htm), "HDNet Films: News" (http://www.hdnetfilms.com/news/index.html), and 2929 Entertainment's "Coming Soon" page (http://www.2929entertainment.com/comingSoon.html), all accessed July 16, 2009.

13. See "About Us" (http://www.showbizcafe.com/en/contact [accessed July 16, 2009]).

14. All content described appears in Rico, "EXCLUSIVE! 8 never before seen clips."

15. Ibid.

16. Johnston, "'The Coolest Way to Watch Movie Trailers,'" 147.

17. See "About Us—Rope of Silicon.com" (http://www.ropeofsilicon.com/aboutus/, accessed July 16, 2009).

18. Brevet, "Soderbergh's 'Che.'"

19. Ibid.

20. Ponto, "Soderbergh Heckled by Anti-Che Audience."

21. See "Staff: About Us" (http://www.justpressplay.net/staff.html, accessed July 16, 2009).

22. In a 2009 interview with Henry Barnes for the *Guardian*, Soderbergh attributes the film's weak performance in South America to video piracy: "We got crushed in South America. We came out in Spain in September of [2008] and it was everywhere within a matter of days. It killed it."

23. IMDb release information shows that *Che: Part One* did not open until May 2009 in Denmark, for example, and in June 2009 in Germany and Austria; *Che: Part Two* followed about six weeks later in most markets.

24. See "IFC Festival Direct" (http://www.ifcfilms.com/ifc-festival-direct, accessed July 20, 2009), and Thompson and Jones, "IFC, SXSW to bow 'Alexander.'"

25. Thompson and Jones, "IFC, SXSW to bow 'Alexander.'"

26. Ibid.

27. In e-mail exchanges reproduced in a *Filmmaker* magazine blog post, 2929 Entertainment principal Mark Cuban writes, "Knowing that the box office is the riskiest component, we pay back part of the ancillary sales to the theaters. We sell a dvd, the theater makes money" (punctuation Cuban's; see http://www.filmmakermagazine.com/blog/2006_04_01_archive.php, accessed July 18, 2009).

28. Bourdieu, *Distinction*, 28.

29. See Barnes, "Hollywood's Blurb Search Reaches the Blogosphere," and Cieply, "Everybody's a Movie Critic."

30. DiOrio, "'G.I. Joe' is AWOL for Critics."

31. Columbia revived the project, but without Soderbergh's involvement. See Cieply, "Money Worries Kill A-List Film at Last Minute."

Bibliography

Abramson, Jill. "Hyperreality TV: Political Fact Meets HBO Fiction." *New York Times*. August 24, 2003. Accessed July 28, 2010. http://www.nytimes.com/2003/08/24/arts/television-hyperreality-tv-political-fact-meets-hbo-fiction.html.

Acland, Charles. *Screen Traffic: Movies, Multiplexes, and Global Culture*. Durham, NC: Duke University Press, 2003.

Albright, Jayson. "Decatur Again Set Aside in 'Informant!' Home Video Release." *Decatur Herald & Review*. February 25, 2010. Accessed June 10, 2010. http://www.herald-review.com/entertainment/movies/informant/article_6d066c96-224f-11df-981d-001cc4c03286.html.

———. "'The Informant' Comes Back Downtown." *Decatur Herald & Review*. May 14, 2008. Accessed June 11, 2010. http://www.herald-review.com/news/local/article_3bacb084-0e66-5818-bcd5-96424f703665.html.

———. "Sun Shines on 'The Informant.'" *Decatur Herald & Review*. May 13, 2008. Accessed June 11, 2010. http://www.herald-review.com/news/local/article_8f22cf97-d010-56e3-b729-7983d9590aa5.html.

Allen, Mike, and Susan Schmidt. "Bush Aides Testify in Leak Probe: Grand Jury Called McClellan, 2 Others." *Washington Post*. February 10, 2004. Page A1.

Altman, Rick. *Film/Genre*. London: BFI, 1999.

———. "Reusable Packaging: Generic Products and the Recycling Process." In *Refiguring American Film Genres*, edited by Nick Browne. Berkeley: University of California Press, 1998.

Anderson, Chris. *The Long Tail: Why the Future of Business is Selling Less of More*. New York: Hyperion Books, 2006.

Anderson, Wes. "My Private Screening With Pauline Kael." *New York Times*. January 31, 1999. Accessed August 10, 2010. http://www.nytimes.com/1999/01/31/movies/film-my-private-screening-with-pauline-kael.html.

Appadurai, Arjun. "Disjuncture and Difference in the Global Cultural Economy." In *Modernity at Large: Cultural Dimensions of Globalization*, 27–47. Minneapolis: University of Minnesota Press, 1996.

Archer Daniels Midland Company. "About ADM and 'The Informant!'" Accessed June 19, 2010. http://www.adm.com/en-US/informant/Pages/default.aspx.

Associated Press. "Porn Star Headlines Soderbergh's New Film." *MSNBC.com*. May 3, 2009. Accessed June 22, 2009. http://www.msnbc.msn.com/id/30485929/ns/entertainment-movies.

Ault, Susanne. "IFC's *Che* Gets Close Theater, VOD, DVD Release." *Video Business Online*. December 19, 2008. Accessed February 4, 2009. http://www.videobusiness.com/article/CA6624248.html.

Baker, Aaron. *Steven Soderbergh*. Urbana, IL: University of Illinois Press, 2011.

Barker, Martin. "News, Reviews, Clues, Interviews, and Other Ancillary Materials—A Critique and Research Proposal." *Scope: An Online Journal of Film and Television Studies*. February 2004. Accessed July 20, 2009. http://www.scope.nottingham.ac.uk/article.php?issue=feb2004&id=246&section=article.

Barnes, Brooks. "Hollywood's Blurb Search Reaches the Blogosphere." *New York Times*. June 7, 2009. Accessed July 15, 2009. http://www.nytimes.com/2009/06/07/weekinreview/07barnes.html.

Barnes, Henry. "Steven Soderbergh: 'I Can See the End of My Career.'" *The Guardian*. July 14, 2009. Accessed July 20, 2009. http://www.guardian.co.uk/film/2009/jul/14/steven-soderbergh.

Bart, Peter. "Beware Falling Stars!" *Vanity Fair*. March 2009. Accessed February 22, 2009. http://www.vanityfair.com/culture/features/2009/03/state-of-hollywood200903.

Baumgarten, Marjorie. "*Out of Sight*" (film review). *Austin Chronicle*. June 29, 1998. Accessed January 22, 2010. http://www.filmvault.com/filmvault/austin/o/outofsight1.html.

Bernstein, Matthew. "Hollywood's Semi-Independent Production." *Cinema Journal* 32.3 (Spring 1993): 41–54.

———. "The Producer as Auteur." In *Auteurs and Authorship: A Film Reader*, edited by Barry Keith Grant, 180–189. Malden, MA: Blackwell, 2008.

Betz, Mark. *Beyond the Subtitle: Remapping European Art Cinema*. Minneapolis: University of Minnesota Press, 2009.

Biskind, Peter. *Down and Dirty Pictures: Miramax, Sundance, and the Rise of Independent Film*. New York: Simon & Schuster, 2004.

———. *Easy Riders, Raging Bulls: How the Sex-Drugs-and-Rock 'n' Roll Generation Saved Hollywood*. New York: Simon & Schuster, 1998.

Bloore, Peter. "Re-Defining the Independent Film Value Chain." UK Film Council. February 2009. Accessed July 6, 2009. http://www.ukfilmcouncil.org.uk/media/pdf/h/b/Film_Value_Chain.pdf.

Boozer, Jack. *Career Movies: American Business and the Success Mystique*. Austin: University of Texas Press, 2002.

———. "Introduction: The Screenplay and Authorship in Adaptation." In *Authorship in Film Adaptation* 1–30. Austin: University of Texas Press, 2008.

Bordwell, David. "The Art Cinema as a Mode of Film Practice." *Film Criticism* 4.1 (1979): 56–64.

———. "Cutting Remarks: On THE GOOD GERMAN, Classical Style, and the Police Tactical Unit." *David Bordwell's Website on Cinema: Observations on film art and FILM ART*. November 15, 2006. Accessed April 20, 2007. http://www.davidbordwell.net/blog/?p=91.

———. "Intensified Continuity: Visual Style in Contemporary American Film." *Film Quarterly* 55.3 (Spring 2002): 16–28.

———. "Not Back to the Future, but Ahead to the Past." *David Bordwell's Website on Cinema: Observations on film art and FILM ART*. November 12, 2006 (with addendum January 25, 2007). Accessed April 20, 2007. http://www.davidbordwell.net/blog/?p=66.

Boucher, Geoff. "Matt Damon: Steven Soderbergh Really Does Plan to Retire From Film-making." *24 Frames* (blog), *Los Angeles Times*. December 22, 2010. Accessed June 7, 2011. http://latimesblogs.latimes.com/movies/2010/12/matt-damon-steven-soderbergh-is-retiring-from-filmmaking-.html.

Bourdieu, Pierre. *Distinction: A Social Critique of the Judgement of Taste*. Translated by Richard Nice. Cambridge, MA: Harvard University Press, 1984.

———. *The Field of Cultural Production: Essays on Art and Literature*, edited by Randal Johnson. Translated by Richard Nice. New York: Columbia University Press, 1993.

Brevet, Brad. "Soderbergh's 'Che' Gets a Bootleg Trailer Release." *RopeOf Silicon.com*. July 31, 2008. Accessed December 8, 2008. http://www.ropeofsilicon.com/article/soderberghs_che_gets_a_bootleg_trailer_release.

———. "UPDATED: International 'Che' Trailer, Clip and New Cannes Poster." *RopeOfSilicon.com*. August 24, 2008. Accessed July 18, 2009. http://www.ropeofsilicon.com/article/hq_international_che_trailer_clip_and_new_cannes_poster.

Brookey, Robert Alan, and Robert Westerfelhaus. "Hiding Homoeroticism in Plain View: The *Fight Club* DVD as Digital Closet." *Critical Studies in Media Communication* 19.1 (March 2002): 21–43.

Brunette, Peter. "*Che*" (film review). *The Hollywood Reporter*. May 22, 2008. Accessed March 7, 2010. http://www.hollywoodreporter.com/hr/film/reviews/article_display.jsp?rid=11169.

Buckland, Warren. *Directed by Steven Spielberg: Poetics of the Contemporary Hollywood Blockbuster*. New York: Continuum, 2006.

Cain, Tim. "ADM Working With Filmmakers on 'The Informant.'" *Decatur Herald & Review*. March 14, 2008. Accessed June 10, 2010. http://www.herald-review.com/news/local/article_17a5a5cf-9245-5009-ab50-2c2332c88515.html.

———. "Don't Expect 'Informant' Hobnobbing." *Decatur Herald & Review*. March 19, 2008. Accessed June 10, 2010. http://www.herald-review.com/news/opinion/editorial/columnists/cain/article_31980cbe-4fde-5c25-b067-5eee057197ac.html.

———. "Extra, Extra, Read All About It." *Decatur Herald & Review.* April 18, 2008. Accessed June 10, 2010. http://www.herald-review.com/enter tainment/local/article_01cd666d-07c6-594f-8ffo-c4402dedebf1.html.

———. "'Informant' Still Lost in Decatur." *Decatur Herald & Review.* September 6, 2007. Accessed June 11, 2010. http://www.herald-review.com/news /opinion/editorial/columnists/cain/article_1f43165d-a0d9-522c-9996 -98af639c219c.html.

———. "You May Be a Little Blurry." *Decatur Herald & Review.* September 17, 2009. Accessed June 10, 2010. http://www.herald-review.com/news/opinion /editorial/columnists/cain/article_37fe7eeo-98a5-57a5-9549-3978a224a32a .html.

Caldwell, John Thornton. "Cultures of Production: Studying Industry's Deep Texts, Reflexive Rituals, and Managed Self-Disclosures." In *Media Industries: History, Theory, and Method,* edited by Jennifer Holt and Alisa Perren, 199–212. Malden, MA: Blackwell, 2009.

———. "Prime-Time Fiction Theorizes the Docu-Real." In *Reality Squared: Televisual Discourses on the Real,* edited by James Friedman, 259–292. New Brunswick, NJ: Rutgers University Press, 2002.

———. *Production Culture: Industrial Reflexivity and Critical Practice in Film and Television.* Durham, NC: Duke University Press, 2008.

———. "Screen Studies and Industrial 'Theorizing.'" *Screen* 50.1 (Spring 2009): 167–179.

———. "Welcome to the Viral Future of Cinema (Television)." *Cinema Journal* 45.1 (Fall 2005): 90–97.

Calhoun, Dave. "The Directors: Steven Soderbergh." *Time Out.* February 21, 2007. Accessed April 20, 2007. http://www.timeout.com/film/features/2633 .html.

Canby, Vincent. "Richard Gere in *Breathless*" (film review). *New York Times.* May 13, 1983. Accessed May 20, 2011. http://movies.nytimes.com/movie /review?res=9E03EED81138F930A25756C0A965948260.

Carringer, Robert L. "Collaboration and Concepts of Authorship." *PMLA* 116.2 (March 2001): 370–379.

Carruthers, Lee. "Biding Our Time: Rethinking the Familiar in Steven Soderbergh's *The Limey*." *Film Studies* 9 (Winter 2006): 9–21.

Carter, Bill. "Media Talk: Two HBO Shows Lose Viewers After Starting Strong." *New York Times.* October 13, 2003. Accessed October 13, 2003. http://www.nytimes.com/2003/10/13/business/media/13HBO.html.

Cellini, Joe. "Mac, Lies and DV Tape: Oscar-Winning Director Steven Soderbergh Cuts His First Digital Film." *Apple.com.* Accessed April 25, 2002. http://www.soderbergh.net.articles/2002/apple.htm.

Chanko, Kenneth M. "Steven Soderbergh Hopes That Three is His Lucky Number." *Boston Globe.* September 26, 1993. Reprinted in *Steven Soderbergh: Interviews,* edited by Anthony Kaufman, 66–69. Jackson: University Press of Mississippi, 2002.

Child, Ben. "Winstone to Play Caesar in Soderbergh's Cleopatra Musical." *The Guardian*. December 3, 2008. Accessed May 2, 2009. http://www.guardian.co.uk/film/2008/dec/03/ray-winstone-steven-soderbergh-cleopatra-musical.

Children's Defense Fund. "Children's Defense Fund Celebrates 30 Years By Honoring Students Who 'Beat the Odds'" (press release). October 10, 2003. Accessed June 28, 2006. http://www.childrensdefense.org/pressreleases/2003/031010.aspx.

Chocano, Caroline. "*The Good German*" (film review). *Los Angeles Times*. December 15, 2006. Accessed April 21, 2007. http://www.calendarlive.com/movies/reviews/cl-et-german15dec15,0,4642786.story.

Chris, Brian. "New Frontier." *Filmmaker Magazine*. Fall 2008. Accessed July 18, 2009. http://www.filmmakermagazine.com/fall2008/redone.php.

Cieply, Michael. "Everybody's a Movie Critic: New Web Sites and Online Readers Chime In." *New York Times*. June 13, 2009. Accessed July 15, 2009. http://www.nytimes.com/2009/06/13/movies/13critics.html.

———. "Independent Filmmakers Distribute on Their Own." *New York Times*. August 13, 2009. Accessed August 13, 2009. http://www.nytimes.com/2009/08/13/business/media/13independent.html.

———. "Money Worries Kill A-List Film at Last Minute." *New York Times*. July 1, 2009. Accessed July 1, 2009. http://www.nytimes.com/2009/07/02/business/media/02moneyball.html.

Ciment, Michael, and Hubert Niogret. "Interview with Steven Soderbergh: *King of the Hill*." *Positif* (October 1993). Translated by Paula Willoquet. Reprinted in *Steven Soderbergh: Interviews*, edited by Anthony Kaufman, 56–65. Jackson: University Press of Mississippi, 2002.

———. "Interview with Steven Soderbergh: *sex, lies, and videotape*." *Positif* (September 1989). Translated by Paula Willoquet. Reprinted in *Steven Soderbergh: Interviews*, edited by Anthony Kaufman, 13–23. Jackson: University Press of Mississippi, 2002.

———. "Interview with Steven Soderbergh: *The Underneath*." *Positif* (April 1996). Translated by Patricia Willoquet. Reprinted in *Steven Soderbergh: Interviews*, edited by Anthony Kaufman, 70–80. Jackson: University Press of Mississippi, 2002.

"Clooney Predicts New Ocean's Eleven Will Attract Heat." Internet Movie Database. November 30, 2000. Accessed June 3, 2010. http://www.imdb.com/news/ni0078374.

Cook, David. *Lost Illusions: American Cinema in the Shadow of Watergate and Vietnam, 1970–1979*. Berkeley: University of California Press, 2002.

Corliss, Richard. "Woody Allen on Ingmar Bergman." *Time*. August 1, 2007. Accessed February 28, 2010. http://www.time.com/time/arts/article/0,8599,1648917,00.html.

Corrigan, Timothy. *A Cinema Without Walls: Movies and Culture After Vietnam*. New Brunswick, NJ: Rutgers University Press, 1991.

Couldry, Nick. *Media Rituals: A Critical Approach*. New York: Routledge, 2003.

Curtin, Michael. "Thinking Globally: From Media Imperialism to Media Capital." In *Media Industries: History, Theory, and Method,* edited by Jennifer Holt and Alisa Perren, 108–119. Malden, MA: Blackwell, 2009.

Dargis, Manohla. "In the Snows of Sundance, a Marked Chill in the Air." *New York Times.* January 22, 2009. Accessed January 22, 2009. http://www.ny times.com/2009/01/23/movies/23sund.html.

———. "Spies, Lies and Noir in Berlin" (film review). *New York Times.* December 15, 2006. Accessed April 21, 2007. http://www.movies.nytimes .com/2006/12/15/movies/15germ.html.

———. "They Always Come Out Ahead; Bet on It" (film review). *New York Times.* June 8, 2007. Accessed June 21, 2009. http://www.movies.nytimes .com/2007/06/08/movies/08ocea.html.

Denby, David. "Bad Behavior" (film review). *The New Yorker.* June 11, 2007. Accessed June 21, 2009. http://www.newyorker.com/arts/critics/cinema /2007/06/11/070611crci_cinema_denby.

Dieckmann, Katherine. "Liar, Liar, Pants on Fire: Steven Soderbergh Comes Clean." *Village Voice.* August 8, 1989. Reprinted in *Steven Soderbergh: Interviews,* edited by Anthony Kaufman, 38–44. Jackson: University Press of Mississippi, 2002.

DiOrio, Carl. "'G.I. Joe' is AWOL for Critics." *The Hollywood Reporter.* August 4, 2009. Accessed August 6, 2009. http://www.hollywoodreporter.com/hr /search/article_display.jsp?vnu_content_id=1003999966.

Directors Guild of America. "Statement of Steven Soderbergh on Behalf of the Directors Guild of America Before the House Committee on Foreign Affairs." April 13, 2009. Accessed April 29, 2011. http://www.dga.org/news /pr-images/2009/Soderbergh-oral-testimony.pdf.

Dooe, Mary. "Steven Soderbergh's Daily Diet." *Studio 360* (blog). April 11, 2011. Accessed June 7, 2011. http://www.studio360.org/blogs/studio-360 -blog/2011/apr/11/steven-soderberghs-daily-diet/.

Drake, Philip. "'Mortgaged to Music': New Retro Movies in 1990s Hollywood Cinema." In *Memory and Popular Film,* edited by Paul Grainge, 183–201. Manchester, UK: Manchester University Press, 2003.

Druxman, Michael B. *Make It Again, Sam: A Survey of Movie Remakes.* Cranbury, NJ: A.S. Barnes, 1975.

Dwyer, Michael. "'Unreleasable' *Che* Finally Goes on Release." *Irish Times.* September 19, 2008. Accessed June 22, 2009. http://www.irishtimes.com /newspaper/theticket/2008/0919/1221689990077.html.

Dyer, Richard. *White.* London: Routledge, 1997.

Ebert, Roger. "*Erin Brockovich*" (film review). *Chicago Sun-Times.* March 17, 2000. Accessed January 17, 2010. http://rogerebert.suntimes.com/apps/pbcs .dll/article?AID=/20000317/REVIEWS/3170303/1023.

———. "*Ocean's Eleven*" (film review). *Chicago Sun-Times.* December 7, 2001. Accessed August 26, 2011. http://rogerebert.suntimes.com/apps/pbcs.dll /article?AID=/20011207/REVIEWS/112070302/1023.

———. "*Ocean's Thirteen*" (film review). *Chicago Sun-Times*. June 7, 2007. Accessed August 23, 2009. http://rogerebert.suntimes.com/apps/pbcs.dll /article?AID=/20070606/REVIEWS/706060301.

———. "*Out of Sight*" (film review). *Chicago Sun-Times*. June 19, 1998. Accessed January 18, 2010. http://rogerebert.suntimes.com/apps/pbcs.dll /article?AID=/19980619/REVIEWS/806190304/1023.

Edelstein, David. "*The Girlfriend Experience*" (film review). *New York*. May 17, 2009. Accessed June 20, 2009. http://www.nymag.com/movies/reviews /56787/.

Eisen, Rich. "Wild Card Podcast: Charles Barkley, Urban Meyer & Steven Soderbergh." NFL Network. January 5, 2011. Accessed May 5, 2011. http:// www.richeisen.nfl.com/2011/01/05/wildcard-podcast-sir-charles-barkley -urban-meyer-steven-soderbergh/.

Elder, Robert K. "Screen Scene: Goyer Happy to Bring Horror to Chicago." *Chicago Tribune*. May 9, 2008. Accessed June 14, 2010. http://www.chicago tribune.com/topic/chi-050908-screenscene,0,2561632.story.

Epstein, Edward Jay. *The Big Picture: Money and Power in Hollywood*. New York: Random House, 2005.

"Even Stevens: Soderbergh, the Man with the Plan." *Film Review* (UK). February 2005. Accessed April 15, 2009. http://www.stevensoderbergh.net /articles/2005/filmreview-soderbergh.php.

Forrest, Jennifer, and Leonard R. Koos, eds. *Dead Ringers: The Remake in Theory and Practice*. Albany: State University of New York Press, 2002.

Foucault, Michel. "What Is an Author?" In *Language, Counter-Memory, Practice: Selected Essays and Interviews*, edited by Donald F. Bouchard, 113–138. Translated by Bouchard and Sherry Simon. Ithaca, NY: Cornell University Press, 1977.

Foundas, Scott. "Che, Cannes and Hi-Def Video." *LA Weekly*. January 15, 2009. Accessed June 20, 2009. http://www.laweekly.com/2009-01-15/film-tv/che -cannes-and-hi-def-video/.

———. "The Sundance Experience: So-So-Soderbergh, and Then Some." *LA Weekly*. January 29, 2009. Accessed June 20 2009. http://www.laweekly .com/2009-01-29/film-tv/the-sundance-experience/.

Gabriel, Trip. "Steven Soderbergh: The Sequel." *New York Times Magazine*. November 3, 1991. Accessed April 28, 2009. http://www.nytimes.com/1991 /11/03/magazine/steven-soderbergh-the-sequel.html.

Gallagher, Mark. "*Traffic/Traffik*: Race, Globalization, and Family in Soderbergh's Remake." In *Authorship in Film Adaptation*, edited by Jack Boozer, 223–252. Austin: University of Texas Press, 2008.

Gans, Herbert. *Popular Culture and High Culture: An Analysis and Evaluation of Taste* (rev. ed.). New York: Basic Books, 1999.

Gardetta, Dave. "The Teenager and the Porn Star." *Los Angeles*. November 2006. Accessed July 1, 2009. http://www.lamag.com/featuredarticle.aspx?id=15460.

Gaut, Berys. "Film Authorship and Collaboration." In *Film Theory and Philosophy*, edited by Richard Allen and Murray Smith, 149–172. Oxford: Oxford University Press, 1997.

Genette, Gérard. *Palimpsests: Literature in the Second Degree*. Translated by Channa Newman and Claude Doubinsky. Lincoln: University of Nebraska Press, 1997.

Gerstner, David A., and Janet Staiger, eds. *Authorship and Film*. New York: Routledge, 2003.

Gibson, Owen. "Steven Soderbergh: 'I Am Sure It's a Scary Idea for the Studios.'" *The Guardian*. January 27, 2006. Accessed June 14, 2008. http://www .guardian.co.uk/world/2006/jan/27/film.owengibson.

Gilbert, Matthew. "'K Street' Is Stranger Than Fiction." *Boston Globe*. September 16, 2003. Accessed June 20, 2006. http://www.boston.com/ae /tv/articles/2003/09/16/k_street_is_stranger_than_fiction.

Giles, Jeff. "The 20 Million Dollar Woman." *Newsweek*. March 13, 2000. Accessed November 22, 2009. http://www.newsweek.com/id/83318.

"The Girlfriend Experience" (press kit). Magnolia Pictures. 2009. Accessed April 14, 2009. http://www.magpictures.com/presskit.aspx?id=d9d8d174 -b85a-48e8-842a-fa0de0675f65.

Gledhill, Christine. "Rethinking Genre." In *Reinventing Film Studies*, edited by Christine Gledhill and Linda Williams, 221–243. London: Arnold, 2000.

Goldsmith, Ben, and Tom O'Regan. *The Film Studio: Film Production in the Global Economy*. Lanham, MD: Rowman & Littlefield, 2005.

Goss, Brian Michael. "Steven Soderbergh's *The Limey*: Implications for the Auteur Theory and Industry Structure." *Popular Communication* 2.4 (January 2004): 231–255.

Grant, Catherine. "Auteur Machines?: Auteurism and the DVD." In *Film and Television After DVD*, edited by James Bennett and Tom Brown, 101–115. London: Routledge, 2008.

Hight, Craig. "Making-of Documentaries on DVD: *The Lord of the Rings* Trilogy and Special Editions." *Velvet Light Trap* 56 (Fall 2005): 4–17.

Hillis, Aaron. "Steven Soderbergh's *The Girlfriend Experience* Tries to Turn a Porn Star Legit." *Village Voice*. March 18, 2009. Accessed April 5, 2009. http://www.villagevoice.com/2009-03-18/film/spring-guide-steven -soderbergh-s-the-girlfriend-experience-tries-to-turn-a-porn-star-legit/.

Hoberman, J. "Behold the Man: Steven Soderbergh's Epic Film Biography of Che." *Virginia Quarterly Review* 85.1 (Winter 2009): 203–209. Accessed April 28, 2009. http://www.vqronline.org/articles/2009/winter/hoberman-che/.

———. "The House Always Wins" (film review). *Village Voice*. May 29, 2007. Accessed June 21, 2009. http://www.villagevoice.com/2007-05-29/film/the -house-always-wins/.

———. "Nostalgia Trip" (film review). *Village Voice*. December 5, 2006. Accessed April 21 2007. http://www.villagevoice.com/2006-12-05/film /nostalgia-trip/.

———. "Role Players and End Games" (film review). *Village Voice*. December 4, 2001. Accessed August 26, 2011. http://www.villagevoice.com/2001-12-04 /film/role-players-and-end-games/.

———. "Soderbergh's *Girlfriend Experience* Porn-Star is a True Character" (film review). *Village Voice*. April 29, 2009. Accessed May 4, 2009. http://www

.villagevoice.com/2009-04-29/film/soderbergh-s-girlfriend-experience-porn-star-is-a-true-character/.

———. "Steven Soderbergh's *Che*: Two Guevara Movies in One Four-Hour Sitting" (film review). *Village Voice*. December 9, 2008. Accessed January 30, 2009. http://www.villagevoice.com/2008-12-10/film/soderbergh-s-the-argentine-and-guerrilla.

Holson, Laura M. "Trying to Combine Art and Box Office in Hollywood." *New York Times*. January 18, 2005. Accessed November 23, 2008. http://www.nytimes.com/2005/01/17/business/media/17clooney.html.

Holt, Jennifer, and Alisa Perren, eds. *Media Industries: History, Theory, and Method*. Malden, MA: Blackwell, 2009.

Honeycutt, Kirk. "*The Girlfriend Experience*" (film review). *The Hollywood Reporter*. April 28, 2009. Accessed June 19, 2009. http://www.hollywoodreporter.com/hr/film-reviews/film-review-the-girlfriend-experience-1003967126.story.

Horton, Andrew, and Stuart McDougal, eds. *Play It Again, Sam: Retakes on Remakes*. Berkeley: University of California Press, 1998.

Hozic, Aida. *Hollyworld: Space, Place, and Fantasy in the American Economy*. Ithaca, NY: Cornell University Press, 2002.

Hudson, Dale, and Patricia R. Zimmermann. "Cinephilia, Technophilia, and Collaborative Remix Zones." *Screen* 50.1 (Spring 2009): 135–146.

Hutcheon, Linda. *A Theory of Adaptation*. New York: Routledge, 2006.

Hyman, Peter. "The Development Hell of *A Confederacy of Dunces*." *Slate.com*. December 14, 2006. Accessed March 12, 2009. http://www.slate.com/id/2155500.

"*The Informant!*" (press kit). Participant Media. August 2009. Accessed June 17, 2010. http://www.participantmedia.com/press/press_kit/the_informant.php.

Jacobson, Harlan. "Steven Soderbergh, King of Cannes: Truth or Consequences." *Film Comment*. July/August 1989. Reprinted in *Steven Soderbergh: Interviews*, edited by Anthony Kaufman, 24–37. Jackson: University Press of Mississippi, 2002.

Jagernauth, Kevin. "Steven Soderbergh Is Doing Second Unit Shooting On 'Hunger Games.'" *The Playlist*. August 4, 2011. Accessed November 27, 2011. http://www.blogs.indiewire.com/theplaylist/steven_soderbergh_is_doing_second_unit_shooting_on_hunger_games.

James, Caryn. "'Party Monster' to Pekar: The New Cinematic Realism." *New York Times*. October 5, 2003. Accessed October 6, 2003. http://www.nytimes.com/2003/10/05/movies/05JAME.html.

Jeffries, Stuart. "Rebel Without a Pause." *The Guardian*. December 16, 2008. Accessed April 14, 2009. http://www.guardian.co.uk/film/2008/dec/16/steven-soderbergh-film-che-guevara.

Jenkins, Henry. "Historical Poetics." In *Approaches to Popular Film*, edited by Joanne Hollows and Mark Jancovich, 99–122. Manchester, UK: Manchester University Press, 1995.

Johnson, G. Allen. "Q&A with Steven Soderbergh: 'I Feel Like I'll Hit the Ceiling of My Imagination.'" *San Francisco Chronicle*. May 21, 2009. Accessed April 17, 2012. http://www.sfgate.com/cgi-bin/article.cgi?f=/c/a/2009/05/21/NSBD17NPRT.DTL.

Johnson, Vida T., and Graham Petrie. *The Films of Andrei Tarkovsky: A Visual Fugue*. Bloomington: Indiana University Press, 1994.

Johnston, Keith M. "'The Coolest Way to Watch Movie Trailers in the World': Trailers in the Digital Age." *Convergence* 14.2 (2008): 145–160.

Johnston, Sheila. "David O. Russell's Folks Saw *Spanking the Monkey* and Weren't Amused. Must Have Been the Masturbation. Or the Incest." *The Independent*. August 10, 1995.

———. "The Flashback Kid." *Sight & Sound* (November 1999): 114–119. Reprinted in *Steven Soderbergh: Interviews*, edited by Anthony Kaufman. Jackson: University Press of Mississippi, 2002.

Kapsis, Robert E. *Hitchcock: The Making of a Reputation*. Chicago: University of Chicago Press, 1992.

Kaufman, Anthony. "Man of the Year: Steven Soderbergh Traffics in Success." *indieWIRE*. January 3, 2001. Reprinted in *Steven Soderbergh: Interviews*, edited by Anthony Kaufman, 157–165. Jackson: University Press of Mississippi, 2002.

———, ed. *Steven Soderbergh: Interviews*. Jackson: University Press of Mississippi, 2002.

Keathley, Christian. *Cinephilia and History, or, The Wind in the Trees*. Bloomington: Indiana University Press, 2006.

Kehr, Dave. "You Can Make 'Em Like They Used To." *New York Times*. November 12, 2006. Accessed November 11, 2006. http://www.nytimes.com/2006/11/12/movies/12kehr.html.

Kelleher, Ed. "Out of Sight." *Film Journal International* (June 1998). Reprinted in *Steven Soderbergh: Interviews*, edited by Anthony Kaufman, 102–107. Jackson: University Press of Mississippi, 2002.

Kendrick, James. "What Is the Criterion?: The Criterion Collection as an Archive of Film and Culture." *Journal of Film and Video* 53:2 & 3 (Summer/Fall 2001): 124–139.

Keough, Peter. "*The Girlfriend Experience*" (film review). *Boston Phoenix*. April 20, 2009. http://thephoenix.com/Boston/Movies/83668-GIRLFRIEND-EXPERIENCE.

———. "*Out of Sight*" (film review). *Boston Phoenix*. July 2, 1998. Accessed January 22, 2010. http://www.bostonphoenix.com/archives/1998/documents/00525266.htm.

Kerr, Paul. "Babel's Network Narrative: Packaging a Globalized Art Cinema." *Transnational Cinemas* 1.1 (2010): 37–51.

King, Geoff. *Indiewood, USA: Where Hollywood Meets Independent Cinema*. London: I.B. Tauris, 2009.

Kirsner, Scott. "Maverick Mogul." *Fast Company* 101 (December 2005). Accessed September 1, 2010. http://www.fastcompany.com/magazine/101/hollywood-cuban.html.

Kit, Borys. "Smokehouse Defecting to Sony." *The Hollywood Reporter*. June 30, 2009. Accessed July 31, 2009. http://www.hollywoodreporter.com/hr /content_display/news/e3i9b66dcb9d0fe519ac2c4fb6907569e5c.

———. "Soderbergh Signs with Anonymous." *The Hollywood Reporter*. March 18, 2008. Accessed November 16, 2008. http://www.hollywoodreporter.com /hr/content_display/news/e3icdc37db19c2bf2ef97950b9c95f37fd4.

Kit, Borys, and Gregg Goldstein. "Warners Axes Picturehouse, WIP." *The Hollywood Reporter*. May 9, 2008. Accessed February 20, 2009. http://www .hollywoodreporter.com/hr/content_display/film/news/e3ie18fbd8cbed3od 57f63f6b5fd4d2499a.

Klinger, Barbara. *Beyond the Multiplex: Cinema, New Technologies, and the Home*. Berkeley: University of California Press, 2006.

———. "Digressions at the Cinema: Reception and Mass Culture." *Cinema Journal* 28.4 (Summer 1989): 3–19.

———. "The DVD Cinephile: Viewing Heritages and Home Film Cultures." In *Film and Television After DVD*, edited by James Bennett and Tom Brown, 19–44. London: Routledge, 2008.

Kramer, Peter. *The New Hollywood: From* Bonnie and Clyde *to* Star Wars. London: Wallflower, 2005.

LaSalle, Mick. "Here's Looking at You, Kid (Nudge, Nudge, Wink, Wink)" (film review). *San Francisco Chronicle*. December 22, 2006. Accessed April 21, 2007. http://www.sfgate.com/cgi-bin/article.cgi?f=/c/a/2006/12/22/DDG NRN3GFQ1.DTL.

———. "A Lucky 'Thirteen' for Ocean and the Gang" (film review). *San Francisco Chronicle*. June 7, 2007. Accessed 20 June 2009. http://www.sf gate.com/cgi-bin/article.cgi?f=/c/a/2007/06/07/DDGDBQ9JN913.DTL.

Lee, Luaine. "*Jaws* Hooked Soderbergh on Filmmaking." *Chicago Sun-Times*. January 12, 2001.

Le Fanu, Mark. *The Cinema of Andrei Tarkovsky*. London: BFI, 1987.

Lem, Stanislaw. *Solaris*. Translated by Joanna Kilmartin and Steve Cox. San Diego: Harcourt, Inc., 1987.

Levy, Emanuel. *Cinema of Outsiders: The Rise of American Independent Film*. New York: New York University Press, 1999.

———. "*The Limey*: Soderbergh's Artistic Meller" (film review). *Variety*. May 24, 1999. Accessed May 2, 2009. http://www.variety.com/review/VE1117 914193.html?categoryid=31&cs=1.

———. "*Out of Sight*" (film review). *Variety*. June 22, 1998. Accessed January 18, 2010. http://www.variety.com/review/VE1117477633.html.

Lim, Dennis. "Having Your Way with Hollywood, or the Further Adventures of Steven Soderbergh." *Village Voice*. January 9, 2001. Reprinted in *Steven Soderbergh: Interviews*, edited by Anthony Kaufman, 148–156. Jackson: University Press of Mississippi, 2002.

Lipton, Shana Ting. "Weapons of Mass Instruction." *Salon.com*. November 5, 2002. Accessed April 17, 2012. http://www.salon.com/2002/11/06/qatsi.

Malcolm, Paul. "Back in Sight: The Return of Steven Soderbergh." *LA Weekly*. July 3, 1998. Reprinted in *Steven Soderbergh: Interviews*, edited by Anthony Kaufman, 110–113. Jackson: University Press of Mississippi, 2002.

Mann, Denise. *Hollywood Independents: The Postwar Talent Takeover*. Minneapolis: University of Minnesota Press, 2008.

Maslin, Janet. "'Out of Sight': A Thief, a Marshal, an Item" (film review). *New York Times*. June 26, 1998. Accessed January 19, 2010. http://www.nytimes.com/library/film/062698sight-film-review.html.

Mayer, Vicki, Miranda J. Banks, and John Caldwell, eds. *Production Studies: Cultural Studies of Media Industries*. New York: Routledge, 2009.

McCarthy, Todd. "*Che*" (film review). *Variety.com*. May 26, 2008. Accessed June 22, 2009. http://www.variety.com/review/VE1117937244.html.

———. "*Erin Brockovich*" (film review). *Variety.com*. March 6, 2000. Accessed January 17, 2010. http://www.variety.com/review/VE1117778755.html.

———. "*The Good German*" (film review). *Variety.com*. December 1, 2006. Accessed April 21, 2007. http://www.variety.com/review/VE1117932224.html.

———. "*Ocean's Thirteen*" (film review). *Variety.com*. May 24, 2007. Accessed August 22, 2009. http://www.variety.com/review/VE1117933755.html.

———. "*The Underneath*" (film review). *Variety.com*. March 14, 1995. Accessed April 18, 2009. http://www.variety.com/review/VE1117903827.html.

Merritt, Greg. *Celluloid Mavericks: A History of American Independent Film*. New York: Da Capo Press, 1999.

Minsky, Terri. "Hot Phenom: Hollywood Makes a Big Deal Over Steven Soderbergh's *sex, lies, and videotape*." *Rolling Stone*. May 18, 1989. Reprinted in *Steven Soderbergh: Interviews*, edited by Anthony Kaufman, 3–12. Jackson: University Press of Mississippi, 2002.

Mitchell, Elvis. "For the New Rat Pack, It's a Ring-a-Ding Thing" (film review). *New York Times*. December 7, 2001. Accessed August 26, 2011. http://movies.nytimes.com/movie/review?res=9F03E5D8123CF934A35751C1A9679C8B63.

Mottram, James. *The Sundance Kids*. London: Faber & Faber, 2006.

Naremore, James. "Authorship." In *A Companion to Film Theory*, edited by Toby Miller and Robert Stam, 9–24. Malden, MA: Blackwell, 1999.

———. "Authorship and the Cultural Politics of Film Criticism." *Film Quarterly* 44.1 (Autumn 1990): 14–23.

——— (ed.). *Film Adaptation*. New Brunswick, NJ: Rutgers University Press, 2000.

Neale, Steve. *Genre and Hollywood*. London: Routledge, 2000.

———. "Masculinity as Spectacle: Reflections on Men and Mainstream Cinema." In *Screening the Male: Exploring Masculinities in Hollywood Cinema*, edited by Steven Cohan and Ina Rae Hark, 9–20. London: Routledge, 1993.

———. "'New Hollywood Cinema.'" *Screen* 17.2 (1976): 119–122.

———. "Questions of Genre." *Screen* 31.1 (Spring 1990): 45–66.

Newman, Michael Z. *Indie: An American Film Culture.* New York: Columbia University Press, 2011.

Nornes, Abé Mark. *Cinema Babel: Translating Global Cinema.* Minneapolis: University of Minnesota Press, 2007.

Nussbaum, Emily. "Reruns: 'Tanner '88' is now 'Tanner '04.'" *New York Times.* February 1, 2004. Accessed February 2, 2004. http://www.nytimes.com/2004 /02/01/arts/television/01NUSS.html.

O'Hehir, Andrew. "Beyond the Multiplex." *Salon.com.* May 24, 2007. Accessed August 23, 2009. http://www.salon.com/ent/movies/review/2007/05/24 /cannes_8/index.html.

Orndorf, Brian. *"The Girlfriend Experience"* (film review). *eFilmCritic.com.* May 8, 2009. Accessed June 18, 2009. http://www.efilmcritic.com/review .php?movie=18484.

Orr, Christopher. *"The Girlfriend Experience"* (film review). *The New Republic.* June 5, 2009. Accessed June 20, 2009. http://www.tnr.com/booksarts/story .html?id=362696of-027f-42ec-b766-b1c271088d99.

O'Sullivan, Michael. "Take Two: A 'Keane' Remix by Soderbergh." *Washington Post.* March 24, 2006. Accessed November 23, 2008. http://www.washington post.com/wp-dyn/content/article/2006/03/23/AR2006032300541.html.

Palmer, R. Barton. *"Blood Simple*: Defining the Commercial/Independent Text." *Persistence of Vision* 6 (Summer 1988): 5–19.

Palmer, R. Barton, and Steven M. Sanders, eds. *The Philosophy of Steven Soderbergh.* Lexington: University Press of Kentucky, 2011.

Parker, Deborah, and Mark Parker. "Directors and DVD Commentary: The Specifics of Intention." *Journal of Aesthetics and Art Criticism* 62.1 (Winter 2004): 13–22.

Patterson, John. "Invasion of the Movie Snatchers." *The Guardian.* September 12, 2003. Accessed May 2, 2009. http://www.guardian.co.uk/film/2003/sep /12/1.

Ponto, Arya. "Soderbergh Heckled by Anti-Che Audience." *JustPressPlay.net.* December 15, 2008. Accessed July 16, 2009. http://www.justpressplay.net /movies/movie-news/4458-soderbergh-heckled-by-anti-che-audience.html.

Prince, Stephen. *A New Pot of Gold: Hollywood Under the Electronic Rainbow, 1980–1989.* Berkeley: University of California Press, 2000.

"Professional Profiles: Jayson Albright." *Decatur Herald & Review.* May 29, 2008. Accessed June 11, 2010. http://www.herald-review.com/special-section/news/business_journal/profiles/article_65700fd8-b5bf-5cdf-91a4 -4bfda83b3ee7.html.

Richardson, John. "The Very Boring Life of Steven Soderbergh." *Esquire.* August 2002. Accessed April 18, 2009. http://www.esquire.com/ESQ0802 -AUG_SODERBERGH.

Rico, Jack. "EXCLUSIVE! 8 never before seen clips from 'CHE'!," *ShowbizCafe. com.* November 12, 2008. Accessed December 8, 2008. http://www.showbiz cafe.com/en/news/exclusive-8-never-before-seen-clips-from-che/1338.

Rockwell, John. "On an Odyssey to Love's Outer Limit." *New York Times*. November 24, 2002. Accessed June 4, 2010. http://www.nytimes.com/2002 /11/24/movies/film-on-an-odyssey-to-love-s-outer-limit.html.

Romney, Jonathan. "Future Soul." *Sight & Sound* 13.2 (February 2003): 13–17. Accessed June 4, 2010. http://www.stevensoderbergh.net/articles/2003 /sightandsound.php.

Rosen, Christopher. "Steven Soderbergh's Liberace Movie with Michael Douglas and Matt Damon Heads to HBO." *Moviefone.com*. October 11, 2011. Accessed November 26, 2011. http://blog.moviefone.com/2011/10/11 /steven-soderbergh-matt-damon-michael-douglas-hbo-liberace.

Rosenbaum, Jonathan. "Neither Noir" (film review). *Chicago Reader*. April 28, 1995. Accessed April 18, 2009. http://www.jonathanrosenbaum.com/?p =6862.

Rosenblatt, Josh. "*Ocean's Thirteen*" (film review). *Austin Chronicle*. June 15, 2007. Accessed August 23, 2009. http://www.austinchronicle.com/gyro base/Calendar/Film?Film=oid%3A481177.

Roth, Elaine. "Black and White Masculinity in Three Steven Soderbergh Films." *Genders* 43 (2006). Accessed May 28, 2009. http://www.genders.org/g43/g43 _roth.html.

———. "'I Just Want to Be a Decent Citizen': Melodrama as Political Appeal in *Erin Brockovich*." *Feminist Media Studies* 4.1 (2004): 49–63.

Routt, William D. "L'Evidence." *Continuum: The Australian Journal of Media & Culture* 5.2 (1990). Accessed July 6, 2009. http://www.wwwmcc.murdoch .edu.au/ReadingRoom/5.2/Routt.html.

Rubin, Nathan. "*K Street: The Complete Series*" (DVD review). *The Onion A.V. Club*. July 26, 2004. Accessed July 28, 2010. http://www.avclub.com /articles/k-street-the-complete-series,11346/.

Rueff, Ashley. "'The Informant' Debuts to Hollywood Hoopla." *Decatur Herald & Review*. September 18, 2009. Accessed June 14, 2010. http://www.herald -review.com/news/local/article_4b55aaca-776f-560f-872e-339df9cc1c41 .html.

———. "Upcoming 'Informant!' Showing a Fundraiser for the Mental Health Association of Macon County." *Decatur Herald & Review*. September 10, 2009. Accessed June 11, 2010. http://www.herald-review.com/entertain ment/local/article_3f8f9139-eb75-533b-8b88-e5068b89fad2.html.

Sarris, Andrew. "Sleeping With the Enemy . . . Of Course, the Enemy is Jennifer Lopez" (film review). *New York Observer* June 28, 1998. Accessed January 19, 2010. http://www.observer.com/node/40697.

Saunders, Rhys. "Damon Watch: Have You Seen Him?" *State Journal-Register*. May 20, 2008. Accessed June 14, 2010. http://www.sj-r.com/entertainment /x1191423991/Movie-extras-take-their-cues.

Schickel, Richard. "In the Heat of the Noir" (film review). *Time*. December 3, 2006. Accessed June 21, 2009. http://www.time.com/time/magazine /article/0,9171,1565553,00.html.

Sconce, Jeffrey. "Irony, Nihilism, and the New American 'Smart' Film." *Screen* 43.4 (Winter 2002): 349–369.

Scott, A. O. "'Erin Brockovich': High Ideals, Higher Heels" (film review). *New York Times*. March 17, 2000. Accessed 17 January 2010. http://www.nytimes.com/library/film/031700erin-film-review.html.

———. "Saluting the Rebel Underneath the T-Shirt" (film review). *New York Times*. December 12, 2008. Accessed December 12, 2008. http://movies.nytimes.com/2008/12/12/movies/12che.html.

———. "Soderbergh and Che, Provocateurs." *New York Times*. May 23, 2008. Accessed May 24, 2008. http://movies.nytimes.com/2008/05/23/movies/23cann.html.

Scott, Allen J. *On Hollywood: The Place, The Industry*. Princeton, NJ: Princeton University Press, 2005.

Sellier, Geneviève. *Masculine Singular: French New Wave Cinema*. Translated by Kristin Ross. Durham, NC: Duke University Press, 2008.

Sellors, C. Paul. *Film Authorship: Auteurs and Other Myths*. London: Wallflower Press, 2010.

Shaw, Deborah. "'You are Alright, But . . .': Individual and Collective Representations of Mexicans, Latinos, Anglo-Americans and Africans in Steven Soderbergh's *Traffic*." *Quarterly Review of Film and Video* 22.3 (Summer 2005): 211–223.

Shohat, Ella, and Robert Stam. *Unthinking Eurocentrism: Multiculturalism and the Media*. London: Routledge, 1994.

Silverman, Jason. "*Bubble* Fails to Rock Tinseltown." *Wired.com*. February 13, 2006. Accessed November 10, 2007. http://www.wired.com/science/discoveries/news/2006/02/70202.

Siskel, Gene. "Candid Camera: *sex, lies, and videotape* Director Faces Reality." *Chicago Tribune*. August 6, 1989. Reprinted in *Steven Soderbergh: Interviews*, edited by Anthony Kaufman, 34–37. Jackson: University Press of Mississippi, 2002.

Snyder, Gabriel, and Stephen Zeitchik. "Movie Biz on the 'Bubble': Pic's Triple Bow Inconclusive." *Variety.com*. January 29, 2006. Accessed November 10, 2007. http://www.variety.com/article/VR1117937061.

Soderbergh, Steven. *sex, lies, and videotape*. New York: Harper and Row, 1990.

Soderbergh, Steven, and Richard Lester. *Getting Away With It: Or: The Further Adventures of the Luckiest Bastard You Ever Saw*. London: Faber & Faber, 1999.

Spates, Alicia. "Singing the Informant Blues." *Decatur Herald & Review*. September 2, 2008. Accessed June 11, 2010. http://www.herald-review.com/entertainment/local/article_6d79e4bc-78d2-501d-aa88-5c07f1e64f81.html.

Staiger, Janet. "Authorship Approaches." In *Authorship and Film*, edited by David A. Gerstner and Janet Staiger, 27–57. New York: Routledge, 2003.

———. "The Hollywood Mode of Production, 1930–1960." In *The Classical Hollywood Cinema: Film Style and Mode of Production to 1960*, edited by David Bordwell, Janet Staiger, and Kristin Thompson, 309–337. New York: Columbia University Press, 1985.

————. "The Politics of Film Canons." *Cinema Journal* 24.3 (Spring 1985): 4–23.

Stam, Robert. "The Author: Introduction." In *Film and Theory: An Anthology*, edited by Robert Stam and Toby Miller, 1–6. Malden, MA: Blackwell, 2000.

————. "Beyond Fidelity: The Dialogics of Adaptation." In *Film Adaptation*, edited by James Naremore, 54–76. New Brunswick, NJ: Rutgers University Press, 2000.

Stanley, Alessandra. "Inside Washington Politics, Turned Inside Out" (television review). *New York Times*. September 14, 2003. Accessed July 28, 2010. http://www.nytimes.com/2003/09/14/politics/14KSTR.html.

Stanley, Alessandra, and Virginia Heffernan. "The Lows: Mullets at Night and Pain in the Morning." *New York Times*. December 28, 2003. Accessed January 13, 2004. http://www.nytimes.com/2003/12/28/arts/television/28HALE.html.

Stewart, Ryan. "Steven Soderbergh: The Girlfriend Experience." *SuicideGirls.com*. May 21, 2009. Accessed May 27, 2009. http://www.suicidegirls.com/interviews/Steven%20Soderbergh:%20The%20Girlfriend%20Experience.

Stringer, Julian. "The Gathering Place: *Lost* in Oahu." In *Reading* Lost: *Perspectives on a Hit Television Show*, edited by Roberta Pearson, 73–93. London: I.B. Tauris, 2009.

Tarkovsky, Andrei. *Collected Screenplays*. Translated by William Powell and Natasha Synessios. London: Faber & Faber, 1999.

————. *Time Within Time: The Diaries, 1970–1986*. Translated by Kitty Hunter-Blair. Calcutta, India: Seagull Books, 1991.

Taylor, Charles. "*The Limey*" (film review). *Salon.com*. October 7, 1999. Accessed May 4, 2009. http://www.salon.com/ent/movies/review/1999/10/07/limey.

Taylor, Drew. "Composer Cliff Martinez Talks Score for 'Contagion' & Working with Steven Soderbergh." *The Playlist*. April 25, 2011. Accessed June 6, 2011. http://blogs.indiewire.com/theplaylist/archives/composer_cliff_martinez_talks_score_contagion_working_steven_soderbergh.

"Thanks to 'The Informant' Cast and Crew." *Decatur Herald & Review*. May 16, 2008. Accessed June 14, 2010. http://www.herald-review.com/app/blogs/letterstotheeditor/?p=3144.

Thompson, Anne. "Sundance: Soderbergh Unveils *Girlfriend Experience*." *Variety.com*. January 21, 2009. Accessed January 30, 2009. http://weblogs.variety.com/thompsononhollywood/2009/01/sundance-soderbergh-unveils-girlfriend-experience.html.

Thompson, Anne, and Michael Jones. "IFC, SXSW to bow 'Alexander.'" *Variety.com*. January 19, 2009. Accessed February 4, 2009. http://www.variety.com/article/VR1117998768.html.

Thomson, David. "Steven Soderbergh." *The Guardian*. February 13, 2009. Accessed May 4, 2009. http://www.guardian.co.uk/film/2009/feb/13/steven-soderbergh-profile.

————. *The Whole Equation: A History of Hollywood*. New York: Alfred A. Knopf, 2004.

Topel, Fred. "Interview: Soderbergh Talks Positions in *The Good German*." *CanMag*. December 10, 2006. Accessed April 13, 2007. http://www.canmag .com/news/4/3/6034.

Travers, Peter. "*Full Frontal*" (film review). *Rolling Stone*. August 22, 2002. Accessed April 24, 2009. http://www.rollingstone.com/reviews/movie/594 8535/review/5948536/full_frontal.

———. "*The Good German*" (film review). *Rolling Stone*. November 21, 2006. Accessed June 21, 2009. http://www.rollingstone.com/reviews/movie/956 9555/review/12626060/good_german.

"Tribeca '09: Bungion Boy Reviews *The Girlfriend Experience, Moon, Passing Strange*, and *Hysterical Psycho!*" *Ain't It Cool News*. May 7, 2009. Accessed June 18, 2009. http://www.aintitcool.com/node/41007.

Turan, Kenneth. "*Ocean's Thirteen*" (film review). *Los Angeles Times*. June 8, 2007. Accessed August 23, 2009. http://www.calendarlive.com/movies /reviews/cl-et-oceans8jun08,0,773906.story.

Tzioumakis, Yannis. *American Independent Cinema: An Introduction*. New Brunswick, NJ: Rutgers University Press, 2006.

Verevis, Constantine. *Film Remakes*. Edinburgh: Edinburgh University Press, 2006.

Waxman, Sharon. "One Player's Journey from Hollywood to Iraq Raises Eyebrows." *New York Times*. May 6, 2006. Accessed July 21, 2009. http:// query.nytimes.com/gst/fullpage.html?res=9D07E3DC1F3FF935A35756 C0A9609C8B63.

———. *Rebels on the Backlot: Six Maverick Directors and How They Conquered the Hollywood Studio System*. New York: Harper Entertainment, 2005.

Wayne, Mike. *Marxism and Media Studies: Key Concepts and Contemporary Trends*. London: Pluto, 2003.

Webster, Andy. "Secrets in the Snow" (film review). *New York Times*. April 28, 2007. Accessed November 9, 2008. http://movies.nytimes.com/2007/04/28 /movies/28wind.html.

Weiner, Allison Hope. "Shyamalan's Hollywood Horror Story, With Twist." *New York Times*. June 2, 2008. Accessed June 13, 2008. http://www.nytimes .com/2008/06/02/business/media/02night.html.

Weiss, Philip. "When the Producer Comes to Town." *New York Times Magazine*. November 11, 2007. Accessed November 15, 2007. http://www .nytimes.com/2007/11/11/magazine/11pohlad-t.html.

Whipp, Glenn. "Nothing Clear-Cut in Noir-Style 'Good German.'" *DailyBulletin .com*. December 9, 2006. Accessed April 13, 2007. http://www.dailybulletin .com/entertainment/ci_4811488.

Williams, Linda. "Melodrama Revised." In *Refiguring American Film Genres*, edited by Nick Browne, 42–88. Berkeley: University of California Press, 1998.

Willis, Sharon. *High Contrast: Race and Gender in Contemporary Hollywood Film*. Durham, NC: Duke University Press, 1997.

Wloszczyna, Susan. "'German' Takes Hard Look at World War II Aftermath." *USA Today*. December 14, 2006. Accessed April 13, 2007. http://www.usa today.com/life/movies/news/2006-12-13-clooney-side_x.htm.

Wright, Evan. "Pat Dollard's War on Hollywood." *Vanity Fair*. March 2007. Accessed March 17, 2009. http://www.vanityfair.com/politics/features/2007 /03/dollard200703.

Zacharek, Stephanie. *"The Good German"* (film review). *Salon.com*. December 15, 2006. Accessed April 21, 2007. http://www.salon.com/ent/movies /review/2006/12/15/good_german/.

———. *"Ocean's Eleven"* (film review). *Salon.com*. December 7, 2001. Accessed August 26, 2011. http://www.salon.com/entertainment/movies/2001/12/07 /oceans_11/index.html.

Zafirau, Stephen. "Audience Knowledge and the Everyday Lives of Cultural Producers in Hollywood." In *Production Studies: Cultural Studies of Media Industries*, edited by Vicki Mayer, Miranda J. Banks, and John Caldwell, 190–202. New York: Routledge, 2009.

Zimmermann, Patricia R. "Digital Deployment(s)." In *Contemporary American Independent Film: From the Margins to the Mainstream*, edited by Chris Holmlund and Justin Wyatt, 245–264. New York: Routledge, 2005.

Index

Page numbers in *italics* indicate photos.

178, 179; as whistleblower film, 172, 178, 179, 182

Eros, 1, 91, 96, 233

ethnicity. *See* race

Expressionism, 40, 41, 67, 94, 172–173, 178; *See also* film noir; *Kafka*

Fallen Angels, 198, 258, 283n68

Far From Heaven, 6, 7, 68, 220, 222

femininity. *See* gender roles, women's

film festivals. *See* Cannes Film Festival; London Film Festival; Sundance Film Festival; Toronto Film Festival; Tribeca Film Festival; Venice Film Festival

film noir, 41–43, 61, 63–64, 94, 172–178, 198, 283n68. See also *Criss Cross*; Expressionism; *Good German, The*; *Limey, The*; *Underneath, The*

Fincher, David, 26, 36, 149

Fine Line Features, 3, 29, 36, 281–282n24. *See also* New Line Cinema

Finney, Albert, 144, 157

Fithian, John, 2, 13, 279n11

Five Easy Pieces, 29–30, 51

Flack, Sarah, 58

Focus Features, 4, 81, 216, 220

Fonda, Peter, 60–61, 65, 284n25. See also *Limey, The*

Foucault, Michel, 86

Foundas, Scott, 115–116, 132, 289nn11,15

Frank, Scott, 153, 255–256

French Connection, The, 59

French New Wave, 53–54, 58–59, 60, 62–63, 66, 132, 180, 268. See also *Cahiers du cinéma*; Godard, Jean-Luc; Resnais, Alain

Friedkin, William, 29, 30, 45, 46, 226

Frogley, Louise, 82

f64 (film collective), 36

Fukasaku, Kinji, 226

Full Frontal, 37, 46, 58–59, 88, 128–128, 200, 206, 283n58, 284n10, 286n23; gender representation in, 142–143, 147–149, 150; location filming of, 142–143, 147–149

Gallagher, Peter, 39, 41, 293n14

Gans, Herbert, 281n21

Garcia, Andy, 157, 158, 292–293n32

Gaut, Berys, 98

gender roles, women's, 21, 39, 142–151, 153, 155, 163, 177, 187, 190, 192, 206, 281n9, 292n24. *See also* masculinity

German Expressionism. *See* Expressionism

Get Carter, 49, 60, 62, 92

Gilroy, Tony, 227–228

Girlfriend Experience, The, 15–16, 37, 44, 81, 91, 99, 110, 111, 124, 128, 142, 149, 205, 212, 217, 235, 290n21; reception of, 115–122, 131–132, 289nn11,12

Godard, Jean-Luc, 45, 62, 63, 67, 69, 115–116, 132, 268

Goldsmith, Ben, 94, 95

Gómez, Antxón, 97

Gondry, Michel, 36

Good German, The, 2, 45, 52, 67, 87, 89–90, 91, 124, 172, 204, 208, 209, 211, 227; production of, 75, 78–85, 143, 290n23; promotion of, 79, 83, 88; reception of, 52, 85, 111, 127–131, 132, 141–142, 260–261, 286n10; and Section Eight, 211, 221; source novel for, 176–178

Good Night, and Good Luck, 1, 7, 68, 78, 88, 211, 212, 217, 220, 279n6

Gorenshtein, Fridrikh, 196, 294n30. See also *Solaris* (1972)

Gould, Elliott, 157, 159, 200, 207–208

Gramercy Pictures, 4, 19–20, 23, 35, 43, 63